Have No Fear

Have No Fear

The Charles Evers Story

Charles Evers
and
Andrew Szanton

A ROBERT L. BERNSTEIN BOOK

John Wiley & Sons, Inc.
New York • Chichester • Brisbane • Toronto • Singapore • Weinheim

This text is printed on acid-free paper.

Copyright © 1997 by Charles Evers and Andrew Szanton
Published by John Wiley & Sons, Inc.

All rights reserved. Published simultaneously in Canada.

Portions of this book are from "The *Playboy* Interview: Charles Evers," *Playboy*, October 1971. Copyright © 1971 by *Playboy*. Used with permission. All rights reserved.

Reproduction or translation of any part of this work beyond that permitted by Section 107 or 108 of the 1976 United States Copyright Act without the permission of the copyright owner is unlawful. Requests for permission or further information should be addressed to the Permissions Department, John Wiley & Sons, Inc.

This publication is designed to provide accurate and authoritative information in regard to the subject matter covered. It is sold with the understanding that the publisher is not engaged in rendering legal, accounting, or other professional services. If legal advice or other expert assistance is required, the services of a competent professional person should be sought.

Library of Congress Cataloging-in-Publication Data:

Evers, Charles.
    Have no fear : the Charles Evers story / by Charles Evers and Andrew Szanton.
       p.   cm.
    "A Robert L. Bernstein book."
    Includes bibliographical references and index.
    ISBN 978-1-62045-693-4
    1. Evers, Charles, 1922–   2. Civil rights workers—Mississippi—Biography.   3. Afro-American politicians—Mississippi—Biography.   4. Politicians—Mississippi—Biography.   5. Civil rights movements—Mississippi—History—20th century.   6. Afro-Americans—Civil rights—Mississippi.   7. Mississippi—Race relations.   8. Mississippi—Politics and government—1951.
I. Szanton, Andrew.
E185.97.E93A3 1997
323'.092—dc20
[B]   96-5766

*To our brothers,
Medgar and Nathan*

CONTENTS

	Acknowledgments	ix
	Collecting History: A Collaborator's Introduction	xiii
	Prologue: What It Meant to Be an Evers	1
1	My Pact with Medgar	3
2	Mama, Daddy, and Old Mark Thomas	11
3	The Wall of Separation	23
4	Whites Messed with Us, But We Couldn't Mess with Them	33
5	Felicia	45
6	Wheeling and Dealing at Alcorn	55
7	Crossing the Line	71
8	The Pure of Heart: Medgar Joins the NAACP Full-Time	77
9	Terrible Years	85
10	Chicago: The Chances I Took	99
11	I Trusted to God and My .45 Pistol	111
12	Turn Me Loose	121
13	You Won't Die in Vain, Medgar	133
14	Taking Over the Mississippi NAACP	145
15	Two Lost Brothers	157
16	Hate Goes on Trial	165
17	Interrupting the Green	179
18	The Next Step up the Ladder	193

19	Lyndon Johnson Said, "We Shall Overcome"	205
20	Black Power	213
21	Losing Martin, Losing Bobby	219
22	Running for Congress: Evers for Everybody	233
23	Call Me "The Mayor"	241
24	Fayette Was Our Israel	249
25	A Black-Skinned Man Running for Governor	265
26	Scolding Richard Nixon about Watergate	273
27	Why I Became a Republican	287
28	The Bridge That Carried Us Across	299
29	Have No Fear	307
	Selected Bibliography	313
	Index	317

ACKNOWLEDGMENTS

WRITING THIS BOOK has been a four-year journey passing through six different states. Among the hundreds of good people I have met along the way, let me single out five for special thanks.

My parents, Peter and Eleanor Szanton, have inspired me to write all my life and have helped me in many specific ways to understand, and do justice to, this particular project.

My brother, Nathan Szanton, has also been a great inspiration over many years, and a thoughtful, enthusiastic reader of this manuscript.

Hana Lane, my efficient, friendly editor at John Wiley, was another wise reader of the manuscript, who nimbly shaped it, believed in it, and saw it through to publication.

My greatest thanks go to Charles Evers. He answered hundreds of questions without flinching. He opened his files to me, took dozens of telephone calls at odd moments, sat for about ten formal interviews and countless informal ones, and even put me up for two long stays in his home. He trusted a man he hardly knew to tell his life story. I hope I have repaid his confidence.

For general assistance with this book, let me thank Franz Allina, Jerry Auerbach, Judy Auerbach, Steve Axelrod, Helen Bernstein, Jason Berry, Ellen Brodsky, Chris Calhoun, Cecily Cook, Levente Csaplar, Frank Curtis, Ken DeCell, Joseph Finder, Marilyn Fletcher, Eric Frumin, Melissa Frumin, Doris Kearns Goodwin and Richard Goodwin, Rob Gurwitt, Grace Halsell, Al W. Johnson, Ray Kemp, Susan Klee, Sydelle Kramer, Lisa Mihaly, Ethan Nelson, William Novak, Ronald Roach, Ted Rybeck, Will Schwalbe, Daniel Steiner, Henry Steiner, Sarah G. Szanton, Sarah L. Szanton, Tom Wicker, Sally Willcox, Mary Beth Williamson, Edith Wojeski, and Ken Wong.

For granting me personal interviews or helping this project in some other especially generous way, I want to thank Ainslie Binder, Peter Edelman, John Gregg, William Kienzle, Kate Kowalski, Neal Peirce, Dan Rather and his assistants Susan Martins and Sakura Komiyama, Yuval Taylor, and Peggy Wiesenberg.

Thanks to the San Francisco Public Library; the John F. Kennedy Library, especially Ronald Whealan, head librarian; the State Library of Massachusetts; the Wessell Library at Tufts University; the Pusey Library and the Widener Library, at Harvard University, especially Cheryl LaGuardia; the Henry Thomas Sampson Library, at Jackson State; the Mississippi Department of Archives and History, in Jackson; the Louis Round Wilson Library, at the University of North Carolina; the Shreve Memorial Library in Shreveport; and the Library of Congress, Washington, D.C., especially Fred Bauman and Ernest Emrich in the Manuscript Division. My thanks also go to *Playboy* magazine, especially to Marcia Terrones, for granting me permission to use material from Charles Evers's 1971 interview.

For the photos in this book, let me thank Charles Evers, Eric Williams and Gerry Matthews at Black Star, and Don Bowden at AP/Wide World.

Let me thank all the people at John Wiley, besides Hana Lane, who helped produce and promote this book, especially Carole Hall, but also Lisbeth Cobas, Dee Dee DeBartlo, Gerry Helferich, Lauri Sayde, Jennifer Holiday, Earl Cox, and the distinguished man who has honored me by publishing this book under his own imprint, Robert Bernstein. Thanks also to Lachina Publishing Services, Inc.

In Mississippi, let me thank Charles Evers's chancery court clerk's staff, especially his daughter, Charlene Wilson; the people of Fayette, especially Milton Braxton and Kennie Middleton; David Westbrook in Crystal Springs; and in Jackson, Margaret Hawthorne, Charles Robinson, and the staff at WMPR; Susan Garcia of the Jackson *Clarion-Ledger*; Lillie McNeal; and Walthena Gregory of the NAACP.

I owe a great debt of thanks to a number of perceptive family members, friends, and experts who read and critiqued this work in draft. Thank you Marcia Allina, Steve Bauer, Carol Cannon, Ed Davis, Toni Davis, Anne Gentile, Joe Gentile, Malcolm McCullough, Priscilla McMillan, Shirley Morrisette, Trish Perlmutter, Marion Pisick, Michael

Pisick, Alex Polsky, Mallory Rintoul, Don Stokes, Sybil Stokes, Joseph A. Trunk, John Urda, Karen Waldstein, Tom Waldstein, Carole Walker, Jim Walker, Curtis Wilkie, and John Williamson.

Finally, let me thank my wife, Barbara Cannon, for years of faithful and ingenious support, on many levels.

COLLECTING HISTORY

A Collaborator's Introduction

FIRST-RATE BIOGRAPHIES can be written a century after the death of their subject; memoirs must be written during the subject's life. That fact brings a lovely urgency to the task. Most people recall life with the best mix of passion, precision, and wisdom within a decade of their sixty-fifth birthday. In 1992, when I first spoke to Charles Evers, he was seventy.

I telephoned his chancery court clerk's office in Fayette, Mississippi, and told him I had researched his life with some care and hoped to help him write a memoir. I told Mr. Evers that I had always been intrigued by civil rights, the nature of leadership, and relations between brothers. I told him I knew he had been a leader in the great movement to gain equality for black Americans. His passionate bond with his martyred brother, Medgar, fascinated me.

I have found the life of Charles Evers even richer than I'd expected. Deeply rooted in Mississippi, he has also traveled widely, with an inquiring mind. If his career has faltered in certain ways, the faltering has been revealing, too. He has not only befriended an astonishing range of people, from presidents to sharecroppers, but has tried to knit their lives together, to convince each that they need the other. His life has been full of ambition, hardship, love, grief, money, sex, and glory. His voice is humorous and blunt, his vision unsparing.

Most national civil rights leaders are tactful, live in large cities, and seek attention. Evers is a straight-talking loner who lives far from the national media centers, in Fayette, a town of two thousand, where in 1969 he won his greatest victory. He has turned down national political jobs. His politics and personal style have often put him on the margin of the national civil rights movement. Few people outside Mississippi know that Charles Evers, more than any other person, brought Mississippi blacks the vote.

I told Charles Evers that a well-told memoir might spread his good name, serve both his career and the history of the civil rights movement. Evers was rushing through the last days of a political campaign. Distracted but intrigued, he invited me down to Fayette to present myself and explain the nature of the book. In August 1992, we first met face-to-face. Evers sat behind his desk in an old shirt and slacks and spoke openly about his life. I described the memoir I wanted to write. He nodded, assenting easily, withholding comment. Even as I came to know him much better, I always sensed something withheld.

The idea of a memoir appealed to him. He likes to sift and make sense of the past. He wanted to talk about the greatness of Medgar Evers, and he saw the book as a vehicle to spread Medgar's fame. When I first told him I hoped to learn about Medgar, Charles Evers said proudly, "You came to the right mule." I told him I also wanted to learn all I could about Charles Evers. What had his childhood been like? He smiled: "Rough and tumble. Toe to toe."

Evers took care that first afternoon to disabuse me of any notions I might have of his purity: "I'm no Democrat. I'm no Republican. I'm an Independent and a sonofabitch. I don't go round pretending I'm a saint. But I can rear back and speak my piece because I know what I am." Later that afternoon, he added, "Nearly all the people you talk to will say something bad about me. I don't care what they say. Most of them don't understand a man willing to die for what he believes in."

One day as I sat with him, under two ceiling fans in his Soul Food Cafe, a phone call came from his best friend, B. B. King, the great blues musician. Evers rose and left me to my notes. Five minutes later, he returned with a smile and a shake of the head: "Thank God, I'm not a worrier like B. B. He just called me from Perth, Australia. I lined up a show for him in a penitentiary round here, and him calling from Australia to find out exactly when he's going on stage. What the hell difference does it make when he goes on? Inmates ain't going nowhere." He smiled again.

Charles Evers knows himself, but few others know quite what to make of him. In 1969, he was NAACP Man of the Year, after becoming the first black mayor in a biracial Mississippi town in a century. Evers has also been a cotton picker, driver, bootlegger, dishwasher, busboy, short-order cook, shoeshine boy, cabdriver, sandwich peddler, soldier, whorehouse owner, deejay, cafe owner, insurance agent, mortician, funeral home director, numbers runner for the Mob, nightclub owner, music promoter, history teacher, football coach, head of the NAACP in Mississippi, Democratic national committee member, author, informal advisor to Presidents Kennedy, Johnson, Nixon, and Reagan, radio host and radio station manager, and chancery court clerk.

After our first meeting in Fayette, I began sifting through books and magazines, oral histories and old news stories in the *New York Times* and the *Chicago Defender.* I began calling Charles Evers about once a month and was moved the first time he ended a phone call, "Keep in touch now, hear?"

Charles Evers is a gifted storyteller. When I seemed skeptical of his stories, he would say, "Check me. You collect history. Whatever I say, check the record." The record almost always bore him out. The few times it did not, he cursed his memory and quickly accepted correction.

I have assembled this memoir under careful ground rules. I have formally interviewed Evers perhaps forty times over the course of three years. I have read his published writings and all of his major interviews. Let me specially thank Grace Halsell, who prepared his brief, previous memoir, *Evers,* and the editors of *Playboy* magazine, who published a 1971 interview. The bibliography makes clear this book's other debts. From all these sources, I have stitched together this book. I have labored to catch the rhythms of his speech. To make his story more fluent and clear, however, I have compressed his words a good deal and gingerly added a few of my own. I have also added some dates and minor details. But Charles Evers spoke every idea in this memoir, most of them to me, and several times.

As I worked, Evers's own motives for the project grew clearer to me. He felt he had been misunderstood. For two years, I buried myself in his memories, in his words and images, looking for patterns.

My second trip to Fayette came in May 1994. Evers invited me to stay in his Fayette home for five days. He designed the house to frustrate potential assassins. For years it had no windows at all, and he still keeps his lights dim. His long living room is filled with photos, plaques, and keys to cities. He has a big dining room and bedroom, a kitchen, barroom, guestroom, and much bright red carpet, but few guests.

Among his rooms, his many pistols, photos, mementos, stuffed animals ("They don't give me no backtalk"), his forty-two plaques, and his shag rugs, I conducted a series of interviews on the run. When I asked him to tell me about racial injustice in Mississippi, he said, "I hope you got a sharp pencil." I followed him nearly everywhere, taking notes, asking questions. When I showed him the manuscript, the project seemed to come alive for him. He answered almost every prying question.

In April 1995, I stayed in his Fayette home again. Over the course of five more days, I read him the entire manuscript aloud, often at night in his home; sometimes in the cab of his black Chevy Cheyenne 3500 truck, as he drove on an errand; sometimes on the site just north of town where, under his close watch, a small crew was sawing boards, hammering nails, and building the bandstand frame for the Medgar Evers Homecoming.

Telling someone his own story, reading to him in his own voice, is a rich but distinctly odd process. Charles Evers was free to reject this version of his life. But he embraced it, interrupting only to question chronology, to ask me to smooth some of his coarser language, or to chuckle and marvel at what he has seen and done. In those five days, he made about twenty-five specific corrections that sharply improved the book. Discussions flowing from his corrections improved the book further.

Charles Evers has two bases: one in Fayette, the other in Jackson, Mississippi's biggest city. Researching this book, I have watched Charles Evers at work as chancery court clerk. I have gotten his guided tour of Fayette, and in Woodville, Mississippi, I have watched him cajole some white storeowners. In the last three years, I have sat with Evers in a small room at his Jackson radio station and watched him promote on the air an earnest group of young black businessmen. I have sat with him at radio station WMIS in Natchez, Mississippi, while

Collecting History: A Collaborator's Introduction xvii

he took phone calls, coffee cup and pistol at hand, and firmly promoted racial equality, respect for the law, and his own soul food restaurant in Fayette. One caller threatened to "get" Evers on his way home to Fayette that night. Charles Evers snorted derision.

Evers seems most himself in Fayette. People constantly stop him on the street or call him at home, wanting to visit, to get help, or to gossip. He is a private man, who sometimes pretends annoyance at the phone calls that keep him company. He lists his phone numbers and reserves a special disdain for "leaders" who hide behind their secretaries and won't mix with the public. "Call me, honey," he urges an old black woman anxious about some minor constituent service. "I'm just three steps away from that phone."

He has the politician's knack for names and faces, for making contact—the quick tap on his truck horn, the wave, the grin, the well-chosen word. He has the timing and effrontery of a born comedian, but he is often a sad, lonely man. He has several smiles: a quick, brilliant one and a slow one. He has a low speaking voice, but a quick, high-pitched laugh and a wheedling laugh of protest. On his radio show, he names local people who have just died and prods listeners to telephone condolences to family of the deceased. Death he understands, and respects.

Charles Evers carries 250 pounds with grace. ("I'll march, I'll picket—but I don't believe in no hunger strikes.") At seventy-three, his face has few lines, his hair little gray. He has dark brown skin and a pencil mustache. He speaks quickly, to cover a slight stammer. He mixes easily with others but has hooded, watchful eyes. He likes some people whom he distrusts, and he is oddly fond of virulent white racists, so long as they fall short of violence. He expects to convert them.

Charles Evers is equally at home in Fayette, in Jackson, or in Angola with Jonas Savimbi. He has constantly opened new doors—to the army, to college, to the NAACP, to the mayor's office. He loves to mingle service with self-interest: to help bring an economic delegation from Senegal to Mississippi, for example, in the process helping Senegal, helping Jackson, and helping Charles Evers.

Charles Evers ran the NAACP in Mississippi at a crucial time, was a voter registration head, a marcher, a boycotter, a pioneer. He now bridges the civil rights movement and the right wing of this country.

His blunt calls for moneymaking, self-help, and Republican Party politics, which have often put him on the fringes of the national civil rights movement, are now enjoying a new vogue. The life story of Charles Evers richly deserves telling.

Charles Evers expects his friends to work hard, to freely pay the price. In assembling this book, I hope I have done that. When recounting some of the risks he has taken in his work, Charles Evers often voices a simple credo: "We all have a job to do." For the last three and a half years, this has been mine.

A final note: Much of the speech presented within quotation marks in this book is drawn from memory and should not be considered a verbatim account. However, Charles Evers and I have made every possible effort to ensure the accuracy of quoted dialogue.

In a very few, clearly marked instances in this book, we have changed the names of minor characters to protect their privacy.

Andrew Szanton

Somerville, Massachusetts
January 1996

PROLOGUE

What It Meant to Be an Evers

When I was a boy in Decatur, Mississippi, my Daddy bought candy sticks, groceries, and snuff at the local sawmill commissary. The commissary was a company store whose prices squeezed the lifeblood out of you. Every Friday or Saturday, Daddy paid his bill when his paycheck came through. The commissary manager was a white scoundrel, Jimmy Boware, who beat and kicked Negroes who didn't pay their bill. Jimmy Boware knew Daddy couldn't read or write much, but he didn't know Daddy could add, subtract, and multiply faster in his head than you could with a pencil.

One Saturday, when I was about nine and my younger brother Medgar was six, we went with Daddy to pay his commissary bill. I can still see that commissary in my mind. It had a countertop in front and shelves around all the walls. It was full of flour sacks: 25-pound, 50-pound, 100-pound sacks. Daddy looked at the bill and saw he'd been overcharged five dollars—big money in those days. Daddy refused to pay.

Jimmy Boware got nasty as a rattlesnake. "Nigger," he shouted, "don't you tell me I'm telling a lie!" Daddy was calm. "Mr. Boware, you're just wrong," he said. "I don't owe that much." "You're calling me a liar, nigger?" His eyes looked like they were dripping poison. Daddy just set his jaw and said, "I don't owe that much and I won't pay it."

Jimmy Boware started behind the counter to get his pistol from a drawer. Daddy blocked his path, snatched a Coke bottle, broke it off at the neck, and pointed the jagged end at Jimmy Boware. Jimmy Boware screamed and said, "I'll kill you, you black sonofabitch!" Daddy said, real soft, "You better not go around that counter. Move another step, and I'll bust your damn brains in." Fifteen mean whites were gathered in that store. What kept them from pulling a gun on Daddy, or rushing him in a group and dragging him off to a lynching tree? Daddy stopped them. He wasn't scared, and he'd have killed a few of them before he died. They knew that.

Medgar and I each grabbed a Coke bottle, to help Daddy. He turned and said, "Get outside, boys." We said, "No, Dad, we ain't going to leave you in here." Daddy had nothing but a coke bottle, but Jimmy Boware was shaking like a leaf. He couldn't understand why a man would die for what he believed in. And that gave Daddy an edge.

Daddy kept his eye on Jimmy Boware and backed us out of the store. Medgar and I wanted to run. We thought they'd come after us. But Daddy hissed, "Don't run. They're nothing but a bunch of cowards." He was right. No one followed us. We walked home down along the railroad tracks, Medgar on one side of Daddy, me on the other. We put our arms around Daddy's waist, he put his hands on our heads. We were so happy. And Daddy told us, "Don't ever let *anybody* beat you. Anyone ever kicks you, you kick the hell out of him." And Daddy sat up that night with a .22 rifle. If Jimmy Boware had come calling, Daddy would have shot to kill. Some thought Daddy was crazy risking his neck, but that's the stock he came from. That was part of what it meant to be an Evers.

CHAPTER 1

My Pact with Medgar

"SLOW DOWN, CHARLIE. You going to get in trouble." Those are the first real words I remember. I heard them a lot as a kid—from Mama and Daddy, from my sisters, and from my younger brother, Medgar. But the way I figured, I wasn't getting in trouble. I was *born* in trouble, just like every Mississippi Negro in the 1920s. Specially so if you were sassy, smart, and strong like I was. Death was walking right behind me all the time, just waiting for me to slip. I paid him no mind.

In my hometown of Decatur, Mississippi, white kids were born in nice, clean hospitals, staffed with young doctors in stiff white coats. I was born in an old bed, in a house filled with flies, with a wrinkled old Negro midwife standing by. Slavery was seventy years gone, but the system I was raised in might as well have been slavery. White folk segregated "the niggers" to hold us in line. They forced us to sharecrop, worked us like mules, walked on us like dirt. We lived in shacks and shanties, went down cheap, and grew old with nothing. Half of us died as children, and the other half were always in danger. You drank that in with mama's milk.

You knew you were a nigger the very first time you rode in a car, couldn't use the bathroom at the service station, and had to relieve yourself in the woods just off the road, hiding from passing cars. One day when I was nine years old, in uptown Decatur, I had to pee real bad. At a service station, I asked for the bathroom. A white man yelled at me, "We don't have no nigger toilets!" I knew he didn't like me, but I couldn't believe he'd forbid me to use his toilet. I thought maybe he hadn't heard me. I asked, "Can I just come in and pee?" He shouted, "No!" I peed all over myself, walked home, and asked my parents why

I couldn't use the gas station toilet. They said, "White folk are like that."

You knew you were a nigger the first time you went driving with older Negroes and they warned you to avoid the highway patrol and never let a white man pass you after dark because he might run you off the road or put a bullet through your head. You knew you were a nigger when you learned you weren't allowed to swim in the lakes of Mississippi. You knew you were a nigger when the nicer restaurants wouldn't serve you and the nicer hotels wouldn't let you spend the night there, or even get a cup of coffee.

You were trained never to say "yes" and "no" to whites—always "yes, sir" and "no, ma'am"—but whites called you "nigger," "hoss," or "boy." You knew you were a nigger each time you went to a white man's home and had to come in the back. They'd walk right in *your* front door without knocking, but even your regular doctor made you come around back. You knew when you looked at the newspapers of Mississippi, and the good that Negroes did was never mentioned, and the evil that whites did to Negroes was never mentioned. God, it hurts a child to be refused and rejected! White folk told us everything black was dirty, stupid, and dishonest. They said God planned it that way. Their movies and newspapers and magazines told us that all the beautiful women were white, and all dark skin was ugly. Nothing destroys a child's self-respect like all the powerful folk assuming he's ugly.

I know that hardship can build strength and character, but no white person would take for an hour what most blacks take all their lives. I know the future is what counts, but like most blacks, I spend too much time fighting bitter memories. White folks ate breakfast cereal in the morning. We'd eat a bowl of rice. White folks had steak dinners. We ate neckbones and day-old bread. White kids were born in homes with running water. We walked down to a spring and took our water home in buckets. White folk had big enamel bathtubs. We had little tin tubs. But being poor wasn't what hurt most. The worst thing was being treated like we weren't human and had no right to be happy. Humiliation built and built until it crushed Negroes like a millstone. How can you explain to your bubbly little Negro son that he's got no right to be happy?

Whites killed Negro men they even *suspected* of desiring a white girl. They would cut their ears off, maybe cut their balls off, and drag their bodies to the sheriff's house or leave them in the road for the vultures. They justified all this by saying the South would be ruined by race mixing. All day, they'd spread this jive about racial purity, and at night half of them would slip into bed with a black girl, like their kin had done for three hundred years. Some of them boasted, "There's my nigger woman," but most of them shut their mouths. Nighttime integration, we called it. Talking white, sleeping black. We got nighttime integration long before we got daytime integration. That's why so many of us are light skinned.

Every southern black family has suffered this, but Mississippi was America's lynching capital. It seemed there was a lynching every day, somewhere in Mississippi. Negroes could be lynched for sending a mean note to a white man, testifying against a white man in court, requesting service in a white restaurant—or just for being uppity. People think Negroes got lynched for trying to rape a white girl, but most of the time rape wasn't even charged. The Ku Klux Klan had everything its own way. Sometimes the Klan burned eighty crosses around Mississippi on a single night. They hated not only Negroes, but Jews, Catholics, Chinese, socialists. All kinds of "foreign elements."

White folk had police protection. Whites who got beaten by cops were either bad white boys, or it was all a big misunderstanding. Law-abiding whites always had the comfort of having the cops and politicians on their side. Mississippi Negroes had no such comfort. The cops were taught to beat us up. The political system was *designed* to keep us down. No misunderstanding about it. We were almost 50 percent of the state, and just 4 percent of the voters. The poll tax and literacy test and brute force kept it that way. Every two-bit politician made hay "cussing the niggers." Every little redneck farmer scared of losing his crop or his wife could thank God he wasn't a nigger and vote to keep the niggers in their place. One politician went down, a new one came up. On the race issue, they were nearly all from the same bag.

There'll always be a few extremists who'll beat and kill folk of another race. That's human nature. But when the police and the politicians wink at these killings and cover them up—that's worse than violence. That's state-sponsored terrorism. And that was Mississippi in my childhood. Cops killed Negroes all the time and called it justifiable homicide. If a white man went on trial for killing a Negro, the jury retired to "deliberate," played dominoes for ten minutes, and came out saying, "Not guilty." White men got in more trouble killing rabbits out of season than they did killing niggers.

I was raised with white people bragging about the Negroes they'd killed. Negro bodies were found in rivers and creeks all over the South. For every Negro we knew was murdered, there were two others buried deep in a forest or fed to the gators. Killing Negroes was a white man's prerogative. They'd kill Negroes just like stepping on a bug. Bad whites killed, bullied, and raped, and hardly a "good white" lifted a finger to stop it. The merchants did nothing, the high society did nothing, the white preachers never preached about it, the police and politicians wouldn't even discuss it in public. Very few Negroes would talk openly about it, either. Too many of us lived as cowards.

White hatred dogged your heels like a shadow. Whites blocked us from registering to vote. Juries were lily-white. Draft boards were lily-white. The police force, fire department—any place with a job that might interest a little boy—was lily-white. White bootleggers were winked at because they knew the local cops and politicians. Negro bootleggers got the law on their neck. On and on and on. Most Negro men worked seasonal jobs, and many lived on three hundred dollars a year.

A very few made it. Leontyne Price, the opera star, was born in Laurel, Mississippi. B. B. King, the blues legend, was born in Kilmichael, Mississippi. I'm proud of Leontyne and B. B. But they're musicians. They weren't trying to change society. And they had to leave Mississippi to make it. Thousands more like them stayed in Mississippi and got twisted or killed by the white man. Strong, independent Negroes got crushed, driven to whiskey or drugs, denied the chance to reach their potential. They were made to do hard, dangerous work, for ten cents an hour, and if they acted uppity, for no pay at all. Medgar and I vowed not only to make something big of ourselves—but to do it in Mississippi.

I should have been able to make it easily in Mississippi. I'm a man born to be out front. I was myself at an early age. I've always worked long hours, made good money, and loved people. I could always reach folk by speaking from the heart. I was a born leader, proud, and without a scared bone in my body. I was born to get rich and rise in politics. But I hit a brick wall saying, "Niggers got no business making money, being proud, or going into politics." I had to struggle so hard to take my place out front.

As a small boy, I played with white kids: Margaret and Bobby Gaines, the Hollingworths, Sonny Boy Jordan, Johnny Keith. We'd scrap like little kids do, but we never had racial problems. Kids left alone are beautiful that way. Until about the eighth grade, these white kids never acted superior to Negroes. We ate together, swam together, slept together. Peas in a pod.

And I have to say that right next to all the white hatred in Mississippi, the meanness, the killings, there's always been a sweet closeness between whites and blacks you don't find up north. It sounds crazy, but it's true. Maybe it's because 90 percent of us in Mississippi are poor. White folk could be generous with black kids that caught their eye. Leontyne Price had an aunt who worked as a maid for the Chisholm family in Laurel. When the Chisholms found out their maid's niece could sing, they helped pay her way through the Juilliard music school, and one of them was in the crowd when Leontyne Price made her debut in New York. That smiling face was a side of white folk that kept us confused.

Decatur had some nice white merchants, like our druggist, Andy May. But Mama and Daddy used to send Medgar and me into Decatur to buy flour and sugar at Charlie Jordan's store. We dreaded going, because the white men hanging around that store would pick on us, push us, call out, "Dance, nigger!" Charlie Jordan didn't mind taking our money, but he was the worst of all. I swore to Medgar one day I'd have my own store and make white folk dance to my tune.

Growing up Negro in Mississippi, the rules were drilled into you: Watch your step. Learn your place. When a white woman passes, get in the gutter so you don't brush against her and defile her. Don't brush against anyone white. Many Negroes told their kids, "It's a white man's world. You just happen to be here, nigger." The Evers family had more pride than that. But when I asked Mama and Daddy, "Why do we have to do like this?" they knew no better than to say, "Because we're colored, son." As a sharp little boy, looking around, you expect more than that from life.

Daddy once bought two mules, Maud and Kate, to haul lumber and pull the grinding wheel at a local sugar mill. Maud never kicked, and she let you crawl up between her hind legs and raise one of her back feet to look at her shoe. So we used Maud every day, worked her hard in the fields all day, and rode her home for dinner. Kate was the opposite. Mean! Could kick the sweetening out of gingerbread without cracking the crust. If she was tired when you came bothering her, she'd kick you to kingdom come. So we kept Kate well fed and well rested. Kate taught me a great lesson: The tougher and more dangerous you are, the better you get treated.

But Mama could see that along with my toughness, I was starting to hate, and she told me hatred solves nothing—just brings down more hatred. I ignored her. Many times Mama would say, "Charlie, you must not believe you can die." I'd answer, "No one dies before their time." And she'd say, "Yeah, boy, but you can rush your time." Mama always knew I'd work for civil rights.

Medgar was the saint of the Evers kids. Slim and small boned, easygoing and quiet, with a real soft voice and a big, happy smile that warmed us all. He'd take long walks alone, kicking a tin can. Never wanted to hurt anyone. Smarter than the rest of us, but he studied more, too. He'd sit on our back porch for hours, reading some dog-eared book or the Negro papers. Medgar didn't like the rough and tumble, but when he set his mind to something, he could be cold as ice. He was always on my butt about something. No one but me thought he'd do civil rights. Medgar always thought of other people's feelings. He always planned what he did, always measured the consequences.

I came from the other side of the street. Charlie Evers was the loudmouthed Evers boy. Big, too blunt. A hothead. Wouldn't back down. Always had to have my say. Rode roughshod over folk if I had to. Acted on instinct, and damn the consequences. I liked to plan for the distant future, but not the near future.

Our whole family was close. My younger sisters Ruth and Liz scratched together very close. But Medgar and I were the closest. We were not only roommates, but bedmates. Medgar shivered easily, always hated the cold. It was my job to keep him warm. At night, in wintertime, those old sack sheets were *cold*. I'd lay down first, warm a spot, then shift over, give it to Medgar. Sometimes, I put my legs on him, just to keep my little brother warm.

Medgar and I did everything together. Built scooters from skate wheels and boards. Fished in creeks and streams. Walked to school and back. When we worked the fields, we rode the same mule, me up front, him behind. We wrestled and boxed. Medgar was clumsy but strong. I got us into many battles around Decatur, mostly with Negro boys. Older boys came courting our sisters, and we'd pound spikes into two-by-fours, lay them under their car tires, and put out all four tires at once. I taught Medgar to swim by throwing him into a swimming hole. I'd have pulled him out if he started to go down, but I wanted him to learn by himself. He learned.

We played with local Negro boys: Cloris Tims, Junior Gardner, Frank Jordan, and Henry McIntosh. Cloris Tims wanted to hunt or play baseball. Frank Jordan liked my sister Liz. I was crazy for Henry McIntosh's sister Lizzy. Medgar's and my room was right at the back of our old frame house. We had to be home by sundown and in bed by eight. Saturday night, we'd kiss Mama and Daddy goodnight, go to our room, crawl out the back window, and join our friends at our hideout down by the washhole, near the railroad tracks.

Henry McIntosh or Frank Jordan would steal some lard, Junior Gardner or Cloris Tims would bring a skillet. Archie Lee Tims would bring bread. Medgar and I brought the meat, maybe a chicken we'd stolen from Miss Atkins. We'd make chicken fry, ease back to bed about midnight. Sometimes down at the washhole, we'd try to kiss the girls, or stick them between the legs in the bushes. I don't recommend this mischief. But in the '30s, we had no TV, no bowling alleys, no basketball courts, or swimming pools. No libraries. Not for Negro kids. So we played and plotted, but never dreamed of carrying machine guns like kids do today.

Medgar and I always knew there must be something more than what the Negro was getting in this white man's world. From the time I was eight and Medgar was five, we vowed to prove black folk could get our share. Plenty of people around Decatur used to tell us, "You Evers boys going to get yourselves killed one of these days." But we refused to stay in our "place." Tell me I couldn't go somewhere or do something, and I was going to find a way to do it.

Medgar and I made a sacred oath as young boys: However much we might trick our friends or white folk, we would never lie to each other. And whatever happened to one of us, the other would carry on.

Sure, young boys promise all kinds of things, but Medgar and I were more proud and serious than most youngsters. We were always planning years ahead, and we carried out many of those plans. Many people in Decatur were surprised to see sweet little Medgar Evers grow up to be such a warrior for civil rights. I wasn't surprised one damn bit. I saw the warrior in Medgar when he was a tiny boy. I helped create that warrior.

CHAPTER 2

Mama, Daddy, and Old Mark Thomas

MY MAMA WAS JESSIE WRIGHT EVERS. My daddy was Jim Evers. Both were strong people. Daddy taught me to fear no one. Mama taught me religion. Daddy was over six feet and two hundred pounds, lean but very strong. He was dark skinned. Mama was just over five feet, brown skinned, real pretty. Late in life she got stout, but as a girl she was a little doll, with fine features. Mama had a full-blood Indian grandmother and an Indian complexion. Tiny little size-four foot, like a bird. Padded around barefoot most of the time.

Mama's first husband was named Grimm. She never talked about him, but Grimm gave her three children: Eddie, Eva Lee, and Gene. With Daddy, Mama brought four more kids into the house: me in '22, Medgar in '25, Liz in '26, and Mary Ruth in '27. Liz was like me: outgoing, pushy, liked money and good living. Mary Ruth was sweet and easygoing.

Mama knew the time was coming when Negroes would need education. She pounded that into our heads. Mama and Daddy were thought strange for keeping their kids in school at harvest time. Liz got some high school before she married, Mary Ruth finished high school, and Medgar and I finished college. In Decatur, Mississippi, very few Negro families got that much schooling.

One of Mama's great-grandfathers was a half-Indian slave, one of the worst slaves they ever had. Caused trouble, took no abuse from anyone. His name was Medgar Wright, and Mama named Medgar Evers for him. Mama's father was half white, and he once shot two white men and left town in the dead of night when someone called him "a half-assed mulatto." There was a lot of spirit in Mama's family. But Mama herself made no trouble. She thought a black man had no business being mayor of any town. She thought a black man shouldn't even walk the sidewalks.

Mama prayed first thing in the morning and last thing at night. She sang hymns as she moved through the house. She knew her Bible, and she made sure her kids knew the Bible, too. She applied Bible teaching to daily life. No makeup for her girls. No alcohol or cigarettes in the home. Poor as we were, we had to be clean and neat. No one ironed clothes like Mama. We had to be morally clean, too. But when Medgar and I were eight or ten, we already hated whites. Mama knew that, and every night she'd pray for us. She told us, "Hatred only breeds more hatred." We couldn't see it.

Mama made all our clothes, from cotton, denim, gingham cloth, old flour and fertilizer sacks. She made her men denim pants and coveralls, her girls cotton drawers and petticoats. She'd sew all night. I wore cheap green tweed pants on Sundays, coveralls and blue jeans the rest of the year. My half sister Eva ran off and married at sixteen so she could have a nice new pair of shoes.

Mama was a maid for Decatur's postmaster, Mr. Jim Tims. But her main family was the Gaines family, a mile down the road. She worked for them six days a week. Left for the Gaines house at sunrise, cooked their meals, washed their dirty linen, cleaned their house, cared for their kids, Bob and Margaret, helped Miss Ann Gaines—all for fifty cents a day. None of the Gaineses but Margaret was ever more than cordial to us, and even Margaret thought no Evers could possibly be her equal.

At 7:00 A.M., while Mama fixed the Gaineses' breakfast, her own kids ate old cornbread, chitlins, and pot liquor. While Mama got Bob and Margaret ready for school, Medgar and I were slopping down the hogs, and Liz and Ruth were ironing their own clothes, combing their own hair. Mama couldn't ready us for school because she had to get the little white kids ready. Mama came home worn out, and right off she had to start washing the Gaineses' laundry. Mama shooed us out of the kitchen while she worked, but we'd slip back in just to be with her. Those small, strong hands were always cooking or working over some laundry. She'd find fault with us, but no matter how tired she was, she always had a smile, a pat on the back.

Mama led us over to the Gaines house, clean laundry perched on her head: twenty shirts, overalls, dresses, socks, and underclothes. A dozen big sheets, cleaned and ironed. Medgar and I'd walk next to her, arms full of clean clothes. Mama would say, "Boys, be careful. Don't wrinkle Mr. Gaines's shirts." Mr. Gaines had a temper. The Gaineses denied us their front door. Mama could care for their kids and cook their food, but she couldn't use their front door. And Mama took such pride in being clean as a pin. All those fresh clothes in our arms, we'd walk in the back door but couldn't go past the dining room. Medgar and I vowed we'd be buried in hell three times before we'd let our own kids get treated like this. "White folk are no better than you are," Mama said. "But they sure think they are."

Mama thought nothing of rising at 2:00 A.M. to fix a meal for company. We raised okra, black-eyed peas, potatoes, and corn in our garden. Mama canned them in the fall. Each fall, we'd kill a hog, cut it up, salt it, and eat it for weeks. Mama baked cookies, and Medgar and I would steal a bunch from her big wooden platter. Mama would ask about the missing cookies. I'd say, "I don't know, Mama." "Charles, don't lie to me!" She'd make me and Medgar open our mouths. When she saw crumbs, her eyes would flash, and she'd slap us across the face. Then she'd fetch her peach tree switch or Daddy's double razor strop: "If you lie about this, you'll lie about something else." She'd beat the stew out of us.

Mama and Daddy never told us how they met. They both came from Scott County. Daddy was a rowdy, handsome devil. He drank too much and hustled, but he always made good money, and by the time he courted Mama he was settling down. They married around 1920. He called her "Grimm." She called him "Jim." They made a good couple. Daddy would walk in the front door saying, "Where's Grimm?"

Like any Mississippi Negro, Daddy couldn't always find paying work. He worked his back off, stacking lumber in the sawmills, working for the railroad. Daddy was more than a hired laborer, he was a businessman. He owned his own property in Decatur, built and rented out two small homes on it, and kept a small farm. He raised cows, chickens, and pigs. Had a pair of mules. Grew vegetables for himself, and cotton to sell. He was a small lumber contractor, too. Lumber's dried in kilns now. In the '30s you dried it in the sun. Daddy had lumber contracts in Hazlehurst, Union, and Decatur, making sure lumber was dried right. He worked for our small family funeral home, too. We never had a whole lot of money, but Mama and Daddy made us appreciate what we had.

Daddy was a small-time businessman. But being in business isn't about size, it's a matter of how you think. And Daddy thought like a tough businessman. He always told us, "Work! If you can't function, you're a has-been." He made his kids work for the luxuries we wanted, and he taught us to believe in work. If I asked for the car, Daddy would say, "You want me to furnish you a car? For how long? Two hours? Three hours?"

"Maybe three hours."

"Well, an ambulance costs three dollars an hour, but a car shouldn't cost that much. We'll make it a dollar an hour."

People said, "Jim, how can you charge your own boy for the family car?" But I'm glad he did. Daddy raised me to think like a businessman. Nothing in life comes free. Whatever you want, work for it. Until you produce something, you mean nothing. Until you turn a profit, own some land, you mean nothing. Ever since I was twelve years old, I've set up businesses wherever I've gone. That comes from Daddy.

Daddy was a strange mix. He swallowed the white man's lie that whites deserved all the best jobs, and Negroes the menial ones. When I asked about any of the better jobs, he'd say, "That's a white man's job." Daddy paid taxes, but he never voted in his life. He never felt entitled. Yet Daddy backed down to no man—white or black. Daddy was a man. Tough and proud. Tall, hefty, and quick. Worked sunup to sundown. Always called a spade a spade. When someone knocked at our door, Daddy went to the door himself. "Who is it?" he'd ask in a big voice. If he didn't like your voice, you weren't coming in his door. Liberals and feminists say different, but sons, daughters, wives, and girlfriends—we all want our man to be tough. A man's not someone with a pair of pants on. A man is someone who stands up. Daddy stood up.

Provoked, Daddy was mean. He tanned our hides with a belt if we showed him or Mama any disrespect. One time Daddy got to talking about those soup lines they had downtown for the sorry unemployed. "Boys, let me tell you," Daddy said. "If the Evers family got in that soup line, I'd kill every one of you, and then kill myself." Daddy didn't allow. Black or white, if someone did Daddy wrong, Daddy raised all kinds of hell. He just didn't allow. In doing this, Daddy taught Medgar and me that most men are timid, measly, and mediocre. Be tough, and they'll fall in line behind you. Other Negroes fell in behind Daddy.

It's amazing Daddy stayed alive, bucking whites like he did in the '20s and '30s, when the Klan was riding high, and killing a Negro was like killing a chicken or snake. White folk said, "Let's go kill us a nigger." For Daddy to act like he did, hold a big family together and teach us how to buck whites—for a Mississippi Negro, that was like being a brain surgeon. My Daddy was about the most remarkable man I ever knew, and he spent most of his potential just trying to stay alive.

Courage kept Daddy alive. Bullies can smell fear. It brings out the sadist in them. Daddy had no fear. When other men got scared, Daddy got angry. When Daddy was roused, he didn't smell like fear, he smelled like danger. White folk can be pretty dumb, but most of them leave danger alone. They couldn't make Daddy crawl, so they called him a "crazy nigger" and let it go.

My Daddy taught me the real truth about Mississippi white men: Most were cowards. Sure, some were tough and a few courted real danger. But most of the meanest, most threatening white racists were cowards. Daddy always told Medgar and me, "If you're scared, you can't do nothing. Show a coward some nerve, and you can back them down." And Daddy taught us another great lesson: If you want to survive very long, with dignity, you better learn to back them down. Either that, or outsmart them—and Daddy wasn't built to dodge trouble.

Negroes walking down a sidewalk in Mississippi could get lynched if they didn't move aside each time white folks approached from the other side. Daddy was one of the only Negroes around Decatur who wouldn't move aside to give whites the sidewalk. Daddy set his course and walked straight on.

Daddy was proud of Medgar and me. He believed in us. He'd say, "Charlie can do it." My full name was James Charles Evers, after my daddy, and everyone said I looked like Daddy, so I had to live like him, too. *I had to be tough as he was.* Daddy stuck up for us. When we told Daddy how Charlie Jordan made us dance in his store, Daddy went straight to Charlie Jordan, told him his boys had been messing with Medgar and me. "And my boys don't make up no story." Daddy told them to stop, and they did.

Daddy always showed me and Medgar how to be a man. When he took us shopping with him for staples in Decatur on Saturday night, we saw the respect he got from whites. Negroes were supposed to slouch, shuffle and grin, scratch their neck, stammer, never look a white man in the eye. Daddy did none of that. He'd say, "Don't scratch, never grin. Stand up straight and look the white man dead in the eye." Daddy didn't mince words, either. White folk respected my fearless Daddy. I could tell by the way they greeted him. Daddy would buy a big round peppermint stick and give it to all his kids. Candy was special, one of the few things Daddy bought with cash.

Daddy had a habit of pointing to a sign and asking, "What's that say?" like he had no time to read it. It took me years to learn Daddy couldn't read or write. No one had ever stopped to teach him. But Daddy was a very smart man, and he was full of good advice: "Don't ride a horse to death, son, unless you're ready to walk." And: "Don't never tear up nothing unless you got something better to offer." I still live by that. Daddy said if you have a favor to ask a man, don't beg or demand, just ask for it straight. Daddy told us, "It ain't what a man says, it's what he does." And, "If you can't pay, don't play." Daddy told us how easy it is to talk about changing things, and how hard it is to do it. He'd say, "Build things, boys. Don't destroy." He'd say, "Don't look back, look forward. Don't look down, look up." When we did wrong, Daddy would say, "Alright, you made a mistake. Don't wallow in it. Don't tuck your head. Just because you stumble, ain't no reason to lay down." And Daddy said, "Only the strong survive." But he also said, "You're strong, so *have no fear.*"

On Christmas Eve in Decatur, the white folks put on a fireworks show. White folks came into town, shooting off sparklers, firecrackers, Roman candles. Medgar and I wanted to see the show, but the Klan had a rule: "No niggers allowed in Decatur around Christmas." Daddy saw his boys wanted to watch the fireworks. He did, too. He and Mama mostly kept us in after dark, but Daddy didn't like white folks crossing him. Daddy put a metal tap on the end of a broom handle and hefted it like a baseball bat: "C'mon, boys. We're going to town. If anyone throws a firecracker, we'll use this on him." And we walked down the road into the heart of Decatur. Daddy busted that ban wide open with no more than a broom handle.

The white folk on that road stared at us, mouths hanging open. Everyone knew niggers out that night were asking for trouble. People were murmuring, "Tough old Jim Evers." Daddy walked on, ignoring their looks, just walking and swinging that broom handle. A white boy ran in front of us to light a firecracker. Daddy told him, "Throw that firecracker and I'll bust your brains out." The boy ran and told his father what Daddy had said. The father came up spitting fire. Daddy stared him straight in the eye and called out, "And that goes for you, too!" For a black man in 1935 to tell a white man, "I'll bust your brains out!"—that was signing his own death warrant. But Daddy backed the white man right down and told him, "You better not come to our house, neither."

We went on, did our shopping in town. Daddy told the shopowner what had happened, and the owner told the white men standing around, "You leave Jim alone. Get on away from here and let Jim alone." They did, and we went home. Man, that impressed me. Every boy wants a daddy tough as my Daddy. Medgar and I told Daddy we expected the Klan that night. We said, "We better set up tonight." "That's right," said Daddy. And we did.

Our house was in Decatur's Negro section, the last house on the road out of town. Anyone coming to our house had a long walk down that road, right in our view. Two other men, Henry and W. J. Roosevelt, sat up with us, holding .22 rifles. We set up a crisscross. No Klukker came down that road. Just before sunrise, Medgar and I got up, picked up our .22 rifles, and walked stiff legged a short way toward town. Looking to kill some Klukkers. No one was there, so we turned around.

Daddy's father, Mike Evers, farmed two hundred acres of corn, peanuts, and potatoes out in Scott County, just west of Decatur. He had peach trees, pecan trees, fig trees, and apple trees until he missed a few tax payments and white folk stole his land. Mike Evers was rough, fought a lot, and taught Daddy to have no fear. Daddy's mother, Mary Evers, was part Creole Indian, with long, straight hair and high cheekbones. All my grandparents died when I was small, and no one talked about any earlier ancestors. We had no birth records, no photos. All I knew of Daddy's family was that they were hard workers and fighters, and that none of them lived to be very old.

Daddy could be sweet. Sunday afternoons, he'd go out in the yard, dip some Tuberose chewing tobacco, then ease inside. We'd go up in his lap and he'd rock us to sleep with great old stories from when he was a boy in Scott County: parching peanuts, hunting possum, stealing watermelon. Swimming with his friends and getting their clothes stolen by white boys. Hunting rabbits with a stick, because his folks didn't trust him with a gun.

Daddy liked to make us smile. When we griped about the rickety old hearse the Evers funeral home used, Daddy would say, "If dead folks don't want to be toted away in this, let them find something better." We tried to make him smile, too. When Daddy chewed Tuberose, he was supposed to spit in a jar. But every now and then, Daddy would roll his lip, swish around some chew, and let fly on the house floor. Medgar or I'd jump up: "Look here, Daddy. Somebody spit on the floor." "Shut your mouth, boy. You know damn well who spit on that floor. Don't you ever be sassing me, boy!"

Mama was proud of Daddy and gave him no back talk. Daddy pointed out that her religion forbade it. Daddy and Mama were very close. They truly loved and enjoyed each other, and that love reached out and warmed everyone in the house. But Daddy's hankering for other women caused trouble. Daddy was tightfisted and we were poor, so the money Daddy spent on his girlfriends hurt us all. Especially Mama. We kids, most of all Eva, sensed what was happening. We pestered Daddy's girlfriends, threw things at them, trying to protect Mama. At first, Mama never spoke of Daddy's girlfriends. It was tearing her up inside, but she wouldn't let anyone speak badly of Daddy.

By '36, when I was fourteen, Daddy's tomcatting got worse. For the first time, Daddy started spending nights away from home. His girl was a family friend, and we knew her kids. Daddy gave them nice clothes, things he never gave us. One day Mama, Daddy, Medgar, and I were sitting around a fire. Mama mentioned the other woman, and rebuked Daddy for neglecting his family. He denied everything. Words flew. I had never heard Mama raise her voice at Daddy. Daddy threatened to beat Mama, so I grabbed a hammer and Medgar a butcher knife. I did like Daddy had raised me to do: I looked Daddy dead in the eye and said if he hit Mama, Medgar and I would kill him. He stormed out the back door. Mama pulled Medgar and me close and cried real heavy. None of us ever mentioned this incident again.

For a few years, Daddy kept on straying. He and Mama would yell at each other, but Mama waited it out. She'd say, "We're just going to pray for him. Someday he'll change." After two years, Daddy broke with the other woman, and the rest of his life was as faithful as Mama could ask. Loyal and devoted. Now, our home was never what you'd call fertile ground for women's lib, but Mama felt her prayers had been answered. On rainy nights, the rain beat a rhythm on our tin roof, and Medgar and I would lie in bed and hear Mama and Daddy laughing and making plans, deep into the night. They lived happily together until he died.

But Daddy's straying left a scar on me. No matter what face Mama put on it, I knew how bad she hurt. After Medgar, Mama was my closest friend. Daddy denied her. I blamed Daddy's women for his flings. They twisted him around their fingers because they wanted the flowers, cards, and candy he bought for them. They coaxed these things out of him, then laughed at him. A boy always hates seeing his big, strong daddy made a fool of. I saw the way the world works: A good wife assumes her man will never stray, and then a pretty woman comes along and takes him. I began hating women.

Mama warned me not to hurt women just to get even with Daddy's girls. But since women had hurt Mama, I thought for Mama's sake I should hurt women back. I never bought a girl flowers or a box of candy or even one valentine. I vowed that no woman would ever laugh at me. I promised Mama no wife of mine would ever see me with a girlfriend. Whatever happened would be out of sight, with no one humiliated. I also promised Mama that when I was a daddy, I wouldn't chase married women. That promise I broke.

Mississippi winters have no snow, but that damp air gnaws at your bones. Our house was full of cracks, and before we started the morning fire, it was cold. Each morning at 5:00 A.M., Daddy told us to make a fire. We said, "Yes, sir." But on some of those real cold mornings, we'd just put one foot out of that warm bed, stomp so it sounded like footsteps, then lay back in that warm bed ten more minutes. One morning we pretended to get up a few times, but we fell back asleep each time until Daddy woke us with his double razor strop. From then on, when he told us to make a fire, we jumped.

But I was a sassy boy, and I often made Daddy mad. One day I was sitting on an old bench at home. Daddy was grouchy. He told me, "You think you can take care of yourself? Then you don't need to be in my house." I said, "Dad, it ain't your house, it's *our* house." Whop! Daddy slammed me off that bench. Mama heard me hit the floor, and she came in: "Now, Jim, honey—" "Shut up, Jessie," Daddy said. "Can't be but one Daddy in this house. When they get so they're telling me what to do, they better get out of this house."

For all of Daddy's strength, there was a basic contradiction in his nature that I never understood. He was sweet, but he was also mean. Too strong and proud to let any white man break his spirit, Daddy never questioned the whole system of racial segregation. He was the toughest man I ever knew, but he wasn't free. Our preacher said, "We're all God's children." So I'd ask Daddy, "Why are we treated so mean?" And tough as Daddy was, he had no good answer. Man to man, no one could whip Daddy, but the system whipped him. He spent so much of his talent just guarding his self-respect. Daddy accepted the system he hated. Medgar and I vowed to be as tough as Daddy, but to never accept the system.

Of my half brothers and half sister, I liked Eddie the most. Gene was a small guy who worked hard and drank a lot. Eva worked for white folk as a maid. But Eddie was a hobo. He rode the rails. Eddie had never left Mississippi, but he traveled all around the state. That was farther than anyone I knew had ever gone. It was a big achievement then for a black man just to have been to Jackson. Daddy never got outside of Mississippi all his life.

Mama frowned on any son of hers being a hobo, and she would knock down even a grown child for showing her disrespect. Eddie knew that. He was always courteous to Mama, never sassed her, but when he wanted to go, he just caught a train. No one could stop him. I loved that. I've always admired people who can't be controlled. Medgar and I wanted to see this hobo world. Catching trains to other towns. The more Eddie described it, the better it sounded. The train tracks ran just behind our house, so one summer we started catching trains to Newton and Union.

One day the Newton train passed Newton without stopping, and headed for Laurel. All of a sudden, we were far from home, broke. If the yardman caught us, he'd beat us, maybe put us in jail. We jumped off the train, and the yardman started after us. Did we ever run. We reached the highway, hitched some rides, and got home the next day. Mama and Daddy had worried. Daddy said, "You're running off because you ain't got nothing to do! You're idlesome." He beat the stew out of us, then worked us like dogs all summer: "Busy men got no time for the devil." Much as I admired Daddy, I couldn't wait to leave Decatur, to get out from under him.

Around '37, Eddie came home with a real bad headache. He was afraid of hospitals, so he stayed home, lay down, and died. From the way he suffered, it may have been brain cancer. When Eddie closed his eyes, I didn't cry, but Mama couldn't get me to eat. I just sat out on our back porch and watched every freight that came by, hoping somehow Eddie was on one of them.

A better role model than Eddie was my Daddy's uncle, Mark Thomas. Mark never got much school, but he was smart and ambitious. As a young man, he'd worked in a funeral home. One day, Uncle Mark was in a train wreck. He got hurt, and he made sure he got paid: two thousand dollars. Uncle Mark took that two thousand dollars and founded Thomas Burial Insurance. He sold policies to the local Negroes; a dollar a month covered the whole family. He branched out, opened his own funeral home, and ran many side businesses.

More than anyone else, Mark Thomas had raised my Daddy, but watching them, you'd never have known it. Daddy would never Tom. Mark Thomas shuffled and Tommed all his life. Whenever white folk were near, he was all "Yes, sir" and "Thank you, sir." But he was shrewd. Mark understood white folk, and he used words to reassure them. He had it all figured: The more he talked to them, the more they liked him, and left him alone.

Mark looked the white man in the eye, told him just what he wanted to hear, just how he wanted to hear it. He'd promise to do what they asked, then go do the reverse. If Mark Thomas saw a white man coming, he flashed a smile: "Morning sir! You're looking mighty fine today." The white man thought he had Mark in his pocket, and he'd promise to help my uncle or his church. Mark would smile even wider: "Yes, sir, I sure appreciate that." Then the white man would try to gossip: "Well, Mark, is Auntie Dorothy Lea going with that white man?" Now, if anyone knew what Auntie Lea was doing behind the door, it was Uncle Mark. But why should he tell some ignorant white man? Mark would say, "Well, I don't know about that, but if I find out, I'll sure let you know, sir."

My uncle played white men for fools and got most anything he wanted from them. Folk today would call him a big Uncle Tom, but look at what he achieved in brutal times. He always worked for himself, got rich by Negro standards, never drew a paycheck from a white man, always kept his freedom, and used his businesses and his good name to help other Negroes.

My Daddy had no use for sweet talk or diplomacy, so I was fascinated to see how Mark Thomas used diplomacy to raise money, keep his freedom, keep his businesses rolling. Mark became my second role model in business, and diplomacy became a new strategy for me. Tough as I am, I've Tommed a bit through the years to help keep Negroes a little safer. A black man can't use just one strategy on the white folks.

CHAPTER 3

The Wall of Separation

THE DECATUR MOVIE HOUSE denied Negroes all the better seats. We had to sit in an upper balcony. We called this upper balcony "the buzzard's roost" because buzzards roost way up high in trees. Medgar and I saw a lot of movies from up there. I thought Hedy Lamarr was the most beautiful woman in the world. I first saw Africa in Saturday matinees of Tarzan of the Apes. Africans looked like fools next to Tarzan swinging on those damn vines. I loved watching him kill lions. I rooted for Tarzan—I didn't see the racism then in those pictures. But in the cowboy pictures—Tom Mix, Bob Steel, Hopalong Cassidy—Medgar and I saw the racism clear as day. The white kids in the good seats downstairs rooted for Tom Mix. Medgar and I always rooted for the Indians.

Cowboys and Indians or Negroes and whites, I always studied who got the upper hand, and why. I saw lots of aggressive white men stomp on passive Negroes. The white man would ask question after question. Many of those questions had no right answer. Negroes were supposed to stumble and lie, and think: Whites are better than us. But I saw this, and all it showed me was that being aggressive was a hell of a lot better than being passive. The trick was to always be the man asking the questions. And if someone accused you of something bad, you should agree with them. People hate for you to agree with them.

When I was ten and Medgar seven, whites in Decatur claimed one of Daddy's best friends, Willie Tingle, had insulted a white woman. Mr. Tingle was a Negro about thirty-five, a laborer in town and a part-time farmer. A real nice man. A white mob started ranting and throwing a fit. They grabbed Willie, tied him to a wagon, and dragged him through the streets of Decatur. Mama and Daddy rushed all their kids off the street. In a beautiful pasture, the mob hung Willie Tingle from a tree, took shotguns and shot his body right in half. When he was dead, the lynch mob laughed, cut him down from the tree, and stripped his body. They left his bloody clothes under the lynching tree to remind us Negroes what happened when we got too fresh.

Most of the Negro men in Decatur stood and watched this. They shuffled their feet and looked away, scared that if they tried to save Willie Tingle, they'd be the next nigger up that lynching tree. The cowardice of those Negroes almost hurt me more than the lynching itself. Medgar and I had known for years that most whites put no stock on our lives. But we expected Negroes to stand up for each other. You never forget seeing your first lynching.

Daddy was Willie Tingle's undertaker. He cut the hanging noose off Willie's neck and hauled Willie to the Evers family funeral home. Willie's body was too mutilated to be embalmed. That lynching left Daddy as upset as I ever saw him. A big helpless look covered his face. One of his best friends had been killed for no reason, with no warning, and with no way to stop it. When Medgar and I made some furious noises, Mama said, "Be quiet. They could do the same thing to you." I said, "Mama, it's a damn disgrace!" She said, "Someday it will change. Let's pray on it." I said, "Mama, we pray all the time. What do it get us?"

Every day for months, Medgar and I saw those rotting, bloodstained clothes each time we passed that pasture. For months, we dreamed about those bloody clothes. To this day, I can still close my eyes and see that lynching in 1932. Years later, I used to go back to Decatur and walk by some of those white folk who killed Mr. Tingle. One of the killers was drying up like a seed. He must have remembered the night he helped lynch Willie Tingle.

After the lynching, Medgar asked Daddy, "Why did they kill Mr. Tingle?" Daddy said, "Just because he was a colored man." Then Medgar asked, "Could they kill you?" Daddy seemed invincible to me. I was shocked when he said, "If I was doing anything they didn't like, they sure could kill me." Boy, it hurt to hear my Daddy say that. I grew up a bit that day.

I was a natural hustler. Church folk had a saying, "Give me the Lord, and you can have the rest." I always said, "Give me the Lord *and* the rest." Ignorant as I was, foolish and naive, I knew no one ever got rich picking cotton. I always knew how to make a dollar. I sold Coke bottles back to the grocery store, a penny a piece. I scoured the fields for abandoned plows, searched towns and railroad sites for metal I could sell as scrap iron. For each one hundred pounds, the junkman gave me a dime. I pressed cigarette foil and sold him that, too, for a few pennies.

Medgar and I read more about Africa in the best Negro newspapers—the *Chicago Defender* and the *Pittsburgh Courier.* Poor as my family was, we subscribed to the *Chicago Defender.* In the 1930s, none of the great white papers told the truth about the Negro. Not a one. So when I was about eleven and Medgar eight, we took our first little step to buck the system. We sent off to the *Chicago Defender* for copies of the paper to sell. The *Defender* always wanted Negro paperboys outside Illinois to spread the word about the Negro. Medgar and I planned to spread the word and make money, too. For a few months, we sold the *Defender.*

Then the local whites said, "Selling papers is a white boy's job. Can't have nigger paperboys." We weren't taking anyone's job, now. No one in Decatur had ever delivered the *Defender.* But seeing Negro boys take initiative and make money made the crackers nervous. And Negroes reading political articles and editorials made the crackers crazy. Politics was white folks' business. Post offices in Mississippi weren't above confiscating a Negro paper that came in by subscription. Whites felt they couldn't let us wise up to how bad they were using us. Decatur's Negroes were even more scared, seeing us deliver the *Defender.* God, there was so much wasted Negro potential in that town! So many Negroes scared they might be the next one up the lynching tree.

Medgar and I stopped delivering the *Defender.* But we'd been taught "An eye for an eye, and a tooth for a tooth." So we figured white boys in Decatur weren't going to sell newspapers, either. The next few times a white boy came around selling the Jackson *Clarion-Ledger,* we laid in wait in the bushes, pulled a toe-sack over his head, tore up his papers, and threw them in the woods. A white boy snitched on us, and his daddy told mine, "Jim, you better do something about those kids of yours." Daddy called us in: "What you been up to?" We told him how the whites wouldn't let us sell papers and how we'd torn up the white boys' papers. Daddy was silent a minute. Then he said, "Well, don't get in no trouble now." From an old-school disciplinarian like Daddy, that was approval! Daddy was proud as hell his boys bucked the whites. Through the years, many folk around Decatur told Daddy, "Your boy got smart with me, Jim." Daddy warned me not to go too far, but he loved having a son as fearless as he was.

Daddy worked his boys hard. We mended fences around our property. We killed chickens, slaughtered hogs, milked the cows, and drove them home from the pasture at night. We fetched firewood and started the morning fire. Three times a year, a truck left a load of wood at our house, and Medgar and I had to cut it into sticks for Mama's cookstove. If we wanted to bicycle to school, we had to buy our bikes with money from painting white folks' houses and cutting white folks' lawns.

Medgar and I saved our money in old Bull Durham chewing tobacco sacks. We each had our own sack, tied to the bedsprings on our side of the bed. We never let Mama and Daddy know how much money we had. If we had, they'd have demanded to know where we were getting it. And a lot of it we were stealing. Medgar and I hated how bad things were for us. "Because we're colored, son" wasn't enough reason for us. There was a big deficit between what we thought of ourselves and how white folks treated us. To fill that gap, we stole from whites.

We picked pecans for an old white widow lady, Mrs. Lizzlie Pace. Mrs. Pace lived behind her store, very near us in Decatur. Almost a neighbor. She fussed over us like we were sons of her own, but she wouldn't pay us worth a damn. We'd work all day, pick almost four bushels of pecans, and get paid just one child's bucket of pecans. So Medgar and I brought a little homemade wagon to Mrs. Pace's barn late one night and took all the pecans we'd picked.

The next day, Mrs. Pace told us some low-down scoundrel had stolen her pecans. We were outraged and promised to fix it so no one could steal those pecans again. We nailed up the barn door tight, but we tore a plank off the side. That night, we hauled off all the bushels again in our wagon. Medgar wanted to quit then. His nerves were thin. But since Mrs. Pace wasn't paying us our due, I had to show her she wasn't so smart. I got Medgar to help me put the pecans in new sacks, and we hauled two hundred pounds worth to a white buyer named Sam Massey. He insisted we only had one hundred pounds, and he wouldn't pay a cent more. So we took his damn fifty cents on the dollar. A few nights later we stole those same pecans from Massey and sold them back to him. White folk thought Negro boys had no nerve for things like that. I took pride in my nerve.

Medgar and I rode our mule Maud to the sugar mill where Sam Massey made syrup. He hired us to harness Maud to a wheel and walk her in a circle all day. We also helped throw in the cane to be squeezed and mashed. Juice from the cane flowed into a machine that strained out the shucks. They cooked the syrup five hours, then poured it into five-gallon cans for market. Our day's pay was one small bucket of syrup. So at night, I'd say, "Come on, Medgar, let's get our pay." We'd slip back down to the sugar mill and carry off two of those five-gallon syrup cans.

My cousin T-Boy was in Decatur. Around 1936, when we were both fourteen, T-Boy and I got a job racking oak wood at the sawmill where Daddy worked. The wood was four feet high and eight feet long. The pay was ten cents an hour. We were still learning the job when a white man named Otto Pearson got mad at T-Boy and kicked him. T-Boy fell over, right off the ramp. I ran at Otto Pearson: "Why'd you kick T-Boy? If you kick me, I'll kill you!"

He glared at me hard but didn't kick. He was just another redneck bully and coward. Otto Pearson found my Daddy stacking lumber: "You better talk to James Charles. He's talking about killing me." Daddy asked, "Charles, did you say that?" "Yes, sir, I sure did. And I meant it, Daddy. If he kicks me like he kicked T-Boy, I'll go get my rifle and kill him." "You go on home," Daddy said. I never worked at that sawmill again, but I didn't mind. I'd made my point.

Working for the white man, nothing was guaranteed. Once, a mean cracker named Cooper hired Medgar and me to haul lumber by truck from Decatur to the town of Lake, one county over, a forty-mile round-trip. Medgar and I worked ten hours a day, Monday to Saturday. A dollar a day. And after all that work, Cooper never paid us a cent. He didn't even explain, just didn't pay. I told Daddy, and Daddy spoke to Cooper.

Daddy came back: "Charles, the man says he ain't got it." "Didn't they pay him for the lumber?" I asked. "Yeah," Daddy said. Three years later I saw Cooper selling cars in Jackson. I asked him for my money, and he still wouldn't pay. I said, "I better not watch nobody buying no car from you." I vowed never to work for whites again, but I made sure I got Mr. Cooper back. I bided my time. Then, years later in Jackson, when I was grown up and he didn't recognize me, I got him. I bought a 1941 Ford off Mr. Cooper, on installment, and never paid him a dime.

I was fourteen, and restless. Daddy said, "An idle mind is the devil's workshop." He'd started hiring out Medgar and me to Sam Massey, for his sugar mill, and out in his fields to pick cotton, corn, and tomatoes. Cotton picking was something I'd vowed never to do. Sam Massey only gave Medgar and me fifteen dollars a month, and Daddy snatched thirteen dollars of it: "What you need with money? You got room and board with me." Any back talk and he'd beat the stew out of us. As Medgar and I reached twelve and fifteen, we tired of this. Real carefully, we asked Daddy for a bigger cut. When he said no, I vowed to leave Decatur. I ran off to Jackson, worked in a white cafe, stayed with a black lady named Mrs. Tims. Mama and Daddy found me after two weeks and made me come home.

I cooked up another plan. I figured if I could move one town south to Newton, Mississippi, attend school, and work there, I could make more money and save most of it. A nice white lady, Mrs. Payne, had a cafe in Newton. She knew my family. Lizzlie Pace recommended me. Mrs. Payne offered me a job in her cafe as a dishwasher, busboy, short-order cook. It was a little thirty-seat bus station cafe, with a counter in front, kitchen in back. I took the job.

Mrs. Payne was as different from Cooper and Sam Massey as night and day. She was about fifty-five, tall, neat, and gracious, with glasses and a lovely smile. She wasn't wealthy, but she dressed well with what she had. Her husband had passed, but her son, Robin, was just a few years older than me. Mrs. Payne was a woman I could talk to. But her cafe still served white on one side, Negroes on the other. Two entrances. I always used the white entrance. When I asked Mrs. Payne why the Negro entrance was so dirty, she just said from now on I should keep it clean. She didn't see the big picture, the way a dirty entrance hurt a Negro inside. But Mrs. Payne was one of the good ones. Later, she hired Medgar, too. She didn't just work us—she taught us, encouraged us. She'd say, "James Charles Evers, you're just as good as anybody, but you're no better than anybody." I worked for Mrs. Payne several years, went to the Negro school in Newton through the tenth grade, even played some raggedy football on the team there. I lived in an attic room over Mrs. Payne's house.

One midday, a drunk white man walked in the cafe and told me to make him a hamburger. From back in the kitchen, I heard him cussing me out: "Dirty black nigger. . . ." I was standing back by the kitchen windows. Mrs. Payne didn't know I was listening. She lit into her own customer: "Listen! I won't have you bothering Charles. He works for me, and if you don't like it, *you get out of here!*" She ate him up. I smiled. Mississippi needed more folks like Mrs. Payne.

When she'd finished, the drunk man said, "Well, he must be your black lover boy." She said, "He's my black son. And don't you mess with him. He's working here, and he's doing what I tell him." By then, the man's hamburger was ready to come off the grill. I put that burger on a bun, hawked and spit on it, put it on a plate, covered it with lettuce, then walked up front to watch this white bastard eat it. When I handed the man his burger, he cursed me again. Before he took a bite, Mrs. Payne ordered him out of the cafe. He made a furious scene. Mrs. Payne got him out, then went back to the kitchen and told me to go back to work, don't pay him any mind. It was folks like Mrs. Payne who kept Medgar and me from being white-hating fanatics.

But all that afternoon, I was a hater. I'd peek out of the kitchen to see who came into the cafe. If they looked like a racist, I'd spit on their hamburger or their scrambled eggs, sometimes four or five times. Silently, I'd say, "You can curse me, but you going to eat my spit!" Then I'd take the order out to their table and watch them eat it. See what hate does to you?

Speaking of hate, let me tell you about the master of talking hate, a politician named Theodore Bilbo. Medgar and I first saw Bilbo back in 1934. He'd already been a state senator, lieutenant governor, and governor of Mississippi. Candidates for president didn't stump in Mississippi, so to us Bilbo was the top of the line. Bilbo was a white man knee high to a duck, maybe five feet four, 140 pounds. But he had a broad forehead and campaigned like a plantation boss: business suit, metal-rim eyeglasses, big white hat, diamond stickpin in his necktie. Had a big voice. Like a lot of little men, Bilbo was rambunctious, hard to predict. But he'd grown up with the peckerwoods, and they loved him.

Others called Bilbo a race baiter, a skirt chaser, a fool, and a demagogue. Some said he took bribes, but no one ever made that stick. Now he was running for Senate. There was no television then—even radio was rarely used in politics. Candidates spoke from the stump. Bilbo made over one thousand stump speeches in that one '34 campaign. We expected Bilbo to entertain us, and he never let us down. He could use Bible phraseology. When he reached the Senate, no one filibustered like Bilbo.

Bilbo once got pistol-whipped for calling a rival "a cross between a hyena and a mongrel, begotten in a nigger graveyard at midnight, suckled by a sow, and educated by a fool." But we forgave his lies, because he entertained us. Bilbo called Jews "kikes," Italians "dagos," and himself "The Man." He called his opponents "liars," "hypocrites," and "buzzards on a fence, waiting for the good white folk of Mississippi to let down their guard." Then Bilbo would warm to his favorite subject: The Nigger. He'd start shouting about how he was going to preserve racial purity by "sending the niggers back to Africa." Bilbo claimed Negroes meant to mongrelize the white race. If he had to lambaste the Negro to stay in office, on a fat salary and a flower bed of ease, Bilbo happily lambasted the Negro.

The race issue was king in Mississippi. White folk themselves should have hated white supremacy, since it kept them from being the good Christians they wanted to be. But the fact was, whoever was harder on the niggers was elected. Bilbo gave the poor crackers what they wanted. He'd start out high-toned, but soon he'd be sweating at the forehead, rearing and stomping, waving his arms: "I believe in white superiority, white domination, and the integrity of my white blood. . . . We have behind us four thousand years of culture, learning, education, and wisdom . . . and the nigger, I got nothing against the nigger, I'm his best friend, but the poor devil is only one hundred fifty years removed from the jungle and eating his own kind."

Most Negroes stayed clear of Bilbo's rallies. But Medgar and I saw Bilbo speak many times, for the entertainment. We might be the only Negroes there, but we didn't mind sitting amongst the peckerwoods. As I said, when someone told me I couldn't go somewhere or do something, that made me do it. Medgar and I went to watch Bilbo clown, and we ignored all the nigger baiting. Northerners can't appreciate a southern rascal. I always could.

On the stump, no one was worse on the race issue than Bilbo. But you don't govern on the stump. As a man, Theodore Bilbo was alright on the race issue. Racists like Bilbo knew much more about Negroes than they ever let on. Bilbo kept a Negro woman down in Poplarville who bore him Negro kids. Bilbo supported Negro education and gave new buildings to Alcorn A&M College, the local Negro college. He had some Negro friends on the quiet. He may have helped Negroes more than any governor we'd ever had to that time. Bilbo's viciousness was an act.

One day, Medgar and I walked to the Newton County Courthouse in Decatur to watch Bilbo spit fire. We sat in the front row, right by the courthouse steps. Bilbo said, "If we fail to hold high the wall of separation between the races, we will live to see the day when"—and then he pointed square at Medgar and me—"those two nigger boys right there will be asking for everything that is ours by right. You see these two little niggers setting down here? If you don't keep them in their place," said Bilbo, "then someday they'll be in Washington trying to represent you." Medgar nudged me in the ribs and whispered, "Ain't a bad idea." I looked up at Senator Bilbo and smiled. Bilbo squawked, "He's even got the nerve to grin at me!" That day Medgar and I decided old Bilbo might be right. One day, Medgar and I might be in Washington representing Mississippi. That day made politics a goal for Medgar and me, something possible even for two Negroes from Decatur.

Mama and Daddy raised us right. We would have done some good with our lives even if we had never met Theodore Bilbo. But I wonder if we'd have fought so hard for civil rights if Bilbo had patted us on the head and said, "Nice nigger boys." We *always* rose to a challenge.

CHAPTER 4

Whites Messed with Us, but We Couldn't Mess with Them

MAMA RAISED ALL US CHILDREN in the Church of God in Christ. We called it the Holiness Church. The Holiness Church forbids drinking, smoking, gambling, and card playing. Mama tithed the best she could: a dollar a month. Tuesday and Friday nights, the church held prayer meetings, but Sunday was the big day. At 5:00 A.M. Sunday morning, Medgar and I started rounding up chickens. Chickens are filthy animals. White farmers kept them in a painted chicken house in the yard. Our chickens lived right outside our door. Medgar and I had to catch those poor chickens and wring their necks. The chickens flopped around in their own blood and died so Mama could cook some rascal preacher his Sunday dinner.

Medgar and I never liked preachers. They knew how to talk, but did they help us get better homes or jobs? The preacher pitied the poor sinners in our shotgun shacks, but when he visited, he expected your best. He lived high on the hog. The deacon of Mama's Holiness Church was Will Loper. He was a Sunday shouter, a dancer, a twister. I called Medgar "Lope" just to tease him, and it stuck. I called him Lope until the day he died.

Mama dumped the chickens in a tub of hot water, and all her kids plucked the feathers. Liz shucked corn. Mama fried the chickens and made sweet potato pie, white biscuits, white gravy, and cornbread dressing. Dessert was blackberry pie, pecan pie, or peach cobbler. Six days a week, we ate second-best food so that preacher could eat our Sunday best. Some Sundays, we all ate together, but mostly the adults ate alone while the Evers kids watched from the next room. Mama might have two or three preachers over at once, praying over the food, talking holy talk, and eating all our sweet potato pie, biscuits, and peach cobbler, with us kids peeking in, hoping some potato pie would be left over.

One Sunday, I said, "Mama, come out! Something's going on in the yard!" and Medgar slipped in the kitchen and stole some thighs and drumsticks. But clumsy as he was, he dropped those chicken parts on the floor. Mama caught him: "Reverend! Come look!" The mean old preacher ran up with a long peach switch and whipped us all around the house. The reverend kept saying, "That's right, Mrs. Evers, we got to break them for stealing. If they steal chickens, they'll be going downtown and stealing."

Mama said prayers at home Sunday morning, then we went to church at 9:00. The kids had Sunday school until 11:00, then went in to the adult church service. The congregation sang, prayed, and danced until 1:00. Then the preacher preached until 3:00. After the service, we'd rush home to eat. We had to be back by 6:00 for a young folk service. Then a prayer service stretched from 7:30 to 8:30. And then we'd start the testimonials. All the members rose and testified, and after each testimonial we sang a song. After that, we took up a collection. Then we'd leave the church and walk the streets collecting money for the preacher. We had to be back in church by 9:30, when the preacher returned to preach a second time.

We spent three months a year in church revivals. Mama had her Holiness revival, but Daddy favored the Baptist revival. We hit other revivals, too. Preachers came from all over. Everyone "saved by grace" was promised they'd see heaven and Jesus when they died. We had convocations, summer revival, fall revival. The third Sunday in August, the revival was in Decatur, and Negroes came from miles around to be saved and get happy.

The big revivals opened with a picnic in a pasture. Everyone spread out their own dinner. Country people in the South are so affectionate. Mama and the other ladies hid their bodies in white all-over dresses but Mama told all her kids to do a lot of kissing. She said, "We're all brothers and sisters." To Mama, kissing someone showed you cared. Mama made caressing and comforting people part of my life. I liked those picnics.

But after the picnic, they got down to the Christianity. The Evers kids had to sit up front stone silent. With all the love in Mama's heart, if we spoke one word during the whole revival, Mama'd tear our fanny up, saying, "Lord, give me strength to whip this boy's behind!" I had a shaggy brown mutt named Trim, with some German shepherd in him. I trained Trim to protect me. Mama could never whip me in the yard without first tying up Trim. I always said, "Whip me first. Get it done." Neither Mama nor Daddy could whip me and make me cry. Mama wore herself out trying, and she had to rest before whipping Medgar. Lope would jump, scream, holler, and run. He cried even before the blows came.

Each night before bed, we dropped to our knees and prayed to God. Mama asked God aloud to help her care for her kids, to help her sons become men the world would admire, not lazy rascals, drunks, or haters. Mama taught us hate was a sin as bad as murder. And she ordered us to forgive all those who hated us. The Holiness Church required that we forgive seven times, if necessary. After our Sunday morning prayers, Daddy'd say, "You're going to church today, and after that, come on home. I don't want you getting in no trouble. But if anyone bothers you, you knock their ass off." So we got a mixture of spiritual and natural teaching. Mama's old raggedy church leaked, so we stayed home when it rained, and Mama read us Bible stories. Daddy'd say, "Y'all go on, listen to your Mama read the Bible. Get your Sunday school lesson." Then he'd ease outside to do some work in the yard.

I loved those Bible stories. I loved Moses saying, "Let my people go." People smile when I praise the Bible, like the Bible's only for the holyroly. The Bible has so much to teach us all—big men and little, strong and weak, devout and backsliding, too. "An eye for an eye, and a tooth for a tooth"—is that holyroly? I loved hearing Mama read the parable of the prodigal son. Luke chapter 15, verse 11: "A certain man had two sons. . . ." The bad son left and "wasted his substance with riotous living." He spent his time amongst whores and thieves, and it didn't matter. The day he came home, his father laughed and killed the fatted calf. I loved that. "Do unto others as you'd have them do to you" was Mama's favorite line. I've tried to follow it. The Bible says a prophet is never honored in his own land. That's very true. And the saying "Yea, though I walk through the valley of the shadow of death, I will fear no evil"—you can't top that. I used to say, "Listen up, Mississippi. Yea, though I walk through the valley of the shadow of the Klukkers, I fear *none* of you!"

I had too much church as a boy and got wild later just to catch up. But the Holiness Church is still part of me. My civil rights meetings and business meetings are religious, and I hug and kiss folks I meet. I don't give a pastor 10 percent, but I might pay someone's water bill. When a man dies poor, and I make sure he gets buried right, that comes from church and Mama. Most of all, the Holiness Church taught us that people do change. God put good in us all, and when evil men see the Lord or see their own death, it works a change on them. As long as there's breath in the body, enlightenment can come. If I didn't know in my heart that people do change, I could never have been a civil rights leader.

Lots of church Negroes just wait to go to heaven and accept that here on earth we're going to live like dogs. Mama never did. She'd say, "You pray— and then you get up and go after it." I'll go off and pray a minute when I'm in a tight spot. I know the Lord's listening. He wants us to believe in Him, but He expects us to go after it. I don't know what the Lord told Martin Luther King, but the Lord's never once told me to turn the other cheek.

People said Charlie Evers was a rough boy, but I always loved the Bible and wanted some sweetness in my life, some way to treat people better than what I saw. Medgar loved to hunt raccoon, possum, and squirrel. I never did. One night I went possum hunting with some grown men. The dogs treed the possum, one man threw a blinding light on him, another clubbed that possum to death. I knew the possum loved his life as much as I loved mine. I ran off when they beat that possum's brains out, and I never hunted again.

And when I was twelve and first fell in love, it was for sweetness, too. Ruby Nelle Willis was a cute Negro girl in the Newton school who lived with her Negro mother. Her white father lived nearby, bragging about his "nigger woman down the street" and his "nigger kids." Negroes were brainwashed to prefer light-skinned women like Ruby, but I loved her for her sweetness. Later I fell in love with Virgene Williams, who was dark but just as sweet. Folks called me a bad boy, but I had Bible stories in my heart, and I knew I was good. Where that goodness would get me, I had no idea.

Miss Ada Adkins, my first grade-teacher, was also my next-door neighbor. She was a tall, heavy Negro woman, with a daughter, Florene. Miss

Ada only had eight years of school, but she was bright as a lamp. If she ever saw the Evers kids in devilment, Miss Ada thought nothing of whipping us. Then she'd tell Mama, and Mama would whip us with a peach switch and tell Daddy, and he'd whip us with a leather belt. But Miss Adkins said, "Them Evers boys will be something one day." She advised us how to act: "You got to stop being so high-strung. Start listening. Don't be so quick to get mad. But you got it. You got the gumption."

The whites had a slogan for our school systems: "separate but equal." Separate, yes. Equal, no way. They were never meant to be. The more honest white slogan was "A dumb nigger's a contented nigger." They did all they could to make us feel dumb. Negro schools were only open mid-October to mid-February, the four months a year when white folk didn't need us on their farms. Late in February, whites closed our school so we could help with their spring planting.

Each morning, the white kids boarded a shiny new yellow-and-black school bus. Medgar and I walked to school, three miles each way, shivering our way down muddy, icy roads, often with no coat or proper shoes. Even then, the white folk couldn't leave us alone. As the white school bus drove past, the driver would slow down so the white kids could lean out the windows, jeer and spit at the dirty niggers, and throw rocks. They tried to force us off the road into a ditch, to make us dirty our clothes. When we reached school, more than likely we were muddy and damp. Medgar always hated the cold, hated the damp. Often we were hungry, too.

White folks had nice school buildings. We had the Decatur Consolidated School, a dingy one-room shack with shingle windows and a shingle top, and holes everywhere. If the white bastards who ran that county sent us to school only in fall and winter, at least they should have given us a half-warm building. But the rain came right in. In December and January, cold winds cut right through that shack. Girls wrapped their feet in raggedy horse blankets. We had an old potbellied stove in the middle of the room. First thing each morning, Medgar and I went for firewood. We came back to see one hundred kids shivering in their hand-me-downs. One hundred kids ages five to fifteen in one classroom, grades one through eight, all together, always cold. It was hard to concentrate.

The white schools had poor teachers, but the Negro schools only required their teachers to read, spell, and do sums. All one hundred of us had just two teachers: Miss Adkins and Miss Anderson. Those two tried to control us, but while they were helping one boy, most of the rest of us would be hollering and carrying on. Our teachers never got trained in how to teach. They had no equipment. So we didn't learn much. When the teachers rebuked us, it wasn't for our schoolwork, but our attitude.

I wanted to be a lawyer so I could use the law to keep white folk off my neck. I knew I needed school to be a lawyer. I learned some spelling, reading, and arithmetic, but I finished eighth grade in Decatur with only a raggedy few schoolbooks. Of the very little I learned in school, a lot of it was racist. My favorite subjects were history and geography, but in eight school years no one ever told me a Negro, Matthew Henson, helped find the North Pole. No one told me Negroes had fought and died in the American Revolution, or how much Negroes had built this country, north *and* south. We never learned what Negroes had done with blood plasma, peanuts, and the clock. The Negroes in our textbooks were beasts of burden, savages with strong backs and weak minds.

Our history books lied to us about the Reconstruction years after the Civil War. They told us Reconstruction was a disgrace. I know about Reconstruction now. That time had its troubles, but it was the first time the South tried racial integration. It was very important, and it could have worked. But in 1877, white folks in Washington made a dirty deal to end Reconstruction. Whites had promised us forty acres and a mule, freedom and dignity. They never even gave us the mule, let alone the forty acres. But I surely didn't learn that in the Negro schools of Mississippi.

Few Negro kids had books at home, either. Fannie Lou Hamer would jump off a truck on the way to the cotton fields just to read a little magazine lying by the road. Medgar was such a bookworm that Mama said he'd be a doctor or professor. But in school we were too cold to read much. Even the teachers were cold. We asked why we had to go to school in a freezing-cold shack when a big new school was standing nearby. Mama explained that the new school was white-only because whites thought they were better than us.

At 3:00 P.M., we started walking home those same three miles, on the same dirty, muddy roads. The white kids drove by in that same big yellow-and-black school bus. And the white folk still couldn't leave us alone. The driver would shout from the window, "Let's see you run, niggers!" Maybe he'd cut the wheel, try to sideswipe us and force us off the road, while a busful of white kids laughed. Medgar and I began picking up rocks and waiting in the bushes on the roadside. I'd be on one side, Medgar one hundred yards past on the other. We'd pelt that bus with rocks. The driver would speed up, scared to stop. Daddy was right again: The white bullies were cowards.

That was the school day for Medgar and me. Four months a year, in one cold room, with two teachers trying to teach one hundred rowdy kids of all ages. And all the white kids in a nice, separate system nearby, hating Negroes, taunting us all they could. I never learned to read, write, and do sums properly. I know deep down what a poor education means, because I'm a victim of one. But I've never let my poor education hold me back. Whenever folks have told me, "You're not qualified," I tell them, "You go to hell. I never had the chance to qualify."

Lucky for me, there's more than one way to get an education. To make ends meet, Mama took in boarders, and Ed Meyers was one. Mama welcomed anyone in her home and at her table—rich or poor, young or old. She wasn't nosy about how they made a living. She didn't condone evil things, but she ignored what wasn't her business. Tramps slept on our porch, and Mama fed them, too. I was a curious little boy who preferred older people to kids my age. These tramps and boarders fascinated me. Around '34, when I was twelve, we got a new boarder, a slicker from Macon, Mississippi, named Ed Meyers. Ed was an ugly little gap-toothed Negro, 140 pounds, wearing a cockeyed cap. He told Mama he worked on a construction gang in Decatur.

Ed had an old Model A Ford. Standard drive. I'd never driven a car, and I wanted Ed to teach me. There was no driving exam then, no license. You just watched a man drive awhile, then got behind the wheel. One day, Ed took me in his Model A over to Shuqualak, Mississippi—up in Noxubee County, near the Alabama line. Coming home, Ed got sleepy, parked the car in a ditch, and fell asleep. I wasn't going to get caught at night so far from Decatur. Mama and Daddy might have beat me if I didn't return by morning. "Ed," I said, "I want to go home."

He said, "You drive it, then." So I took the wheel and drove the thirty miles home without hitting anything or going off the road. The car jerked all the way, and Ed didn't sleep too well. I thought he'd cuss, but he liked having a little driver. Soon, that Model A and I were taking Ed all over Mississippi. Ed liked to climb in the back seat and fall asleep. I soon found out why Ed was so sleepy, and why we were driving so far. Ed Meyers didn't work on any construction gang. He was a bootlegger. And that Model A was loaded with bootleg whiskey—white lightning, homemade stuff made from fermented corn, sugar, and an acid that could knock you flat.

By law, Mississippi was dry. Every time liquor hit the ballot, the preachers got up on their hind legs about demon rum and sent out whole congregations against that bill. Good people were always ashamed to admit they drank, and the church folk whipped the bill. The result was you couldn't buy liquor from a decent store anywhere in Mississippi.

But Mississippi was full of big drinkers, so bootleggers met the demand. Some of the bigger bootleggers sold their brew from little "grocery stores" with a few cookies or canned sardines. But most bootleggers had no store to pay rent on, no hired help. They sold to anyone, black or white, young or old, seven days a week, twenty-four hours a day. They delivered, even in the dead of night. Even in Tennessee, the wet state to the north, you couldn't buy liquor on Sundays, but you could in Mississippi. You bought homebrew for sixty dollars, sold it for one hundred dollars, and cleared forty dollars a week—good money for a Mississippi redneck, and great money for a Negro.

I loved the sound of forty dollars a week. I decided to bootleg myself, but I had to take care because Daddy hated alcohol as much as decent folk hate crack cocaine today. Folks came by our house buying pints from Ed Meyers. My parents knew something was going on, but I never told them just what.

Daddy told a story on himself about the evils of whiskey. As a young hustler, he'd gotten drunk one day and started jumping up on tables, clearing them off with his feet. At one table a "little bitty old nigger" five foot tall, 130 pounds, said, "You get up on that table, and I'll whip your big old ass." Daddy jumped up on the table and cussed him. The little man snatched the table down, and Daddy went down hard. "He beat me, stomped me, kicked me all over," Daddy would tell us. "Then he snatched that half-pint of whiskey from my pocket and busted it over my head." Daddy rarely drank after that.

Ezra Wonley was the main Negro whiskey seller in Decatur. He was no more than five foot seven and 140 pounds, and wore overalls and a cap. A lot of people sold bootleg on the side, but Ezra was our only real full-time bootlegger. He was a likable man, with many friends, and he did well for himself, but Daddy was bitter against Ezra. He'd say, "Old sorry Ezra don't work nowhere, don't do nothing but bootleg whiskey." Medgar and I would say, "Daddy, he's got more money than we do. And his kids go to school well dressed." "You shut up!" Daddy'd say.

I played along with Ed's bootlegging for a time. But even at twelve, I told myself, "Whatever I can do for you, I can do for myself." I began buying whiskey where Ed Meyers was buying. Or Medgar and I would say we were going fishing, and then we'd go buy gallon whiskey jugs from an old white bootlegger. We made blackberry wine, put it in a big jug, let it set four weeks, then sold it for a nickel a glass. We also found where Ezra Wonley stashed his whiskey, began stealing some of it and hiding it in a ditch behind our house. Ezra sold his whiskey for fifty cents a pint; we charged a quarter.

We picked up half-pint bottles from barrels and ditches, washed them out, and filled them with whiskey. We brought the bottles out to an open field where we could scan for cops on all sides. We sat on a stump and sold stump whiskey. We had plenty of customers. Every Friday, I brought maybe twenty-five half-pints of bootleg whiskey to four local honky-tonks. They sold them for me for a dollar through the weekend. They kept a quarter; the rest was mine. Monday I went back to collect my money or my whiskey. If they didn't have either one, we had a little session.

Bad bootleg can give you the jake leg, so folks wouldn't buy a bottle till you "knocked the poison off it" by taking a slug yourself. That was trouble for me because I didn't drink. Business fell off till I hired a drinker to stand right by me, take a swallow in front of each customer, and knock the poison off.

Around then, I lived for a time with my great-uncle, Mark Thomas, the one who owned a funeral home. Since I knew how to drive, Mark sent me in one of his hearses to collect bodies for his funeral home. I saw parts of many all-day funerals, with folk shouting and screaming, almost getting down in the hole with the dead man.

When Uncle Mark was gone, I'd drive the hearse to Vicksburg. I paid a man there to buy me some sealed whiskey and carry it to his garage. I'd pick it up. I took Medgar with me in the hearse, laid him down in the bed like a corpse, and hid the whiskey under the bed. Then I'd hit the siren on that hearse and come rolling down those country roads, through little redneck Mississippi towns, watching people scatter.

Medgar and I'd come to a little town, slow down. The old white sheriff would be standing there. He'd wave at the hearse, thinking, "Good. Another nigger getting buried." I'd look back at him real solemn till we got clear, then we'd laugh all the way to the next town. We'd reach Forest at dusk, drive into the ambulance shed, fetch the cot for hauling the dead, unload the whiskey, and haul it by cot to the embalming room. I'd cover my half-pints of whiskey, scotch, bourbon, and gin with bottles of embalming fluid.

The white man told me I was a poor, stupid Negro. Well, sure I was poor, but I was going to get rich. Sure I was a Negro, and proud of it. And stupid? I *knew* that wasn't true. I loved outsmarting white folk—Mrs. Pace with her damn pecans, all those old redneck cops trying to stop my bootlegging. I was a big local bootlegger before I could legally buy a drink, even in a wet state like Tennessee.

One day Mama was leaving for the Gaines house. Medgar and me tried to come along, to play with Margaret and Bobby. Mama looked at us strangely, and told us, "You can't play with them no more." That was it. A curtain just dropped down. We went from good friends to no friends at all, overnight. We couldn't understand—these were our friends. Mrs. Gaines must have taken Mama aside and said, "Jessie, you know Margaret's becoming a woman now, so it's time you told Charles and Medgar. . . ." She didn't have to draw Mama any pictures. There was an unwritten rule in the South: Whites could mess with us, but we couldn't mess with them.

Medgar and I weren't fit to associate with our white friends anymore. When Margaret Gaines saw us on the road, she'd stop and chat. But the Tims boys turned on us and never looked back. One day in high school, I saw one of the Tims boys working in the Newton bank. I smiled, went over, and called him by his first name. His eyes narrowed and his face got strange and tight. He said, "Listen, James Charles, you call me 'mister.' " I said, "What?" I couldn't believe he'd do me like that. I'd known this boy all my life, we'd swum together, pulled cockleburs from our feet together. And now he ordered me to call him "Mr. Tims."

But whites took all kinds of liberties with us. Old white peddlers came to the door, just as friendly as they liked. Most stores were far off, and Negroes lacked the time or money to buy in town. Some of them couldn't stand being harassed in town, or they didn't have clothes fit to wear in town. The peddlers knew this. So they came door-to-door, selling on installment: peaches, pecans, watermelons, eggs, chicken. Half-rotten beef, barely washed.

The Lott's furniture man brought cheap, broken-down furniture to the door and sold it on credit. If you missed one damn payment, he took it all back and sold it to someone else. Medgar and I flattened a few tires on the Lott's furniture truck. The Raleigh Company peddler came selling cake mix, spices, all kinds of junk. He'd walk right through our front door without knocking and go find Mama. If she was in her bedroom, he'd sit smack on Mama's bed and say, "I'm your Raleigh man. What you need today?"

The peddler I hated most was Old Man Tobe. Tobe was a tall, skinny white man with a long, thin nose, sandy hair, high-top shoes, and overalls with suspenders. Winter and summer, he wore the same old black hat. He was always toting a basket of cucumber and squash. Peddled tomatoes and eggs Saturday mornings. Toted everything in a basket on his head. He'd barge right in the front door. Never knocked. And Tobe wanted more than a few dollars. He looked around each house he went in and guessed about the goings on. He'd say, "I'm tired," and sit down on Mama's bed to gossip. I could never get in a white woman's front door, but a white peddler could walk right in our front door and cozy up on Mama's bed.

So Medgar and I told our Negro neighbors to stop buying from Tobe. They told us to mind our own business: "You Evers boys going to get in trouble messing with these white folks. Y'all too biggity." As much as I hated those peddlers, I got just as mad at the Negro women who bought their damn wares. Mama was no better than the rest. Whatever the peddler was selling, she was buying: Bibles, brushes, hair tonics, cure-alls—you name it.

I decided Lope and I would take care of Old Tobe. In the path in front of our house, we dug a hole five feet wide and three feet deep, just like Tarzan did in the movies. We laid straw and pine needles in the hole, laid sticks across the hole, and covered them with a little dirt. The next day, we watched from up in a tree as Tobe walked that path. He went down hard, spilled his eggs and tomatoes, saw us run, and told Mama. She said Tobe could have broken his neck, and she whipped us.

White girls would bother us, too. Decatur was a small town, and spunky white girls found it dull. There are some older white ladies from Decatur who make me smile when I see them now, because when they were fifteen and sixteen, every chance they had, they were getting a little thrill by pulling at Medgar and me. I was once a dishwasher in Hattiesburg, and one white waitress would lean down and rub her breasts on my back. When she wouldn't stop, I quit. Another white lady would ask Medgar and me to wash her windows, then pull on our legs as we stood on the ladder, and ask us were we men or little boys. There's many a black man buried in Mississippi because a white woman lacked the guts to say, "Yes, I asked him. You leave him alone."

CHAPTER 5

Felicia

FRANKLIN ROOSEVELT came in as president in 1933. He believed like my Daddy: "The only thing we have to fear is fear itself." I loved that line, kind of adopted it. Roosevelt's New Deal hired Mississippi Negroes for the Works Progress Administration (WPA) and the Civilian Conservation Corps (CCC). The WPA reached Mississippi in '35 and built highways, sewers, and parks. Negroes worked mostly on Negro projects, but the CCC offered good-paying work when jobs were damn hard to find.

In 1939, I was seventeen. Daddy wanted to get me a local WPA or CCC job. But I wanted to join the military. With a war coming, Mama and Daddy didn't want me shot, but I liked the soldier's uniform, and I had to leave Mississippi. The service could get me overseas, show me the world. I knew there had to be a lot more than Mississippi. Like thousands of American Negroes, I knew life outside had to be better.

In '39, the air corps and the marines wouldn't take a Negro, but the army had Negro units. I was a year too young, but big and tough enough to lie my way in. They sent me to a Negro unit at Camp Shelby, in Hattiesburg. But the army found out I was underage, yelled, "Why'd you lie?" and sent me home. In Forest, Mississippi, I went back to work in the funeral home of Mark Thomas. But I'd got that little taste of the army, and I wanted more. I reenlisted at eighteen, and returned to Hattiesburg.

I was too young to see that I was doing just what the white man wanted. Peckerwoods couldn't lynch every smart-ass nigger who came along. They loved seeing one volunteer for the army, with war coming. Put the nigger on the front lines, let him die for his country, and come home in a pine box. Easier than hanging him from a tree. Now, white boys from the best southern families didn't serve on the front lines. They might wear the uniform, but they weren't being groomed to die like we were. The Great White Fathers of Mississippi kept the fair-haired white boys out of harm's way.

I soon left Hattiesburg. The army sent me to Camp Claiborne and Camp Polk, in Louisiana; Fort Knox, Kentucky; Fort Sill, Oklahoma. I was always learning, vowing to make something of myself. At Camp Claiborne, I got in engineering training school, learned carpentry and bridge building. At Camp Polk, I got special training. At Fort Knox, they wouldn't let me into officer candidate school. At Fort Sill, I was an orderly at headquarters.

Damn hard work, and when I came home on furlough I told Medgar how bad it was. But when he was just seventeen, still in high school, Medgar volunteered, too. The Evers boys didn't give in—not to the white bullies of Decatur, and not to the U.S. Army. We vowed to use the army to see the world and learn how to defend ourselves, so white folk couldn't mess with us.

They trained me, then assigned me to the 334 Engineer Battalion, with the Corps of Engineers. My battalion had a few Negro officers who had somehow survived the racism at officer candidate school. My favorite, Lieutenant Crabtree, from Bowling Green, Kentucky, was a smart man and a nice man. All the Negroes loved Crabtree and hated a white officer named Crane. And for every Crabtree, there were three like Crane. Every enlisted man in the 334 Engineer Battalion was Negro, but nearly every officer was a white man who treated us like dirt. They'd been ordered not to call us "niggers," but they looked at us with such hate. They put strangling restrictions on us, made us clean latrines for hours at a time. Nearly starved us. They put us in disgusting living quarters, handed us vicious punishments for the tiniest infractions, or for no infraction at all.

And you know what? I still preferred the army to life in Mississippi. I knew that even if the army told me to duck bullets in a foxhole, I'd have a little piece of freedom. I could travel, learn new skills. When Medgar joined the army, he felt the same. The army brought us around the South and then across the world, taught us how to care for ourselves, and how to kill. Deep down, we were both full of hate. We both wanted to kill some white folk in Mississippi. It tickled us to have the U.S. government teaching us how.

At some southern army bases, Negroes couldn't go to the white PX, couldn't go inside the white officer's club, couldn't even parade with white men. When the inspector general came to inspect our troops, he had to inspect my Negro battalion separately. White men never let a Negro soldier forget that most white men hated us.

But white *women*—that was another thing. Just like back home, there were women who wanted to go to bed with a Negro. But now we weren't in Decatur, Mississippi, anymore, so it was easier to arrange. I looked forward to using every white girl I could. Use them and dump them, just to avenge everything the white race had done and was still doing to Negroes. Hate poisoned my mind.

In 1942, the army transferred me to Fort Leonard Wood, Missouri, where blacks and whites used the same PX. I met a friendly white girl who worked there. She smiled, asked me questions, teased me. We went to the service club together, drank coffee, and talked. She invited me up to St. Louis. I went up there on furlough, stayed at the Jefferson Hotel in the Negro quarter. She came down, and we made love. She was the first white girl I ever had.

In my six months at Fort Leonard Wood, we grew very close. We truly cared for each other. If a woman loves you, cares for you, and worries over you, no matter her color, it touches you. This woman cured some of my hate. We never discussed marriage; not in the South, in 1942. But even after being transferred to another army camp, I still went up to St. Louis to see her. She opened my eyes, showed me love's got nothing to do with race.

Medgar's time in the army was a lot like mine. He was placed in an all-Negro unit with white officers. A port battalion. They fought two years in the European theater: England, Le Havre, Liège, Antwerp, Cherbourg. Medgar had some bitter experiences in the war. On Omaha Beach, he saw lots of dead soldiers, saw how horrible it is to kill a man. Medgar was young, and he fell in with the men around him. He began swearing, took on some rougher attitudes. One white officer saw Medgar was smart and told him to keep a proper attitude. Go to college, make something of himself. But most of the white officers were so mean to Medgar. Medgar was always very proud of being a veteran, but he never got over some of the racial prejudice he'd suffered in the service.

Like me, Medgar found white women liked a Negro soldier. In France with his unit, Medgar met a local French family and fell for their daughter. In Mississippi, Medgar could never have touched her. In France, he walked with her, kissed her in public. Her parents liked Medgar and supported this. To a Mississippi Negro, this was amazing. To the French, Medgar was a soldier first, an American second, and a Negro third. Going with this French girl made Medgar even more sure the racism we'd grown up with in Mississippi was unnatural and could be changed. It convinced him black and white could live in peace.

In 1943, I went overseas for the first time—to Sydney, Australia, to Melbourne, and then with the combat engineers to New Guinea, our staging ground for invading the Philippines. Was New Guinea ever a godforsaken place! For eighteen months, we slept on the ground, crawled through mud, fought off bugs, ate and drank coconuts, and sweated like fools. We drilled, cooked, drove trucks, built floating pontoon bridges, opened up roads, and cleared away airfields. I fell off a truck and smashed the same left knee I'd hurt playing football for Newton High. And we waited and waited. I've never been able to sit quietly, and doing nothing drove me crazy. You almost welcomed a Japanese raid just to kill the boredom.

In basic training all the white officers had abused me. But after I got overseas, I got promoted: private, corporal, battalion sergeant major. You got promoted by how much you got done. I was a foreman in charge of construction, very active and hardworking. I got things built without a blueprint. I got barracks repaired. As a battalion sergeant major, I chose which people to dispatch to which jobs. I liked controlling my time. If I made 6:00 A.M. reveille and 11:00 roll call, most of the day was my own.

There was plenty of money to be made in the army if you had the eye. While I ran the barracks, I ran crap games for a twenty-five-dollar-a-night cut. No cut, no crapshooting. I put my money in a big box, changed it to big bills, kept it in a tobacco sack in my shirt pocket. I never smoked, drank, or gambled. Too expensive, too hurtful to the body. I hardly spent a cent. Each GI got a few bottles a week beer ration. I sold mine. I bought beer at the PX for two pesos a bottle, about fifty cents, and resold it for three pesos a bottle, seventy-five cents. GIs were always short on money, so I started a loan outfit, at 100 percent interest: Loan you five dollars, you pay me back ten. You'd be surprised how many customers I had. I sent lots of money back home to Mama and Daddy.

The U.S. Army put us in New Guinea to keep the Japanese from overrunning Australia. Tropical warfare gave many GIs malaria, dysentery, anemia, hookworm. Our walkie-talkies didn't work well in the jungle. During one night raid, I ran for a foxhole, tripped, and broke my left knee a third time.

New Guinea had no civilization. Just the bush people. And no women in sight. The New Guinea natives were almost as dark as Africans and had no education, spoke no English. So we couldn't talk to them. They were friendly, as soon as they saw we weren't trying to kill them. But the U.S. Army didn't trust these people. The army forbid us from fraternizing with them and told us some of them had diseases or were "cooperating with the Japs."

Then we left New Guinea for the Philippines. The army invaded the Philippines in stages. We invaded Leyte in October of '44, Luzon in January of '45. The idea was to secure a beachhead, drive south, take Manila, open Manila Bay, then clean up by taking the little southern islands. We never had enough engineers or equipment in the first assaults. There was great confusion. I was a day behind the invasion of Luzon, and when you were fighting the Japs and you were a day behind, you were right in it.

I was almost killed once in New Guinea, out of sheer carelessness. During a night march just before we left for the Philippines, I walked behind a huge truck just before it rolled back and smashed the truck in back of it. But all this time, I never killed anyone, never even fired a shot. I saw plenty of death. I supervised a first aid unit in my battalion and did a little first aid there. I got my face rubbed in injury and death. But I was never even scratched. The Lord took care of me.

When we cleaned out the last Jap holdouts, we moved into Quezon City. The Philippines sure weren't New Guinea. The land looked like Florida, with beaches, palm trees, thick, heavy bush. But the Philippines also had real cities. After all that time in New Guinea, downtown Manila and Quezon City looked like Memphis to me. Booming. Close to a million people. Quezon City was just northeast of Manila.

Real pretty city, full of old Spanish buildings, social clubs, dance clubs. They spoke English.

We had to drill and cook and clean latrines all week, but the army gave us evenings and weekends to mingle with the Filipinos. So you had a lot of American GIs stationed far from the battlefield, on an evening pass or a three-day pass. Like most young men far from home, these GIs wanted to meet pretty girls and take them to bed. Most of them didn't care who, they just wanted a girl in bed. They'd had their fighting, now they wanted some fucking.

I'd grown up in business, had set up businesses wherever I'd been. I was always alert to a new business opportunity. The natural business to set up in the Philippines was whoring. I watched awhile, just observing and mingling. The Filipinos had plenty of what they called "pom-pom houses"— whorehouses, love shacks. The country was poor, village families crowded into the city, and lots of girls were ready to go to bed for money. But the pom-pom houses were far from the army camps. I knew most of the GIs. When I met some pom-pom girls, I decided to hook them up, and afford the GIs a place to indulge.

A few GIs had brought some girls back to their tents and tried to set up as a cathouse. Pitiful. The tents were filthy, the girls were dirty and ugly, and there were long lines to get in. Some GIs brought their own pom-pom girls to the tent but couldn't wait to get inside, so there was wholesale public fucking. Disgusting! Very mismanaged. From the start, my pom-pom girls were clean and pretty, the tents were clean, and the lines were short. I made sure those huts had hot and cold running water. I changed the sheets three times a day.

I treated the girls well. I left them free to come and go, never tried to stop girls from leaving the business, never threatened or abused any of these girls. I never took them to bed, either. Why would anyone want to put his dick where fifteen other dicks had been that same day? Think of the diseases you could catch. To me, a cathouse was a business—no more, no less.

I started with one GI tent in Manila. Three or four girls. I expanded quickly to rented huts and ended up with a string of four brothels: the one in Manila, a hut on the outskirts of Manila, a hut in Quezon City, and my biggest house, on Quezon Boulevard. Filipino pimps procured the girls for me. I paid my girls five pesos a throw, and charged the GIs twenty pesos a throw—about five dollars. Lieutenants or captains paid twice as much. I bet I was the only U.S. soldier in the Philippines fighting a war with one hand and running a whorehouse chain with the other. I was proud to provide a service. My superiors knew all about it. The military police never lifted a hand to stop it. I bribed them a little, but there was no need. Some of those MPs were my best customers.

I kept my huts open twenty-four hours a day. No one got more than a few minutes a throw in my houses. Profit required me to rush them in, rush them out, like an assembly line—fifteen minutes, tops. Lucky for me, the GIs took pride in how many girls they screwed, not how long they could screw one girl. Fifteen minutes was all they wanted. I stood at the door, giving my customers the once-over. The drunk, dirty, or looking for trouble, I tossed out. But my cathouses served the well behaved of all races. Black, white, Chinese, Japanese, Filipino. I've always been an integrationist.

I couldn't supervise all four huts at once. When I wasn't there, I left one of the girls in charge—like a house mother in the Girl Scouts, except these weren't Girl Scouts. If I was running pom-pom girls like that today, I'd have GIs not paying, causing trouble. But in '42, GIs were politer. Besides, owing me money, where were they going to go? We were all in the army. I'd have gotten my money back. I made over three thousand dollars from those brothels, when most Mississippi Negroes made three hundred dollars a year.

Fighting a war and running an illegal business didn't take up all my time, so I decided to study law. Philippine universities didn't require a high school degree. I entered the University of Manila business law school. Classes were in English, taught by GIs and Filipinos. When I started, I knew nothing about business law, couldn't tell you about negotiable instruments and contracts, to save my life. I learned a lot in Manila.

In '44, I fell in love hard with another law student at the school, Felicia. Her last name was something like Esteneslo. Felicia was part French, part Filipino. Five foot three, 125 pounds, with the finest black hair I'd ever seen. Her father was vice mayor of Manila. In those days, women really worked for their men. Felicia washed my clothes by the banks of a river. Beat them on rocks. Fixed all my shirts just how I liked them. She was so different from the other girls I'd known. So kind, so good to me in every way. Felicia looked out for me, showed me how much a woman could care for me. Taught me a lot about love.

We never even came close to having sex. Those Filipinos were Catholic, and Felicia was 100 percent Catholic: absolutely no sex before marriage. Some girls say never, but late at night, they don't mean it. To Felicia, never meant *never*. Not before marriage. She went with me for a year before she unbent enough to kiss me. And that's as far as it went. Here I was, a handsome man running a string of thriving cathouses, and I couldn't get laid because the only woman I wanted wasn't giving it away. But that was fine, since I truly cared for her. You don't need to take a woman to bed to love her deeply. Felicia taught me that, too. I'd never known a woman so pretty and so chaste. Lovely in every way. Doing business with whores all the time, I welcomed her purity.

Felicia really understood me. She knew how I felt, what I cared about. In her quiet, sweet way, she told me she needed me. So many women try to change a man, try to make him what *they* want him to be. Felicia helped me be the man *I* wanted to be. Part of this was Filipino culture. They love *you,* not what you do. But Felicia had a special natural kindness. She knew I was in business with pom-pom girls, but she never poked into that. She was happy to love the part of me I chose to share with her.

Finally, I asked Felicia to marry me. She said yes. We needed her daddy's approval. He didn't care for me much, but he was happy to have us marry, as long as Felicia stayed in Manila. The Filipinos were scared the Japs would come kill them, but they had no hatred for Americans or Negroes. They were too busy trying to stay alive to think much about race. Felicia's daddy was a big man in Manila, and he expected Felicia to stay in Manila. But I had to get back to Mississippi. Mama and Daddy were getting old. They needed me to support them and help run the family businesses.

I'd have ignored Felicia's family and brought my girl home to Mississippi, but for one thing: Felicia was white. She was part French, part Filipino, but to Mississippi she was white, and I was still a nigger. It was that simple. And in 1945, Decatur, Mississippi, couldn't handle that. I would have risked not only my life but Felicia's, too, bringing her home as my wife. Felicia didn't understand racism. It broke my heart explaining it to her. I put my arm right next to hers: "See how much darker I am? That's why we can't live in Mississippi." Finally, she understood.

When Medgar's battalion was transferred, he and his girl had the same trouble. They couldn't live together in Mississippi. So Medgar came home alone, too. I never saw Medgar's French girl except in a photograph, but I know Medgar loved her deeply because we often talked about finding our girls and living in peace in some Central American country where no one cared about race.

When I heard of my transfer back to the states, Felicia begged me to stay. I couldn't. My last night in Manila, Felicia's folks trusted me enough to let Felicia come to my tent. We sat up all night, talking, kissing, and crying. At 7:00 A.M., Felicia walked me down to a landing ship transport, LST458, with her mama, her daddy—the vice mayor of Manila—and all her little sisters and brothers. I boarded the ship. Felicia cried and screamed and squeezed. I was holding her tight, while her mama was trying to pull her loose. Finally, I let go. We sailed out of that harbor. I hadn't got sick once coming over. On the forty-two days going home, I vomited every day. Losing Felicia was that big a shock to my system. She and I stayed in touch for ten years, but I was never much of a letter writer. Then I lost her for good.

Felicia's the only woman I've ever really loved. Of all the girls I've had since then, I've never been in love with any of them. I've been content, but never deep in love. I've never known hair as fine as Felicia's, never known a woman so understanding. When I lost Felicia, I took all that passion, all that desire and threw it into the civil rights movement.

CHAPTER 6

Wheeling and Dealing at Alcorn

WHEN I WAS MUSTERED OUT of the U.S. Army in 1945, I'd earned an honorable discharge and saved three thousand dollars in cash. I brought it home to Decatur, and a few months later, Medgar came home from France and joined me. We found some changes. With some of our army pay, Daddy had put in four new rooms and indoor plumbing. Mama had replaced her woodstove with an electric stove. But Mississippi seemed all stuck in the past—so much the same that Lope and I almost couldn't believe all this had happened to us, in France and Belgium, New Guinea and the Philippines.

Fighting World War II woke up a lot of Negro GIs, especially in the South. We'd risked our lives for our country overseas, fought for democracy, and seen places without racism. We had to ask ourselves, if the United States was the world's greatest democracy, why were we second-class citizens? When France had so little racism, why did Mississippi have so much? Medgar and I couldn't bring home to our free country the white girls who loved us overseas. And in our democratic country, we couldn't vote. Mississippi whites could kill us just for trying to do either one.

Medgar had a cute French girl writing him letters. And I had a gorgeous Filipino girl who hoped to marry me, writing me letters every day. Medgar and I loved those letters. Mama hated them. She was scared white folks in Decatur would find out her boys were writing love letters to white girls. White folks could lynch you for less than that. It didn't matter if the girl was a foreigner. White was white. Mama pleaded with us to stop writing our girls. Much as we loved Mama, we had to refuse her. We just wrote quietly.

But over time, I lost touch with Felicia. It was too painful writing her, knowing I'd never have her. If Mississippi hadn't been so brutally racist in 1945, Felicia and I would be happily married now, probably living in Mississippi with ten children. Felicia is the only damn woman I ever really loved. Now, I chase younger women, and I tell them all I'm not a marrying man.

James Lusk Alcorn was a hot-tempered old Mississippi white man around the time of the Civil War, who couldn't stand the thought of Negroes at the University of Mississippi (Ole Miss). In 1872, with Negroes demanding to go to college, he gave us our own school: Alcorn Agricultural & Mechanical. And seventy-five years later, Ole Miss was still lily-white, and Alcorn was still the best way for local Negroes to better themselves. In '46, Medgar and I decided to go to Alcorn. Mama and Daddy were all smiles. The GI Bill was paying our tuition. We started Alcorn's high school program, got a diploma, then started college. I was a year ahead of Lope, and we were roommates. I was still my brother's keeper.

Alcorn turned out a lot of teachers for the Negro schools. We had a sprinkling of GIs, but most of my classmates were country boys, green kids who just wanted enough schooling to make forty dollars a month teaching. Medgar and I held ourselves above these country boys. We came from a stronger family than they did, we were older and had served overseas in the war. We had more guts.

On Freshman Day all the Alcorn freshmen met. A teacher explained where all the buildings were and what activities we could try out for. Someone said we'd need a class president. I stood up: "I'm the president of the freshman class." Another freshman, Harvey Cole, of Laurel, Mississippi, jumped up, outraged. "You can't do that!" I said, "Why can't I? I'm twenty-three years old. I fought in the war, risked my life overseas. I got three businesses going. I've stood up to white folk all my life. Can you match that?" No one spoke for a minute, then a greenhorn piped up, "Well, I want to be president. Let's at least put it to a vote." I said, "Put it to a vote, then!" I won in a landslide.

I made a good class president. I encouraged the other students, and because I was older and had seen the world, they believed me. I knew how to mediate, how to lead a meeting, how to inspire folk. I led a strike against Alcorn's miserable food. We blocked the cafeteria. I led a strike against the class facilities. I led a movement to get the deans to stop treating us like babies. And I got things done. The college was run by a bunch of Uncle Toms installed by the white power structure. Those Toms would tolerate some change as long as we didn't embarrass them in front of their white masters. But they were all afraid to rock the boat. I knew what a lot of activists never learn: If you hash things out too long, it all blows up. You must be able to take the concessions you can get, and move on.

For a Negro school in Mississippi in 1946, Alcorn did alright. We had some dedicated teachers, like R. Jess Brown. But the school gave us a false picture of Negro history. We used the same old white racist textbooks that described us as savages and Reconstruction as a terrible evil.

Alcorn also lacked supplies. Our Business Department had one typewriter. Our Science Department had one test tube. I never got a solid academic foundation at Alcorn, never learned any chemistry, physics, math. To this day, I couldn't pass a stiff grammar school test. Medgar went out for business administration, but I knew business already, so I went out for social studies. I was too restless to learn much.

I still planned to be a lawyer, to advise black folk about the law. In 1945, Mississippi Negroes couldn't get legal advice. There were almost no Negro lawyers, and white lawyers wouldn't lift a finger to help us. I never wanted to prosecute anyone. I wanted to know the law, to know how much trouble I could get in, or my people could get in, and still get out.

Medgar and I both played football for the Alcorn Braves. I played center. I'd snap the ball to the quarterback, turn and hit someone. I played the game rough, mixed it up on the line. Medgar was smaller, and quicker, and didn't like the rough stuff on the scrimmage line. He played halfback, at six foot, 170. He made all-conference and I didn't, because Lope was the better athlete. I didn't mind. I was a more natural leader than Medgar, a three-year starter and elected team captain of a team that was Southern Association champs two years running. That was more than enough for me. But we never knew just how good we were, because white teams wouldn't play us.

Medgar ran track, edited the school paper, was a debater, a glee club singer. He made good grades, built up his vocabulary. We both avoided the fraternities. Neither of us smoked or drank. Medgar was gentle and polite. He worked a lot of part-time jobs, watched his money, and planned for the future. He was president of the junior class. Medgar was studious, disciplined—all the things I wasn't. But he was a rebel, too. He planned to test his belief in Negro equality. He read the papers, followed current events, and itched to get out in the world.

While Medgar was thinking about the vote, I was thinking about the dollar. Medgar chased civil rights. I chased girls, civil rights, and the dollar. I was the naughty one, Medgar the good guy. I gave till it was enough. Medgar gave till it hurt. I hustled, wheeled and dealed. I was damned if I was going to leave Alcorn and start teaching for forty dollars a month. I planned to get rich quick.

By 2:00, classes were done. Time for business. Medgar and I bought fresh peanuts from a local farm and roasted them in our room. Late at night, when people got hungry, we'd holler, "Peanut man! Peanut man!" Ten cents a bag. Saturday nights, Alcorn students watched Hollywood movies in the chapel. I'd buy bologna, salami, cheese, peanut butter, and bread and make a hundred sandwiches. When the movie let out, the kids were hungry, but the local grill was closed. I'd walk outside the dorm shouting, "Fresh-made sandwiches!" They'd run to their windows: "Come on up!" I made sandwiches for five cents, sold them for thirty-five. One year, I snuck thirty-five pounds of fresh ham from the football banquet. I left my girl at the banquet, went back to the dorm with Medgar, warmed up that ham, and opened the door a crack to let the smoke waft through the building. At 11:00 P.M., the banquet let out some hungry clowns, and we sold sandwiches for a dollar that night. Made over a hundred dollars.

Bootlegging whiskey was where Lope drew the line. He'd always helped me bootleg back in Decatur. As his older brother, I'd drawn him into it. But now he became a high-minded gentleman. Like Daddy, he was appalled I'd sell bootleg. I said, "Lope, whiskey money looks just like chopping cotton money. It's all green." I didn't feel like a student—more of a businessman taking classes.

But my best scheme was my taxi service. Alcorn was eight miles from any bus stop, seventeen miles from Fayette or Port Gibson. No one on campus had ever offered taxi service. The dean of men and the dean of women gave me permission to taxi folk to Port Gibson, Fayette, Natchez, and back. My cab was the '41 Ford I'd taken off Mr.

Cooper, the man who'd once hired me and worked me but wouldn't pay me. I charged a dollar a head to Port Gibson. Natchez cost a dollar fifty. I picked up dry cleaning in Port Gibson, charged GIs fifty cents to cash their government checks in Port Gibson. "Don't like my price, you can ride in my cab and cash the check yourself. A dollar each way." So I got folks coming and going. Almost everyone at Alcorn rode with me: students, teachers, the deans, even J. R. Otis, our president. I loved having my own vehicle. I kept my eyes open on those trips and learned a lot about my passengers. I drove students to places they didn't belong. Teachers, too. Some teachers even bought my bootleg.

Back then, lots of noble, high-minded civil rights folk sat on their asses debating whether we should be called "Negroes" or "colored people." Of all the bullshit! I warned Medgar to avoid that garbage. I'd say, "Lope, let's get money for our people." Medgar loved to fish, and I'd talk about getting rich so we could buy a big fishing yacht on the Mississippi River. Lope would say, "Charlie, don't be so crazy about money." That burned me. I'd say, "Lope, without money, how do you eat? How do you sleep? You can't be free if you're broke." We loved each other, but we had some awful scraps. As close as we were, we'd still claw and fight.

I just always had to be making money. Summers, Medgar and I and a bunch of friends drove to Chicago to work the meatpacking houses. We worked for Swift and Armour, on the docks, in the slaughter pens. No need to interview for those jobs. We just walked into the Swift Personnel Department. They hired lots of college kids, from Alcorn and the University of Illinois. We stayed wherever we could get a small room. Trucking beef, hanging beef, rotating beef. Cleaning out big containers, working inside the coolers. We always worked hard and left a good work record. All we wanted was money enough to get a little farther ahead.

Medgar and I had always wanted to vote. As soldiers, we'd worked like dogs and risked our lives fighting for freedom, democracy, and all the principles this country was founded on. But we couldn't vote. The law said we could, but the whites of Mississippi made sure we couldn't. Now, as tough, proud young men, Medgar and I hated that. Racism had kept me from marrying Felicia. I had a deep personal grudge against racism. Medgar and I *knew* voting was the key to power. Decatur had nine hundred whites registered to vote, but not one Negro. Even the president of Alcorn told Medgar and me not to register. Boy, that stung. But in 1946, as Alcorn students, Medgar and I decided to go to the Newton County courthouse to register to vote.

I knew that courthouse. It was the same courthouse where Senator Bilbo had spoken when he ran for U.S. senator in 1934. That was the day Bilbo had seen Medgar and me sitting up front and had told the crowd that if they didn't watch out, niggers like us were going to grow up and represent them in Washington. Now twelve years had passed, Medgar and I were war veterans, and Theodore Bilbo was running for a third term as a U.S. senator.

One day soon after Medgar and I announced that we planned to register to vote, a white clerk in town, Alton Graham, told Daddy, "If your boys don't want trouble, they better not try to register." A few days later, we went up to register. I went by home to see Mama on the way. She was washing clothes with my sister Liz, standing in front of a big tin bucket, soaping the clothes with lye soap she'd made herself, churning those clothes with an old stick. Mama was so afraid. She wasn't saying a word, but I saw her lips moving. She was praying for us.

Medgar and I reached the courthouse. Whites blocked the door. Alton Graham said, "Who you niggers think you are?" I said, "We've grown up here, we fought for this country, and we think we should register." Alton Graham shook his head. When we insisted, he and some other whites threatened us. There was quite a commotion.

The old circuit clerk, Mr. Brand, hurried over. He was a little man, no more than five foot five. He handled registration, marriage licenses. He knew Mama and Daddy, probably knew Medgar and I were war veterans. He hated to see anyone get hurt. He said, "Come here, Charles, and you, Medgar." Mr. Brand was a decent man, like almost half the whites in Mississippi. They didn't want murder and bloodshed, but they didn't dare embrace us and get branded "nigger lovers." White gangs would whip a nigger lover even sooner than they'd whip a bad nigger, because bad niggers were known to be dangerous, and most nigger lovers were peaceful.

Mr. Brand took us into a private room. We convinced him the poll tax didn't apply because we were veterans. "Now, look," he said. "I have no right to tell you not to register, but if I were you I'd just go back and wait. The time will come when you can register." But I kept thinking about crawling around in that mud in New Guinea, fighting for my country. Now I was going to be counted as a man. I told Mr. Brand, "We've waited too long already." He looked very sorry. He said, "You're going to cause trouble." I told him, "I don't care what kind of trouble comes down. I want to register." Mr. Brand looked at us a long time, then walked us in and let us register.

But registering was less than half the battle. Voting was the key. Before the election, Alton Graham and some other haters called on Daddy at home to warn him: "Your boys better not come vote, because we're going to get them if they do." White bigots came by Daddy's house every night to warn him. Uncle Tom Negroes came to see Medgar and me. The message bearers would say, "Take your names off the books before some Negro gets hurt."

Mama knew she couldn't get us to take our names off the books, but she let us know she was worried sick. Daddy was just the opposite. Didn't say much, but Lope and I knew he was so proud we were sticking to our guns. He loved to see any Negro defy the whites. To see his own sons do it made him proud as hell. If he worried about the risk, he never told us.

The election came. Senator Bilbo was raving, "The best way to stop niggers from voting is to visit them the night before the election." Medgar and I heard this, and we said silently, "Come on and visit us! We'll kill you all!" No one visited us.

On election day, Medgar and I recruited some old friends to join us: my good friend A. J. Needham; A. J.'s brother, C. B. Needham; and two others, Bernon Wansley and a man named Hudson. We went to the polls early to beat the crowd. When we reached the courthouse, we found 250 rednecks, dressed in overalls, holding shotguns, rifles, and pistols. Some were sitting in pickup trucks, others standing around the courthouse square. God! I'd never seen so many Klukkers, bigots, and hatemongers, never seen so many guns in one place, not even in the army. And mean, silent white men holding those guns.

We tried to ignore them, but a bunch of them were blocking the courthouse doors. We stood on the courthouse steps, eyeballing each other. I had a long-handle .38 with me and a switchblade knife in my pocket. I'd learned as a young boy that white folks feared knives more than guns. Now I tucked the .38 away in my pocket, held the switchblade in my hand, and headed for the door.

The old circuit clerk, Mr. Brand, scurried over again: "You Evers boys come from a good family. Why go looking for trouble like this?" We looked at him real solid but said nothing. Mr. Brand kept on: "Charles, you and Medgar, you all go back, you're going to cause trouble." I said, "Let me tell you something, Mr. Brand. We're going to vote—or else we're all going to hell today. It's up to you. Now, give us our ballots." Mr. Brand turned tail and scooted back into the courthouse.

The six of us split up. The courthouse had three doors. I told A. J., C. B., Bernon, and Hudson to try the side door. Medgar and I went in the front door. We planned to meet in the clerk's office for our ballots, but armed rednecks blocked all the entrances. I hoped to talk my way through, but most of them were strangers. Then at one door, I spotted a familiar white face: Andy May, a nice man with a drugstore at the south end of Decatur. The Evers family had bought toothpaste from Andy May for years. I considered him a friend—would have liked to see him anytime. I was really glad to see him now. I thought he'd help us get in that door and cast our votes. I said hello to Andy May.

Andy patted the gun in his hip pocket and hissed at me like a snake: "Listen, nigger, ain't nothing happened to you yet." Hate dripping from his words. Oh, that hurt. I knew the other Klukkers hated me, but they didn't know me. Andy May knew me. I'd always thought he was a good man. When I saw he was nothing but a hater, something died inside me. I thought, "So what if these rednecks kill me?" I really wanted to die. Had stopped guarding my life. But I wouldn't give Andy May that satisfaction. I pointed to the .38 peeking from my side pocket, flashed my switchblade: "Ain't nothing going to happen to me!" I pushed by Andy May, and Medgar and I walked right into the courthouse. Our four friends kept close watch, trying to protect us. We got into the clerk's office. We even got hold of our ballots.

But we couldn't reach the ballot box. The Klukkers had locked it away inside a back office. About twenty of them blocked the office door. A row of about seven men, three deep, all of them armed. When they saw Medgar and me, they surged forward. Two whites jammed their shotguns up under our ribs. Medgar wanted to stop there, but I was a reckless 180 pounds, armed and determined, fed up with white folks, and furious at Andy May for turning on Medgar and me. I saw fear in the eyes of those crackers, just like Daddy had taught us. I taunted them, told them how yellow they were. Not a one made a further move. I said, "Medgar, I'm going through." Medgar said, "No, Charlie, don't try. It ain't worth it."

I realized I wanted to die. I meant to die fighting for Negro rights. The Klukkers were cowards. They liked defending white rights, but they didn't want to die doing it. Those big old Klukkers were shaking like leaves on a tree. Dozens of them, big-bellied, rednecked, armed to the teeth—and scared to death. I told them I planned to vote. One of them said, "You niggers can't come in here." "Why not?" I asked. No answer. Andy May walked up beside me: "Evers, ain't nothing happened to you yet?" I answered, "Ain't nothing going to happen to me!"

As Medgar and I waited, white folks we knew came over to break the standoff. They told us to go home before anyone got hurt. A white man we'd raked leaves for urged us to go home. A white lady who knew Mama begged us to leave while we were still alive. The county sheriff sat watching us. He wasn't going to let us vote, but he didn't try to beat us or even arrest us. He knew he might have to kill us first, and he didn't want to do that.

Finally, Medgar said, "Come on, Charlie, let's go. We'll get them next time." Medgar didn't want to die that day. And he didn't want me hurt, either. I'd stopped guarding my life, but Medgar guarded it for me. After a long time, I let Medgar lead me away. Going out, I told Mr. Brand and all the other white folks, "You've beaten us, but you haven't defeated us. We'll be back. And one of these days, *you're* going to want to come in the door. And we ain't going to let you in!"

Andy May shouted on our way out, "You niggers better get away from here before something happens!" I looked at him, cold as ice: "Ain't nothing going to happen to us but what happens to you, too! And you better not follow us down the street." Medgar and I called A. J., C. B., Bernon, and Hudson. We all backed out of the building, just like Daddy had backed out of the sawmill commissary when Jimmy Boware threatened to kill him. A white man yelled after us, "You damn Evers niggers going to get all the niggers in Decatur killed."

Many of Decatur's Negroes were watching now, peeking out from behind posts and cafe windows. Most of them thought the whites would try to kill us. Sure enough, after we'd gone a mile, some whites drove up, leaned out their car windows, and said, "We'll take care of you tonight!" I said, "If you weren't cowards, you'd get out of the car and take care of us right now." They sped off. Another car full of rednecks drove up and taunted us. I pulled my .38: "You see that! I'll blow your brains out if you step out of that car!" They sped off, too. A. J. and C. B. Needham cut through the white school grounds, and the other boys left. Medgar and I went down the street. A big group of cussing white cowards followed, chanting, "We'll get you tonight, niggers!" We pulled our guns. "All right, crackers. Come on down here. Now." Outnumbering us ten to one, they turned heel and ran.

We sat up that night at Daddy's house, waiting for them. Medgar in the barn, me in the garage. The U.S. Army had taught us how deadly crossfire can be, and we had a crossfire ready for anyone dumb enough to mess with us that night. No one came. I could easily have been killed that day, but it wasn't my time.

Medgar and I never forgot that day. After risking our lives in a war for democracy and free elections, we had come home and were nearly killed for trying to vote. We were told that we weren't good Americans because we believed that all men are created equal. More than any other single thing, that day in Decatur made Medgar and me civil rights activists. The way whites guarded that ballot box, we knew voting was the key to power. We talked about the pact we'd made as kids that if ever one of us went down, the other would carry on. And one year later, in the '47 county elections, Medgar and I did vote. We had to ignore a lot of threats, but for some reason Decatur didn't guard the ballot box with white goons. Medgar and I were the very first Negro voters in Decatur. By then we knew liberating Mississippi from the Great White Fathers would be a lot tougher than liberating Europe from the Nazis.

But change was stirring in Mississippi. Theodore Bilbo died in 1947—of complications from cancer of the mouth. That had to be poetic justice.

Medgar and I did other civil rights work as Alcorn students, working with a Negro called Dr. Theodore Roosevelt Mason Howard. Everyone in the United States should know the name T. R. M. Howard, after what Dr. Howard achieved against the odds he faced. Dr. Howard lived up in Mound Bayou, Bolivar County, Mississippi, north of Greenville. But he'd been born, schooled, and got medical training in Kentucky and Los Angeles. He moved to Mound Bayou, a little Negro town founded by ex-slaves on land once owned by Jefferson Davis. Dr. Howard had seen the world, and even gotten rich. In 1950, T. R. M. Howard must have been the richest Negro in Mississippi. Made money hand over foot.

Dr. Howard was tall, light skinned, balding, with a mustache. Wore a bow tie, white hat, and black glasses. Had a big voice and a wide smile. He was very generous with his money. He had a big farm, worked by sharecroppers, and he raised pheasant and quail. Folks said he'd made big money betting on horses. He drove a red Buick convertible, and his wife drove a Cadillac.

Dr. Howard had founded Tarborian Hospital in Mound Bayou and was surgeon in chief there. Tarborian was no grand hospital, more like a medical clinic. But it was heaven next to what the local Negroes were used to. Dr. Howard was also a very fine general practitioner. Half of curing rural people is getting them to believe in you and to follow your treatment. Dr. Howard made all the Negroes around Mound Bayou believe in him.

He could have sat on his cash like most of the rich. He could have lived it up in Harlem. But T. R. M. Howard came to Mississippi, a state with no real city, no wealthy Negroes, very few Negroes with any schooling at all. And he became the toughest, most outspoken Negro in the state. He was never afraid to rock the boat. He took on a system stacked against him. Outsmarted it where he could, bucked it when he had to.

Freedom Day was an annual event Dr. Howard ran. There was a parade, but Dr. Howard also set up meetings on that day. There weren't many Negroes willing to buck whites, and Dr. Howard wanted to know us all personally. He sent for Medgar and me. Dr. Howard was so outspoken, it was dangerous even to be seen with him. Not too many Negroes from outside Mound Bayou were tough enough to go to his party. But Medgar and I went, and we helped Dr. Howard register Negro voters. Whites threatened us, threatened Daddy, but most of all they threatened Dr. Howard. He never flinched.

T. R. M. Howard was always pushing young Negroes to buck the old racist system. He built us up, encouraged us, organized us. We were just scratching the surface of the racist system in those days, waking up Negroes who'd been passive and ignorant all their lives. But Dr.

Howard always made us feel important. He'd break down the evil of racism into parts. "Who put you in jail?" he'd ask. "The cops," we'd answer. "Alright, now who appointed the cops?" "The mayor," we'd say. "Well, who elected the mayor? How you going to vote him out of office?" Dr. Howard showed us the power of the vote. I can still hear him: "We've got to register to vote. We can't be afraid."

That was informal talking. But on the stump, T. R. M. Howard was amazing. People call Martin Luther King Jr. the Negro orator of the century. T. R. M. Howard was as good, or better, and I heard them both in their prime. T. R. M. Howard had no formal congregation. His speeches weren't caught on a tape recorder or movie camera. He never got the exposure. But that man had a big, booming voice. He could take a crowd up into a frenzy and bring them right down when he wanted.

Around '48, Medgar and I wrote to the NAACP, trying to join up. NAACP stands for National Association for the Advancement of Colored People. Mississippi whites said it stood for Niggers, Apes, Alligators, Coons, and Possums. The NAACP was the oldest, best-respected civil rights group in the country. It was about the only civil rights group Lope and I had heard of. The NAACP was founded in New York in 1909, and from the start bucked segregated housing, jobs, schools. The NAACP had been in Mississippi since 1918. The national NAACP president was Walter White, a great man.

Medgar and I were honored the NAACP had heard of us. They had hundreds of southern branches but were still called a northern group. They wanted us to help open new southern branches and perk up the old ones. And we did. Medgar and I disliked all the NAACP regulations, disliked being run from New York, but we were young and fired up to be working for the top civil rights group. We knew we'd hardly ever hear from the top brass up in New York.

One time I did go up to New York, just to meet the baseball star Jackie Robinson. My role models were Negro lawyers and businessmen—not athletes. But Jackie Robinson of the Brooklyn Dodgers was a great pioneer. He integrated major league baseball when I was at Alcorn. A great athlete catching hell for being a Negro in the white man's league. I wrote Jackie and asked if I could come up and see him. He didn't know me from Adam, but Jackie was always willing to meet a young civil rights man. In 1948, there weren't many of us. Jackie answered my letter, said sure, come to New York. That's how I met Jackie Robinson.

Medgar was a damn romantic. He had neat, studious, long-haired girlfriends—shy and untouchable. I liked a sassy older woman who knew the world. I planned to get rich. I wanted my woman to help—at least buy me a few shirts. I'd been overseas too long, staying faithful to my lovely virgin, Felicia. Now I had to sow my wild oats. Alcorn only had one test tube and one typewriter, but it had *plenty* of pretty girls. I was older than most students, vocal and visible on campus. I had money to spend. For wheels, I had Evers family funeral cars and my taxi. Girls came along and liked my sleepy eyes. Whenever one had nice legs, nice hair, I sought after her. I took her to dinner, spent good money on her, and whenever I could, I took her to a hotel in Vicksburg.

Three of my best girls were Nannie Laurie and two girls I'll call "Christine" and "Claudia." I met them around the same time and started balling all three. Within three months, Christine was carrying my child. I said, "If it's mine, that's all you got to say." I was determined to provide for my child. Balling women is great, but if you can't pay, don't play. I was ready to pay. A month later, Nannie Laurie was carrying my child. I told Nan the same thing: "If it's mine, that's all you got to say." I knew I could support two babies. Then Claudia got pregnant. I said, "Okay, baby, if it's mine. . . ." I was beginning to wonder how long this would go on.

Christine, Nan, and Claudia—each one expected to be my wife. Their mamas and daddies expected it, too. Even my own Mama and Daddy were after me. I put Mama through so much pain over this. The first she knew I even had a girlfriend was when I told her I had three girls pregnant. This wasn't how the Holiness Church did things. Everyone said, "Charlie, do what's right," which meant I should get married. Hell, I'd have had to be a Mormon to do right by all three of these girls. I was still mad at women for attracting men, then trying to control us. Each time I got close to a woman, I loved her to a degree. But deep down, I was mad at all women for the pain Daddy's girlfriends had brought our family.

I knew one thing: I had to finish school. I knew building a Negro business and pursuing civil rights in Mississippi would bring on lots of white resistance. I kept thinking any woman I married would try to scale back my business and civil rights work and press me to take some forty-dollar-a-month job. To hell with that—and to hell with marriage. Christine told me, "You got to marry me." I said, "I don't got to marry a one of you! I'm finishing school." I'd always promised Mama and Daddy I'd get a degree.

But when Claudia, my third girl, got pregnant, word reached President Otis. One of the deans called me in, said he and Otis knew I'd been keeping company with Christine, Nan, and Claudia. He told me to stop knocking up people's daughters: "Charles Evers, you choose one of those three, and marry her." Then he sat back and looked at me like he meant it. But I knew something about this particular dean. As one of my taxicab passengers, he'd visited a place he shouldn't have been visiting. After a lot of talking, this one dean and I struck a deal: I would forget about any trips he'd taken in my cab, and he would pretend I'd done my part and married one of those girls.

But the Alcorn chaplain had no part of the deal. Folks asked why the "marriage" was never announced in the school paper. The Reverend was a good man who knew something was wrong. He lectured me. And I believe Christine took her story to the dean. President Otis must have stepped in, because Alcorn threatened to expel me unless I married one of those three girls. I was class president, student body president, captain of the football team, and near to getting a college degree. I couldn't let them expel me.

I got a marriage license at the old courthouse and came back to Alcorn. Nan and Claudia were away. I said, "Christine, honey, we're getting married." The chaplain married us by phone. I took the license to him, and he filled it out. I mailed in the papers, and we were hitched. It was legal and official but we had no ceremony, no witnesses, no honeymoon.

Within three months, I'd dissolved the marriage. I still liked Christine and admired her. I had nothing against Christine but what I had against all the cute women I'd ever met, except Felicia: They used their beauty to cut into their husbands' freedom. I couldn't allow that. And in the back of my mind, I always had to be free in case Felicia ever became free. Folks asked me, "What you got against marriage, Charlie?" But no woman was going to treat me like women treated my tough old Daddy.

Christine had our baby, a lovely girl she named Charlene. Nan had our baby, a girl she named Pat. When Claudia was due, I wanted a boy, but Claudia gave me a cute baby girl, Carolyn. I always provided plenty of money for my little girls, never backed away like so many men do. After all, none of my little daughters had asked me to bring them into the world. People would ask why I stuck my neck out for civil rights, and I'd joke, "Hell, you can't stay in the sack *all* the time." But in Mississippi, civil rights wasn't something to pick up and put down. Our lives were at stake. Bringing three babies into the world made that even clearer to me.

Medgar thought I was crazy, slipping around with all these girls. Medgar aimed to marry, settle down, and have four kids. But Lope never had the same girlfriend more than a month until he met a Vicksburg girl, Myrlie Beasley. Myrlie was raised by older female relatives. She was cute and real smart. Made Alcorn's honor roll, even won second place in the Negro Masons' statewide oratory contest. She put herself through school playing the piano. But Myrlie had been raised by women. They'd told her, "Don't rock the boat." Myrlie's daddy wasn't a Jim Evers, and she'd never met a man like Medgar, who insisted on full equality between black and white, right in Mississippi. This was totally new to Myrlie.

Medgar wasn't big on hugs and kisses. He didn't tell Myrlie he loved her for a whole year. But Lope hadn't been hurt by Daddy's girlfriends like I had, and one night his senior year, he told me he was marrying Myrlie. Said he loved her and she'd make him a good wife. I said, "Lope, no woman would make you a good wife." I had a crazy vision of Medgar and me with $10 million and two big houses, high on a hill. We'd both have lots of kids, but no wives. We'd have a great big gate hooked up to an electric box to recognize voice commands. No one could come in without our say-so. I was going to get filthy rich and set us up on this high hill. Myrlie didn't fit into my dream. Lope and I'd been so close all our lives. Myrlie was the first person to come between us.

On December 24, 1951, Medgar married Myrlie Beasley. Everyone thought I should be Medgar's best man. Mama and plenty of people tried to talk me into it. I helped pay for the wedding, but I didn't attend. Medgar understood. Myrlie made Medgar happy, which wasn't easy. She was tough and smart. She stuck with him, even when he gave himself to the civil rights movement. My problem wasn't with Myrlie, but with anyone coming between me and Medgar. Deep down I'd never wanted Medgar to marry. It was supposed to be just the two of us against the world.

I was still at Alcorn when the army called me back and sent me to Fort Hood, Texas. One day I got a telegram from Eva and Liz. Our baby sister, Mary Ruth, was dying. Mary Ruth had married Curtis Hawkins, a good man she'd known since we were kids in Decatur. I drove straight through to see Mary Ruth. When I walked in her hospital room, she hugged and kissed me. A few days later she died in my arms. Brain cancer. She was the youngest of the Evers children, so sweet and trusting. Twenty-one years old.

Seeing Mary Ruth die like that made me think about my own death. I decided I'd be happy to die for civil rights, but I sure didn't want to die in Korea. The army was deferring married men. Claudia was married, Christine was off somewhere, so I said, "Hello, Nan." I married Nan in '51. I had another reason, too. Kids born outside marriage weren't respected much. I didn't care what folks said about me, but I couldn't stand them calling my little girls "bastards." So I married Nan, left the service for one last semester at Alcorn, and got my degree.

Nan and I stayed on the books for twenty-two years, but we didn't act married for long. Here's how I see marriage. For most men, it's a lie. If they're not off making babies with a girl down the street, they're looking at her and wishing they could. I'm a man who could never live a lie. Married to Nan, I had plenty of women on the side. But out of respect for Nan, I kept them private. I never denied any of my children, did well by them, and they all loved me. But I told my girlfriends right off that I wasn't ever going to take them to the altar. Marriage is a damn trap.

Looking back now, I'd say Alcorn gave me a good eighth grade education, at best. But at that time, it was all we had. Neither Medgar or I followed our major. Medgar went into the insurance field. I kept hustling, traveling, meeting people. I've learned nearly all my lessons from life. Not from books.

CHAPTER 7

Crossing the Line

IN '51, NAN AND I MOVED to a room in Philadelphia, Mississippi, over the funeral parlor of my great-uncle Mark Thomas. I managed the funeral parlor for Mark and picked up nineteen dollars a month teaching history and coaching football in Noxapater, Mississippi, north of town. Between teaching, bootlegging, and undertaking, I cleared a hundred dollars a month.

I put my little daughter Pat in third grade at the Noxapater school where I taught. The Noxapater schools were better than those in Philadelphia, and I'd vowed to give Pat the best schooling I could. My school sent Pat back to the run-down Philadelphia school. The Noxapater principal was an Uncle Tom who insisted Pat was in the wrong district. When I wouldn't back down, that damn Tom had me jailed. For all of the trouble I'd seen, all the bullies I'd crossed, I'd never before been arrested or jailed. The jail was a calaboose hardly bigger than a phone booth. Passing whites cussed me. I waggled my finger at them. Pat was crying. I told her through the bars of my cell, "Don't worry, baby. I'll be in more jails before I'm through. But Daddy will be back!"

Proud as I was of teaching, I never felt comfortable at it, because I'd never been properly schooled myself. So I left teaching and took over Mark Thomas's funeral parlor full-time. I also picked up my bootlegging. Daddy never could figure out where I got cash to help pay his bills. He suspected the truth. Once he asked me flat out: "You bootlegging?" Of course I was bootlegging. I said quickly, "Daddy, you know I'd never bootleg."

In '52, when Medgar graduated from Alcorn, Myrlie wanted to move to Chicago, but Lope refused to leave Mississippi. Myrlie and her aunt and grandmama expected Medgar to find a good Negro job as a postman or teacher. But Lope had bigger ideas. One of T. R. M. Howard's companies in Mound Bayou was an insurance firm called Magnolia Mutual. Dr. Howard hired Medgar as an insurance agent, and Lope moved his family to Mound Bayou. No white company would have hired Medgar to a white-collar job, but Dr. Howard did.

Medgar rose at dawn and drove into Clarksdale. He worked the Negro side of town, selling Magnolia Mutual life insurance, hospital insurance, burial insurance. So many Negroes died before their time—they always needed insurance. Medgar worked hard. Anyone could see he was honest. Customers liked and respected him. The company made Medgar district supervisor for the whole Clarksdale region. Later he became Magnolia Mutual's agency director.

As district supervisor, Medgar traveled all through the Delta: Bolivar County, Leflore County, Sharkey County. After being in college, seeing Europe at war, Medgar hated being stuck in these rural Delta counties. He saw whole families there picking cotton, living like slaves. Medgar vowed to improve these people's lives.

Like me, Medgar dreamed of being a courtroom lawyer for Negroes, like the great NAACP lawyer, Thurgood Marshall. We both started thinking of this even more after we met Thurgood for the first time, in early May of '54. Dr. Howard brought Thurgood to a rally in Mound Bayou. Thurgood spoke about freedom and mingled with eight thousand Negroes, some from as far away as Detroit and Chicago.

Life was slow in Mississippi, and whites didn't mind humoring some nut railing about big changes. If he was Negro, they just called him a "crazy nigger." But if you did like Thurgood, went beyond talking and started working to change things, you'd crossed a line. You'd become an agitator. It was a big decision to become an agitator in Mississippi, because any harm that came to an agitator had to be his own fault. If he'd only shuffled and Tommed, said "Yes, sir, boss, all us Negroes are happy," he'd never have been jailed, beaten, or lynched. So any lynchings, jailings, or beatings were his own fault. That's how white Mississippi thought.

For all the tomfoolery we'd pulled as boys, and despite having insisted on registering to vote as college kids, Medgar and I had never been true "agitators" until we started putting in a lot of time with the NAACP around '52. Whites in Decatur forgave us for coming home from the war with fool ideas of equality, and acting biggity at Alcorn. But around '52, Medgar and I crossed that line and became agitators. You better betcha we did. And white folk couldn't forgive that. No matter how much they liked the Evers boys as men or respected our family, they hated the Evers boys for becoming agitators. I started sleeping with a gun under my head.

Inspired by T. R. M. Howard in Bolivar County, Medgar set up an NAACP branch in the town of Cleveland and revived the old NAACP unit in Mound Bayou. Driving through Mississippi, Medgar couldn't use most of the gas station bathrooms, so in '52, he and Dr. Howard paid a Negro printer in Jackson to print up forty thousand fluorescent bumper stickers that read DON'T BUY GAS WHERE YOU CAN'T USE THE RESTROOM. Medgar put those bumper stickers on his Magnolia Mutual car and on all the cars and hearses in the Evers family funeral business. He gave out that bumper sticker to hundreds of Negroes statewide—whoever would take one. Even doing that was dangerous. The NAACP sent out its membership cards in unmarked envelopes and held many meetings in secret, in pastures or in old barns.

Amzie Moore was another one who crossed the line. Amzie had been with the U.S. Air Force in Burma during World War II, then came back to the Mississippi Delta. He'd worked at a post office, joined the NAACP, and traveled the Delta with a barbershop quartet that did more civil rights work than singing.

Another man who crossed the line was Aaron Henry. Aaron was a pharmacist in Clarksdale. His drugstore was a meeting place for civil rights work. Aaron was an adviser to Medgar and me, he was our friend, our lawyer—almost a third brother. Aaron had earned a degree from Xavier University around '45 and began working for the NAACP. By '52, he was president of the local branch.

Another bold one we used to see at Mound Bayou Day was Mrs. Fannie Lou Hamer. Fannie Lou had some kind of polio as a girl. It never got treated, and it left her with a limp. But Fannie Lou Hamer was strong. Five feet four, close to two hundred pounds, with a powerful singing voice and a way with words. No education to speak of, but a great speaker. A real strong lady in every way.

Fannie Lou was born Fannie Lou Townsend in 1917, twentieth child to a sharecropper. Fannie Lou's daddy died young. Her mama was blinded by a sharecropping injury. Fannie married Perry Hamer, and they lived on the Marlow plantation outside Ruleville. Fannie Lou fit right in with T. R. M. Howard, Medgar and me, Aaron Henry, and Amzie Moore. We were the boldest Negroes in the state. We got to be a kind of family.

Around 1950, I had met a bluesman named B. B. King. B. B. had been playing in Memphis, but he was from Indianola, Mississippi. He was a short, dark, slim, handsome guy, always smiling. B. B. was three years younger than me, and our birthdays were just five days apart. He was a deejay, had his own radio show. In '53, he recorded in Jackson with the bluesman Sonny Boy Williamson. He began touring the South, playing club dates. Amzie, Aaron, Fannie Lou, Medgar, and B. B.— these were my best friends.

Standing over us were the big Mississippi politicians. Not only were they all white, they were all white men who loved racial segregation. There was Senator James O. Eastland, there was Senator John Stennis, and there was Congressman Jamie Whitten. In '41, James Eastland owned fifty-eight hundred acres of cotton, and Fannie Lou Hamer lived in an unheated shack in the very same county. Eastland was appointed to the U.S. Senate. Jamie Whitten won a special election after prosecuting gamblers who'd slipped into the state from Tennessee. Whitten was a wily lawyer who always claimed the press caused race violence, and Mississippi needed the poll tax to fund our public schools. Eastland, Stennis, and Whitten were all youngsters. Power in Congress came not from brains, heart, or fairness, but from seniority. So Mississippi elected agreeable young white men to Congress, let them rise up the ranks until they had great seniority and power. That's what Eastland, Stennis, and Whitten did. I called them "the Great White Fathers."

In late '53, our state NAACP branches elected me state voter registration chairman. Whites didn't bother to gerrymander the districts. Southern registrars were always white. Negroes brave enough to register to vote got a poll tax, then a literacy test: "Read and interpret to the satisfaction of the registrar this section of the Mississippi constitution." That constitution had 282 sections! How's a Negro sharecropper going to interpret it to satisfy a cracker registrar sworn to keep niggers off the rolls? If he did, the registrar would ask, "How many bubbles in a cake of soap?" "How many hogs on a forest path?" The NAACP took Negro college grads smart as a whip, prepared them for that test, and they were flunked by redneck registrars who hadn't finished sixth grade.

The registrar also asked you where you worked, so they could run and tell your boss that you were trying to register. That got many Negroes fired. If a Negro somehow passed the literacy test, paid his poll tax, and bucked his boss, he might hear from a white vigilante with a shotgun. See, the whites were so confused, they told black folks we couldn't be good Americans until we gave up this idea that all men were created equal. But we wouldn't give it up.

Medgar and I grew up with very few heroes. We loved Joe Louis and caught his fights on the radio. We admired any Negro who could beat up a tough white man without being lynched. Joe Louis knocked those white boys down and got paid for it. But Daddy and Joe Louis, and later Jackie Robinson, were about our only heroes.

Around '51, Medgar and I had found a new hero: Jomo Kenyatta of Kenya. The Negro newspapers had our own kind of patriotism. We backed the Declaration of Independence, the Constitution, and the Supreme Court, but we rejected war, segregation, and racism. Most southern whites hated that. The Jackson *Clarion-Ledger* ignored colonial Africa wanting freedom, but the *Pittsburgh Courier* didn't. Lope and I read articles in the *Courier* about a strong new Kenyan leader, Jomo Kenyatta. We learned all we could about Kenyatta—in the papers, from friends, reports on shortwave radio. Hodding Carter's paper up in Greenville covered Kenyatta. Even the Memphis papers and the *Jackson Daily Courier* ran a few articles on him. Fearless. They all said Kenyatta was fearless. I loved that word.

Kenyatta ran a militant movement called Mau Mau in the British colony of Kenya. Mau Mau was a plan to kill white colonial masters on a secret schedule. Kenyatta had traveled, schooled himself abroad, returned to Kenya in '46. Kenyatta always seemed to be in jail, or threatened with detention. But whites didn't scare him. He vowed to press on until Kenya was free, and die if he had to. That inspired Medgar and me so much. We wanted to free *our* people. In '52, Kenyatta created a state of emergency in Kenya. Fighting there lasted through '56. When Medgar and Myrlie had their first child, Medgar tried to name him Kenyatta Evers. Myrlie named him Darrell Kenyatta Evers.

Why not really cross the line? we wondered. Why not create a Mau Mau in Mississippi? Each time whites killed a Negro, why not drive to another town, find a bad sheriff or cop, and kill him in a secret hit-and-run raid? To avoid suspicion, one of us could drive home, the other take a bus. We thought this was how to teach righteousness to whites. We bought bullets, made some idle Mau Mau plans, but Medgar never had his heart in it, and over time we dropped it. Medgar was a sweeter man than me. It took me longer to purge my system of all the hate that whites had put in there.

CHAPTER

8

The Pure of Heart: Medgar Joins the NAACP Full-Time

THE UNIVERSITY OF MISSISSIPPI has always been the high-toned college in Mississippi. In '54, no Negro had ever studied there. In early '54, Medgar decided to apply to the Ole Miss law school. I pressed him to hold his ground, no matter what. Medgar asked Alcorn to send his records to Ole Miss. The Jackson *Daily News* ran the headline: NEGRO APPLIES TO ENTER OLE MISS.

Our old white neighbor, Jim Tims, recommended Medgar. Mr. Tims was an Ole Miss alum and felt secure enough as Decatur's postmaster to recommend Medgar. But most local whites thought Medgar applying was an outrage. Mississippi state pride required that its best university be high-toned, and Ole Miss couldn't be high-toned with nigger students. Case closed.

Myrlie was scared Medgar would get beaten or killed for what he'd done, and based on what happened to Negroes who tried to integrate Ole Miss later, her fears were justified. Medgar just said, "You have to make sacrifices in order to make progress." Medgar and Myrlie visited Mama and Daddy in Decatur. Medgar said he was applying to Ole Miss; Myrlie said she was pregnant. Daddy disapproved of what Medgar was doing and told him, "Your first duty is to your family." Medgar jumped up and left the dinner table. He wouldn't be told by anyone, not even Daddy.

Eight months after Medgar applied to Ole Miss, he heard from Mr. James "J. P." Coleman, the state attorney general. Coleman was an Ole Miss alum, a cagy farm boy who'd already been a district attorney and circuit judge, and later became our governor. James Coleman was no

Klukker, but he wasn't above bald-faced lying to preserve the status quo. Coleman once testified in Congress that Mississippi did not intimidate Negro voters. J. P. Coleman thought the Negro had never lived who deserved to study at Ole Miss. Coleman invited Medgar to Jackson and asked him why he wanted to attend Ole Miss. Medgar said he was a loyal taxpayer who just wanted the best legal education in the state. That was Ole Miss.

Coleman asked, Had the NAACP put Medgar up to this? Medgar said no. Lope was quiet, polite, well-spoken. He kept saying all he wanted was the best legal education in Mississippi. Coleman praised Medgar for not being a radical and just wanting a fine education. He offered Medgar a full scholarship to a fine out-of-state college and pressed him to accept it.

But J. P. Coleman didn't know that under Lope's kind, gentle face, he was tough as nails. He'd been a debater at Alcorn, he'd been talking civil rights all his life, and Jesus Christ come down from the cross to defend segregation couldn't have budged Medgar an inch. Medgar turned the scholarship down. J. P. Coleman flushed, asked Medgar where he planned to live while at Ole Miss. Medgar said, "I plan to live on campus in a dormitory, to use the library, eat in the dining hall, and attend classes. But I assure you, I bathe regularly, I wear clean clothes, and none of the brown of my skin will rub off. I won't contaminate anything." Wily J. P. Coleman couldn't get the best of Medgar. They said goodbye, neither man liking the other.

A few months later, Daddy collapsed in the bathroom, fell into the tub with a stroke. Daddy had rarely seen a doctor. Any time someone went in a hospital, Daddy'd say, "Now, don't eat anything there. Hospitals got germs." But now Daddy needed a hospital. Decatur had none, so we rushed him north to Newton County Hospital, the white hospital in the town of Union. We brought Daddy down to the basement, where they took Negroes. I looked around and almost cried. It was freezing cold. Water was dribbling from the pipes. Rats and roaches were running around. A line of Negroes was stretched out on cots. There were no doctors or nurses anywhere.

I couldn't believe big old Daddy, who had defied so many death threats, was going to die like this. I pleaded with the hospital staff to bring Daddy upstairs, give him a room, at least put him in a ward. They said no. I raised all kinds of hell, but it did no good. People were sick and dying all over, and the staff had no time for a brash young Negro bending the rules to help his Daddy. They told me I was lucky they took Daddy in the basement.

Daddy was in the hospital for a week. A decent hospital might have saved him, but deep down in the basement, he died. No dignity, no kind of care. The hospital called me with the news. I was too shocked and angry to cry. I jumped in a funeral parlor hearse and raced down to the hospital. As a mortician, I knew how rough a morgue treats bodies. No one was going to treat Daddy like that. At Newton County Hospital, I collected Daddy and started loading him in my hearse.

A white doctor came by. He expected Negroes to cry like a baby when their daddy died, then let white folks handle the arrangements. Here I was, eyes dry, picking up Daddy in a nice vehicle I owned myself. That white doctor tore into me: "How in hell can you pick up your own dead father in a hearse? You have no heart." Well, I've never turned the other cheek. I said, "You got heart enough to leave my daddy down in a damn, dirty basement and let him die! Sure, I'll carry him in my own hearse. I'd rather do it than see one of you do it." I rolled Daddy out, put him in my hearse, and drove him to Philadelphia.

I couldn't let Daddy go. I wanted to embalm him myself, but Medgar and the whole family said no. I had Saul Ruffin, the Evers Funeral Home mortician, embalm Daddy. But I watched Saul extract the blood from Daddy's body so Daddy wouldn't decay too fast. The deceased's family is never supposed to watch the embalmer work, but since I owned the funeral home, no one could stop me. When Saul was done, I dressed Daddy myself and went upstairs. I couldn't sleep, couldn't get outside my grief. Those were bad days.

I broke down at the church funeral. Couldn't hold back the tears, collapsed, almost passed out. First, I'd seen my brother Eddie die, then Ruth, now Daddy. One of the greatest men I've ever known never lived to see Medgar and me grow up and change things. Smart, tough, and hardworking as he was, if Daddy had been born fifty years later, there'd have been no limit to what he could have achieved. But for all he was, Daddy never thought a civil rights movement could work. Kicking one white man's ass, he remembered with pleasure. But kicking segregation's ass? No. Jim Evers lived fifty years too soon.

While Medgar waited for an answer from Ole Miss, the U.S. Supreme Court, run by Earl Warren, ruled on the *Brown vs. Board of Education* suit brought by Thurgood Marshall and the NAACP. On May 17, 1954, the Supreme Court called racially segregated schools unconstitutional. The Supreme Court called that old "separate but equal" a sham. White public schools would have to let in Negroes, even in the South. That was a huge victory for Thurgood, the NAACP, and the schoolchildren of this country. In his apartment in New York City, Roy Wilkins of the NAACP took down a bottle of Scotch and drank toasts with his wife to the health of Earl Warren.

In the redneck South, believe me when I tell you, whites drank no toasts to Earl Warren, because the white South had been taught that racial integration would disgrace everything in the South. Sandlot baseball, barbershops, and beauty shops would be disgraced. Jesus Christ and the Christian church would be disgraced. Pickup trucks and fishing and Friday night football and country music and all their Confederate ancestors would be disgraced if the white South integrated. Most of all, the white maidens of the South would be defiled by Negroes. I could never see why white men were so touchy about their women. When they'd warn me to keep away from white girls, I'd ask them, "Are you taking care of your woman? Does she love you?" "Yes, uh huh," they'd say, trying to sound tough. "Then you ain't got nothing to worry about."

But whites learned as kids that civil rights was a Communist front meant to pollute pretty white girls. No wonder whites resisted us. No wonder they stepped up their abuse of the NAACP. Texas got an injunction against the NAACP; Virginia passed six bills to keep us quiet. Georgia sued the NAACP over its tax exemption; South Carolina banned all NAACP members from working for municipal, county, or state government. Alabama courts outlawed the NAACP outright. Louisiana revived an old anti-Klan law that made political groups file membership lists with the state. Louisiana made the state NAACP branch list its members publicly, which almost ruined us in Louisiana for a while.

But Mississippi was the worst. The Jackson *Clarion-Ledger* called May 17, 1954, "A black day of tragedy." White folk called it "Black Monday." Our senator, James O. Eastland, brayed like a jackass. He told the rednecks, "You are not required to obey any court which passes out such a ruling. In fact, you are obligated to defy it." The *Brown* decision sent all kinds of white Mississippians into the Klan—

men who had never before pledged themselves to "keeping the niggers down." Now, they felt they had to.

But lots of white Mississippians couldn't join the Klan. Lawyers, doctors, preachers, and businessmen wanted to keep the nigger down, but legally. Lynchings embarrassed them. These "respectable" folk in Jackson, in the Delta, on the Gulf Coast needed their own group. In the summer of '54 they formed the White Citizens Council. They meant to buck school integration and the mongrelization of the races. Citizens Councils sprung up around the state and went wild about Mau Mau. They tarred Medgar as the "The Mau Mau admirer" and boycotted Falstaff brewing, Philco radio, and Philip Morris tobacco based on hearsay that these companies backed the NAACP.

I liked the *Brown* decision more than the rednecks did, but much less than Roy Wilkins did. I knew full, instant integration would fail. When you build something to last, you must first lay the foundation. I said, let's integrate every first grade in '55. School districts without an integrated first grade commit a felony. In '56, integrate every first and second grade, in '57, every first, second, and third grade, and on down the line. Over the next twelve years, black and white kids could have grown up together. But liberals couldn't wait. They integrated the whole system overnight, and forced sixteen-year-old whites into school with sixteen-year-old Negroes. These kids had already learned hate. It takes time to break prejudice down, but Negroes had heard "It takes time" for too long. When I favored gradual integration, some Negroes called me a Tom.

The greatest man in the NAACP was Thurgood Marshall, the head of its legal department. Thurgood was a light-skinned, straight-haired Negro, a cool dresser, smart, relaxed, a talker and a joker. Thurgood was a warrior. He always had a big mouth, but like T. R. M. Howard told us, you must study the system oppressing you. Study the legal system, study the political system. Beat them at their own game. Thurgood learned how to run a case, file a motion, examine a witness, and charm a judge. Thurgood was the great Negro lawyer I'd always dreamed of being. He used the white man's justice system to turn the white man's school system upside down.

The Mississippi Board of Higher Learning turned down Medgar's Ole Miss application, saying he'd failed to submit recommendations from white folk in the state. Jim Tims wasn't white enough for them.

Medgar wanted to sue his way into Ole Miss law school, but there were only about five Negro lawyers in all Mississippi. If one took our case, he'd be arguing to a white judge and jury. No way we could break all that down, so we attacked racism another way.

I pushed Medgar to apply for a formal job with the NAACP. Partly because of the *Brown* decision, the NAACP people were preparing a big push in Mississippi. They wanted to hire their first state field secretary for Mississippi. I thought of applying for the job myself, but their salaries were too damn small. I had to be a millionaire. And I couldn't work in a tight organization. Aaron and Medgar wanted folks to like them. I didn't care what folks thought. Aaron and Medgar told me to be more tactful. It just wasn't in me. I was bullheaded—not an organization man.

So Medgar applied instead. Applying to Ole Miss had made him a big symbol to the Negroes of Mississippi. The NAACP saw that. Dr. E. J. Stringer was a Negro dentist and president of the NAACP branch in Columbus, Mississippi. Dr. Stringer told the NAACP how good a man Medgar was. In late October 1954, Dr. Stringer introduced Medgar to Gloster Current, the NAACP director of branches. Medgar's courage, his work ethic, and his passion for civil rights were clear as soon as you met him. Gloster Current advised Roy Wilkins to hire Medgar.

In November '54, not even thirty years old, Medgar became the first state field secretary for Mississippi. In mid-December of '54, Aaron Henry and I helped Lope open his NAACP office on Farish Street in Jackson. From that one office, we built the NAACP till Mississippi had more members and local branches than any other southern state. Aaron Henry was president of the NAACP, a part-time, unpaid job that left him free to run his drugstore in Clarksdale. I advised Medgar and signed up new NAACP members. But Medgar was field secretary. Full-time, with far more action than either Aaron or me. He made forty-five hundred dollars a year.

Let's talk a minute about the NAACP. The NAACP doesn't go around screaming, "Black Power!" The NAACP is organized. It had a plan: First, get Negroes the vote; then, end lynching; then, take on broader issues. The NAACP branches have been mother and father to black folks in our state. The NAACP got an antilynching law passed, brought the *Brown* case to the Supreme Court, and won it. But on the state level, we took care of mostly the little stuff: A woman needed money to help her husband's little weekly paycheck. Folk brought us sick children they couldn't get to the hospital or a dead daddy they couldn't afford to bury properly. Medgar and I were on the job twenty-four hours a day. We'd get up at 2:00 A.M. some days, drive two hundred miles just to see someone.

The Congress of Racial Equality (CORE) and a few other little civil rights groups also worked in Mississippi in the '50s. I was never tempted to join them. They were full of tough young kids who could yap, yap, yap, but they had no financial base. Lots of black leaders never learn: It takes money to change this country. The NAACP knew that. They knew how to raise money. The NAACP has been the most forceful black group ever in this country.

On the other hand, I never got along with Roy Wilkins, Gloster Current, and the meddling NAACP brass in New York. No one controls Charles Evers. There were NAACP folks in New York I liked. I liked Robert Carter. I liked John Morsell, a sociologist and a mouthpiece for Roy Wilkins. Herbert Wright never did me wrong, far as I know. But I clashed with Roy Wilkins, and I couldn't stand old Gloster B. Current, director of branches and field administration.

No matter the problem, Roy always wanted to go through the courts. He'd say, "Citizenship is rooted in law and must be secured by law." But I'd grown up in Mississippi. I knew our state courts weren't worth a damn. I might hire a white lawyer to represent me in a personal case, but I wasn't dumb enough to depend on a white judge to grant me my civil rights. No way. I said, let's boycott, go into the streets, anything short of violence to get justice. The NAACP never wanted to hear that.

I had another beef with the NAACP. I was fascinated by the tiny number of Negroes who got rich. How did they do it? I told the NAACP to focus more on showing poor Negroes how to make money. Charles Diggs was a Negro from Detroit, president of House of Diggs, the biggest Negro funeral home on earth. In the '50s, he even got himself elected to Congress. How did he do all that? I always said the NAACP should feature guys like Charles Diggs more, hook them up with young Negro businessmen. You must be willing to buck a group when it's off course. I bucked the NAACP.

Medgar couldn't buck them. Had to toe the NAACP line best he could, even when he thought it was wrong. He had to design NAACP programs, put them in, run them, go to conventions, make strategy, hold press conferences, organize and inspire the Negroes of Mississippi, and get them to resist racism. Medgar had to take phone calls from everyone, from Negro sharecroppers to dirty white bigots. Medgar had to investigate racial violence and put out the real facts, because the cops claimed the killer was always "Person or persons unknown." Lope did a hero's job.

Lope could have investigated racial violence full-time, but he was also supposed to improve things for us. And Medgar had no leverage on whites. Jackson had very few northern-run businesses, a small Negro middle class, a tiny Negro business community. The big Jackson paper, the *Clarion-Ledger,* was a Negro-hating rag. With Negro jobs in Jackson controlled by local whites, Negroes were scared to ask for justice. Medgar urged them to protest. He used moral persuasion on the white folk. But in Mississippi in the '50s, moral persuasion on race was almost a lost cause.

Where else could we look for help? President Eisenhower was Medgar's old commander in the European theater, fighting the Nazis. But he didn't give a damn about Negroes, and we got nowhere telling him about civil rights. We told Congress about the lynchings and injustice, but guess who ran the Senate Judiciary Committee? Senator Eastland of Mississippi. No man ever worshipped segregation more than James O. Eastland. The top Senate committee on justice was run by a man with *no idea* of what justice was.

Medgar got death threats. Mississippi highway patrol, city cops, police detectives sat in front of NAACP headquarters, watching who came and went. When they saw a Negro they didn't like, they'd take his picture or follow him home, try to scare him. If a Negro joined the NAACP, his boss fired him. If he was a farmer, he lost his crop loan at planting time. If he rented land, his rent went up. If he owned, the bank foreclosed. Stores cut off his credit. When the waters got rough, some Negroes folded, left the NAACP, and left Medgar more lonely and exposed. Lope took it in stride. He trusted the pure of heart to stay on. Most black preachers were safe from white violence because most whites respected the church. But Medgar had no church to protect him. His commitment was total. Look all over the world, you'll never find a better man than Medgar Evers.

CHAPTER 9

Terrible Years

THE YEAR 1955 WAS A TERRIBLE ONE for the Mississippi Negro. When we tried to free ourselves by getting the vote, whites threatened us, beat and killed us in counties all over the state. And for a while America's white folks didn't seem to care.

In Humphreys County, each white employer got a voter list. If one of his Negroes was on it, he'd say, "Get off the list or get off my payroll." Those who stayed registered got a personal call from a white man: "You've been in this town a long time. Want to stay here? Get your name off that list." He'd threaten violence. Soon we were down to thirty-five registered Negroes in Humphreys County.

In Belzoni, the Humphreys County seat, Reverend George Lee, the town's NAACP president, signed up four hundred more Negro voters. Whites in town growled at him to get those names off the voting rolls. He refused. Whites bullied Negroes till the total of Negro registered fell to ninety-two by May 1955. On May 7, Reverend Lee walked out of the tailor shop with his Sunday preaching suit, and someone shot off the whole bottom of his face. The biggest Negro in Belzoni, brutally murdered downtown, in broad daylight. We hoped this killing would shock the nation, but nothing happened. The cops made no arrests—didn't even investigate.

Medgar looked into Reverend Lee's murder. The white powers in those little Mississippi towns bucked NAACP investigators all the way. They couldn't have cared less how Negroes had suffered. We pointed out Reverend Lee was found with lead pellets in his mouth. The white sheriff said, "Maybe they're fillings from his teeth."

Within a few weeks, Belzoni only had one Negro left on the voting rolls, a man named Gus Courts. Gus ran a little grocery store. His landlord tripled the rent. No one would give him groceries on credit. One night near Thanksgiving, Gus Courts was standing behind his grocery counter when a white man drove by and shot Gus in the abdomen and arm. No whites cared. When Gus healed, he left Mississippi for Chicago.

In Brookhaven, Lincoln County, Lamar Smith was an NAACP member good at getting out the vote. A white man or men murdered him on August 13, 1955, in Brookhaven, in broad daylight, with many witnesses, right in front of the county courthouse. A grand jury never indicted anyone.

In Jefferson Davis County, around '55, white officials began a reregistration campaign. Negroes registered to vote had to reapply. That brought the county total of registered Negroes down from about eleven hundred to sixty.

The Mississippi NAACP had over forty-six hundred members in 1955, and only about seventeen hundred in 1956. Medgar and I were furious about losing Negro voters to white threats. Meanwhile, the U.S. government was in Geneva, Switzerland, lecturing the Communists about free elections in *East Germany!* President Eisenhower didn't care about free elections in Mississippi, and we couldn't get the country to care.

Finally, in August of '55, we got the national attention. A fourteen-year-old Negro from Chicago named Emmett Till came to visit his family in Money, Mississippi. On a dare, he flirted with a white woman. He was just playing, but the woman's husband came at night with his brother, snatched Emmett Till from his cabin, shot Emmett Till in the head, tied a cotton gin fan around his neck with barbed wire, and dropped him in the Tallahatchie River. His body floated up, bloated and beaten, one eye missing, a bullet in the skull. Medgar took a photo of it, then went home and cried.

We all knew the killers would go free. Four NAACP folk risked their lives anyway, looking into the Emmett Till murder: Medgar, Aaron Henry, Amzie Moore, and Ruby Hurley. Amzie Moore worked for the NAACP in Cleveland, Mississippi. All four dressed like field hands and slid around the Delta, looking for criminal evidence, trying to convince folk who'd known Emmett Till to risk their lives by being legal witnesses. Whites harassed them, but they pressed on. Medgar wanted to shame all America with the story of Emmett Till. He wanted to make the civil rights struggle a mass movement.

T. R. M. Howard spread word of the Emmett Till case to the papers. Emmett Till's mama did her part. The Klan wanted to get Emmett Till out of sight quick, shove him in the ground. Emmett Till's mama wouldn't play that. She took his body back to Chicago for an open-casket funeral. There'd been killings like this for centuries, but times were changing. This was big news. Even in foreign countries, people wanted to know why a black boy had been murdered just for being fresh.

The publicity forced a trial. In September of '55, in a red-brick courthouse in Sumner, Mississippi, the killers were tried. Charles Diggs came down from Detroit. Dr. Howard helped the prosecution, ignored lots of death threats. Medgar got Emmett Till's great-uncle, an old preacher named Mose Wright, to testify about the killing, and then got Mose Wright safely away from any lynch mob. The jury declared the two killers not guilty. The killers bragged to reporters how they'd done it, even sold *Look* magazine the story of the whole dirty plot. And they were never convicted of a damn thing.

I began to organize little NAACP meetings around Philadelphia. Neshoba County was so mean we had to get our NAACP materials sent in unmarked envelopes. We had to have secret meetings in barns and pastures. Ruby Hurley and Fannie Lou Hamer helped spread the word among local Negroes.

Ruby Hurley had been with the NAACP since 1943 and had founded the NAACP office in Birmingham in '51. I'm a male chauvinist who hates a bossy woman in charge, and was Ruby Hurley bossy! But as a woman, she got away with things that Medgar, Aaron Henry, Amzie Moore, and I couldn't. All white folk knew Negro women in some kind of way. If they didn't practice nighttime integration with them, they had one as a cook, a nurse, housekeeper, or babysitter. Even most of the real mean old white racists cared about a few Negro women somewhere. And because a woman's smaller than a man, whites were less scared of a Ruby Hurley or a Fannie Lou Hamer than of Medgar or Charles Evers. So we put Fannie out front, right in the trenches, and she did us proud.

Late in '55, Medgar moved his NAACP office from Farish Street to a two-story Negro-owned concrete and steel office building in Jackson. We called it "the Masonic Temple" and also "the Black Capitol of Mississippi." It had lots of Negro businesses and was a symbol of

Negro ambition. Mississippi's first Negro senator, back in Reconstruction days, was a former slave named John Roy Lynch. The Masonic Temple was on the street named for Senator Lynch—Lynch Street. Having his office on Lynch Street was a symbol of how deep Medgar's troubles ran.

Around 1955, I met Nelson Rockefeller for the first time. I knew what his family had done for Negroes. The Rockefellers and the Kennedys were the only two powerful families in this country who backed civil rights before it was fashionable. The *only* two. And the Rockefellers saw the light before the Kennedys. I'd heard Nelson himself was a special friend of the Negro, so I bowled my way in to see him, at one of his little receptions up in New York. I knew once I was in, he'd like me. And he did.

Nelson impressed me from the start. He was so warm and outgoing, and loved people. And like most good leaders, he knew how to listen. He wasn't the governor of New York State yet, but he was on his way. He didn't care if his views were fashionable. He didn't care about liberal or conservative. Nelson cared about right and wrong. Racism was wrong. Segregation was wrong. The civil rights movement was right. This was the kind of powerful white man that I'd always been looking for in Mississippi. In 1958, we heard Rockefeller had become governor of New York in a big upset. I wasn't surprised—just happy for Nelson and for the cause of civil rights.

Nelson Rockefeller was governor of New York for fifteen years. And as governor, he did more for the Negro than any governor in the country. And not just do-good liberal social programs. Nelson hired Negroes to good jobs. His family bank, the Chase Manhattan, hired more blacks than any bank in the country. Rockefeller had Jackie Robinson as a Negro advisor and supported Jackie through thick and thin.

I made myself an informal advisor to Nelson. We weren't close friends—most years we only spoke about four times a year. But Nelson had friends all over the world, and I was one of them. He always made me feel special: "You're terrific, I want to tell you." He hated red tape and loved touching people, just like me. He spoke from the heart, just like me. Nelson could tell a joke, and take a joke. He spent money freely but didn't waste money like most of the rich do. He spread it around, bought things of value, and never apologized for being rich. I wanted to get rich and do just the same.

In 1955, I was out to prove how much money I could make. I did six different jobs at once around Philadelphia, Mississippi. I started with three: Great-uncle Mark's funeral parlor, selling burial insurance, and bootlegging. With Daddy dead, I didn't care who knew about my bootlegging. It was a natural business for me. Many respectable folks bootlegged. No one knew more Bible than Fannie Lou Hamer, but even she and her husband bootlegged and kept a juke joint to make ends meet.

My fourth job was more adventurous. Downstairs of a hotel in Philadelphia, I started a Negro cafe. Negroes in Mississippi had never been able to sit down and enjoy a milk shake. The best we could do was to buy one at a drugstore take-out stand. My cafe finally gave Negroes a place to sit down, order a Coke or a milk shake, and relax, just like white folk. I built this cafe into the Evers Hotel and Lounge. I brought in real good musicians and made it a club, with my own house band. I featured good food and liquor and cute waitresses. The place was jumping.

My fifth business was a Negro taxi service. Negroes said, "Mississippi won't allow no colored cabs." I started my own cab company anyway—first Negro cab company ever in Mississippi. I converted a car into a cab and drove it myself, from a cabstand one hundred yards from my cafe. I was primed for a fight. I barely heard a squawk. The white cabbies did give me one rule: "You can't pick up passengers at the bus station." I said, "You big enough to stop me?" No one stopped me. I bought another car and hired a man I called Obiedow to do my driving for me.

I was still finding new ways to make a dollar. My sixth job was as a deejay. I'd bought advertising for the Evers Funeral Home on WHOC Radio, Philadelphia. WHOC was owned by whites, the Cole family. But not everyone who looks like the enemy is truly your enemy. In '54, even Philadelphia, Mississippi, one of the meanest white towns on earth, had at least two white families who helped the Negro openly: the Cole family and the Lewis family.

Greenville, Mississippi, had the Carter family. Good white folk. Hodding Carter Jr., published a liberal newspaper that fought racism proudly, and he caught hell for his editorials. A few other good white folk around the state worked to change the system. But let's not get carried away about how many of these folk there were. Half the whites in Mississippi now say they worked for civil rights in the '50s and '60s, "behind the scenes." They were "the silent majority," "the quiet majority." Let me tell you, that was no "quiet majority." "Stone-mute majority" is more like it.

A lot of white folk wanted to do right, but the atmosphere was so sick they were scared to speak up. They disliked lynchings but lacked the guts to stop them. So instead they'd warn us. In small southern towns, word spreads like wildfire. At the first sign of race trouble, white folks warned the niggers they liked. All my life, whites have tipped me off about white plots against me. Against everything their culture taught them, many white folk admired us. Even the Klan had a few who said, "Leave that poor nigger alone." Mayor Clayton Lewis tipped me off to many ugly things that whites in Philadelphia had in store for me. Saved my ass a few times, maybe saved my life.

The Cole family helped me, too. They owned WHOC Radio, and they owned a big wholesale company. They had many Negro employees and treated us as people. Now, the Evers family was paying WHOC good money to sponsor a radio show. A few times a day, a white boy came on and reminded the listeners about the Evers Funeral Home. But the ads had no feeling. The station owner was Howard Cole. I told Mr. Cole we weren't getting our money's worth for those funeral home spots. He said, "Then you do them." Just like that. Asked me down to the station to do the show myself. Now, in 1954, in Mississippi, Negroes weren't on the radio, on TV, or in the papers except to be mocked or charged with a dirty crime. A few Negro musicians got on the air, but never a Negro anchorman on TV. Never a Negro columnist in the newspaper. And no more than one or two Negro deejays in all Mississippi, if that many.

But Medgar and I planned to change that, and now Howard Cole gave me the chance. I came down to WHOC, and Howard showed me how to spin records, how to operate the board. After watching for three days, I jumped in. WHOC was "1490 on your radio dial." I called my show *The 1490 Club*. Never read any copy. Everything was live. I just spoke the ads, spoke to my listeners from the heart. Played good, hard rhythm and blues. B. B. King, Muddy Waters. Took requests, too.

I was one of the very first Negro deejays in Mississippi history. I grew a big, loyal audience. Negroes loved hearing one of their own on the radio. They liked the songs I played, bought the products I promoted. I had a gift for reaching people. I loved doing that show. Howard Cole got to shake things up, help the Negro, and make money, too.

As soon as I saw I could reach lots of black folk, I started sneaking in civil rights messages on the air. I'd play a B. B. King song, read an ad, then say, "Pay your poll tax." Play Muddy Waters, read an ad for the Evers Funeral Home, then tell my listeners to register and vote. As time went along and no one stopped me, I got bolder. Every time I signed on or off, I'd say, "Pay your poll tax. Register and vote. If you can't register to vote, pay your poll tax anyway. Become a full-fledged citizen of this community."

With all these six jobs, I was making good money. Got myself a bank account, just like a white man. Some Negroes said, "James Charles, you're high on the hog." I said, "Go to hell! I'm working six jobs at a time, putting in eighteen hours a day to get what I got."

On December 1, 1955, cops in Montgomery, Alabama, arrested a Negro named Mrs. Rosa Parks for not giving up her seat on the bus to a white man. A Negro named E. D. Nixon started a boycott of the Montgomery bus system. He asked the Montgomery NAACP to join him. The NAACP people did like they'd been told: They began checking with Roy Wilkins in New York. E. D. Nixon knew that was bullshit—he had to launch his boycott quick. So he turned to the black churches. The Dexter Avenue Baptist Church had a new preacher, Martin Luther King Jr. Martin was just twenty-six, but he was smart, well schooled, and had studied how Gandhi in India had freed his people through nonviolence. Martin led the boycott.

When Walter White died in '55, Roy Wilkins became executive director of the NAACP. Roy had come to work for Walter White back in 1931, running the NAACP magazine, *The Crisis*. Roy was real smart but worked too much from the head. The same time Roy Wilkins took over the best civil rights group in the country, Martin came out of the black church, a preacher willing to fight white racism in the streets. A great orator who wanted action. A man nonviolent as Gandhi, but tough as nails. A man who worked from the head *and* from the heart. And Roy Wilkins couldn't handle it.

Negroes in Montgomery got threatened, arrested, and beaten. But after a year, they won the right to sit anywhere on those damn buses. In 1956, the big question in civil rights was whether Negroes around the country should copy the Montgomery bus boycott. Should the NAACP march, boycott, and sit in? Martin said yes. Roy said no, keep the movement in the courts. Roy said direct action would only work where Negro boycotts could cripple the local economy. They could do it in Montgomery, but not in most towns.

Roy Wilkins was jealous of Martin. We all knew Martin's bus boycott had integrated the buses of Montgomery. Roy insisted NAACP legal action did it. He and Gloster Current opposed boycotts, sit-ins, or marches. In '57, after Roy rejected direct action, Martin helped found his own group, the Southern Christian Leadership Conference (SCLC). Medgar and I soon got in touch with the SCLC and met with Martin. Roy Wilkins and Martin did *some* work together. At the end of '59, they announced a joint drive to register over a million Negroes to vote. But Roy showed his true colors in '57 when Medgar volunteered to be an assistant secretary to the SCLC. Roy told Medgar to get right out of the SCLC. Once an NAACP man, always an NAACP man. Medgar obeyed Roy and got out, but I liked direct action, and I did little favors for Martin as he set up the SCLC.

Martin impressed me right off. He was short and stocky, a snappy dresser with good manners and a serious face. Out of the pulpit, he spoke with common sense. In the pulpit, he really moved people. A common organizer must rustle up his crowd. His crowd's in working clothes and tight with their money. But a preacher's got a congregation, ready for a sermon and expecting to fill the collection box. Martin was the son and grandson of Baptist preachers. He liked the perks of being a preacher.

But from the start Martin was so much tougher than most preachers. And he could make a decision. He liked to hold to his decisions once he'd made up his mind, but he was easy to talk to, always willing to listen. And he was down south, where the need was, looking evil right in the eye. Roy Wilkins only came down to Mississippi on special occasions. He came down May 17, 1959, to celebrate with Medgar and the Mississippi branches the fifth anniversary of the *Brown vs. Board of Education* decision. But mostly he kept his ass safe up in New York.

In '56, the national NAACP convention was in San Francisco, and Medgar was a delegate. That's where he first met Martin. Medgar wanted the NAACP to use marches, boycotts, and sit-ins. He invited some other delegates back to his hotel room, to talk about how the NAACP could follow Martin's lead. Medgar even invited Martin to Jackson, told him his presence alone would raise the spirits of Mississippi Negroes.

But Roy Wilkins and Thurgood Marshall were damned if they would follow Martin's lead. Thurgood Marshall called desegregation "man's work." Roy was more of a diplomat. He pushed through a resolution saying the NAACP executive board would give "careful consideration" to Martin's tactics in Montgomery. But Roy and Thurgood always favored the courts, the courts, the courts.

Medgar bought himself a big old Oldsmobile, with a big V-8 engine. It had to be big enough to sleep in since most hotels wouldn't take Negroes. It had to be able to hold its own with any redneck car that might try to run Lope off the road. For the next nine years, day and night, Medgar used that car for his work. He drove over one hundred miles an hour sometimes, down many back roads. He put thousands and thousands of miles on that Oldsmobile.

Medgar really had two jobs. One was selling local memberships in the NAACP—that meant making civil rights sound safe and civilized. His other job was to investigate and publicize the white man's race crimes, many of them committed against civil rights folks. That meant scaring local Negroes. The last thing they wanted to do was to join the NAACP. So there was a conflict in Medgar's job, and it wore him down.

I organized people in my vocal, sassy way. I'd talk big, cuss guys out, take guys on. "Don't wait around," I'd say. "Let's get it over." Medgar was as militant as I was, but always quiet, levelheaded. He kept his careful plans private. He'd bide his time, then step forward. Medgar was in the American Legion and the YMCA. He was a Baptist, a Mason, an Elk. I was a loner. Medgar's main goal was the vote. I believed that maybe a Negro could buy his way up in this country. I was after the dollar.

Whites in Mississippi hated seeing me prosper. Even the nice ones choked up when a local Negro built a fat bank balance. And nothing riled the peckerwoods more than seeing a Negro who wouldn't crawl, shuffle, or beg. The Citizens Council boasted that they had mayors, police chiefs, and bank presidents as members. They were proud of being law-abiding. But the Citizens Council was just the Klan without the bedsheets. The Country Club Klan. A bunch of college graduates who liked to enforce segregation with guns.

Some prominent folks in the Citizens Council decided to drive me out of town. They came after me and the Cole family that owned WHOC. They made '56 a terrible year for me. They didn't care if I was working eighteen hours a day, taking risks, holding down six jobs. To them, it was simple: No nigger should be making good money or telling niggers they were a white man's equal. And I was doing both.

White folk hated that Medgar was NAACP field director and I was chairing voter registration. They knew we aimed to destroy their power over us. They resisted that tooth and nail and, between '52 and '55, cut the rolls of Negro voters in Mississippi from twenty-two thousand to eight thousand. In February 1956, I started a Philadelphia chapter of the NAACP, and things went from bad to worse.

Finally, the racists went all the way. A white friend called: "Charles," he said, "there's a Negro coming to your house. He'll ask you to drive your cab down to the county line. Don't go. Some Klansmen are waiting there to kill you." My friend said this Negro had already been paid for the job. It was a Negro I knew well, a man with nothing much against me. He was going to lure me to my death strictly for the cash.

Soon enough, this very Negro came right to my front door. He stood on my front step, rang my bell, casual as can be. My blood boiled. I opened the door with a .38 in my pocket, livid to see him so friendly. But I acted innocent.

"Charlie," the man said, "carry me down to the county line."

I said, "Isn't Obiedow around here someplace? He'll take you."

The Negro said, "I want *you* to carry me. Want to talk to you about something."

"I'm going to stay in," I said.

"Come on, come on," he said. "I'll give you five dollars."

"You're going to tempt me," I said. "Come on in the house a minute."

It was my life or his. He'd started something, and I was glad to finish it. Soon as he stepped inside, I grabbed him, called him a dirty sonofabitch, and beat him to the ground with a sawed-off baseball bat. I might have killed him, but Nan was screaming. I said, "Get this bastard out the house before I kill him." She did.

But the white racists turned up the heat. They pressured the man who owned my restaurant building to revoke my lease. They held up my restaurant license. They drove by my restaurant and shot in the windows. Cops kept raiding my hotel, rousting everyone out of bed. Even my best customers got tired of that. The Citizens Council cut off my bank credit, threatened Negroes who bought my burial insurance or used my funeral parlor. They leaned on the man who sold me caskets and embalming fluid until he cut off my credit and then stopped selling to me, even for cash.

One Friday night, I got tough with my listeners: "Either be registered to vote by next Monday evening or please don't tune in to 1490 again." The Citizens Council told Howard Cole, "Evers is talking too much about paying the poll tax. We don't want these niggers voting!" They threatened to pull their ads if Mr. Cole didn't cancel my show—and that would have been just the start. They said, "Put this nigger off the air, or we'll put you through hell! Is it worth going through hell for one nigger?"

When I reached work Monday, Howard Cole was almost crying. He told me what the Citizens Council had said, and he said, "I can't let you go on the air no more." I could have talked Mr. Cole into giving me one more chance. But those Citizens Council boys played rough, and I didn't want to cost him WHOC. I resigned and put my deejay career on hold.

The Citizens Council fixed it so I couldn't renew my cab license, couldn't get insurance on my taxi fleet. Then they began staging incidents. They'd ram my hearse or one of my cabs, and those who rammed me would sue me for their "injuries." They were slapping suits against me everywhere. Any fair judge would have thrown every case out of court, but the Citizens Council easily made Charles Evers pay damages and fines.

One day, I was parked at an intersection, in front of an old glove factory. A white lady with the Citizens Council tore out of a parking lot and rammed me. Clearly deliberate. Cops were there in a flash. Ticketed me for running a stop sign. The woman sued me, claimed I'd hurt her back. Most of my witnesses were scared to testify. The court ruled I owed this woman five thousand dollars, and five thousand dollars then was like fifty-thousand dollars today. I was flat broke. I'd have liked to appeal, but not one lawyer would take my case.

I couldn't raise the five thousand dollars. The court took almost everything I had. They couldn't take my car, since I hadn't paid for it, but they attached all my property. I had to sell all my businesses. I went looking for work so I could feed my wife and three little girls, but I couldn't find a decent job anywhere, and I knew I was only suited to work for myself, anyway.

Finally, I tossed in the towel. I told Medgar, "I better move north and make money. You stay here and carry on. I'll send money back, and buy up property." Medgar was so worried about my safety he *insisted* I go north. But I never left the civil rights movement. I went north to escape the racists of Philadelphia and to make money so I could fund Medgar's work. I had no plan and hardly knew a soul up north. But I knew somehow I'd get rich.

In the '40s, over three hundred thousand Negroes left Mississippi for towns like Chicago, Detroit, St. Louis. Gus Courts was up in Chicago. But I hated leaving Mississippi. You want to choose when to go. You hate to be chased from a place where your family has deep roots. I felt like the prodigal son. I told Medgar, "Anytime you need me, I'll be back. Day or night." Medgar reminded me of our pact: If one of us went down, the other would carry on, all the way to the end. We shook on that real solemn.

Whites walked into our home and auctioned off every last stick of furniture. Stripped the house bare. The four-hundred-dollar dining room suite I'd bought Nan at Christmas they auctioned for one hundred dollars. When the auctioneer was through, it was goodbye Mississippi. I was so broke, my friends had to take up a collection just to get me traveling money. I got twenty-six dollars in nickels and dimes, sent Nan and Pat down to live with Nan's mama, and pointed my Ford to Flint, Michigan. I thought I'd start with an auto job.

I drove up old Highway 51, then turned on Highway 57 just outside Illinois. On the outskirts of Chicago, I was almost out of gas. At a service station, the white attendant saw my Mississippi plates, saw me counting out gas money from my old piggy bank. He told me, "No charge." I tried to pay, but he wouldn't take it. In tears, I took the gas station's address and vowed to pay them back as soon as I made some money in Flint.

But I was just outside Chicago when my money ran out, so I headed for Chicago instead of Flint. I thought I'd stay with my sister Liz and her family for a while. I was determined to get rich. I didn't give a damn how.

CHAPTER 10

Chicago: The Chances I Took

MAN, IT STARTED OUT ROUGH IN CHICAGO. I was broke, almost desperate. Ten years before, while I was an Alcorn student, I'd worked in Chicago a few summers, so I knew something about the slaughterhouses of Swift and Armour. But moving to Chicago at thirty-four, to stay awhile, was all different. When I reached Chicago in '56, I saw I didn't know one side of the street from the other.

Until I got on my feet, I had to stay with my sister Liz in her little rented apartment. Liz worked for one of the packing companies, and her husband worked for the city. I told Liz how the whites drove me from Mississippi and auctioned my furniture. Liz said, "Well, you can sleep here. It'll cost you fifteen dollars a week." Liz always knew the value of a dollar, but I never thought she'd charge her own brother rent when he was broke. Liz thought I had cash squirreled away somewhere. She put me in a little room with her two little girls. Wedged me in with my little nieces.

After three nights of that, I went out and found the cheapest apartment I could. A nasty basement place, with water dripping all day through the pipes. I went back to Swift and took a sixty-dollar-a-week packinghouse job—8:00 to 4:00, hauling beef in the stockyards. I ate day-old bread and neck bones, fifty cents at a time. Had no steady girl. I was alone in my basement apartment but for the rats and roaches. It took me almost two years before I could send for Nan and Pat. And then times got worse. Pat got every little sickness that came along. I worked like a dog to support Nan, send Pat to the doctor, and send money home to Medgar and Mama.

I'll never forget those who helped me then. Gladys Mazique was a friend of Liz and my stepsister Eva. The Maziques put me up for nothing, but they couldn't help me get rich. I remembered Al Benson, a Negro from the Delta, who'd come up to Chicago and become a deejay with his own show on WVON. Al knew a lot of people. I called him, and he said sure, he'd like to see me. Al took me out to the racetrack, the first track I'd ever seen. But when I told him I was broke and needed work, Al just winked. No one who'd known me in Mississippi could believe I was broke. Al Benson did nothing for me. Those first months in Chicago were hard.

But I kept my eyes and ears open. A friend at Swift found me a second job, at a Hilton Hotel downtown, near Michigan Avenue. No colored boys were allowed on the second floor of the hotel, but they hired us as ground-floor washroom attendants. I also worked at the Ambassador East Hotel, a fancy North Side place. But I liked the Hilton best. I'd get off work at Swift, head straight to the Hilton, and work there from six to midnight. Handed out towels. Used a switch broom to brush the dandruff off white folks' leisure suits. Got three dollars a night—plus tips.

The Hilton got a lot of convention business. Many of the convention folk were rednecks from Mississippi, Alabama, Georgia. I'd hated them all my life. Hearing that Deep South accent put me in a mean mood. If some redneck had a few drinks, lurched into the washroom, and dropped his money, I put my foot on it. If he staggered in blind drunk, I'd roll him, pick every penny from his wallet, stuff the wallet back in his suit pocket, and hustle him out. With my salary, tips, and stealing, I made a hundred dollars some nights.

Some old lush would come in: "Hey, boy! Where can I get a half-pint?" I began buying whiskey at a liquor store on my way to work. Sold it for five dollars a half pint. I got them girls, too. Cabbies at the bus station and train station told me where the whores were. I brought girls to the Hilton, set them up with men, and paid them for their time. Collected from the johns myself, just like in the Philippines. I wasn't a pimp, now; a pimp takes money from whores to protect them. These whores didn't pay me; I paid them. But I was trafficking in whores, alright. "Running girls," I called it.

Sometimes, a john came in the washroom: "You want to make ten dollars?"

"Doing what?"

"Go get me a colored woman and bring her to my room."

"You got the wrong man. I don't do nothing like that."

"How the hell you make money?"

"Just like I'm doing, brushing you down."

In Mississippi, white men took black women, and Negroes got lynched for looking at a white girl. So I wasn't going to help any white man get a black girl in Chicago.

Then I met an old Negro who needed weekend help at his bar, a cozy joint on Fifty-ninth Street, lit with little colored bulbs. Five dollars a night. For two long years, I did nothing but work those three jobs, save my money, and sometimes go to church Sunday. I went less than I should have, but the Lord took care of me.

I was a washroom attendant at the Palmer House in Chicago when Conrad Hilton, owner of the Hilton hotel chain, spoke at the hotel. All the hotel managers and big shots came to hear him. I was a greenhorn at business at that level, but one thing Mr. Hilton said really hit me: "Own everything you can, and run nothing." He said there are lots of good people to run a business for you, so draw a salary, oversee the business, but don't run it. Conrad Hilton had a concession on everything in his hotels—even the shoeshine stand. I vowed to do the same as soon as I had real money again. And I planned on getting it, by hook or by crook.

Not even three jobs could make me rich. One night I had dinner with a friend I'll call Preston and his wife. I won't use Preston's real name because he's a well-known preacher now—no sense making trouble for him. But in '56—well, believe me, Preston wasn't preaching. That night at dinner, I told him I'd been chased out of Mississippi, and had to get rich in Chicago. He said, "Come work for me." I said, "What kind of business you in?" He said, "The policy business." He meant illegal gambling, the numbers, the Mob. My mind started wheeling. The only Mississippi Negroes I'd ever known to get rich were the Jones boys of Vicksburg, and they'd done it in Chicago, in the numbers. There were a lot of Jones boys, and word had reached Mississippi they'd all become millionaires. So Preston's offer stirred my blood.

But I took pause. I said, "I don't know a thing about the policy business." Preston said, "I'll teach you." And he did. He taught me well. It wasn't the schooling Daddy had in mind, but I learned the policy business—a dangerous, very rich business, no more, no less. Dirty, easy money. Preston carried three guns with him when he did business. He had seventy-five people working for him at his peak, and he took in as much as fifteen thousand dollars a day. This was my ticket to getting rich.

Today, it's strange to think I was once deep in the Chicago underworld: gambling, call girls, nightclubs, the rackets. I did a lot of wrong things. I never sold drugs only because there was none to sell. I studied the scene, took in every fact Preston told me, then jumped in. I began as a field runner for a syndicate, dropping policy and picking it up.

The Mob controlled the big numbers. It was a loose group, really many different groups fighting for the action. The Mob had run the Jones boys from Vicksburg clean out of Chicago. Had killed some of them and taken over. In the end, all the numbers money went to the Mob. Negroes ran some policy games, whites ran others. Negroes managed and ran my policy game. When I got in the numbers, I started meeting all kinds of guys: white, black, Italian, Jewish. Everyone focused on making money. No one hated me for being a strong black man. They expected me to be strong. Working with the Mob helped me start to get over my hatred of whites.

As a runner, I saw to my own station. I collected money and dropped it off. Midnight, I'd get off from my Hilton Hotel job and set out on that policy route. Only took an hour. I always carried two guns: a .38 pistol and a sawed-off shotgun, a carbine. But I expected no trouble, and got none. Preston gave me all the addresses, showed me the quickest routes.

In Mississippi, the cracker police were too slow and dumb to catch me. I'd enjoyed eluding those old lead-foot cops. In Chicago, things were different. The Mob was in with the cops. You didn't outrun them or outsmart them. You paid them off. Just part of operating costs. Cops didn't charge much. Between Swift, the Hilton, the bar, and dropping policy, I made two hundred dollars a week.

There was nothing friendly or casual about the numbers racket. It was rough, and it was enforced. You did what you were told, or they'd take your job, maybe even kill you. But turn in your money, and no one asked questions. When a Mob bagman was cut in half, his body stuffed in a trunk—that man hadn't been turning all his money in. I was never that stupid.

Only took three weeks to learn the policy game. I wanted a bigger challenge, more money. It was the old story: Anything I can do for you, I can do for myself. So I told the syndicate I was starting a wheel of my own. They had the map of Chicago divided up. Each part of the syndicate had a piece of the city. I found two mostly Negro parts of Chicago that the Mob didn't reach: one on the South Side, one on the West Side. I stayed inside those areas. I only took syndicate crumbs, but they were sweet crumbs. They could have killed me, but I didn't mind. I could have been killed anytime in Mississippi for urging Negroes to vote. Death had been walking right behind me since I was a small boy.

Preston never knew I'd started my own wheel. He fell sick, almost died, and promised God in the hospital that if he ever got well, he'd quit the policy business and become a preacher. Next time I saw him, he was holier-than-thou and couldn't be bothered about policy. I began my own game with five hundred dollars. The first night, I let someone hit for one hundred dollars. For a week, I let no one hit, just took all the money in. That gave me cash enough to operate. Then most every day, I'd rig the game so someone won a small amount, but most everyone lost. I was my own runner. I picked up my customer numbers myself and put them in a bowl. People played from their own apartments. You knew the little guys by the address and the amounts they bet. None of my customers ever saw the numbers in the bowl. I never catered to any rich customers. Little guys who win the numbers love to spread the word: "Hey, I caught Evers for one hundred dollars!" Best advertising you could have. A few times I got way ahead and let someone win three thousand dollars. Business boomed. The numbers is fast, fast money.

The police thought I was running a Mob game and let me alone. I had to keep paying the cops off, but I didn't mind. Running cathouses in the Philippines, I'd paid off the MPs. In Chicago I paid off the cops, and it was easy pickings. Oh, once or twice, a rookie cop carried me down to the station. He'd drop me off to get charged, tell the desk sergeant, "I caught this man dropping policy." Well, all the top cops in the precinct knew I was a runner for the Mob. *Not to be messed with.* The desk sergeant would ask a few questions, but he just wanted a hundred dollars. After the rookie cop left, the desk sergeant would say, "Present yourself to the jailer." I'd peel a hundred dollars from the roll in my pocket, hand it to the sergeant, and walk past the jail cells and out of the station.

I never overplayed my hand. I was satisfied to skim $400 to $500 a week. I hardly paid taxes. Saved a bundle. From my profits, I funded a lot of Medgar's civil rights work. I'd send him $100, $200, $500, $1,000. I sent money to Mama, too, for the rest of her life. I visited Mississippi every couple of months, tried to help the NAACP all I could. Talked with Medgar every week about strategy and tactics. We were always jawing over the phone about one thing or another.

Medgar was such an angel, he ignored money. So I was a sonofabitch who sent him money. I paid down Medgar's house note. I helped him buy a station wagon. I never had the heart to tell him just where the money came from. He'd have called it "dirty money." I told Medgar to grow some black businesses. We had the same old scraps: Medgar sought after justice, I sought after money. I had economic answers to black suffering. Medgar wanted *political* answers—new voters, and a new civil rights bill in Congress.

In '57, we got that civil rights bill—our first since Reconstruction. The '57 Civil Rights Act was a compromise, but it set up a commission on civil rights, a civil rights division in the Justice Department, and penalties for denying us the vote. Senate Majority Leader Lyndon Johnson of Texas pushed the bill through because he aimed to be president and had to be more than a peckerwood from Texas. Medgar pushed for that bill, too. It was a way to teach civil rights to the whole nation. None of us knew then how much that bill would help the Evers family.

Medgar kept looking for ways to reach a large white audience. In '57, a few Negro kids got into the best public high school in Little Rock, Arkansas, and the governor of Arkansas wouldn't allow it. President Eisenhower had to send in the National Guard to integrate that school. Jackson TV station WLBT had a panel show on how "the Little Rock Crisis" might spread to Mississippi. There wasn't a Negro on the panel to explain Negroes had a legal right to attend Central High. Medgar asked WLBT's manager, Fred Beard, for airtime to give the Negro side. When the bastard refused, Medgar wrote the Federal Communications Commission to ask if we could force WLBT to give time to the Negro side. The FCC said no. In February of '58, Medgar wrote

Dave Garroway, host of the *Today* show on NBC. J. P. Coleman had talked race on the *Today* show, so Medgar asked if he could come talk race. He was always asking, "Why can't the Negro do it, too?" Dave Garroway turned him down.

In '58, Mississippi had twenty thousand Negroes registered to vote. By 1960, we had it up to twenty-six thousand. But whites kept beating and lynching. In '59, they said Mack Charles Parker of Poplarville jumped a white girl. Two days before his trial, a mob dragged Mack Parker from jail, threw him in a car, shot him, and dropped his body into the Mississippi River. The FBI turned over the evidence to Mississippi lawmen. A grand jury did nothing.

In '58, a Negro preacher and part-time college professor named Clennon King applied to Ole Miss. The State of Mississippi said only a crazy nigger would do that and got him committed to the state madhouse. And in 1960, when a Negro named Clyde Kennard applied to Mississippi Southern College, cops in Hattiesburg arrested him for having told another Negro to steal five bags of chicken feed. The other Negro testified, was freed and handed a job. Clyde Kennard got seven years on a chain gang. And as a convicted felon, Kennard was barred from any state college in Mississippi. When Medgar called the Kennard sentence "a mockery of justice," cops arrested him for contempt of court and fined him one hundred dollars. Somehow, the Mississippi Supreme Court voided the conviction. Even they thought that was going too far.

In '59, the Mississippi legislature had a committee investigate the NAACP. The hearings spread propaganda that the NAACP was full of Communists and took direction from outsiders. The committee wouldn't let Medgar testify. Our own state legislature almost banned the NAACP in Mississippi.

On March 11, 1958, Medgar was coming home from an NAACP conference in Greensboro, North Carolina. About 1:00 A.M., he got on a Trailways bus from Meridian to Jackson. He sat right behind the driver, who told him to move back to the Negro section. Lope refused. The driver went for help. Local cops mounted the bus, took Medgar inside the bus station, and told him to sit in the back of the bus. They asked him who he was and why he was breaking the law. He said he was NAACP and he was breaking the law because it was wrong. The cops told him if he and the NAACP really cared about race relations in Meridian, he'd sit in the back of the bus.

Medgar still refused. The bus was forty-five minutes late when the driver finally left, with Medgar sitting up front, thinking he'd beat the racists. But five blocks from the station, a cab drove up from behind, and the screaming cabbie pushed his way onto the bus and punched the left side of Lope's face so hard it went numb. Medgar defended himself but never threw a punch. Not a passenger tried to help. Finally, the bus driver got the cabbie off the bus, and the bus rolled on. Medgar was still sitting up front.

I was down visiting Mississippi when this happened. Someone called, told me how the white cabbie had done Medgar. I grabbed a shotgun, jumped into an Evers family funeral car, and roared into Meridian. I drove straight to the bus station where the cabbies waited, and I stalked inside *brandishing* my shotgun. I saw a crowd of rednecks and shouted, "I'm Charles Evers! Which one of you sonsofbitches hit my brother? I'll blow your fucking brains out!" I held my gun, dared them to do something or say something. They looked back, scared and speechless. I stalked out. No one followed me as I drove off. Lope was furious when he found out what I'd done, but I didn't care. I just remember driving those lonesome roads back to Philadelphia, wondering why I hadn't been killed already. Why was God protecting me like this? He must've had some special purpose for me. What was it?

Mama died on Mother's Day, 1959. Ever since Daddy had died, she'd been miserable. Medgar saw her a lot more than I could. I wish I'd seen her more. Mama had kept up with current events. She'd been so proud when Medgar became NAACP Field Secretary. She was scared of the death threats he got, but Medgar had been such a polite little boy, and I'd always been so feisty and ragged. *I* was the hothead. Mama thought I'd be the one killed by whites. Until the day she died, Mama worried more about me than about Medgar. She hated the chances I took. She never stopped telling me, "You must not believe you can die." And then she died. I felt very sad, and also restless.

I'd run my own policy game three years, and I started thinking about getting out. Then the Summerdale police scandal hit. Summerdale was a North Side district. Around 1958, the local papers found out a Summerdale burglar had been pulling jobs with help from eight uniformed Chicago cops. That didn't surprise me, but it shocked white Chicago. After a lot of hoola about how the city had been disgraced, the police commissioner resigned.

Mayor Daley's new top cop, Mr. O. W. Wilson, was a little bitty gray-haired man, the dean of the crime school at the University of California. He looked old and weak, didn't know Chicago. How could he overhaul and control a big-city police department? But that's just what he did. O. W. Wilson was a smart, tough little man. He hired a lot of new cops and bought them better equipment. He put in an Intelligence Unit to fight organized crime, and he told those boys to get results. No more taking protection money. When I saw O. W. Wilson playing rough, busting folks, I got out. People say, "You can't quit the Mob." Well, I did. I was smart, but maybe I was lucky, too. I broke a few rules and still got out when I wanted. No broken legs, not even a scratch. The Lord was watching out for me.

I bought myself a building at seventy-first and Vincennes, on the South Side. I opened my first liquor store and tavern, and called it Club Mississippi. A legitimate club, with no whores. My security guards didn't allow cursing, drunks, or fighting. Then I sent for my musicians from my old Evers Hotel and Lounge in Philadelphia, Mississippi. They made a fine house band. I brought my old waitresses up to Chicago, too. I served good food at Club Mississippi, and if another club sold beer for seventy-five cents a glass, I sold it for forty cents a glass. People packed my place, even a few whites, and I made all the money back in volume.

I met most all the great Negro musicians in Chicago—especially the bluesmen. Most of them were from Mississippi, so we had a lot in common. They'd played fish fries, juke joints, and parties down south, then came north. I knew John Lee Hooker, Bobby Bland, Memphis Slim—all kinds of musicians.

I got Elmore James to play with my band. I used to pick him up at his mean old South Side apartment, haul him to Club Mississippi, and listen to him play "Dust My Broom." A great blues player, and he had no car, no money. I used to scrap with Leonard Chess, who owned Chess Records and recorded Elmore, about how little he paid him. Leonard said, "All my performers are making money. They signed a contract." I said, "Leonard Chess, you dirty skunk. You know damn well Elmore can hardly read and write."

I knew Muddy Waters real well, too. Muddy was five years older than me. He'd been raised in Clarksdale, Mississippi—Aaron Henry's hometown. He'd been in Chicago since '43, driving a truck, working a mill, before he hit as a bluesman. "Hoochie-Coochie Man," "Rollin' Stone," "Got My Mojo Workin'," —Muddy was the best. I also did music promoting in Chicago. James Brown, the Hardest Working Man in Show Business, played a show in Chicago. When I bought a hundred tickets, James Brown asked to meet me. We've been good friends ever since.

Just outside Chicago, in Argo, I opened a second tavern. The Palm Gardens was a front for my gambling joint. I had a policy wheel down in the basement. God, the money was good. We packed that place. Mississippi Night on Tuesday night drew on all the people around Chicago up from Mississippi. Thursday night, we had Celebrity Night and put anyone on stage with any kind of talent.

My third tavern was the Subway Lounge, on the West Side. I loved its address: 1313 West Thirteenth Street. The Subway Lounge was another front, with gambling, a policy wheel, call girls, too. For four years, I had ten call girls working for me. I made money off of them and learned how cruel men can be to women. I saw pimps beat women, kick and stomp them. But my call girls never walked the streets, and I never lifted a hand against them. One day, outside the Vernon Hotel at Sixty-second and Vernon, I was walking with one of my call girls when we ran smack in to my wife, Nan. Hello, Nan. Nan met my eyes, kept walking, and never asked me about that woman because she knew I'd have told her the truth. Nan and I were living in a place at Sixty-second and Normal. Down in the basement, I put in a vault, sealed it off, and stored my money.

I put my own jukeboxes and vending machines in my taverns. One day some Mob hoods came calling. They said the Mob owned the jukeboxes in Chicago. I said, "Go to hell! In my place, I can't keep what my customers feed the jukebox? Put a Mob jukebox in here, and we'll bust it apart." The Mob sent in six more white guys to threaten me, but I don't scare. I sent a mean old Negro named Lonnie into some of the

Mob-run clubs, with an old squirt can full of molasses. He'd squirt that molasses in the jukebox coin slot. I don't know how many jukeboxes we messed up. We fought them.

I didn't worry about payback. The Mob heads were never involved, like they'd have been if I'd stolen policy action or policy money. Jukeboxes aren't worth killing over. But I never went without a gun. I took weekly target practice, shooting bottles at a rifle range between Argo and Robbins. The first man who came in my club shooting, I'd have blown his damn brains out.

And by now I had my own hoods. I won't name names because a lot of my hoods have gone straight. But I had some. I had to be tough in Chicago. I was working in a tough city, with a payroll and my reputation to protect. I never killed anyone, but I ordered some folks beaten up. I had to. Just keeping the world in line. People who did business with me said, "Charles Evers, you're a bastard, but I trust you." To me, that was great. Or they'd say, "I hate you, but you're fair." That was all the praise I needed.

I started bootlegging again. Illinois was a wet state, but it had some funny laws about booze. No selling it after 2:00 A.M., or before noon on Sunday. Hell, that's when business was best! I moved my bar down to an after-hours place I called the Club House. Despite Mr. O. W. Wilson, I found some cops who would do business with me. I paid them off and opened for business. Did very well.

Three good things came my way around 1959. First, my friend Al taught me a good business lesson. Al's liquor store next door to mine carried all kinds of crazy liquors that Negroes couldn't afford. I stocked the basics: Gordon's, Gilbey's, Old Taylor. And Al outsold me every day of the week. I said "Al, how come you selling so much more than me?" He said, "Charles, folks want a big selection. They ain't got the money for the exotic, but they hate for you to know that. Before they buy that pint of Gordon's, they want to see the fancy stuff." I started stocking a wide selection.

The second good thing that happened was that one of the big Jewish groups approached me. They'd heard of the Evers boys and admired our civil rights work. They knew rednecks had chased me out of Mississippi. So for several years, they paid all medical bills for me, Nan, and Pat. I've never forgotten that.

The third good thing that happened was running into a Negro named Mr. Lemons, up from the Delta. He knew I'd been rich in Mississippi. Mr. Lemons said, "What the hell you doing packing meat? You got a degree. Come teach for me." He lived in Robbins, Illinois, a Negro town just south of Chicago. He was chairman of the Robbins-Posen School Board. He ended my meatpacking career and made me a history and geography teacher and basketball coach in a Robbins middle school. I made thirty-eight hundred dollars a year, more than my official pay at either Swift or Hilton. The kids loved me.

It was a crazy life, teaching school with one hand, running whores with the other. But I had to get rich and send money down to Medgar. I bet I was the only bootlegging, policy-running schoolteacher in Illinois. I always worried some night one of my students, or one of their parents, would see me in a club next to the policy wheel or talking business with a call girl. Thank God it never happened. I kept my Robbins life in Robbins and my Chicago life in Chicago.

Dr. T. R. M. Howard moved up to Chicago about when I did. Driven from Mississippi, too. Rednecks had shot out the windows of his clinic so many times that his patients stayed away. Dr. Howard gave me my annual physical in Chicago. But Chicago cut me off from a lot of civil rights work. I should have been closer to Medgar. I was a racketeer, bootlegging, raising hell, and running women while Medgar was trying to free the Negro. I went where the money was, but Medgar could never have left Mississippi. His commitment went so deep. He'd say, "Mississippi is a part of the United States. I'll be damned if I'll let the white man lick me!"

Even in exile in Chicago, I was serving civil rights. I came south for voter registration drives. And if I hadn't made money in Chicago, Medgar would have been poor, and being poor would have tied his hands more than he cared to admit. Medgar never knew how I made my living in Chicago. When I told him I was working with the Mob, Medgar said, "Charlie, don't those people kill you?" I said, "Not if you don't owe them." Mama never knew how I made my money. No one really did. It was easier that way.

CHAPTER 11

I Trusted to God and My .45 Pistol

I FIRST HEARD OF ROBERT KENNEDY IN 1960, when his brother, John Kennedy, was a Democrat running for president. I was backing the Republican, Richard Nixon. So were most Negroes. Nixon was a tough young man who'd spoken out against racism for years. He'd been to Africa and met Martin Luther King in Ghana. Negroes thought he'd carry a much heavier load on civil rights than President Eisenhower ever had.

The Democrats looked worse. Lyndon Johnson, the vice presidential nominee, was a conservative Democrat from Texas. He'd helped pass the Civil Rights Bill of 1957, but Johnson didn't have his heart in civil rights. No one in our movement knew Johnson well, and to us John Kennedy was just a rich young Irishman from Massachusetts. Hubert Humphrey was the civil rights Democrat, and Kennedy had whipped Hubert pretty good in the primaries. So Negroes weren't rushing to support John Kennedy for president.

Robert Kennedy ran his brother's campaign like most northern white politicians would: arrogant, selfish, vain. High on the hog. Cut off from poverty and racism. He'd barely thought about the problems of Negroes or poor folks. He seemed to like segregation. He was as much a part of the status quo as General Motors, and I thought Bobby Kennedy would lie through his teeth to defend the status quo. Newspapers called Bobby rude. Rival politicians said he'd do anything to win. Bobby was ruthless about political strategy, but underneath, he cared about fairness.

While John Kennedy ran for president in 1960, Martin Luther King's life was in danger. Martin was on probation on a trumped-up charge of driving with an out-of-state license. When he led a sit-in at an Atlanta department store, Martin broke probation. A judge named Oscar Mitchell hit him with four months hard labor. At 4:30 one morning, they put Martin in handcuffs and leg chains and took him from the county jail to a remote penitentiary. Many Negroes thought he'd be lynched on the way. Martin's wife, Coretta, was five months pregnant and very scared.

Two of John Kennedy's civil rights aides, Harris Wofford and Louis Martin, decided Kennedy should call Coretta Scott King, tell her he didn't like how they were treating her husband. They got word to Sargent Shriver, who put it to John Kennedy. Kennedy called Coretta and said he was concerned about Martin. He didn't promise a thing, but that phone call meant the world to Coretta.

At first, Bobby fumed about that phone call. He called Louis Martin and Harris Wofford "bomb throwers" who'd cost his brother some southern states and probably the election. That was one side of Bobby. But then Bobby began thinking: Why was a decent American like Martin Luther King doing jail and hard labor for using an out-of-state driver's license and breaking probation? For one reason: Because Martin was a civil rights leader. So Bobby phoned Judge Mitchell: "Are you an American or not? If you're an American, get that man out of jail." He made that call thinking it would hurt the Kennedy campaign down south. That was another side of Bobby.

Whites didn't hear about those Kennedy phone calls before the election, so they didn't cost Kennedy with whites. But word of the call to Mrs. King flew out on the Negro grapevine, to churches, ball fields, and beauty shops. Overnight, Negroes across the nation switched to Kennedy. Medgar and I campaigned for Kennedy in Mississippi. I came down from Chicago and met John and Robert Kennedy for the first time. John Kennedy barely beat Richard Nixon in the election, so we told the Kennedys it was that call to Coretta that made John Kennedy president of the United States.

The NAACP did its part. In January of '61, the NAACP began poll tax campaigns in Jackson, Clarksdale, Meridian, and Vicksburg. Medgar led the Jackson drive with Carsie Hall. Short, dark, and heavyset, Carsie walked and talked just as country as he could be. But he was one of the only Negro lawyers in Mississippi. Medgar and Carsie had two hundred people on the phone and going door to door. Negroes lined up at the courthouse to pay their poll tax and register. Exactly 3,818 Mississippi Negroes paid that poll tax. NAACP workers went house-to-house, taking the names of Negroes who'd been kept from voting.

Since Negro votes had elected John Kennedy president, we thought his government might help us to vote. Kennedy had bucked the status quo by getting elected so young. Change was in the air. The NAACP gave the Justice Department eighty-six "affidavits of complaint" based on our poll tax campaign. But John Kennedy had other things in mind. In April of '61, Kennedy sent a bunch of exiled Cuban leathernecks down to take Cuba at the Bay of Pigs. Fidel Castro kicked their butt. The way I heard it, John Kennedy told Fidel, "I might send down seven thousand more to take your country. What would you do?" And Castro said: "I'll send you back seven thousand dead bodies." John Kennedy didn't know whether to shit or go blind.

April 1, 1961, Medgar met with John Doar of the Justice Department about voter discrimination. John Doar and Burke Marshall were two in the Justice Department who cared about civil rights. But Attorney General Bob Kennedy ran the Justice Department, and in early '61 Bobby cared no more about civil rights than John did. The king of the Justice Department didn't want justice; like most white men, he wanted order. Early in John Kennedy's presidency, Bob Kennedy told *Meet the Press* that the Justice Department lacked the men and even the right to protect Medgar. He wouldn't press the FBI to guard Medgar. He entrusted Medgar to Mississippi's Great White Fathers. Bobby made gestures to protect a few civil rights leaders, but in early '61 he didn't identify with civil rights *as a movement*. He didn't want racial justice if it meant stirring up whites and losing the South and the '64 election to the Republicans.

In '63, after whites threw Molotov cocktails at the homes of Medgar and our NAACP president, Aaron Henry, the NAACP filed a formal complaint with the Justice Department and asked it to protect Aaron and Medgar from terrorists, like any big white leader would have been. A statute covered this kind of terrorism, but the Justice Department hardly lifted a finger.

The FBI didn't care about racial justice, either. It wanted order and the status quo. The head of the FBI, Mr. J. Edgar Hoover, was shriveled up before his time. People say Martin Luther King hankered after women. J. Edgar Hoover loved counting Martin's women. Well, let me tell you: J. Edgar Hoover ran the whole FBI without a woman anywhere. Not a woman agent, not a secretary, not even a file clerk. No one ever saw J. Edgar Hoover with a female anytime, anyplace. So who's talking about whom?

Hoover didn't want the FBI going near civil rights. The FBI men had to work with small-town police chiefs all over the South. Why step on the police chief in Decatur, Mississippi, when they might need his help on a case someday? J. Edgar Hoover was buddies with our Mississippi senator, James O. Eastland. As head of a Senate security subcommittee, Eastland worked hand in glove with the FBI. He and Hoover had the same fear and hatred of subversives. Hoover wasn't going to rock the boat and ruffle James O. Eastland.

As chairman of the Senate Judiciary Committee, Eastland could bottle up any civil rights bill in committee. Thurgood Marshall worked his way up in Washington, and in 1961 was appointed as a federal appeals court judge. Senator James O. Eastland had to approve the nomination. Senator James O. Eastland aimed to make a U.S. district court judge out of Harold Cox, an old racist friend of his from Sunflower County. One day in a corridor, Eastland told Bobby Kennedy, "Tell your brother if he gives me Harold Cox, I'll give him the nigger." Thurgood Marshall was one of the great lawyers of the century. To Senator Eastland, he was "the nigger."

Before '63, the FBI did almost nothing for civil rights. These G-men worked in pairs, in dark pants and white shirts, holding briefcases. They didn't impress me one bit. They'd say, "The FBI investigates crime that's been committed. We can't do anything to stop crime." Pure bullshit. The FBI had the right to arrest rioters, lynchers, or anyone doing violence to a U.S. citizen. They hated to do it. Someone recently made a movie called *Mississippi Burning*, which painted the FBI as our friends, and to this day many whites believe the FBI stood for civil rights. That's dead wrong. I was there, and I know. I never relied on the FBI for anything. I trusted to God, to other Negroes, and to my .45 pistol. Not always in that order.

Because whites were doing so little for civil rights, Negroes had to carry the load. James Farmer of CORE ran Freedom Rides in '61 to integrate bus facilities in the South. Negroes got on buses moving across state lines. Sat in white waiting rooms in southern bus stations.

Testing segregation, showing injustice to the nation. Pushing the federal government to enforce our rights. Roy Wilkins tried to get Farmer to stop. To Roy, Freedom Rides meant violence, and too much NAACP money for bail and lawyer fees. Medgar was a loyal NAACP man. Publicly, he opposed the Freedom Rides. Privately, he backed them.

The Freedom Riders hit Mississippi in May of '61. When CORE ran out of bail money, the NAACP put in about three thousand dollars. My good friend Jack Young represented the Freedom Riders. Jack was a Negro about fifteen years older than me, who'd gotten a law degree right in the teeth of racist Mississippi. Jack worked for the post office twenty years, passed the state bar exam when he was forty-three, and went straight into civil rights law. A wonderful man.

Aaron Henry did his part, too. In December of '61, Clarksdale Negroes ran a campaign to force downtown merchants to hire them and call them "mister" and "miss." The Coahoma County attorney, T. H. Pearson, gave Aaron Henry two choices: halt the Negro campaign or go to jail. Aaron refused to halt the campaign. The chief of police, Mr. Ben Collins, was waiting right there. T. H. Pearson said, "Take this nigger to jail." No arrest warrant, Ben Collins just took Aaron to jail. The same day, they jailed six other Negroes for the same crime. That was Mississippi justice.

Medgar regretted that he couldn't build a strong NAACP chapter at Jackson State, the black state school in Jackson. In March of '61, he asked Jackson State students to protest on campus, and he matched them with activists from Tougaloo College nearby. But civil rights work was taboo at Jackson State because the whole faculty could be fired by white politicians. Then in '61, James Meredith, a twenty-eight-year-old student at Jackson State, decided to integrate Ole Miss. The day after John Kennedy was inaugurated, Meredith asked Ole Miss by mail to register him.

James Meredith's boyhood had been a lot like mine and Medgar's. His home around Kosciusko, Mississippi, had holes in the walls and no running water, but his mama kept a clean house and his daddy owned a radio. Cap Meredith told his kids, Better die than be humbled by whites. On Cap Meredith's eighty-four acres, he brooked no meanness from whites. Like Medgar and me, James Meredith loved the beauty of

Mississippi and hated its racism, wanted to change the state, and was ready to die trying.

On January 29, 1961, Medgar became the first man outside Jackson State to hear Meredith's plans. Lope advised Meredith to reach Thurgood Marshall at the NAACP Legal Defense Fund in New York. James Meredith was skeptical of that. He wanted quick, drastic change. In nine years in the air force, he'd found integration could work. He was a soldier at heart, who planned to fight segregation like a war: Invade the enemy stronghold, dodge their fire, die in the fight if you must, but go down fighting.

Medgar brought Meredith home, and they called Thurgood Marshall. Thurgood wanted to represent Meredith but needed proof Meredith was who he said he was. Meredith expected Thurgood Marshall to take his word, and he hung up the phone on Thurgood. Medgar patched things up, wrote off for James Meredith's documents, and sent them on to Thurgood. Thurgood gave the case to a veteran lady lawyer named Constance Baker Motley, one of his assistant counsels. She was smart, patient, and tough. In May of '61, with her help, James Meredith filed suit to get into Ole Miss.

June 1962, Ole Miss brought criminal charges against Meredith for applying from the wrong county. They said rejecting him had nothing to do with race. Then our state legislature passed a special senate bill making it a crime for anyone accused of a felony to enter Ole Miss. Our mean governor Ross Barnett warned Bobby Kennedy there'd be a riot if James Meredith got in Ole Miss. Burke Marshall in the Justice Department spoke to Ross about thirty times on the phone, Ross trying to keep James Meredith out of Ole Miss, Burke telling Ross to keep order. Three times, Ross Barnett kept James Meredith out of Ole Miss by breaking court orders.

When Meredith reached Ole Miss, whites asked, "Who cooked up this stunt: Medgar Evers, the Communists, John Kennedy?" Truth is, Medgar wasn't itching to integrate Ole Miss after what he'd been through, after whites had sent Clyde Kennard to prison and Clennon King to the loony bin. And Medgar knew that James Meredith didn't make the ideal test case. Meredith had guts, but he was a strange, mystical dude. He made up his own mind to integrate Ole Miss.

Medgar wanted an armed guard posted at Meredith's home and told James Meredith to never go anywhere alone. James Meredith rejected the protection. Medgar was in danger, too. During the worst of the Meredith mess, Medgar and Myrlie were barricaded in at home, couches piled up in front of their windows. Medgar was nonviolent, but he had six guns in the kitchen and living room. He needed them.

Around July of '62, I flew down to Jackson to see Medgar. Lope took a week's "vacation"—gave the NAACP six hours a day instead of eighteen. I warned him, "You're foolish, Lope. You'll work yourself to death and no one'll even appreciate it. You'll end up poor as you are now." When I left, I gave Medgar and Myrlie fifty dollars, and told them to have fun. Myrlie convinced Medgar to go down to New Orleans with the money. First thing Medgar did when they hit New Orleans was call the local NAACP chapter. No one was in, or Lope might have had a working vacation. Medgar always paid the price.

On September 30, 1962, whites rioted to keep Meredith out of Ole Miss. The highway patrol was there. Hitler had his SS troops; Mississippi had its highway patrol. A segregationist army. Many highway patrolmen were former Klukkers. Hell, some of them were current Klukkers. Lay down the sheet and put on the badge, lay down the badge and put on the sheet. The highway patrol let those white folk riot all night. Men on Governor Ross Barnett's own staff threw Molotov cocktails. By morning, the Feds controlled the town, but it took fifteen thousand army troops and a federalized National Guard. Two men died in the riot. Hundreds got hurt, including over 160 federal marshals.

In late '61 and through '62, a big change had come over Bobby Kennedy on civil rights. He learned, as much as any white man could, how it felt to be a Negro in this country. During the Ole Miss riot, Bobby Kennedy sat up in his office, at the controls. He could have put an assistant in charge and gone home to bed. When he didn't, I knew Bobby Kennedy was my kind of man. He stuck close to the action, guiding the Feds at Ole Miss, protecting those he could. As I came to know Bobby, his door was always open. He answered his phone on nights and weekends. From '62 to '64, Bobby did more than any other white man to help the Negro. Without Bobby, Mississippi would have had a lot more lynchings. Bobby was the first attorney general in my lifetime to care about the Negro.

James Meredith stuck it out at Ole Miss, always afraid of being shot. Late in '62, whites shot at his father's house. John Doar of the

Justice Department stood by James Meredith, but it's hard to go to school guarded by federal lawyers and U.S. marshals. And a whole other round of this was coming at the University of Alabama. Negroes meant to integrate Tuscaloosa, but a peckerwood named George Wallace was running for governor of Alabama, vowing to "stand in the schoolhouse door" to keep the niggers out. Keeping us out of the best state university was just part of it. George Wallace and his kind wanted to shut Negroes out of all important decision making about the future of the South.

Fannie Lou Hamer refused to be kept down. Until 1962, Fannie Lou Hamer lived on a Mississippi plantation. Then she heard James Bevel speak, and James Forman of the Student Nonviolent Coordinating Committee (SNCC). She knew a night policeman in Ruleville was kin to one of Emmett Till's killers. She'd gone to the hospital in '61, and the white surgeon had sterilized her without asking her permission. Fannie Lou wanted children, and she complained to the doctor, but what could she do? When the chance came to stump for civil rights with the SNCC, she grabbed it. *This* was what she could do. Fannie Lou volunteered to register to vote.

She went to a civil rights meeting, then took a bus to Indianola to register. The registrar asked where she worked, then took a big black book and told her to interpret a section of the Mississippi constitution on "de facto" laws. Fannie flunked. She told us, "I knowed as much about a *de facto* law as a horse knows about Christmas Day." Driving back to Ruleville, a cop pulled them over, charged them with driving a bus too yellow. You didn't know that was a crime in Mississippi, did you? For trying to vote, the plantation owner threw Fannie Lou off his land. But he told her to just take her name off the rolls, and everything would be the same. Fannie Lou told him, "That's just what I'm trying to get out of."

The SNCC folk were committed, but they needed grassroots folk like Fannie Lou. She knew the land, the local customs, and who could be trusted. She could quote Scripture: "Be not deceived, for God is not mocked; whatsoever a man sow, that shall he also reap." She'd also say, "I ain't ever heard of no one white man going to get a Negro. It's always a mob. They the most cowardly people I ever heard of." But Fannie forgave them everything. When a Negro vowed to hurt whites, she'd say,

"Baby, you got to love them. Hating just makes you sick and weak." And Fannie Lou sang "This Little Light of Mine" in a soulful voice and told how it came from the Bible: "A city on a hill cannot be hid." Fannie was tough. She mimicked and mocked big-talking Negroes who wouldn't pay the price. Fannie Lou was just what the SNCC needed. Whites did so little for us that Negroes like Fannie Lou Hamer had to carry the load.

CHAPTER 12
Turn Me Loose

NINETEEN-HUNDRED-SIXTY-THREE was the 100th anniversary of old Abe Lincoln's Emancipation Proclamation. It was a brutal year for civil rights. Lope and I were so happy in June of '63 when Jomo Kenyatta won a huge election victory and finally became prime minister of Kenya. But the whole rest of the year was brutally hard. Back in the '50s, the NAACP had named 1963 "Emancipation Centennial" and set a goal of conquering all racism in America by '63. Medgar drove himself to meet that target.

Whites denounced Medgar as an "outside agitator." Lope would ask, "How can I be an outside agitator? About the only time I've ever left Mississippi was to serve my country in war." Medgar knew that pioneers must pay the price, but he and Myrlie had three kids now—Darrell, Rena, and Van. He had to wonder what this life of his was doing to them.

On January 10, three hundred white students at the Ole Miss cafeteria jeered at James Meredith, "Go home, nigger!" The Ole Miss administration tried to clamp down on that kind of thing, but they blamed James Meredith for provoking it.

On January 14 in Montgomery, George Wallace took the oath as governor of Alabama. In his inaugural, he promised, "I draw the line in the dust. . . . Segregation now, segregation tomorrow, segregation forever." Wallace was a vicious-looking little man, terrified someone might show him some love. Wily George Wallace didn't want to fix Alabama's schools or economy, so he went up in the hollows and railed at "the nigger." Talked hate and destruction. Posed as defender of the white South. Those poor, gullible peckerwoods sat right up, and the dollars poured in. Wallace played the old game: Hold the peckerwoods down. Tell them only hate and segregation can keep them above the nigger.

In February, President Kennedy made his biggest civil rights stand: four concrete proposals to cut into racism. But the governor of Mississippi, Ross Barnett, was saying all the southern states should resist federal "usurpation."

In April, Martin started an antisegregation protest in Birmingham. When it was done, over two thousand demonstrators had been arrested, including Martin. Negroes tried to peacefully integrate stores and restaurants, and cops came at them, with police dogs snarling, fire hoses blasting. Confined in prison, Martin wrote one of the classics of our movement, "Letter from Birmingham Jail."

In the spring of '63, Medgar led a series of mass protests aimed at integrating Jackson's shops and restaurants. The Klan heated up in response. On Good Friday, someone threw a Molotov cocktail into Aaron Henry's house in Clarksdale. Aaron's whole family could have died, but the cops took notice only because Congressman Charles Diggs was Aaron's guest at the time. On April 20, someone blew a hole in the roof of Aaron's drugstore. A month later, late at night when Medgar was still at work, Medgar and Myrlie's home was hit for the first time. Some white bastard threw a Molotov cocktail on the driveway. Myrlie hosed out the flame, but she was scared. The Jackson cops blamed pranksters.

By May, the weather heated up, and tempers flared. On May 28, four Negro students and a white professor at Tougaloo College sat in at a Jackson lunch counter. A white mob poured ketchup, mustard, and sugar on them, hit them with spray paint, and beat them. Whites poured salt in the white professor's head wound. An ex-cop kicked a Negro student's face bloody. Later that day, two thousand Negroes poured into a local church. Medgar asked, "Who's ready to march?" All two thousand rose.

On May 31, 1963, hundreds of Negro kids marched into downtown Jackson. Jackson cops, sheriff's deputies, and state highway patrolmen with riot guns arrested about six hundred kids. Sent them in trucks to a temporary jail at the fairgrounds. Medgar got Roy Wilkins to come down to Jackson. On June 1, Jackson cops arrested Medgar and Roy for picketing in front of Woolworth's. Medgar was holding a sign: END BRUTALITY IN JACKSON. All Medgar aimed to do was to end brutality in Jackson, and the white leadership in town treated him like a criminal.

Allen Thompson had been mayor of Jackson for twenty years, ever since Jackson was just a country town. Now it was the only real city in Mississippi. Mayor Thompson was a short, sturdy man. Jackson's biggest booster. He didn't see any brutality in Jackson. He saw a city with paved streets, good race relations, and good Negro jobs. "Hell," he'd say, "we even got a Negro golf course." That's the kind of ignorance Medgar was fighting.

They freed Medgar and Roy Wilkins on a thousand-dollar bond. Negro children marched again that day. About one hundred more were arrested. On June 1, the Jackson City Commission and Mayor Thompson agreed to three Negro demands: hiring Negro cops and school crossing guards; integrating city facilities; and giving Negroes better city jobs. But they refused Medgar's key demand to set up a biracial committee to start ending racism in Jackson.

Except in a few all-black towns, Mississippi had not one black elected official in '63. So the boycotts and marches made Medgar our biggest Negro. Medgar even got a local TV station to give him about an hour of TV time. Many whites called Medgar the most dangerous man in Mississippi. The white supremacists branded him Satan. Targets that big shouldn't take the heat alone, but when Medgar followed the boycotts with a voter registration drive, Roy Wilkins and most others left Jackson. Lope never complained. Roy offered to transfer him to California. Lope refused. He'd say, "I may be going to heaven or hell. But I'll be going from Jackson."

June 6, the comedian Dick Gregory and the singer Lena Horne came south to help integrate Jackson. Dick Gregory loves poor folk. I once gave out thirteen thousand turkeys at Christmas with Dick Gregory. Lena Horne asked the NAACP to send her south. She paid her own way. Medgar met Lena and her band at the airport, got them settled. Lena was shocked by how demanding and dangerous Medgar's job was. Seeing Medgar ready to die put her in awe. Lena hated seeing Medgar without drivers or bodyguards. The city of Jackson hated outside agitators like Lena Horne and Dick Gregory stirring up the Negroes. The city got a county judge to give a temporary injunction against demonstrations. Medgar held a civil rights rally anyway, and he brought Lena Horne.

Medgar knew that by openly fighting the system, he'd signed his own death warrant. He knew the Citizens Council had him on its death list. When the mailman brought Medgar parcels and no one was home to accept them, his neighbors were too scared of package bombs to take them, either. Medgar and Myrlie took precautions. They watched TV from the floor in case of sniper fire. They made sure none of their furniture faced a window. They never let Darrell, Rena, and Van play in the street or in vacant lots, and they never let them outside at all after dark. They taught them to hit the floor and crawl to the bathtub if they heard screeching brakes, explosions, or shooting. They tried to make it a game: "That's what Daddy did in the army." But the kids knew better. Darrell told Medgar, "Daddy, please be careful." You hate to hear that from your own little son.

But Medgar didn't protect himself enough. He wanted James Meredith to have armed guards, but not Medgar Evers. Lope was always naive. His idea of security on the road was driving his Oldsmobile eighty miles an hour, scanning behind for trouble. One Klukker phoned Medgar, spun the cylinder of a pistol by the phone, and said, "This is for you." But with death threats hanging over him, Medgar had no fear. People asked if he was afraid. Lope said, "I don't have *time* to be afraid." At the very end, he began saying, "Whenever my time comes, I'm ready." He didn't mind dying for the movement; he just hated the thought of leaving his family alone.

In June 1963, I was still living in Chicago and making good money. I was bending the law in my taverns, but I wasn't breaking it. I'd bought a twenty-two-unit building at Sixty-second and Normal. I lived on the first floor of that building and sent most of the building's rent money down to Medgar for his work. Medgar was living in northwest Jackson, in the first decent Negro subdivision there.

Medgar called me from Jackson on Sunday night, June 9. He never knew just how I made my living in Chicago, but he knew I'd worked with the Mob. He knew I'd had to buck some mean Italians to own my own jukeboxes. He knew I wasn't doing all this according to Hoyle. He'd say, "Charlie, I don't know about you." I'd say, "Medgar, you take care of the Klukkers, I'll take care of the boys up here." On this last Sunday night, Medgar said, "Charlie, be careful. Because it's worse up there than it is down here. Them dagos will kill you!" I said, "Now, you be careful. Because it's worse down there. You better watch out for those peckerwoods."

We had lots of these conversations. He'd tell me to stop messing with the Mob: "Charlie, they going to kill you! Why you do business with those people?" I'd say, "Look, Lope, do you want to die poor? I'll handle these cats up here. I ain't going to steal their money, and they ain't going to kill me. Put that out of your mind." This last night, I told Medgar, "You know those Klukkers are after you, and if they get you they'll feel they got everything under control." "Don't worry about me," Medgar said. "I'm going to make it."

Medgar was catching flak from the NAACP. I'd urge him to do something, and he'd say no, we can't break the rules. Always the damn NAACP rules. I'd say, "Lope, you're going to have to tear up the rules." But Medgar wrote all those reports to Roy Wilkins in New York. Lope always cared too much what folks thought of him. Until '63, Medgar mostly did what Roy Wilkins asked, but in '63 Medgar began stepping out on his own. If Roy Wilkins had fired Medgar that year, I wouldn't have been a bit surprised.

Medgar was always warm, upbeat. Never too busy to talk. Never too tired to help. Racists got his unlisted home number and poured out their hate. There's a technique to taking those calls. If you hang up, they call back. If you talk back, it gets worse. So you just lay the phone down and let them yell. When no more sounds come from the receiver, you hang up. That's what Myrlie and I did. But Medgar talked to the haters, in his sweet, even voice, for as long as they'd listen. Lope was always decent, but underneath, he was as tough as Mama, Daddy, and I had raised him to be. He worked round the clock for months at a time. He was threatened, cuffed, clubbed, and shot at. He was beaten over the head with a snub-nosed revolver. His house was stoned and firebombed. He just could not be intimidated. I was so proud of that.

By '63, the NAACP had twenty-some Mississippi chapters. Lope was all day filing complaints, sending out press releases, driving reporters to crime scenes. He did too much—let people take advantage of him. I always challenged him: "Why do you let the NAACP send you all over the place and not pay you for those trips? Why don't you make Roy Wilkins give you a bodyguard?" Medgar always brushed it off.

Friends urged Medgar to leave Mississippi, at least for a while. But Medgar would say, "A man's state is like his house. If it has defects, he tries to remedy them." Lope had to stay and fix Mississippi so Darrell and Rena and millions of other Negro kids could be free. But the summer of '63 was going to be Medgar's first long vacation in years. He and I planned a trip to South America. In '62, Medgar had seen an ad in a Mississippi paper for a land deal in Brazil. He'd called me in Chicago, primed to buy forty acres of land for both of us. I listened a few minutes, then said, "Get it." So Medgar bought deed to forty acres, fifty miles north of Brasília. We'd never seen our land. We dreamed of someday living down there, in two big houses on a hill, Lope fishing for bass, me raising cattle. Medgar wouldn't have given up Myrlie, but she'd have moved to Brazil if he wanted.

When I could finally afford a nice car, I didn't want to flaunt my money, so I had a '48 Chevrolet, then a '52 Dodge. But in '63, I'd bought myself a brand-new Cadillac, black with all the trimmings. Medgar and I planned to drive down to Brazil in the Cadillac, see our land, relax a month, then drive back to Chicago for the NAACP convention. That last Sunday night, Medgar and I discussed our Brazil trip for a long time. We both felt some premonition of danger. Medgar's death threats were now coming daily—and not just against him, but against Myrlie and the kids. When you have no time to be afraid, what you get are premonitions. We both ended up crying. I asked Lope, "You want me to come down there now?" He said, "No, you're due to come anyway next week."

It was time to hang up, but we didn't want to hang up. Medgar and I had squabbled and scrapped all our lives. But when Medgar started getting daily death threats, we stopped scrapping. Myrlie felt the same. You couldn't afford to get mad at Medgar. You might not see him again. Medgar ended the call: "Careful now. I'll see you in a week."

Two days later, on June 11, 1963, two Negroes got in the University of Alabama. So much for "Segregation now, segregation tomorrow, segregation forever." George Wallace raged about this, and so did hundreds of thousands of his followers. Things got a little hotter.

The night of June 11, President Kennedy made a beautiful TV speech on the need for civil rights—the best civil rights speech John Kennedy ever gave. It was tough, it was true, and it showed how much he'd learned in office. President Kennedy said that civil rights was a clear-cut moral issue, and that no white man would stand for what Negroes had to stand for every day. Kennedy ended by saying, "This nation, for all its hopes, and all its boasts, will not be fully free until all its citizens are free." He was telling white folks that Negro rights was *their* fight.

Myrlie sat up in Jackson with her kids, watching the president's speech, thinking how pleased with it Medgar would be when he got home. Medgar worked such long hours that his kids almost never saw him come home, but that night Myrlie let Darrell and Rena stay up to greet their daddy. They sat up, watching the late movie on TV. Waiting for Medgar.

That same evening, someone else was waiting for Medgar to come home. A white Mississippi man named Byron de la Beckwith drove to Joe's Drive-In Restaurant on Highway 49, a few hundred feet from Medgar's home. Byron de la Beckwith was a small, dark-haired man, about forty. Like Medgar, he'd served in the war. The marines. Got wounded in the Battle of Tarawa and came home a hero.

Beckwith's Mississippi and Medgar's Mississippi were like night and day. Beckwith's mama came from big white families in the Delta. Beckwith's mama's daddy had served in the Confederate cavalry. Beckwith's daddy was a farmer in California, but when Beckwith was a small boy his mama had brought him home to Greenwood, Mississippi, "Cotton Capital of the World." Beckwith was raised there, went to Mississippi State, returned from the war, married, and bought a home in Greenwood.

Like Medgar, Beckwith worked after the war as a salesman in the Delta. While Medgar sold insurance for T. R. M. Howard, Beckwith brought New Deal cigarettes and snuff to country stores. He and Medgar could have passed each other on the road. After New Deal Tobacco went bust, Beckwith sold fertilizer.

Beckwith was a type we all knew in the South. He wore dapper white suits, acted gentle to friends and courtly to white strangers. He considered himself refined and genteel. But he hated Negroes and Jews. Just mention racial integration, and he'd blow up. Beckwith was hatred with a dapper face. He was ready for a race war. He collected and traded guns, kept a shoulder holster. Sundays after church, he took target practice at a rifle range next to the VFW hall. He was a crack shot.

In 1954, a few days after the Supreme Court said school segregation was unconstitutional, Beckwith heard a cracker judge from south Mississippi named Tom Brady analyze the case. Speaking in Greenwood to the Sons of the American Revolution, Judge Brady said a Negro was lower than a chimpanzee, and that the federal government wanted a race war in Mississippi. That was all Beckwith needed to hear. He joined the Citizens Council, passed out leaflets against integration. He quit the Episcopal Church because his church rector was too liberal. Some said he brought a pistol to church in case any Negroes tried to worship there.

Beckwith called Negroes beasts without souls and said, "God put the white man on earth to rule over the dusky races." In '57, he wrote the Jackson *Daily News:* "I do believe in segregation like I believe in God. I shall make every effort to rid the U.S. of integrationists." He wrote the National Rifle Association: "Gentlemen: For the next fifteen years, we in Mississippi are going to have to do a lot of shooting to protect our wives, children, and ourselves from bad niggers." Beckwith's wife divorced him in 1960, saying he'd beat her and told her he'd kill her if she told anyone.

That night of June 11, Beckwith's car was easy to spot. It was a white Valiant with a trailer hitch and a shortwave radio antenna. Beckwith parked it in the Joe's Drive-In lot, facing Medgar's home at 2332 Guynes. He walked through the hot evening air to a thick clump of honeysuckle, 150 feet from Medgar's home. He lay down behind a sweet gum tree, next to his high-powered Enfield rifle. And just like Myrlie, Darrell, Rena, and Van, he waited for Medgar Evers to come home.

Medgar had worked a long day in a heat wave. He left the NAACP office, went to a civil rights rally at New Jerusalem Baptist Church on Whitfield Street. Aaron Henry was going to a pharmaceutical convention in Texas. Medgar drove Aaron to the airport. He stayed at the civil rights rally till near midnight. He dropped off Gloster Current and said, "I'm tired, I'm tired." He took Gloster's hand and held it. Then Medgar drove home.

Myrlie told me later Medgar had talked a lot about death. He'd been telling friends, "I'm looking to be shot anytime I step out of my car. Everywhere I go, someone's been following me." On both Monday and Tuesday, Medgar talked with Myrlie about dying. When he left the house Tuesday, he held Myrlie a long time in his arms and kissed each of his kids. Busy as he was, he called Myrlie three times that day, just to hear her voice. The last thing he told her was how much he loved her and the kids.

Twenty minutes past midnight, the whole family jumped up when Medgar's '62 Oldsmobile pulled in the driveway. Medgar must have been happy. He always felt safer at home than on the road. Darrell and Rena ran to meet Medgar at the door. Myrlie turned on the light in the carport and followed. Medgar was so dog-tired, he dropped his usual precaution. He didn't leave the car by the right-hand door, where he'd have been shielded by the car and the house. He opened the left-front door and stepped out on the driveway, wearing a white shirt, carrying paperwork and sweatshirts that read JIM CROW MUST GO. Byron Beckwith found Medgar in the telescopic sight on his rifle, got Medgar right in his crosshairs. The lit carport gave him a perfect view. For a crack shot like Beckwith, it was easy pickings.

No real southerner ever shoots a man in the back. You might taunt a man to his face or even brandish a gun, but you don't shoot from behind, at night, hiding behind a bush. That just isn't how it's done. If Beckwith had spent five minutes talking to Medgar, he couldn't have pulled the trigger on that rifle. But he and Medgar had never met, and that damn backshooter Beckwith shot Medgar down in cold blood. After the gun blast, Beckwith ran off through some tangled underbrush. He knew he'd got Medgar; blood was all over the driveway. The softnose bullet ripped through Lope's back and chest, sailed out his body, through his kitchen wall, off his refrigerator, and landed on a countertop.

Myrlie and the kids heard the car stop, the car door open, then a rifle blast. Darrell and Rena pulled baby Van off the bed and hit the floor like they'd been taught. Myrlie pulled open the front door. Medgar was staggering toward her, blood everywhere. Most men would have collapsed. But he'd found his keys and pulled himself just short of the door. Then Lope fell face down in a pool of blood. Myrlie screamed and screamed. The kids came running. Myrlie tried to keep them from seeing their Daddy die, but they stood over Medgar, begging him to get up. Two neighbors, Thomas Young and Houston Wells, came out armed and seeking the gunman. When they saw no one, Wells pulled out a mattress, and they lifted Medgar on it. Lope's heart was still going, his mouth was moving, but he couldn't speak.

An ambulance took Medgar to University of Mississippi Hospital, but Myrlie already knew Medgar was gone. She pulled the children back in the house and asked God for the strength to endure. Inside an hour, a hospital employee called and told Myrlie that Medgar had died fifteen minutes after reaching the hospital. Myrlie was a thirty-year-old widow. On the way to the hospital, Medgar found his voice. He ordered, "Sit me up!" And then he said his last words, "Turn me loose."

Hundreds of Negroes who had known Medgar began calling the house or coming by with thoughts and prayers. Lots of white folk came, too. Whites who'd never cared one bit about Medgar when he was alive got interested in him real quick when he was dead. Cops were there, police detectives, reporters, crowds of rubbernecking tourists. Killing uppity niggers was old hat in Mississippi: George Lee, Lamar Smith, and so many more. But Medgar Evers was the biggest Negro Mississippi had ever known.

The Justice Department folks had been fiddling for months over whether they were "authorized" to defend Medgar. They got authorized quick, and asked to help. The FBI people had never lifted a finger for Medgar when he'd needed it. Now *they* wanted to help. The White House wanted to help. John and Jackie Kennedy sent Myrlie separate telegrams of condolence. Vice President Johnson said the authorities would "close ranks" and "leave no stone unturned" until they found the killer. Even white politicians in Mississippi had to pretend to be shocked and upset by his killing. Southerners don't do much pretending, but in the first months after Medgar was gunned down, there was a whole lot of pretending.

Mayor Thompson of Jackson had always known damn well the danger Medgar was in, and he had never once tried to make Medgar's work safer or easier. Medgar was so clean and straight, and Allen Thompson always tried to tarnish him, cast him as a crooked outsider meddling in Jackson. When Beckwith killed Medgar, Allen Thompson flew straight home from a Florida vacation, brought Negro leaders to city hall, and issued a statement that he and every citizen of Jackson was "dreadfully shocked, humiliated and sick at heart" about Medgar's killing. That dirty skunk had the gall to say that he and Medgar had worked out lots of racial problems in face-to-face meetings. Like he was Medgar's friend. Made me sick.

Jackson's district attorney, Bill Waller, announced a reward for finding the killer. Started it with fifty dollars of his own money. Mayor Thompson and the city offered a five-thousand-dollar reward. The Jackson *Clarion-Ledger*, a newspaper that had always treated Medgar like a dirty dog, put up a one-thousand-dollar reward. They, too, talked about leaving no stone unturned to find the killer. Even Ross Barnett criticized the killing. Old Ross said, "Apparently, it was a dastardly act."

For a few days, Myrlie hated these people—for being white, for ill-wishing her husband when they might have saved him, and for pretending to care just as soon as they couldn't. But slowly, Myrlie stopped hating. She saw she'd been blessed to be married to Medgar for eleven years. She realized Medgar belonged to millions of people and that his death must serve some purpose. She said in public that killing Medgar would stop nothing, that the NAACP would pick up right where Medgar had left off. Myrlie's a very strong woman. In those first days, she handled herself with grace.

Jackson police detective John Chamblee stood in Medgar's driveway and traced the shot to the honeysuckle thicket. He saw a little clearing there and called another city detective, O. M. Luke. In some vines, Detective Luke found a 30.06 Enfield rifle. The gun's serial number, 1052682, was traced to Beckwith. The six-power Golden Hawk scope that attached to the rifle was also traced to Beckwith. It had Beckwith's fingerprints on it.

At 3:00 A.M. Wednesday morning in Chicago, I was coming home from my tavern, tired but happy. I'd made good money that night. I closed the joint, got in my '52 Dodge, and drove home. When I reached my apartment, lights were on everywhere. I could smell trouble. I hated having strangers in my home. Nan and I had few visitors—none at this time of the morning. But through my apartment window, I could see lots of shadows of heads. Something was very wrong.

I always packed a .38 pistol in Chicago. I grabbed it then. Before leaving the Dodge, I craned my neck, looking for someone I knew. The street and sidewalk were empty. I pushed away the old, horrible fear that Medgar was hurt. Hell, I'd just talked to Lope two days ago. He must be alright. I'd worried about him so many times before, and he'd always pulled through. More likely something was wrong with my daughter Pat. Pat was always sickly. Maybe she was going to the hospital. I jumped out of the car, .38 in one hand, money sack in the other. I ran to the front steps, ran up to the porch, and eased toward the door. I didn't want to go in.

Someone opened the door, and I slid inside. The house was full of people. A dozen friends of Nan's were in the front room alone. Every last one of them looked at me real solid, but no one said a word. I said, "What's wrong? Where's Pat? She sick?" Someone said, "No, she's asleep." Nan walked up to me and motioned down the hall: "Come on back here, Charles." She had a funny look on her face. I froze a little, and she pulled me down the hall, into a little room at the back of the house.

"What's wrong?" I said. "Something happen to Medgar?" By then, the way everyone was acting, I just knew it. Nan had gotten that phone call from Myrlie, the one I'd always dreaded getting. Nan looked me straight in the eye. She said, carefully, "Yes. They shot him." My worst nightmare come true. Whites had shot Medgar, the man who was all I had. My mind froze, but I clung to Daddy's old boast: *You can't kill an Evers*. I thought of the cowboy movies Medgar and I'd watched from the buzzard's roost in the movie house back in Decatur. The bad guys wounded the hero, but they never killed him.

I looked back at Nan and tried to make my voice natural. "Aw, well," I said, "They probably just winged him." White folks were such lousy shots. I said, "They can't kill the Evers boys. They been trying too long." Nan said, real soft, "No, Charles, he's dead."

CHAPTER 13
You Won't Die in Vain, Medgar

THE NEXT TWELVE HOURS ARE A BLANK. I knew my brother and best friend was gone, but as I lay down in bed, I didn't believe it. Nan was beautiful. She'd always given me room. Now she stuck close when I needed it. She helped pack my case and plan my trip, but she didn't try to run me. At eight the next morning, someone drove me to O'Hare Airport and put me on the first flight to Jackson.

Just one thing I knew: I was going to succeed Medgar as head of the NAACP in Mississippi. Someone said, "Don't go down to Jackson, Charles, they're going to kill you, too." Someone else said, "He's dead, Charlie, and you better watch out or you going to be dead, too." I knew the moment I took Medgar's job, my life wasn't worth a plugged nickel in Mississippi. But I had to go.

Like the prodigal son, I'd spent my time amongst the whores and thieves, and now I was coming home. I'd pledged to carry on Lope's work if he ever went down. But I didn't come to my senses until morning when I stepped off the plane in Jackson. I said, "I'll never go back to Chicago. I should never have left Mississippi. I left everything I had."

God, how I hated every white man! I thought I'd stopped hating whites up in Chicago, but now all my old hatred poured back. And how I hated Charles Evers, too. If I'd stayed with Lope in Mississippi, I might have saved his life. As kids, meeting the bullies side by side, we felt invincible. Medgar and I meant to fight racial injustice side by side all our lives. But I'd left too soon to make money, and left Medgar to fight alone. I'd sent money south, but it was Medgar who'd stuck it out in Mississippi, given Negroes a voice, shown whites the light. For seven years, I'd sidestepped the battle. Medgar had insisted I go live up in Chicago, but I'd gone and left him alone. I hated myself for that.

I accepted the passing of Mama and Daddy. I never accepted Medgar's death. Nan tried consoling me: "You couldn't have helped Medgar anyway, Charlie, if you'd been down there." Myrlie said the same: An expert marksman with a top-notch rifle doesn't miss. In my mind I knew that, but in my heart, I knew I'd have found a way to protect Lope, like I'd done hundreds of times before. Maybe I'd have seen something move in that honeysuckle. Medgar had no gun. I'd have damn sure been packing a gun. *I could have saved him.* That thought kept me awake at night—ate away at me. When Lope needed me, I'd been gone.

Medgar's death left me all alone. I asked God to keep me from breaking down. Medgar and I had always believed that crying was weak. I thought of that scared old maid back in Decatur who'd say, "One day, you boys'll get yourselves killed." Now she was half right. I kept thinking of Medgar's goodness. He was well-known, but never flamboyant. He'd say, "Don't hate them, Charlie. Don't hate them." But when they killed him, I hated. God, I hated. I was composed on the outside. People told me I was holding up pretty good. But inside I wanted to kill a whole lot of white folk.

Dan Rather got a tip about Medgar's murder just a few minutes after it happened. Dan had come to know and admire Medgar while covering the story of James Meredith integrating Ole Miss. Rather and his crew chartered a plane from Tuscaloosa right away. He reached Medgar's home near dawn, before any other reporters. Dan Rather looked like any other young reporter with a camera crew. When I arrived from Chicago, he politely introduced himself.

I threw Dan Rather out of the house and off the property. I told him I didn't want him and his TV camera anywhere near our grieving. But Dan's a tough man. He said he'd be happy to leave the house, but this was a big story and he was going to be filing reports to CBS News in New York, from out on the street. I started to realize how big Medgar had grown. This wasn't just a lynching—it was a political assassination. And the civil rights movement was finally a mass movement.

For days, Dan Rather followed us around—at Medgar's house, at the funeral. Dan was more than a radio and TV reporter covering a story. He saw the venom in me and kept talking to me, not as a reporter, but as a man. He couldn't say, "I know what you're going through," because he didn't. But he had a feeling for it when very few whites did. Dan was from Texas, and he knew how whites treated Negroes down south. He said, "Charles, not every white man is like the man who killed Medgar—not even down here." Dan Rather made me see how awful the killing made him feel, as a southern white man. Dan treated me like a friend when the whole white race looked pretty bad. Dan consoled me at the funeral home, went with me to the morgue, stood nearby, heard me out, made sure I was alright.

I told Dan Rather I wanted to kill some white folk. He said, "I know it's bad, Charles, but you can't do that. You can't let yourself do the same thing they did." It was Dan Rather and a few other whites that kept me from killing a whole lot of white folk.

Medgar meant so much to so many. Bill Russell, the basketball star, called me after Medgar went down, said he'd do anything to help. In July, I called him in Massachusetts, told him if he didn't mind risking his life, he should come down to Jackson and run some basketball clinics. He came down. Couldn't relax all three days he was in Jackson. He was shocked I slept with a pistol in my hand. But he gave the first integrated basketball clinics ever at the Jackson Auditorium. Everyone left us alone—the mayor, the police—even the Klan.

When Medgar was killed, Fannie Lou Hamer was in jail in Winona, Mississippi, getting the mess beat out of her under police supervision. When she got out of jail and learned Medgar had been murdered, Fannie Lou burst out, "Something got to break!" Lena Horne was in the *Today* show studio in New York, waiting to do a live TV interview, when she heard about Medgar. Lena went numb and vowed she'd never go back to Mississippi. She said, "I think my heart broke that day." The *Chicago Defender,* that weekly paper that Medgar and I had tried to deliver around Decatur, made Medgar's killing the top story two weeks running.

At the Texas pharmaceutical convention, Aaron Henry turned on the *Today* show in his hotel room, saw Medgar's picture on the screen, and wondered what Medgar had done to make national headlines. When the TV said Medgar'd been murdered, Aaron was destroyed. Medgar was his closest friend.

Roy Wilkins was destroyed, too. Roy had no kids of his own and knew few young folk well. He didn't know how to treat the younger generation. But Roy loved Medgar. If Roy Wilkins ever hated whites, it was the day a white man murdered Medgar in cold blood. Roy called the murder a "cold, brutal, deliberate killing in a savage, uncivilized state." Roy announced an NAACP offer of ten thousand dollars for information leading to the killer's arrest and conviction. The National Urban League and the American Guild of Variety Artists each put up a thousand dollars.

Medgar's killing shocked Martin Luther King and his family. Martin and Medgar had worked together so closely, so often. Martin had just promised Medgar he'd come to Jackson to speak at one of Medgar's rallies. Martin was on the road, between a plane and a speech, still high after President Kennedy's TV speech on civil rights, when a local SCLC man told Martin the haters had killed Medgar Evers. Coretta King took Medgar's killing real hard—as prophesy that one day Martin would be gunned down, too.

The NAACP started a fund to educate Medgar and Myrlie's kids. Eartha Kitt helped raise thirteen thousand dollars at one Hollywood party. The *Chicago Defender* and the *New York Post* also raised money for that scholarship fund. Common people around the country sent money. Old folks on measly fixed incomes sent us part of their retirement nest eggs.

I began knocking on people's doors, saying I was Medgar's brother and wanted a favor. They'd let me in. I knocked on the door of Joe Louis, the ex-heavyweight champ who Lope and I'd always admired so much. When Joe Louis found out I was a civil rights man, and "brother of slain civil rights leader Medgar Evers," he let me in. He and his wife, Myra, couldn't have been nicer. Cassius Clay, the successor to Joe Louis, had won the Olympic gold medal in boxing in 1960. Cassius had done radio spots asking Negroes to register. I wanted to meet him. All it took was, "I'm Medgar's brother." He calls himself Muhammad Ali now, he's one of the most famous people on earth, and we're still friends. Ruby Dee and Ossie Davis, Eartha Kitt—I met many Negroes in those first years who I wouldn't have met but for Medgar's murder. I also got closer to Nelson Rockefeller. All these people were so outraged by Medgar's killing and wanted so bad to *do something* for civil rights that they were happy to do the little things I asked.

Medgar's murder sparked over seven hundred demonstrations around the country. Los Angeles nearly had a race riot. In New York, Negroes sat in the offices of Mayor Wagner and Governor Rockefeller. In Danville, Virginia, the police broke up a protest and sent fifty Negroes to the hospital.

We had to assume Medgar's killer would keep shooting at top NAACP folk, right down the line. The NAACP asked the U.S. marshals for twenty-four-hour protection of fifty of us out front on civil rights. The marshals said no. Aaron Henry asked the Clarksdale cops for protection. They said they couldn't spare a man. When Aaron hired his own guard, the Clarksdale cops somehow spared a man to come to Aaron's home, arrest the guard, and confiscate his gun. That made the Negroes of Clarksdale so mad they gave Aaron guns enough for ten lifetimes. Aaron put another guard in the living room, and the Clarksdale cops let him be.

The '57 Civil Rights Act made killing Medgar a federal crime: conspiring to keep Medgar from exercising his civil rights. That drew the FBI into the case. The FBI had always hated civil rights work, but after Medgar died, Bobby Kennedy began pushing the FBI to infiltrate the Klan, learn who was killing Negroes. The FBI started to help us. J. Edgar Hoover himself opened a big FBI office in Jackson.

A few days after Medgar died, two FBI agents came around to question me. The wound was so raw, I was struggling to get hold of myself. Those FBI agents strolled into my office and said they had reason to think *I'd* killed Medgar! My best friend in the world, and him killed in Jackson when I was in Chicago. I stared at them FBI bastards, speechless, then threw them out of my office on their ass. If they hadn't gone quick, there might have been another killing. These hotshot G-men, protectors of law and order we heard so much about, wanted a whitewash. But give the FBI credit, they played rough with a white informant and cracked the case. Less than ten days after Beckwith killed my brother, FBI agents arrested him. J. Edgar Hoover himself announced the arrest.

The FBI didn't want to prosecute, so they gave Beckwith to the Jackson police. The Jackson cops knew Beckwith did it. They were shamed at all the evidence. They'd found his Enfield rifle in the honeysuckle patch. They'd found his telescopic sight there, too. They'd found a fingerprint on the rifle that matched the right index finger of

Byron Beckwith. When they arrested Beckwith on June 22, 1963, he had a small mark over his right eye, just like from a telescopic sight. It should have been an open-and-shut case.

The big-shot district attorney William Waller amazed us by preparing to try to convict Beckwith. No one in Mississippi could remember a court convicting a white man of killing a Negro. Beckwith was held without bail, a slap at the Klukkers. But three-fourths of the whites in Mississippi were solid behind Beckwith. The jailer let Beckwith keep part of his damn gun collection until he went to Jackson for trial. On July 8, 1963, the day Beckwith was arraigned in Jackson, a Citizens Council group met in Beckwith's home and announced a fund to pay the legal bills of Beckwith and other whites charged with civil rights abuses. The White Citizens Legal Fund helped raise sixteen thousand dollars for Beckwith's defense and got Beckwith a law firm that had Governor Ross Barnett as a partner. Beckwith looked like he was home free.

Roy Wilkins, Gloster Current, and some of Roy's yes-men came down to fix up Medgar's funeral. They wanted a whole lot of hoola. I said, "We're going to give my brother a simple burial." Medgar had never wanted a big burial. Myrlie didn't want one, either. But days passed, and we saw we couldn't keep the burial of Medgar Evers a simple, local thing. Medgar belonged to the nation and to the world. Newspapers in Europe were writing about his murder.

Within a day after Medgar died, Robert Kennedy called me. We'd never before spoken man-to-man. Bobby said he and the president felt terrible about Medgar's murder, and he would personally run the murder investigation. He said he knew we'd want the funeral in Jackson, and he planned to attend. We arranged for him to stay with me during that time. But Bobby said the Kennedys wanted to bury Medgar, with full military honors, in Arlington National Cemetery, where America buries its biggest soldiers and heroes.

Flattering as that offer was, Myrlie and I took pause. Medgar was a man who'd always refused to leave Mississippi. Some of his best friends thought Medgar belonged in Mississippi soil. But Arlington Cemetery had two big advantages. First, Medgar had been so proud of being a veteran. Second, Arlington tends its graves. Some Mississippi graveyards have weeds growing up every which way. And Myrlie and I hated the thought of some Klukker digging up Medgar's grave or burning a cross by it. So we chose Arlington.

We had to prepare Medgar for the funeral. I kept after Myrlie to choose Medgar's burial clothes. She kept putting it off, trying to hold on to Medgar. Medgar wore his hair in a medium-short low English. He needed a last haircut before his funeral, so I brought a barber down to the morgue. Seeing Medgar lying dead in the morgue shocked me. When the barber left, I was alone with Lope. I cried. I was so glad Mama hadn't lived to see her sweetest child gunned down like this. I stayed with Lope's body a long time. I promised him, "You won't die in vain, Medgar. I'll get even if it's the last thing I do."

We held an open-casket funeral on Saturday, June 15, in the Masonic Temple, where Medgar's office had been and where he'd held so many NAACP meetings and events. In 103-degree heat, four thousand people packed the temple auditorium until there was no room to stand. A thousand people more stood in the stifling air outside, paying their last respects to Medgar Evers. Negro buildings had no air conditioning then. We all sweated like fools. Roy Wilkins and Ralph Bunche were there. So were James Meredith and his wife, and Ruby Hurley, Charles Diggs, Dick Gregory, Ralph Abernathy. Dr. T. R. M. Howard came; he'd given Medgar his first job after college. Martin came, too, in shirtsleeves, dressed like a common hardworking Negro, the only one there not sweating. Local TV was there. A *Life* magazine photographer almost stood on the coffin to get the shot he wanted of Myrlie.

I was too broken up to give a eulogy. The eulogies of Dr. Howard and two or three others went by in a blur. I've always done poorly in the heat, and I was just starting to understand Medgar was gone forever. But one thing hit me from the eulogies: *Medgar had really stopped hating.* All the eulogies said the same thing, in different ways: The closer Lope came to knowing for sure that whites would kill him, the less he hated whites. Medgar had grown while I was up in Chicago. Tough as he'd been in '56, he'd grown tougher by '63. And sweet as he was in '56, he'd grown sweeter by '63. He used to hate the whites almost as bad as I did, but I realized at his funeral that the night he was killed, Medgar Evers did not hate anyone. And that just amazed me.

The funeral ended, and the crowd started out of the temple. Myrlie said she couldn't make it. I said, "Don't break down now, Sis." Myrlie looked at me and said, "Do you realize this is the last time Medgar will ever be in this building?" Boy, that was hard to swallow. We got in some cars and rode a mile down Lynch Street in that hot sun to the Collins Funeral Home. Hundreds of marchers left the Masonic Temple, walking east down Lynch Street. Many were teenagers. Some sang "We Shall Overcome." Others chanted: "We want the killer! We want equality! We want freedom!" On North Capitol Street, Negroes began throwing bottles. John Doar of the Justice Department shouted out who he was and told them wrecking property achieved nothing. A Negro kid stepped up, "This man is right!" and most of the bottle throwing stopped.

But some of the crowd took their rocks and Coke bottles toward the business district, hot for revenge. The cops were always ready to fight us. "You can't parade without a permit," they'd say. "You're damn niggers," is what they meant. This day, some Negroes taunted the cops. In back of the Jackson cops stood the state highway patrol, with helmets, police dogs, riot guns, and automatic rifles. They charged and beat the marchers, pushed some in garbage trucks, hauled them to the state fairground, and put them in livestock pens. They arrested 158 people, including 13 preachers.

After the funeral, I helped load Medgar's casket on a slow train through the South, to Washington, D.C. I left Nan and Pat in Jackson and flew to Washington with Myrlie, Darrell, and Rena. Medgar's youngest boy, Van, was too young to go, but Ruby Hurley went, and so did Medgar's funeral director. On the plane, Myrlie gave an interview to *Life* magazine. I sat alone, scared to think.

In Washington, a civil rights delegation met Medgar's train and took his body by hearse to a funeral home. A thousand mourners marched in back of the hearse. A Washington NAACP delegation met Myrlie and me and the others. The secretary of the interior sent his chauffeur and private car, whisked us off to a fancy hotel called the Mayflower. Plainclothes cops guarded the hallways for us. The hotel manager knocked himself out for us. No one let us pay for anything. It was all very confusing. When white folk finally warm up, they tend to overdo it.

Wednesday, June 19, we brought Medgar's body to the church of E. Franklin Jackson, John Wesley AME Church. None of us knew Reverend Jackson well, but John Wesley AME was a big church, and the reverend backed civil rights to the hilt. In '63, most Negro churches still feared to openly join our movement. A year before, Medgar had addressed two hundred people at this church. Now we opened his casket, and twenty-five thousand people paid their respects.

Real quick, it hit me what Senator Bilbo had said almost thirty years before: If the white folk of Mississippi didn't hold down Negroes like Medgar and me, then someday we'd be in Washington, D.C., representing Mississippi. Now here I was, with Medgar's body, in Washington, representing Mississippi. I thought, "Well, Senator Bilbo, looks like we're here." Then I went all to pieces. They had to carry me off someplace before I could pull myself together.

We started out from Reverend Jackson's church for Arlington. I saw the casket carried out the church door. I helped load the casket into the hearse, to cross that river to Arlington. Driving to the cemetery, my mind was a mess. I know one thousand marchers escorted our car. Lots of common folk stood along the route, heads bent, paying their last respects to Medgar. Many were white. When our car pulled up at Arlington, I couldn't get out. I just sat, trembling. Myrlie had to plead before I got out of that car.

About 11:00 A.M., we had a simple service in a little chapel on the grounds. Then we drove to the grave site. It was peaceful, full of big trees. Medgar would have loved it. At the cemetery, soldiers played taps and covered Lope's casket with a U.S. flag. They gave Myrlie the flag. Then they buried Medgar. I kept thinking about Senator Bilbo's words, and how Medgar had always hated the cold. Now we were laying his body down in the cold ground.

All through the service, Bobby Kennedy stayed right with me. I'll never forget how hard he tried to console me. I needed every bit of Bobby's help to keep from going crazy with the pain. He could have just come to the funeral, given his sympathies to Myrlie, and left. Men less important than Bobby would have done just that. But Bobby wasn't built like that.

Roy Wilkins made a great speech at Arlington Cemetery. It was tough, and it was true. Roy said one man had pulled the trigger on Medgar, but that the whole southern political system had put that man behind the rifle. Roy said Medgar had always believed in his country, and that now we'd have to wait and see if Medgar's country believed in him. The *Chicago Defender* ran a front-page editorial on Medgar and a huge headline: HERO GRAVE FOR EVERS.

Next morning, President Kennedy brought Myrlie, the kids, and me into the White House. I'd never seen a president in the White House before. President Kennedy's secretary introduced us all to the president. We shook hands. Kennedy was warm and gentle. He told Myrlie she was a brave woman. She was real quiet. The president gave little gifts to Darrell and Rena. Then he turned to me, and we started talking, mostly about Medgar.

President Kennedy had been thinking a lot about civil rights even before Medgar's murder. That same day, he'd sent Congress the bill that became the Public Accommodation Act of 1964. John Kennedy had been raised to think the southern white man was a rascal on race but had Negro welfare at heart. Now Kennedy was seeing the other side of the white southerner—the cold killer. And it shook him up. President Kennedy seemed to fear I'd hate all whites. He said a couple of times, "Not all of us are like that."

President Kennedy saw that he didn't understand the South, and that he better learn about it from the Negro side. He began by asking a lot of questions, and I answered. At one point, he said, "I hope this doesn't make the Evers family hate." Near the end of our talk, he said, "I will do anything I can to keep something like this from happening again. We can't let your brother die in vain."

John Kennedy knew that life could end overnight. He'd lost his own brother in World War II. All the Kennedys were fighters who met trouble head-on. I felt the same way. I admired their toughness. But that day I didn't hold up my end of the conversation. I didn't feel like talking. Medgar was dead. That was all I could think about.

President Kennedy signaled that our talk was over. He called in a photographer, and we all had our pictures snapped with the president. He signed a copy of the civil rights bill and gave it to Myrlie. Then Kennedy said, "Anytime you need me, all you have to do is call." He gave us his personal phone number and said to call not just if Negroes were in danger in Mississippi, but if we ever felt we needed to talk about Medgar. The last thing John Kennedy told us was, "You know, they'd kill me, too, if they could."

In the next months, I stopped by the White House several times. Never needed an appointment. Phoned a few times, too. The president and Mrs. Kennedy couldn't have been kinder or more considerate. Bobby Kennedy not only urged me to call, day or night—*he called me.* That was the difference between Bobby Kennedy and John: John told me to call when I needed him; Bobby didn't wait. For months after Medgar was murdered, Bobby always called me at least once a week. And I called him many times—at sunrise or deep in the night, whenever I had the need.

Bobby had a tremendous curiosity. And in June of '63, he kept asking, What's it like to have your brother and best friend suddenly murdered? How do you go on?

Until Medgar was killed, I'd assumed Bobby Kennedy wanted to protect the status quo. But in June of '63, I learned Bobby had no love for the status quo. He was a politician, he worked the system, but he wanted to force change. I saw that Bobby and I were going to get on real well. Registrars closed their books to us? Alright, Bobby sent some of his top men into the Deep South to bring lawsuits to open them. Bobby Kennedy's Justice Department sued some of them mean white registrars and sent G-men into Mississippi to protect us. Bobby was never too busy, never too tired.

When Medgar was killed, Martin called Roy Wilkins, suggested they jointly announce a national day of mourning and a memorial fund in Medgar's name. Roy told Martin to butt out, because Medgar was an NAACP man. The top NAACP brass in New York often kicked sand at the top brass from the SNCC, the SCLC, and CORE. But the foot soldiers, those risking our necks down south, knew that Klukkers and racism were the enemy, not other civil rights groups.

I appreciated what Martin said about Medgar, and when I told Martin this, we grew closer. I loved Martin as a speaker. His voice was so soothing, and pitched just right. He was well-read, could quote long passages from memory. He was eloquent and clear, with a gift for reaching the white moderate—folk like Mr. Brand, our circuit clerk in Decatur. I loved hearing Martin talk.

But talk isn't half as good as action. What I truly loved Martin for was leading all those marches. Running those strategy sessions. Making those phone calls. Leading people. In those first dark months after Medgar died, I had to throw myself into the cause. Martin set me such a great example. We got to where we'd do anything for each other. Whenever one of us had a march or demonstration, the other would help round up a crowd. He stayed in my home whenever he was in town. He knew he was safe with me.

In December of '63, the NAACP gave Medgar a posthumous Spingarn Medal, its big yearly prize for Negro achievement. For years, I never went to an NAACP meeting, church meeting, or rally without someone praising Medgar Evers. Folks said with all the dangers he took on, he was lucky to reach thirty-seven. Hundreds of whites called or wrote me saying they were sorry about the murder. A few wrote, "That nigger got what he deserved," but most of the letters were sad and kind. Folk wrote me, wrote Myrlie, wrote the NAACP. Some sent money. Lots of southerners couldn't sign their letters, but they wrote, "Keep up your work. You'll win in the end."

Aaron Henry said Medgar's murder freed him from a fear of his own death. Medgar knew it doesn't matter how long a man lives. It's what he does while he's here. Medgar did more than a lifetime's worth. Nothing important comes free. All great social change requires suffering. The American Revolution took a lot of lives. The westward movement took a lot of lives. The civil rights movement took a lot of lives, too. Every race of people that's ever been set free, its leaders paid the price. Medgar paid the price, every day. And one day he gave his life.

CHAPTER 14

Taking Over the Mississippi NAACP

THE DAY BEFORE MEDGAR'S FUNERAL, some Negroes in Jackson were talking about who should succeed Medgar. I told them, "Look no further, because I'm taking his place." Medgar and I had always said if one of us went down, the other would carry on. No one else could do Medgar's job like I could. From the day he died, I had to be the main civil rights leader in Mississippi. It never occurred to me to duck that job or even to consult Myrlie or anyone before taking it. I *knew* Medgar wanted me to take it. I kept silently telling Medgar, "I deserted you once, Lope. I won't desert you again." I told journalists covering the funeral that I was taking over. Two days before Medgar was even in the ground, I was sitting in his old office, running the state NAACP.

Myrlie was shocked when I took Medgar's job. Four years later she wrote a book saying Medgar had no plan for me to succeed him if he went down, but he might have wanted *her* to. What that meant to me was that Lope didn't tell Myrlie much about his deepest thoughts on civil rights. Myrlie's a good woman, smart, tough, and talented. She made Medgar a good wife. But in the early '60s, she did too much bitching and griping for my taste about Medgar's job being too dangerous, too hard on his family. In my opinion, Lope would never have turned the Mississippi office over to Myrlie.

Roy Wilkins was just as shocked as Myrlie when I took the job. Roy was shaving one morning with the radio on when a report came on that the NAACP had picked Medgar's successor: Charles Evers. Roy almost slit his throat. He planned to name Medgar's successor, and it wouldn't have been me. The NAACP fellas in New York weren't sure what I'd been doing in Chicago, but they knew I'd been mixed up in some bad business. Roy knew I didn't turn the other cheek. He didn't know I'd bankrolled a lot of Medgar's civil rights work. And he wanted Medgar's successor to be a loyal, obedient NAACP man. Roy wanted Medgar to go down in history as a peaceful Negro whose only crime was wanting Negroes to be free. The last thing Roy wanted was Medgar's rough, tough big brother coming out of the Chicago rackets to soil Medgar's memory and tarnish the NAACP.

Well, the last thing Charles Evers wanted was to take orders from Roy Wilkins up in New York. That New York NAACP office was full of backbiting, and it moved at a snail's pace. Even Roy called his job "riding a dinosaur." Roy, Gloster Current, and the boys in New York sat up in their ivory tower, chipping away at racism by lobbying Congress and filing lawsuits. Roy thought the courts could end lynchings, segregation, housing and job discrimination. He thought the right lawsuit could end segregated travel. I'd say, "Roy, how you going to go through the southern courts when the judges and juries down here aim to keep us down?" I told him Mississippi needed grassroots campaigns, new Negro voters, strikes, and boycotts. Roy Wilkins called my appointment "temporary."

Roy Wilkins was a smart man who worked hard. He was a good writer, diplomat, and troubleshooter—things I never was. He was a good speaker, especially when he dropped his text and spoke from the heart. But he wasn't a southerner. He spent his time making speeches, testifying to Congress, sitting in city council meetings, lecturing at churches and women's clubs, and drawing up the budget. Even there, Roy was weak. Both in honest business and in the numbers, I'd handled $5,000, $10,000, all the time. But Roy Wilkins, head of the whole damn NAACP, couldn't send but $1,000 for bail money or legal fees, without an okay from the NAACP board. Hell, I'd made $4,000 in one weekend, selling whiskey!

When Roy came down to Jackson for Medgar's funeral, he brought Gloster Current. Gloster ran the NAACP branches, directed their programs. He was a proud man who guarded his turf and did a lot of Roy's dirty work. The three of us talked face-to-face. I said, "I'm taking Medgar's place, finishing what Medgar begun. You got no choice. I'm going to live up to my pact with Medgar. If you don't like it, you can choke on it."

Roy had few choices. The only man in Mississippi besides me who had really earned the job was Aaron Henry. Aaron had more dignity and restraint than I had, but Aaron didn't want the job—he wanted me to take it. Roy found the Negroes of Mississippi stood with me. And with the memory of Medgar's murder so close, he just couldn't refuse an Evers. So he gave me the job permanently. Today, a lot of coffee-drinking, do-nothing civil rights folks say they wanted to succeed Medgar in '63. But back in '63, let me tell you, *very few* wanted to succeed Medgar. How many people do you know who want to get their head shot off by the Ku Klux Klan?

Roy Wilkins said, "We can't name you without convening the whole NAACP board." I said, "Convene the board, then! But I'm taking this job." Gloster and Roy said, "We can't afford to pay more than five thousand dollars." Roy probably knew I'd been living high on the hog. I said, "Keep your damn five thousand dollars, Roy Wilkins, and stuff it! I'm the Mississippi State field secretary." Roy saved face by announcing he'd given me the job, but I took it. With or without the official title and Roy's blessing, I was taking up Medgar's work. Gloster Current told me when my first big speech would be and said Roy would help write it. I said, "Gloster Current, you stuff it, too, because I don't work from a blueprint." The boys in New York never did digest me too well.

Something deeper was going on than who would succeed Medgar and how they would run his office. I hated Roy Wilkins and his cronies for abusing Medgar's decency. Never reimbursing him right for all the traveling he did on the job. Never protecting him. Roy knew the danger Medgar was in, but he never furnished him a bodyguard or a driver. Medgar drove forty thousand miles a year, often at night, on dirt roads full of rednecks. He needed to ride with a tough driver-bodyguard, a Negro who packed a pistol and loved civil rights. But Medgar never got that man. I blamed Roy.

Roy Wilkins was a northern liberal: heart in the right place, head in the wrong place. *He* didn't travel with bodyguards, so why would Medgar need any? Roy was also so tight with money. He wouldn't approve travel vouchers for first class on planes. He watched the telephone bill like a hawk. He hated us taking cabs. But Negroes all over Mississippi worshipped Medgar. After Beckwith killed Medgar, Negroes lined up to protect me, drive a car for me. Medgar could have hired a bodyguard for next to nothing.

So it was something more than money. Roy Wilkins was jealous of competing civil rights groups like the SCLC. Maybe he feared giving Medgar Evers a bodyguard would cast a shadow on Roy Wilkins. Then Medgar was killed, and Roy acted like, this is what happens when you march in the streets. White folks retaliate. Roy implied that Medgar's direct action campaigns had brought on his murder, and the NAACP brass had been helpless to stop it.

Bullshit! *I'd* failed Medgar the most—I was his older brother and protector, the bodyguard he never hired. I'd loved and understood Medgar best, and I should have hired him a bodyguard myself. Hell, I should have been right beside him when he stepped out of his car that last night. Medgar was also at fault. When no one else guarded him, he should have guarded himself. But I knew in my heart the NAACP had failed Medgar, too. Roy had tremendous pain over Medgar's murder, but no guilt at all. That burned me.

In Medgar's old office, I looked at the old humps and dumps he had for furniture. Lope felt so many Negroes were so poor, he had no right to relax. Scuffling alone up in Chicago, I'd lived much better than that. Medgar had a dusty country rag for a carpet. I threw it out in the hall and ordered wall-to-wall carpet. Medgar had a broken-down desk and an old broken chair. I ordered a big new desk, a new desk chair, and two handsome new chairs for visitors. Medgar never had blinds. I ordered blinds. Medgar kept his records in an old pasteboard box. I ordered filing cabinets. Hot as that room got in June, Medgar had no air conditioner. I bought a brand-new window-unit air conditioner. I said if I'm going to go through hell, let's be comfortable. I spent over three thousand dollars fixing up that office and sent all the bills up to Roy Wilkins in New York. Roy almost went crazy.

A few months later, one of Roy's top assistants came down from New York to explain Medgar's job. He started giving me all kinds of detail on the do's and don'ts. I said, "I don't need you to tell me a damn thing!" I don't wear tight-fitting clothes, I don't wear a seat belt in my car, and I don't let any man tell me what to think or say. I was hard on Roy Wilkins, Gloster Current, and Ruby Hurley. I bucked most of what they did. I spoke out at national board meetings, to reporters, anytime I had something to say.

If you need me to get somewhere, lead me there. If you're smart enough and tough enough to lead me, I might follow. But if you send me somewhere alone, don't tell me anything! Roy Wilkins never led me anywhere, but he tried to send me a lot of places. So there was never any love lost between me and Roy Wilkins. Roy didn't love people he couldn't control.

Around 1941, Roy and Thurgood came down to Mississippi, dressed up like sharecroppers, to investigate a lynching. But most of the time when Roy wasn't traveling up north, he was at the NAACP offices at 20 West Fortieth Street, in Manhattan—all decked out in Stacy Adams shoes, sitting in a high-backed swivel chair, behind a huge mahogany desk, raised off the floor so he looked down at you. He was surrounded by neat stacks of papers, with secretaries buzzing around. Roy dressed in white suits and long black coats and smoked those pricy cigars while I was down in Mississippi, sweating, ducking, and dodging.

It was natural for the NAACP boss in Mississippi to play local politics. But Roy and Gloster Current had the same old speech: "The NAACP does not endorse any candidate or party. We never suggest to anyone for whom they should cast their vote." I heard that bullshit a hundred times, but I always favored the candidate who was better for Negroes, and I'd tell anyone who asked. If that candidate asked me to speak for him, I spoke.

Roy wanted monthly written reports on how many branches I'd visited, how many miles I'd driven, how many calls I'd made. Ducking and dodging in Mississippi, why should I waste time filing reports to Roy sitting safe up in New York? Why should any man in New York know how to fix Mississippi better than a man who's lived there all his life? I always felt that Roy Wilkins, Gloster Current, and Ruby Hurley looked down on southern Negroes, hated seeing us on our own. No real southerner takes handling from a man sitting up in New York City. Roy wanted me to be "his man in Mississippi." I've never been anyone's man but my own.

Gloster or Roy would phone, "Where's your report?"

I'd put them on the defensive: "I been in jail four or five times. Didn't you know that?"

They'd say, "Yes, we knew that."

So I'd say, "Then why do I got to put it in a damn report?"

Gloster Current threatened to fire me. I said, "Go on, fire me! I'll take all the money and all the state branches and start a group called the Mississippi Movement." Mississippi was quite a showpiece for Roy Wilkins. He fund-raised off our lynchings and depraved conditions. If I'd been fired, the Mississippi branches would have come with me in a minute. Every damn one of them. You better betcha they would have.

Wrong as Roy Wilkins was on most things, he was right to fear I'd get violent. I have a sin to admit. Part of the reason I came back to Mississippi was to kill white folks. At times, in those first months back, I wanted to kill every white man I could—just kill, kill, kill until a white man struck me down and ended it. See, with Medgar dead, the world had caved in on me. I knew Lope expected me to go on. Some days that was all that kept me going. I was filled with hate. Hate for myself, hate for whites. Hate like a sickness. I knew Mama in heaven expected me to forgive—seven times if necessary. But I couldn't. I felt sick even looking at the mayor of Jackson, Allen Thompson, with his short, stocky body and pug white face. I know that Allen Thompson is a good man at heart. He may even have silently wished our movement well. But in those days he always seemed to be solid against us. In those days, in my anger, I used to tell him every time I saw him: "You dirty bastard. You got Medgar's blood all over your hands." Allen Thompson hadn't been elected mayor of Jackson by laying down in front of his enemies, so we were at each other's throats for a while.

I returned to the secret plan Medgar and I'd shared years before—Mau Mau killings. I loved the idea of a secret Negro movement of strategic insurrection like Jomo Kenyatta's Mau Mau movement in Kenya. My Mau Mau in Mississippi would run like this: For every Negro the whites killed, I'd kill two whites back. I'd float around Mississippi, killing one white man a week. Kill one in Jackson, ride a bus to Clarksdale and kill one there. Board the bus and kill another in Meridian or Tupelo. Roam the state, picking off the leading racist in each county. Find out where they lived, and knock them down, one by one. Do each killing a different way. Poison a man's coffee here, stab a man there, shoot someone else. As a mortician, I knew a lot about how to make men die.

I got really unhinged and dreamed of killing thousands of whites, small-timers right alongside the big shots. Poison a pot of coffee a day, each time in a different town. Organize an army of Negro maids and cooks to poison white folks' coffee. Grind up glass real fine and sprinkle it in white folks' hamburger so it ground up their intestines. Organize Negro bellhops and mechanics to kill the whites they served. Terrify the state.

Seeing Medgar's killer in the Hinds County courthouse, I could have broken his dirty, slimy neck. But I told myself, "Kill him, and you're as low as he is." Beckwith was a little man, and if he didn't get punished in this world, he would in the next. The men I planned to kill weren't the Beckwiths, but the Great White Fathers who ran the towns, the courts, the counties. Men like John Stennis, James O. Eastland, and Allen Thompson. I was a good rifleman in the army, and I'd kept in practice. I could have hit them from a fair distance. I truly felt the only way to stop whites from killing Negroes was to kill them first. Old friends from the South Side of Chicago sent down guns and ammunition. I began choosing my first target.

I'd come down to Mississippi for Medgar's funeral without having time to pack. Soon as I got settled in Jackson, I flew back to Chicago for a few weeks to collect my money, pack up, and move south for good. Nan had been living in the house at Sixty-second and Normal all alone. Poor Nan. Loyal and kind, there when I needed her. Never asked a lot of questions or tried to run me. I treated Nan poorly, never told her my plans until they were made up.

Nan hated being in the house alone, so without telling me, she got a mean old black mutt to keep her company. She couldn't control the dog, so she kept him in the basement. I went down in that dark basement to get my money from the vault, and a huge, strange dog jumped out at me. I yelled, "Damn, Nan! Put that sonofabitch out of here!" I counted out a huge amount from my vault, threw it in a suitcase, and came down to Jackson. I got myself two little homes in Jackson: a private office at 3554 Queens Road Avenue, and a place at 1037 West Pearl for personal business.

Carrying out Mau Mau would have killed me. But in the first months after Medgar was killed, I wanted to die. I took Negro friends driving and challenged about every white racist highway patrolman in Mississippi. I drove alone too. I'd always liked being alone. Anyone could have gunned me down with a rifle, like they had Medgar. Folk called me brave, but death had been walking right behind me since I was a baby. By '63, he was one of the family. I said just one thing to those gunning for me: "Give me a chance. Don't hide in no honeysuckle, now. Make it a fair fight." But if a white man drew a gun, I was ready. Those first months after Medgar's death, I did many things reckless enough to have got me killed. I always told Negroes, "If you let the white folk mistreat you, you're dead already. If they ain't hiding under sheets or in big groups, they're scared to death. Stand up to them." I told Negroes to remember their Franklin Roosevelt: "The only thing we have to fear is fear itself."

Aaron Henry and Martin Luther King were just as brave as me, but less reckless. Aaron Henry acted more like Medgar's brother than I did: quiet and pleasant, fearless and relentless. Racists bombed Aaron's house in '63, set it on fire. Aaron said, "Don't hate them. We're going to get them." He refused to carry the white man's hatred. Aaron's house has been shot up with a high-powered rifle. His drugstore's been bombed, and the plate glass windows knocked out many times. Through it all, Aaron and I worked together to recruit strong leaders and build the NAACP in every town in Mississippi.

It was probably Aaron who asked a man named Allard Lowenstein to come down from Raleigh, North Carolina, in July 1963. Al was a young Jewish college professor raised in New York, a gifted speaker, a civil rights activist. He'd been to South Africa, and he often said the racial abuse in Mississippi was worse than apartheid in South Africa. Most college professors sit around and study the problems instead of fixing them. Al wasn't that kind at all. He was a little like Bobby Kennedy: great enthusiasm and ambition, great energy, and a knack for political strategy.

Al was well schooled and knew a lot about the legal system. He traveled outside Mississippi a lot, but he'd always come back, driving his beat-up old Volkswagen. He stayed in my house many times. As a Jew, Al Lowenstein knew about persecution. He got riled up when anyone suffered any kind of persecution.

Al Lowenstein was the first white northerner I'd ever met who knew the value of voter registration. He brought a lot of young white volunteers down to help Robert Moses and Aaron Henry and me to promote the Mississippi Freedom Democratic Party (MFDP). In the fall of '63, we ran Aaron Henry as the MFDP candidate for governor of Mississippi, in a mock election. We set up polling places in places where whites wouldn't bother us, like Negro churches and schools.

Aaron got eighty thousand votes, and white folks still said Negroes didn't want the vote.

But as much as I admired Al Lowenstein and loved Aaron Henry, Martin Luther King was truly the man. Martin proposed a great March on Washington for the summer of '63, and Martin made that March on Washington famous. Roy Wilkins opposed the March on Washington as too expensive. On August 28, 1963, 250,000 people—black and white, rich and poor, of all creeds, colors, and faiths—marched in Washington, D.C., to support more civil rights bills. It was about the biggest march Washington, D.C., had ever seen.

At the Lincoln Memorial, Martin gave the keynote speech, "I Have a Dream." I was standing, unarmed, 20 feet from Martin as he spoke. I've heard a lot of great speakers: Theodore Bilbo, T. R. M. Howard, all the Kennedys, Jesse Jackson. And I'd heard Martin many times before. But the "I Have a Dream" speech is the greatest speech I've ever heard. Buy a recording of that speech. It's no highfalutin talk. It has no big words. No matter your race or schooling, you know what Martin means. You feel that powerful message. He doesn't grovel or preen, just hits the mark straight on. When Martin said "My dream is rooted in the American dream," he told whites what Negroes had been telling whites for years. We don't want nothing but what you want: good schools, good doctors, safe neighborhoods.

But Martin took these old ideas of integration and racial justice and put them across to the white moderate like no one else has ever done. His "I Have a Dream" speech told whites, We love the same Bible you do, the same Declaration of Independence and Bill of Rights you do. Let us be Americans, too. *Let us live the American dream, too.* Martin knew we had to reach that moderate, the man who said, "Let's go slow." Martin convinced that man that one hundred years was slow enough. They played that "I Have a Dream" speech on radio and TV all over the country, and millions of white people heard Martin and surrendered a little piece of their racism.

But great as it is, the "I Have a Dream" speech makes me sad. It's Martin's most famous speech, and "I have a dream" is Martin's most famous phrase. They've made Martin into a damn idealist: Martin the dreamer. Let me tell you: Martin was the least dreamy man you ever saw. He was a planner, a marcher, a tireless worker. He stayed up all night planning campaigns, fought for justice, always moving, thinking, conferring with paupers and mayors and presidents. Inspiring his SCLC troops. Marching, protesting, bargaining. We all dream. Martin's greatness was not his dream, but how hard and how smart he worked to make that dream come true.

Within three weeks of the March on Washington, on September 15, 1963, whites bombed the Sixteenth Street Baptist Church, a Negro church in Birmingham. The bomb exploded during Sunday services. Four little black girls came to Sunday school to pray and got their brains blown out. That bomb sent me back to Mau Mau. I got deep into my planning. I had guns everywhere—guns in all my vehicles, guns in every room of my house.

What stopped me was all the signs I saw of Medgar's nonviolent work. Everyone told me how much they respected Medgar's quiet ways. Even whites stopped me on the street in Jackson to tell me Medgar shouldn't have been killed. M. B. Pierce, the chief of police, came to me: "Charles, I know how you feel. Not all of us approve of this." Fannie Lou Hamer was saying, "Soon as you hate somebody, you can't ever hope to see God's face." Negro ministers were all over, praying over Medgar's body, praying over me. And having been raised a Christian, that took a hold on me. I knew God didn't condone Mau Mau. I could still hear Mama telling me, all those years, "Do unto others as you'd have them do it to you."

I wrestled with myself. My heart was troubled. Sometimes white folk seemed innocent. Sometimes the whole white race seemed guilty as hell. A well-meaning white man would tell me, "Bless you for being so kind and forgiving," and I'd smile at him and think, "You're just too dumb to know I hate your white guts." Myrlie had some of the same thoughts. The battle inside me got so hot that some days I felt my head would explode. Each day in Medgar's old office, I felt his presence. I talked to Lope in the spirit and heard his soft voice: "That's not the way, Charlie. Hate someone, and you only end up hating yourself." Medgar was always so proud the NAACP was nonviolent. For Medgar to live on through me I couldn't kill, or run girls anymore. I had to reform myself.

If I killed ten whites as payback, the Klukkers would have won by making me think like a Klukker. The cops would have tracked me with dogs, hunted me down, and killed me. All the newspapers would have screamed what the bad Evers boy did, and how Medgar had also followed Jomo Kenyatta and Mau Mau. They'd have blamed my killings on the NAACP and Kenyatta and Communism and everything but the white racism at the heart of it. And I would have tarnished everything Medgar Evers had achieved.

Slowly I moved away from Mau Mau, and threw myself into other plans. Thank the Lord, I gave up that madness. After many nights on my knees asking God to take away my hate, the murderous mood finally lifted, and the thirst for revenge left my mind. I could avenge Medgar's death better by doing what Medgar did. Changing minds in Mississippi. Using the system. Killing not white folk, but the old white way of life. I started buying up property. I decided to picket and boycott the whites and put blacks in business. I decided Medgar and I had been right back in '46, when we fought our way into the Decatur courthouse, trying to vote. Voting was the key to power.

I lost touch with most of my friends from the taverns and the syndicate of Chicago. I'd left that part of the world and rejoined all the Negroes of Mississippi maimed by whites for the crime of wanting better. Hundreds of them I knew by name. The thousands I'd never known, I *felt* I knew them. The next few years, I drove thousands of miles a month, through dusty towns and bottomland. I started quick, while the memory of Medgar's killing was fresh in all our minds. We filed lawsuits to integrate schools, but we also set up clinics to help Negroes register to vote. I registered every Negro I could get my hands on and got them out to vote so someday we could elect some Negroes. I fought the economic fight *and* the political fight. Medgar would have been proud.

I always tell leaders the plain truth. We needed marches, sit-ins, and voter registration down south, and I pulled no punches telling Roy Wilkins. But I was one of the few who did. Hundreds of southern NAACP branches were too timid to tell Roy the truth. Groups like the SNCC hit a little southern town, signed up voters, started marches. Roy took offense. He wanted them to work through scraggly NAACP branches that were doing nothing. Roy would fume that the SNCC and the SCLC got the credit, and the NAACP paid the bills. Aaron Henry and I ignored Roy and encouraged the SNCC.

Blacks in Mississippi have always had to help each other just to survive. When I got sick, I could pick up the phone and five Negroes were at my door. When any local Negro got sick, we'd see about them, but the Evers family had a special meaning to Mississippi blacks. I never claimed to be *the* single black leader in Mississippi, but I spoke the truth and risked my life every day. Too many Negro leaders had made big promises, then got bought off or scared off by whites and left the state or gave up. So I always stood up to whites and stayed in Mississippi. I'd hear whispers: "Charlie Evers is lining his own pockets, selling out civil rights." Well, sure I was making money! I'm always a businessman. But I'd never sell out civil rights. If I'd needed fifty thousand dollars for surgery, give me ten days, and poor as my people were, I'd have got it. So why should I sell out civil rights?

I picked a series of racist towns in Mississippi. In each town, we'd present the government, the chamber of commerce, board of education, and the school system with about twelve demands. Integrate all school facilities. Hire Negro store clerks. Hire Negro policemen. Hire Negro deputy sheriffs. This long list came down to one simple thing: We're as good as you. Treat us right! The hardest demand for the bigots to swallow was giving Negroes courtesy titles: "Mr. Evers," "Mrs. Evers," or "Miss Evers"—no more "boy," "girl," and "nigger."

We'd organize real tight and give these towns ten days to meet our demands. If they spurned us, we'd march, picket, and boycott. Forcing change takes two things: pressure and negotiation. You try to negotiate away injustice. If negotiations fail, you apply pressure, negotiate some more, and cut a deal. Some folks like to negotiate but hate to apply pressure. That's no good. Some like to apply pressure but have no skill or faith in negotiating. That's no good, either. You need pressure *and* negotiation. Some have said I'm too aggressive to negotiate. That's bullshit. Sure, I'm quick and strong and hard to predict, but that kind of man strikes the best bargains. I'm always ready to deal.

Organizing is hard work, and those who jump in for the glamor get in trouble. I joined the Negro community in each town I went into. I organized real well, but never tried to take over these towns. In Natchez, Port Gibson, Woodville, Hazlehurst, and Crystal Springs, I always consulted local Negro preachers and teachers and other leaders. I always shared power and credit. You had to. Not only because it was right, but because you never knew if you'd be alive to complete a job. You left a structure so the work could go on without you.

CHAPTER

15

Two Lost Brothers

ON NOVEMBER 22, 1963, President John F. Kennedy was shot dead in Dallas. If John Kennedy had lived, he might have been the greatest president ever. Now he'd never have the chance. White folk in Mississippi laughed and shouted with joy when John Kennedy was killed. Hearing the news snapped me back to Medgar's murder, and the day John Kennedy had brought Myrlie and me into his White House office and told us on our way out, "You know, they'd kill me, too, if they could."

Bobby had called me so many times when Medgar was taken. Bobby had many friends, but not many knew how it felt to have your favorite brother shot dead. So I rushed to the phone, told Bobby I was on my way. If I'd asked if he wanted me to come, Bobby would have acted brave and said no. You don't ask a man at a time like that—you just come. I left right away for a Washington hotel. I saw Bobby in some of his darkest moments, right after the killing. We did some hard talking about our brothers. When I left, we were very close friends.

For all their money and power, the Kennedys were a lot like the Evers family. Both families tried to make the world better, to free people from poverty and misery. Both families believed in paying the price. Both Medgar and John wanted equality and justice for all and thought no price was too big to pay for it. Both of them paid the ultimate price. Most white folk don't believe John Kennedy was killed for pushing civil rights, but I know he was.

Bobby and I were twins: hotheaded, good-hearted, ambitious, and tough. We had guts, but no tact. We prayed and brooded alone. We both liked the telephone, and we always talked once a week. We were both natural leaders who liked politics, but not politicians. When

Bobby saw a politician drawing attention, he'd say, "God, he's stuck on himself!" We both judged issues on the merits first, the politics second. We had few staff meetings, liked to talk straight, hash things out face-to-face, man-to-man.

But our strongest link was having our favorite brother gunned down by the haters. Bobby lost his older brother and I lost my younger brother, so we needed each other. Losing our brothers to murder, the same year, for the same reason, brought us so close. Both of us thought a lot about death. We'd visit our brothers' graves at Arlington. Bobby wished he'd have died in John's place. I was past that, but I'd look down at Medgar's headstone and think, "Why's Medgar gone, and Beckwith still here, boasting about killing him? I know God works in mysterious ways, but shit. . . ." I kept a big photo of Medgar in my office; Bobby kept a big photo of John in his. We'd look at those pictures and wonder what our brothers would have done in our shoes.

Growing up poor in Mississippi, my love of the poor came natural. Bobby had grown up rich. The Irish weren't lynched in Boston. Bobby had the best doctors, the best of everything, and grew up assuming America was the land of the free and the home of the brave. I knew it was no damn such thing. But as John Kennedy's time in office went on, Bobby cared more and more about the Negroes. He was baffled by white peckerwood hate. As President Kennedy took on poverty and civil rights, Bobby began to embrace the Negro struggle, not just the legal side but the moral side—not just on paper, but in his heart.

After John Kennedy was killed, Bobby identified even more with the victims of this world: poor folk, Negroes, the powerless. When John was snatched away for no reason, Bobby learned how it felt to be a Negro in this country. Now Bobby *understood* the evil of lynching for the first time. Bobby always asked questions. He started peppering me with questions about life as a Negro. All my answers came down to one thing: "Bobby, we don't want any more than you do: a decent job, decent schools for our kids, a bed in a decent hospital when we get sick, and a chance to vote. And we can't get those things because we're Negroes."

Bobby would say, "Is it really like that?" Angry at the thought. "Yes, Bobby." I told him how hard the Evers boys had to fight just to get to grade school, walking through all that rain and sleet, jumping into ditches when the white kids' bus came down the road at us. Bobby looked so sad. "Damn!" he said. "Is this America? I just didn't know it happened like that." Like Medgar and Martin, Bobby had a very strong, *simple* idea of what America could be and should be. That simpleness gave Medgar, Martin, and Bobby a lot of their power.

Bobby would grow quiet, then say, "How can I change this?" I'd say, "Bobby, you can do lot of things. You got a famous last name. Use it. You know a lot of folk in high places. Use your influence to make them change things." Bobby was late learning, but when he finally saw the depth of racism in this country, he went hog-wild and pig-crazy. He busted his ass to end injustice and inequity. He was viciously outspoken at times. Dogmatic, and wouldn't even try to be nice until he'd convinced you. But he was kind, he was deep, and he was dedicated. I knew Bobby Kennedy much better than John Kennedy. I liked and respected John, but Bobby I loved like a brother. I loved Bobby almost like Medgar.

Bobby wasn't a liberal; he did things. I never wanted his talk or money, just action. And he gave it to me. Bobby and I would cuss and fuss, but Bobby used his influence to help the Negro, and I loved him for it. Without Bobby, there would have been a hell of a lot more beatings and murders in Mississippi.

Lyndon Johnson was the new president. He was a southerner, so we doubted him on civil rights. I'll never forget the first time I met Johnson. Soon after Medgar was killed, President Kennedy had set up a White House meeting on the civil rights bills coming on. He called in black leaders from all over the country to share our ideas. Seemed like five hundred of us were crammed in rows and rows of chairs, in a big White House conference room. President Kennedy came in, spoke briefly, then left in a rush. Vice President Johnson stayed behind, and I had a chance to take his measure.

Johnson was well over six feet and two hundred pounds, bone faced, with brown, graying hair, a long, sharp nose, and a nice pair of shoulders. Most Negroes feared Johnson. He'd pushed through the Civil Rights Act of '57, but he was still a white southerner with a mean voting record. Johnson had an arrogance we didn't see in John Kennedy. When Kennedy made Johnson first vice president, then head of the Equal Employment Opportunity Commission, we feared Johnson would be one of the worst racists ever up in Washington. I'd phoned Johnson and left some messages. He'd never answered. Now, here I was finally meeting LBJ, trying to decide if he was a good man or just another hater sent to pacify and put us off.

In that room with Lyndon Johnson was a Negro named Louis Martin. Louie Martin and I were almost like two peas in a pod. We'd both been in the insurance field and had lived in Chicago. We thought alike. Louie was richer than me, but just as tough and blunt. He'd founded a newspaper in Michigan. He'd edited the *Chicago Defender.* He'd worked on every presidential campaign since 1944 and helped John Kennedy win the crucial Negro vote in 1960. Louis Martin knew the Negro churches, the NAACP, and the newspapers. He was a fun lover, a deal maker, and a power broker. After John Kennedy won the 1960 election, he made Louis assistant chairman of the Democratic National Committee and told him to pass along Negro concerns to the White House.

Lyndon Johnson sat over in the corner, next to Louie Martin, listening quietly. One Negro leader after another got up and told how he'd suffered and what he deserved from the federal government. Speaker after speaker told how hard it was being a Negro and how the Kennedy people should help us. I looked over at Lyndon Johnson to see how he was taking this. Johnson was looking at us Negro leaders like we were from outer space. Then Johnson leaned over to Louis Martin and whispered something.

Louie jumped up: "Wait a minute. Wait a minute. Y'all are talking all this civil rights. You're talking about what you want and what you demand." Louie Martin glared out at all five hundred of us and said, "Now, listen. You're in Washington, D.C. And the only thing folks in Washington understand is, 'How many votes you got?' Folks here count votes—not hollering and suffering. So don't waste your time telling the vice president here all your demands. What the president and the vice president want to know is how many votes can you turn out for the Democrats next election?"

I looked out at LBJ. He'd bowed his head and smiled, like a man in church telling the preacher "Amen!" I thought, "You dirty scoundrel. You ain't *no* different from the rest!" I was mad enough to have bolted, but I sat and watched Lyndon Johnson. Louis Martin kept saying, "What matters in this country is money. What matters in this city is votes." Louie Martin said, "You ain't got money and votes, so go on home and get busy. You're up here hollering and screaming, but you haven't done your homework. We can't do anything for you here until you've done something for yourselves. Round up some votes."

The third time I heard "round up some votes," I raised my hand and kept waving it. The vice president saw me, turned to Louis Martin, pointed at me, and said, "That gentleman over there—see what he wants." Finally, Louie turned and said, "Charlie, what you got to say?" I let go, full blast: "Here you tell us to go home and round up some votes. But Mississippi won't let us vote! Registrars keep us off the rolls by asking, "How many bubbles in a cake of soap? How many pigs on a forest path?" You know we can't vote in Mississippi. How can you tell us to go back and round up votes?" Lyndon Johnson looked at me funny, but I was too mad to let up. "Mr. Vice President, it was white folk who elected you. Because in Mississippi we ain't had the right to vote. If you and Louie Martin think we vote in Mississippi, you're the same damn fools you've been all your life! Maybe they vote in Texas."

Johnson said, "Yes, in Texas, the colored have been voting all along." But he saw my point. He never blew up, like I'd expected. He respected me for talking straight. He turned to Louie Martin and said Negroes had to be assured the right to vote. Then Johnson asked me, "If we get you the right to vote in Mississippi, can you turn out Negroes to support our ticket?" I said we'd need more than the right to vote. We'd need federal protection so we could exercise this right without getting shot. I was thinking of Gus Courts and the Reverend George Lee, and about Medgar.

I was mad enough to punch Louie Martin, but he was right. We had to line up Negro voters. I went home to Mississippi and worked even harder. We launched a voter registration drive and signed up thousands of new Negro voters. Next time I saw Louie, he said, "Charles, I hated to do what I did in that meeting, saying all that about votes and money. But I had to." I said, "Louie, you did right. If you hadn't been that cold and hard up in Washington, I'd have been too soft down here in Mississippi. If you'd sugarcoated the problem, we'd have fewer Negro voters today." And after that day of straight talk in the White House, I never had any trouble getting a phone call through to Lyndon Johnson.

I met with President Johnson many times in '63, '64, '65. I liked and trusted him more each time. Johnson was strong and could make a decision. He bent Congress to his will to carry out John Kennedy's program. He knew you must put in your reforms quick, in the dead man's name, while the politicians are ashamed to oppose you. They dig in their heels later, but for a few months they'll respect the dead.

Lyndon Johnson knew the value of symbols. At his inaugural ball, he walked on the floor and danced with a Negro, the wife of his special counsel. Eyebrows raised. How many presidents had ever danced with a black woman in public?

On July 2, 1964, Lyndon Johnson put that Civil Rights Act of 1964 through the Congress. Negroes could eat in white restaurants, drink from white water fountains, swim in white swimming pools, and play in white parks, all through the South. That bill helped integrate the public schools and got us jobs, too. Lyndon Johnson pushed an old folks' hospital program so southern Negroes could finally see proper hospitals.

As a southerner, Johnson knew all the southern rascals—James Eastland and John Stennis and Jamie Whitten from Mississippi; Strom Thurmond from South Carolina; Herman Talmadge and Richard Russell from Georgia; Russell Long from Louisiana. Johnson had been plotting with these rascals for years. Now he challenged them. Johnson had a sharp eye. He knew Jamie Whitten liked to control the federal farm programs. He knew Ross Barnett claimed literacy tests just kept fools out of state government. Johnson watched those southern big men like a hawk until he got enough on Eastland and Stennis and Thurmond to say, "Now, wait here, buddy. I want this civil rights bill passed."

Let's also praise Hubert Humphrey for the Civil Rights Act of '64. After Lyndon and Bobby, Hubert was the best white friend we had in the '60s. I loved his jolly, confident face. He'd grab hold of you, put his hands on you, showing he cared. I've always liked that in a man. Humphrey had seen poverty and prejudice as a young man. He spoke his mind on moral issues, pushed civil rights way back at the '48 Democratic Convention. Humphrey helped LBJ get the Civil Rights Act of '57 through the Senate. In 1960, Hubert ran for president as "the civil rights candidate." In May of '63, he convinced President Kennedy to beef up the civil rights bill.

People told Humphrey to lay low, forget civil rights so he could be vice president in '64. But Hubert felt racial justice in his heart. He just *knew* all men were created equal. In January of '64, Humphrey became floor leader for the civil rights bill, worked like hell to guide LBJ's Civil Rights Act through Congress, and Johnson made him vice president anyway. Humphrey hired many Negroes on his staff, kept civil rights out front, and in his heart. Never got enough credit for it. Republicans like Charles Percy and Jacob Javits were in that coalition, too. It's a damn myth that all the real civil rights work was done by Democrats.

But passing the '64 bill wasn't enough. We had to test that bill. We held a mass meeting in Jackson in July of '64, with singing, clapping, and speaking. A few days later, Chester Lewis, a Negro lawyer from Kansas City, came south, and together we led a group to the capitol in Jackson. We reached the governor's office. The white flunky there wouldn't let us in, so we held a press conference in the hall. The governor wouldn't hear us, but CBS did. Chester Lewis read our statement, demanding action on civil rights, and we answered reporters' questions. On my way out, I drank from a white-only fountain and let the water run out my black mouth back onto that fountain.

CHAPTER 16

Hate Goes on Trial

ON JANUARY 27, 1964, Byron Beckwith went on trial in Jackson. For eight days, folk packed that little courtroom. Because something much bigger than Byron Beckwith was on trial. Hate was on trial.

Myrlie was there, and James Meredith too. It was a strange trial—partly a sham, partly an honest effort by the white district attorney, William Waller, to convict Beckwith. Myrlie helped Bill Waller all she could. Once the spectators at the trial signed in and got frisked, we could sit our black butt down next to the whitest white man. Most of us didn't want to—we didn't like them any more than they liked us.

Bill Waller was thirty-seven, a seventh-generation Mississippian. While they were impaneling the jurors, Waller asked each man, "Do you think it's a crime to kill a nigger in Mississippi?" It took four days for Bill Waller to find twelve Mississippi white men willing to say in public that killing niggers was a state crime. Beckwith's lawyers made sure all the jurors were men because women had more scruples than menfolk about Negroes being murdered. But not even prosecutor Bill Waller wanted a single Negro on the jury. An all-white jury was a given.

Beckwith claimed he was a hundred miles off, in Greenwood, when Medgar was killed. Two cops swore they'd seen him there. Beckwith's lawyer pointed out that Medgar had named his son after Jomo Kenyatta. Bill Waller showed the jury Beckwith's threatening letters to newspapers and magazines on the need to keep the nigger down. Waller showed Beckwith's Enfield rifle found in the honeysuckle, Beckwith's telescopic sight with his prints on it, the mark over Beckwith's right eye made by the telescopic sight. Waller had witnesses place Beckwith's car at the scene just before Medgar was shot, and witnesses who'd heard running toward the drive-in just after the shot. Waller proved the bullet that killed Medgar could only have come from one gun in the whole world: a 30.06 Enfield rifle. Beckwith didn't deny that his rifle had killed Medgar—he claimed the rifle had been stolen just before the murder. Convicting Beckwith of first-degree murder should have been an open-and-shut case.

But in February of '64, Byron Beckwith's jury deadlocked at six to six. That hung jury ended trial number one. They held a second trial in the Hinds County courthouse, but on April 17, trial number two ended in hung jury number two. They were deadlocked eight to four, and the eight was for acquittal. Beckwith had boasted he'd get off, and he did. Mississippi lacked the guts to convict a white man of killing a Negro, no matter how blatant the deed, no matter how big the Negro. Hate was tried, and it went free.

After the second trial, whites in Greenwood raised Beckwith's ten-thousand-dollar bail quick. Publicly, they said Beckwith hadn't killed Medgar. So why'd they admire him so much? When Beckwith returned to Greenwood, he got cheers, welcome signs, everything but ticker tape. Most whites in Mississippi were glad someone had finally brought down that Evers nigger. They'd mutter, "Medgar Evers was getting too big. It had to be done." They gave Beckwith the hero's role, and he played it to the hilt. Slicked his hair back, wore his finest clothes. Smiled and waved at spectators. Defense lawyers tried to keep Beckwith off the stand, but he wanted to testify so he could finally be someone: Defender of the White South. All the newspapers ran features on him. Thousands of dollars poured into his defense fund. General Edwin Walker, a big John Bircher, came from Dallas to shake Beckwith's hand.

The government made Beckwith's jail time a damn slap on the wrist. When they moved him from Rankin County jail to Hinds County jail, the warden said, "Glad to see you." And Beckwith said, "Mighty glad to be here, sir!" If that bastard hadn't killed my brother, why was he glad to be in jail? The warden kept Beckwith's gun collection out of his cell, but he let Beckwith wear his own clothes, even gave him a radio and TV. Knowing how Mississippi jails treated civil rights workers, it made me sick. They even gave Beckwith a card table and typewriter so he could write his memoir. He called it *My Ass, Your Goat and the Republic.*

In December of '64, the U.S. government bought land in Greenwood from Beckwith. The damn General Services Administration wanted to build a post office and said they'd picked the site before the trial. But they still paid twenty-five thousand dollars to the man everyone knew killed Medgar Evers. Is that how you treat a killer? Pay him taxpayer money? It looked like a damn bounty. I kicked up sand with the postmaster general, the Justice Department, everyone I knew in Washington. It did no good.

During one of those trials, Governor Ross Barnett himself walked up to Beckwith in court, shook his hand, and clapped him on the back. A governor supposed to represent all the people of Mississippi embraced a cold-blooded killer, right in front of the jury! Ross Barnett's official statement called Medgar's murder a "dastardly act." But hugging the killer in court—that was the real Ross Barnett. That handshake and embrace told every juror and spectator in the room that Beckwith had done right to gun down Medgar Evers. That hug was so mean to anyone who loved Medgar. Myrlie had to watch it from the witness stand.

But hung juries meant at least one man in that jury wanted justice. Bill Waller hankered for high office in Mississippi yet pushed for a conviction, so he must have guessed the tide was turning on white supremacy. And the Jackson police cooperated with the prosecution. That doesn't sound like much, but in Mississippi, in '63, it was a lot. We all expected the jury to play two hands of gin rummy, then come back and turn Beckwith loose. Instead, the jury sat ten days and came back hung. That was progress.

Prosecutors finally dismissed the case in 1969. For years, Byron Beckwith was a special guest at Klan rallies. He'd tell them, "Killing that nigger gave me no more inner discomfort than our wives endure when they give birth to our children. We should be willing to do as much."

Violence against blacks isn't just beatings and lynchings. It's also unlit streets with no cops on foot patrol. When I took Medgar's job, I knew Jackson State was dark and dangerous at night. I asked the city to light the area. They said this was "being studied" by the Engineering Department. Jackson State students squawked about the area. Two local pastors told Mayor Thompson about it. A committee met with Thompson about lighting the area or putting in an overpass. Mayor Thompson did nothing.

February 3, 1964, was a cold evening. Mamie Ballard, a popular Jackson State girl, was walking in the unlit area in front of Alexander Hall. A white man, Jesse Aldridge, drove by, hit her by mistake, broke her leg. The cops sent him on. Jackson State students began marching and yelling, blocking traffic. The school was tearing down a building nearby. Students took bricks from the construction site, threw bricks and bottles.

I walked the Jackson State campus, telling kids, "None of us is afraid, but this is no way to get what we want." The crowd dispersed, but at a campus basketball game, activists passed out leaflets urging kids to demonstrate. Crowds rioted all night. Not a cop was hurt, but the Jackson cops, "returning sniper fire" from phantom snipers, shot three Negroes with buckshot, then waited with roadblocks, more buckshot, attack dogs, tear gas, and armed vehicles. Over two hundred Negroes wanted to march against the police blockades, or even march on the Hinds County courthouse, where Beckwith was being tried. Anything could have happened then.

Early the next day, February 4, James Meredith and I moved through the crowd, trying to keep peace. I said, "Your grievances must stay here on campus. If you're such heroes you want to die for a traffic light, go ahead. But they will shoot you. They showed that last night." When I spoke to nine hundred Negroes at an NAACP rally that night, I promised protest marches all over Jackson until race barriers fell. But I've always hated riots. You don't have to throw bottles and break windows to make white folks take notice. March one hundred Negroes down to the Public Service Commission and stand quietly outside the window, and they notice. Get 100,000 Negroes not to pay their light bill and gas bill for one month, I guarantee you they notice. No need to throw rocks. Money talks in this country.

The riot cooled, and Jackson State kids formed a grievances committee. Jesse Aldridge was charged with failing to yield to a pedestrian. The Jackson *Daily News* said that "Mississippi law enforcement officials have a fine record of acting coolly and efficiently under fire." And Mayor Thompson said no one had told him the campus was dangerous. He said he would put a stoplight there, but "would not tolerate violence in the city." So how could he tolerate his own cops?

Most of the best white liberals didn't hire Negroes on their own staffs. For years, George McGovern had no blacks in his inner circle. Teddy Kennedy might have had one. Ed Muskie might have seen a Negro on TV. I'd ask them, How can you discuss racism when you have no black friends? I even had to push Bobby Kennedy. I said, "Bobby, practice what you preach. Get some Negroes on your staff." He said, "I don't have any?" I said, "No, you don't." He said, "Get me some." Bobby got miffed at me a few times, but unlike most politicians, Bobby wanted to be pushed. So I sent Bobby some Negroes. I helped bring Bobby together with Earl Graves, a young man schooled in Baltimore, very aggressive. Bobby liked him. Earl came to work for Bobby in '65.

One day in '64 I was leading a march on Capitol Street in Jackson and one of those damned U.S. marshals jostled me, shoved me off some steps. Now, I'm not Dr. King; I don't turn that other cheek. I jumped up and told the man just what he was. We yelled awhile, and one of the network TV cameras caught it. Bobby saw it on the news. Next day, I was talking to Bobby. He said, "Charles, you lost your cool, didn't you?"

I said, "Bobby, if there were some Negro U.S. marshals, I might not get so upset. How come we got no Negro U.S. marshals down here?" Bobby was caught off stride. He said, "There's *none*?" I said, "Not a one." He said, "Well, find me one and he's yours." That's how quick Bobby made up his mind. I found Bobby a Negro named Milton, a Jackson schoolteacher. Within six months, U.S. Marshal Milton was on duty—the first Negro U.S. marshal in Jackson. U.S. Marshal Milton did a fine job. The first person he served papers on was Charles Evers. I was always protesting something in those days. When I saw how Milton was doing me, I said, "You sonofabitch!" But I was chuckling.

The summer of '64 was Freedom Summer. Over one thousand young white kids came down to Mississippi to work for civil rights, many from prominent northern white families. Some Negroes didn't want their help: "Rich white northerners—what can they do in one summer?" But those kids helped us keep hate on trial. They worked with us, lived with us. Some got beaten alongside us. These white kids saw how the racist system worked. Before the kids came, the Klukkers only had to watch a few racial agitators. It wasn't hard to keep us all covered. With one thousand new agitators in the state, the Klukkers couldn't swivel their shotguns around quick enough. That took pressure off folk like Charles Evers.

The Freedom Summer kids didn't know Negroes and whites couldn't drive in the same car. They didn't know a black man and a white woman couldn't share a meal. Local whites saw these kids drive with us and eat with us, and some of them accepted it. And many of those Freedom Summer kids went home and educated their schools and their families. Thirty years later, many of them are still working for racial justice.

Andrew Goodman and Michael Schwerner were white Freedom Summer kids who came down from New York to work on voter registration. Aaron Henry and I met Andy Goodman in Jackson. He was a pleasant twenty-year-old kid. After half an hour, we sent him over to Meridian to join the other civil rights volunteers. From Meridian, Andy Goodman got in a car with Mike Schwerner and a twenty-one-year-old Mississippi Negro named James Chaney. A black church had burned in Longdale, and on June 21, 1964, Goodman, Schwerner, and Chaney drove toward my old home of Philadelphia, Mississippi, to investigate.

Klukkers abducted those kids on the way and brutally murdered them. Everyone knew the Klan had done it, but the three kids were officially called "missing" for over a month. Then on August 7, federal officials dug up their bodies inside a dam. God, I regretted sending Andy Goodman to Meridian. Bobby Kennedy called and asked what could he do. I said appoint another Negro deputy marshal. Bobby did it.

Goodman, Schwerner, and Chaney got a lot of press because Goodman and Schwerner were white, but Klukkers beat up and killed Negroes all the time. Someone bombed Negro property in McComb, Mississippi, on September 23, 1964. Two days later, someone bombed the home of the white mayor of Natchez, John Nosser, after he'd publicly sympathized with the Negro. Someone bombed the home of Willie Washington, a Negro contractor in Natchez, for the second time in three months. Two days later, a bomb hit the home of I. S. Sanders, a civil rights Negro. After the last of these bombings, I telegraphed President Johnson to stop this "mounting reign of terror." And I warned him, "I cannot and will not be responsible for the action which the Negroes take upon themselves."

I kept a gun in every corner of every room of my house. I kept armed guards outside my home, around the clock. When I traveled, I tried to stay in a motorcade, talking to my guards by walkie-talkie. I felt whites would probably get me, but not like they had Medgar—not in the back, with no return fire.

Aaron and I went to Washington, D.C., to tell the big wheels in the Democratic Party to overthrow the white bigots running the party in Mississippi. Here we were trying to bust the Democratic Party in Mississippi, but Aaron still wanted to be a Democrat working with the Mississippi Freedom Democratic Party. Not only did Aaron want the MFDP to be all-Democrat, he wanted it to stay all-Negro. Of all the bullshit! I said, "I will *not* become what I'm trying to destroy. We need an integrated group." I held that line hard, so the MFDP kind of froze me out.

The '64 Democratic National Convention was in Atlantic City. Aaron Henry and Fannie Lou Hamer led the MFDP there, trying to replace Mississippi's all-white delegation with an all-Negro one. They didn't want me, so I stayed home, registering black voters. But I watched the convention on my little TV. In the midst of a lot of camera seeking, Fannie Lou Hamer told her story on network TV. A national audience saw the power of Fannie's message. Some big wheels at the convention tried to cut a deal to give the MFDP two seats. But to Fannie Lou, that was just window dressing, and Fannie Lou Hamer was no one's window dressing. She said on TV, "We didn't come all this way for no two seats!" They rejected the deal and came home angry, vowing for more at the '68 convention.

Folks mentioned Bobby for vice president on Lyndon Johnson's ticket, but LBJ scuttled that. Bobby was restless. In the summer of '64, a rumor reached Mississippi that Bobby would step down as attorney general and run for the U.S. Senate from New York. But I ignored New York politics. I was busy trying to get Negroes the vote in Mississippi.

Then Bobby called me to say he was running. "Bobby," I said, "How can you run for the Senate from New York when you don't even live in New York?" Bobby chuckled: "I'm going to get an apartment there." We talked on, and he asked for my support. The more I thought about Bobby as a senator from New York, the less I liked it. John Kennedy had been dead less than a year, and Bobby couldn't handle the emotion of a tough campaign. And suppose he won? Would the Justice Department still enforce civil rights? And if Bobby came into New York, wouldn't Nelson Rockefeller pitch a fit? The Rockefellers and Kennedys hated each other.

I went up to Washington, almost begged Bobby to stay on as attorney general. He thanked me for my concern, folded his arms, worked his shoulders up and down: "Charles, let me tell you something. When they scream and holler for you the most, that's the time to get out. The time to quit is when you're loved the most. Because the same people that scream you up, one day they'll scream you down." That made no sense to me in '64. I wanted Bobby enforcing federal civil rights law. But Bobby knew that most politicians cling to the hard-won victories of the past. Not the Kennedys. They kept moving. Bobby insisted he needed my help running for the Senate. I said "Bobby, what about Dr. King, and Roy Wilkins? They got more pull and know-how than I do." He said, "No, I want *you*." I agreed to do all I could.

August 22, 1964, Bobby formally announced. He stayed at the Carlyle Hotel in Manhattan, then moved to a New York apartment. I did all I could for him. As much as I love my freedom, I took direction from Bobby Kennedy. We argued like cats and dogs at times, but I loved him. I went to New York, spoke for Bobby. Told mostly black crowds what Bobby had done for us. I praised Bobby to Nelson Rockefeller, and praised Nelson when I was talking to Bobby.

Traveling with Bobby opened my eyes. I was used to cheap little Mississippi campaigns. The Kennedys opened their wallets and campaigned in style. We flew in the *Caroline,* the private plane John Kennedy used to beat Nixon in 1960. It had plush seats, magazines, a stewardess. On the ground Bobby went by motorcade. I went with him to Buffalo, Syracuse. In Rochester's Third Ward, the Negro section, Bobby got a huge reception.

Sometimes I was Bobby's advance man. I'd walk into a hotel, set everything up for Bobby's speech, make sure he had a crowd. In October, I endorsed Bobby with a column in the *New York Post,* telling what Bobby had done for Negroes all over the United States. I wrote about the James Meredith case, and since Andy Goodman and Mike Schwerner were New Yorkers, I told how Bobby had jumped in to help us when Goodman, Chaney, and Schwerner were murdered.

One day on the *Caroline*, I saw Bobby practicing reading a speech. It was painful to watch. Bobby Kennedy, the most passionate man around, sounded like a damned tongue-tied schoolboy. Bobby could improvise a fine speech and take questions real well, but he couldn't read a speech worth a damn. I can't either—it's unnatural. Speaking comes from the heart, not the page. Negroes knew that, because whites never let us read much.

I walked over: "Bobby, the hell with that! Don't read your speech. Get up and greet people. Tell them how you hate racism, poverty, injustice. Just talk." Bobby was a white man, taught at the finest schools, so he wanted to work from the page. His white advisors expected him to work from the page. But I said work from the heart. Stubborn Bobby kept reading his speeches for a while, but in Syracuse he finally did it my way. Eight hundred people met him at the local airport, many of them college kids. Bobby kicked away that prepared text and just talked. The kids ate it up. From then on, Bobby mostly talked his speeches.

The Kennedys and the Rockefellers, with all their good deeds, have always been denigrated for being rich. What kind of jive is that? You social activists: Stop hating money. Money makes this world go around. The Kennedys are rich because Joe Kennedy Sr. was a hell of a businessman. Old Joe Kennedy's fortune bankrolled the Kennedy's idealism. The Kennedys could have holed up in their Palm Beach compound, living like kings. Instead, they chose to work hard to fix this country and this world.

And rich or not, Bobby began walking with the poor and lowly. Many politicians have tried to help the poor, but very few politicians have ever identified with the poor. Politicians aren't poor to start, and they get richer in office. But Bobby grew, changed, cast off his mistakes. John Kennedy's death made Bobby take a deeper look at life, a deeper look at the poor, the lonely and outcast. Many times he felt just like they did. We'd sit on the *Caroline* talking about poverty, not just in this country but all over the world. Bobby'd say he hated poverty for causing despair. I'd look in his face, and I *knew* he was thinking of his murdered brother.

Change takes time and hard work. But Bobby never quit working to understand the world. And the more he understood, the more he saw how easily he could have been on the other side. One day after a campaign stop in Niagara Falls, New York, Bobby was sitting on the *Caroline* with his legs crossed over and a big hole in his shoe. I said, "Bobby Kennedy, what you doing campaigning for senator with shoes that got holes in them?" That's an old campaign trick, to wear shoes with holes—it shows how much ground you've been traveling without thinking of yourself. But Bobby meant it. He looked me in the eye: "Millions of people can't do any better than this. My having holes in my shoe is by choice, but millions of people have to wear them like this."

People called Bobby a cold, ruthless politician. Win at all costs. But Bobby was so warm inside, and he took amazing chances. Once in that New York campaign, a nasty reporter in a crowd said, "Mr. Kennedy, is it true you're only seeking the Negro vote?" That got Bobby's goat and his face got hard. He said, "Let me tell you something. If I can get the Negro vote, the Irish vote, and the Catholic vote—the hell with all the rest of them!" Hearing Bobby say that scared the hell out of me. I caught up with him later that day: "Bobby, you're crazy! How could you say you only need the Negroes, the Irish, and the Catholics?" He looked at me: "I had to do it, Charles." He felt he had to talk tough.

Another time riding with Bobby, I asked him, "How's Ethel?" He said, "She's fine. She's pregnant now." It must have been about her ninth child. I laughed, "My god, Bobby. You're just like a southern redneck. You control your woman by keeping her barefoot and pregnant!" Bobby flushed. After a minute, he smiled: "Well, I don't think she's barefoot." I said, "Alright, but god, Bobby, she's pregnant every nine months!" I enjoyed kidding Bobby about his family because deep down he was real shy. He'd squirm, try to brush it off, but he was always loyal to his family and always answered back some way.

Now, the NAACP brass backed Bobby's opponent, the incumbent Republican senator, Kenneth Keating. Keating was a little man from Rochester, about sixty-five, a moderate Republican who'd backed civil rights since the '40s. Later he became a judge and a U.S. ambassador. Keating had made the right votes on Negro issues, and the NAACP brass wanted Keating to keep his Senate seat.

Soon as I joined Bobby's campaign, Roy Wilkins called and told me to support Keating. I said, "I don't give a damn what Keating's done. Bobby's my man." Roy said, "Don't mix the NAACP with politics."

My younger brother and best friend, Medgar Evers. I did a real good job of making Medgar a civil rights leader, but I didn't protect him enough. He worked hard for civil rights all his life, and in June 1963 he was murdered for it. (AP/Wide World Photos)

At Medgar's funeral. Medgar's little boy, Darrell, is on the far left. Medgar's wife, Myrlie, is trying to console him. I'm on the right, still in shock. Listening to the eulogies, it hit me: The closer Medgar had come to knowing whites would kill him, the less he hated whites. (AP/Wide World Photos)

From left: Gloster Current, Roy Wilkins, and me. Gloster and Roy wanted me to be "their man in Mississippi." But I've never been anyone's man but my own. No real southerner takes handling from a man up in New York City. (William Sartor, Black Star)

Addressing the faithful in a church in Natchez during our protest work there. In the '60s, I was always protesting something. (William Sartor, Black Star)

With Ted Kennedy, greeting Martin Luther King Jr. at the Jackson Airport in 1966. Martin was a great talker and a great doer. Next to Martin, I always felt like a sonofabitch. (Bob Fitch, Black Star)

Here's Bobby Kennedy campaigning in a black part of Detroit in May 1968. Bobby Kennedy was always working hard, always reaching out to all people. And blacks loved him for it. After my brother Medgar, Bobby Kennedy was the best friend I ever had. (Andrew Sacks)

June 1968, in Los Angeles. I'm shattered inside, but trying to tell a newsman about Bobby Kennedy, outside the hospital where Bobby is dying. My brother Medgar . . . John Kennedy . . . Martin Luther King Jr. Now Bobby. In a five-year period, all my heroes had been shot to death. (AP/Wide World Photos)

On Monday, July 7, 1969, a scorching hot Mississippi day, I took the oath and became the first Negro mayor of a biracial Mississippi town in a century. All I did was my duty. That's Nan next to me, and Pet Thompson swearing me in. (AP/Wide World Photos)

Jackson State University, May 1970. I'm talking to students after Mississippi law officers shot up all five floors of a girl's dormitory, claiming they saw a sniper. Down on the ground, these dirty officers of the law killed two black bystanders: Phillip Gibbs and James Green. (AP/Wide World Photos)

In my race for governor of Mississippi, my staff and I campaigned hard: in a Piper Cherokee three-seater, in fancy air-conditioned cars, in battered pickups, and many times on our own two feet. (John Messina, Black Star)

This picture shows me doing business behind a desk at my campaign office. Behind me on the wall is the greatest man I've ever known and the only man who ever really understood me—my younger brother, Medgar. (John Messina, Black Star)

I loved campaigning. Touching Negroes, pulling them close, squeezing backs—challenging them to vote and to make their friends and family vote. All this came natural. (AP/Wide World Photos)

Campaigning for governor of Mississippi in November 1971. People like you to smile and shake hands like a man. (John Messina, Black Star)

When Bill Waller beat me in the race for governor in '71, I told my supporters, "We may be beaten, but we ain't defeated!" (AP/Wide World Photos)

I was a delegate at the 1972 Democratic National Convention. The convention wasn't much fun, but I was able to get a black man, Basil Paterson, named vice chairman of the Democratic Party. (Dan McCoy, Black Star)

I was a Mississippi delegate to the 1992 Republican National Convention. In 1989, I had formally joined the Republicans, because deep down, too many Democrats want the poor to stay poor. To hell with that. (AP/Wide World Photos)

I said, "I'm risking my life to get Negroes the freedom to vote, so don't tell me who to vote for!" I said, "I'm not doing this as the NAACP. I'm doing it as Charles Evers, Bobby Kennedy's friend. No one tells me who my friends are."

Bobby started the race seventeen points up. He had the Kennedy money and many political friends in New York. Also, the election came with the presidential election, and as a Democrat, Bobby gained by appearing on the ballot with President Johnson because LBJ was much bigger in New York than the Republican, Barry Goldwater. But Keating had advantages, too. He had a kind old grandfatherly face and silver hair. He took care not to endorse Barry Goldwater. The *New York Times* endorsed Keating, and he moved up in the polls. Keating went after the Jewish vote hard, saying Bobby had dealt with a Nazi company as attorney general. Keating sought the Italian vote by claiming Bobby had smeared all Italians, and the Negro vote by charging Bobby had abandoned the Justice Department.

The '64 New York State NAACP convention was held in Buffalo on Friday, October 2. Eugene Reed and William Booth were there, state presidents of the NAACP. Big folk sat up front, and behind them a few thousand of the rank and file. The NAACP invited Senator Keating. For the keynote address, they asked me to tell how the NAACP was beating long odds in Mississippi. The brutality we faced in Mississippi made our work seem kind of glamorous to those in New York. The NAACP didn't invite Bobby Kennedy. The banquet began, and one prominent Negro after another filed up to the podium to endorse humanitarian Senator Keating, not racist Robert Kennedy.

Next to last came Senator Keating himself. His advance text attacked Bobby viciously, but Keating knew most of the NAACP delegates liked Bobby, so he told reporters he stood by the advance text, but he delivered a smoother speech. First solemn old Keating said Bobby had turned his back on civil rights by leaving the Justice Department. Keating had the nerve to say that Bobby was a Johnny-come-lately on civil rights, while Keating was our old friend. And the NAACP brass sat there, urging him on! I had to sit at my table all night, as Keating and his henchmen tore Bobby down. I bit my tongue, almost cried. People passed me little notes. Gene Reed knew I liked Bobby Kennedy, and he'd already warned me not to rock the boat.

Just to make sure, during the other speeches, Gene sent me a note: "Charles—I know Bobby's your man. But not here."

My keynote address topped off the evening. I said, "I won't talk about civil rights or the NAACP, but I'm going to speak about Bobby Kennedy if I never get invited back to Buffalo." I said, "You're lucky to have a man of Bobby's caliber running for senator. Bobby's one of a few whites in power who cares about you, and if we in Mississippi were lucky enough to have Bob Kennedy running for *dogcatcher*, he'd get every Negro vote in the state." I told how many of us Bobby had got out of jail, how he'd helped stop a race war in Birmingham, how he'd helped the Freedom Riders integrate bus travel, how he'd opened up the attorney general's office, appointed the first Negro U.S. marshal, used troops or the threat of troops to get James Meredith into Ole Miss and Negroes into the University of Alabama. I told how Bobby had stuck with Negroes through all our tribulations. I told Bobby's whole story on civil rights.

The more I talked, the madder I got. I ripped the NAACP for inviting Keating to our convention but not Bobby. I ripped the other speakers for kicking Bobby. I turned to Keating: "Senator Keating, everything you've said here about Bobby Kennedy is untrue. During all the time that all the Emmett Tills were beaten and murdered, bub, we in Mississippi knew nothing about you, Senator. Sure, you voted right, but that's all you did. Show me one Negro on your staff. You got the worst Negro poverty in the world in Harlem and Bedford-Stuyvesant. No jobs, maniacs running around on dope. What have you done up there? Bobby Kennedy means more to us in Mississippi than any other white man I know. I want every Negro who believes in me to vote Bobby Kennedy for senator." I ended by saying, "I wouldn't be alive today but for Bob Kennedy."

The NAACP rank and file hollered, "We want Bobby! We want Bobby!" And Roy Wilkins and company had a hissy fit. Afterward, not one man on the rostrum would talk to me. They stalked out of the hall. I was lucky I had cab fare back to the hotel. The NAACP brass forced me out of my hotel room, threatened to fire me. I said, "Go ahead and fire me! Keep your damn five thousand dollars a year." But I said they'd never take the Mississippi field office from me because Medgar, Aaron Henry, and I had built it from two branches to sixty-four, and I wasn't letting go.

And after all that, my speech did some good. The NAACP never formally endorsed Kenneth Keating for senator, and Bobby Kennedy was elected the new U.S. senator from New York, by seven hundred thousand votes. And more than once I *did* try to make peace between him and Nelson Rockefeller. Nelson would start fuming about some "arrogant, ruthless" thing Bobby'd done. I'd always stand up for Bobby and smile and say, "Remember, now, Nelson, Bobby's our senator."

CHAPTER

17

Interrupting the Green

PEOPLE DON'T REBEL when they're all the way down, scratching out a living in the dark. They rebel when they see a chink of light. The year 1965 was our chink of light. I'd always known democracy could help us, but '65 was the first year we really saw it. In early '65, a state group called the Mississippi Economic Council made national news by telling whites to obey the Civil Rights Act of 1964.

Big businesses in the state began to reject segregation as bad for business and tourism. By the end of '65, Mississippi started to drop the poll tax and the literacy test. Now they got cute with us: gerrymandered districts; at-large elections; higher qualifications for running for office; appointees instead of elections.

Also by '65, Paul Johnson, who'd gotten elected our governor with Klan help, quit promoting violence against Negroes. Governor Johnson was still publicly dead set against integration. As I saw it, he was still playing the role of a bald-headed bigot who hated race mixing with every bone in his body. But now Paul Johnson fought us only in court. He publicly condemned lynchings and cross burnings, and in '65, from the governor of Mississippi, that was real progress. Paul Johnson was elected as a hard segregationist, but he governed as a moderate.

I wanted Roy Wilkins to help us by calling a national boycott of Mississippi products. But I began turning away from the NAACP, looking for federal help. I wanted Lyndon Johnson to withhold federal funds from racist state agencies.

On January 22, 1965, in Jackson, cops charged Allie Shelby, an eighteen-year-old Negro, with making indecent gestures at a white girl. Within a few days, they'd given him six months in jail, scuffled with him in the jail, and sheriff's deputies had shot him dead. A coroner's jury called it "justifiable homicide." I was furious. Reverend D. D. Rushing and I ran a mass meeting at Cade Chapel in Jackson. We planned a big protest march, but four state judges barred Negroes from even protesting the murder at the county courthouse. NAACP lawyers warned us to obey the injunction. I walked to the courthouse with four of my aides and told the county to suspend the killer deputies. We used Allie Shelby's burial to show the nation injustice in Mississippi. Around the nation, the NAACP staged mass meetings to protest the Shelby killing.

In February of '65, at a U.S. Civil Rights Commission hearing in Jackson, I told how whites had killed George Lee and Lamar Smith, how they used fear, delay, and literacy tests to keep us from voting, how whites kept Negro candidates off the radio, burned our voter registration offices, and stole the tax exemption from Negro churches pushing civil rights. I told about Schwerner, Chaney, and Goodman, the martyrs of Freedom Summer. Then I told the U.S. Civil Rights Commission to conduct a new voting census, to send federal registrars to run voter registration, and to write laws so Negroes could recover cash when we got beaten for exercising our civil rights. Again, I said we want what whites have: no more, no less.

A civil rights march isn't like a voter registration drive. Civil rights marches dramatize the abuse you suffer; signing up voters builds your power base. We needed both. Civil rights marches got us on CBS News. Celebrities joined us. But sometimes the microphones, TV cameras, and movie stars only got us sympathy. Voter registration was hard work, with no CBS News, no celebrities, none of the glamor of a big march. But it wasn't a symbol, it was real. Each new Negro voter brought us closer to the day we could force the Great White Fathers to respect us or lose reelection. I liked marching, but I *loved* voter registration.

On Sunday afternoon, March 7, 1965, at the peak of Martin Luther King's protest work in Alabama, came the first Selma march, to support passage of the voter registration bill. Martin had been traveling up north, came south dog tired, and let friends convince him to rest for the weekend. No one expected Selma to be a bloody march. Little John Lewis led Andrew Young, Hosea Williams, James Bevel, and six hundred others on a peaceful, orderly march out of Brown Chapel and up to the Edmund Pettus Bridge.

When the marchers reached the bridge, the state troopers beat them with bullwhips and billy clubs. They beat John Lewis down to the ground. He rolled, got up, staggered, and kept walking. Troopers beat John Lewis again and again. Fractured his skull. Teargassed the Negroes on that bridge and trampled some of them under horses. John Lewis kept on marching.

TV cameramen caught the beatings on the Pettus Bridge and put them on national TV. Whites in California, Vermont, and Ohio saw blood running down the bridge like water, and many understood our movement for the first time. I feared the march would end, the cameras would leave, with no follow-up, no voter registration. But Selma brought us new voters, too.

On March 21, 1965, Martin led thousands of marchers on the second Selma march—five days from Selma to Montgomery. Army troops and federalized Alabama National Guard guarded the march. It ended with a rally in Montgomery. Afterward, on Highway 80, a car full of Klukkers murdered Viola Liuzzo, a white civil rights worker. The FBI proudly arrested four Klukkers in the car—one in their car was an FBI informant. But the informant was wearing a gun. So why didn't he stop the killing before it started?

When the White House wanted to talk to a Negro about Mississippi, they often asked Aaron Henry or me. On April 21, 1965, I joined some other southern Negro leaders meeting with LBJ. I didn't tell the NAACP for a few days, and Gloster Current pitched a fit. Gloster and Roy gladly reaped the benefits of all of our marches and boycotts, but they hardly gave us a cent. When dirt-poor Negroes got jailed, the NAACP often refused to go our bail. I had to put up property bonds and start local bail committees.

When Gloster and Roy ordered me to keep the NAACP out of the streets, I'd tell them, "I won't tell you how to run New York, and you don't tell me how to run Mississippi." Roy would say, "Well, we won't back you," and I'd say, "Then you're crazy as hell. Someone else will."

In July of 1965, a big group of us went to Clarksdale and took our racial grievances to the mayor and the city council. The Clarksdale cops told us we were parading without a permit and put two hundred and fifty of us in jail. They put Aaron Henry and me in a cell with twenty other civil rights workers. It was July, over ninety degrees. We weren't helping the movement in there. I said, "Hell, I'm bailing myself out."

But Aaron stayed on a whole week. They made him clean the commodes. They chained him to a garbage truck and made him hobble through the streets of his own neighborhood, plucking garbage—a great man whose "crime" was marching for equal rights! Aaron's a good, nonviolent Methodist. He never stopped smiling. I got the NAACP in New York to agree we had to bail Aaron out. They may have even paid his bail. I went to get Aaron. Near his cell, a redneck was jawing, "If niggers like you were run out of town, we'd have a better town!" I said, "Come on Aaron, you crazy bastard! *I got the bail money! Let's get out of here!*" "No, Charlie," he said, with a smile. He felt the longer he stayed in jail, the more he'd inspire Clarksdale. I was mad as Goliath.

When President Johnson wanted the voting rights bill of 1965, he told Congress, "The Negro may go to register only to be told the day is wrong, or the hour is late, or the official in charge is absent." Johnson saw how it *felt* to be a Negro in America, and he aimed to change it. I was working in Jackson one day when I got a call from the White House. Lyndon Johnson himself was on the line: "Charlie, I want you up here as a witness when I sign the voter rights bill into law." All I could say was, "Thank you, sir. I'll be there." He said a few more words and signed off. I hung up and realized I had no idea when the ceremony was being held.

I got up there just in time, and on August 6, 1965, I stood beside Lyndon Johnson, with about twenty-five other civil rights leaders, when LBJ signed the voting rights bill at his huge presidential desk. Johnson was handing out pens he'd used to sign the bill. I grabbed Lee White and got him to get me one of those pens. I still have it. Many folks in the South busted our asses registering Negroes, but that Voting Rights Act of 1965 out of Washington helped a hell of a lot. It put a real change in the air.

In June of '65, the Mississippi state legislature convened in special session at the capitol in Jackson to rewrite state voting laws to square with federal law. The Mississippi Freedom Democratic Party gathered outside the capitol. We said since Negroes couldn't vote in Mississippi, state elections were a sham, white leaders were a sham, and their special session was a sham. They arrested close to five hundred of us on

June 14, and over two hundred more the next day, including me and John Lewis. The official charge was parading without a permit and leafletting without permission of the city council. The real charge was being uppity niggers who dared to call them false representatives of the people. That's why we got arrested, and we all knew it.

People ask me if I enjoy breaking the law. The answer is no. I've broken the law proudly, but I'd rather not do it. You need law, and you try to abide by it. But if a law's immoral, you test it. If the cops and the mayor are morally wrong, you test them. Pressure, then negotiation.

To avoid integrating, Jackson and Natchez had shut their public swimming pools, even some public parks. At the end of July 1965, I wired Nicholas Katzenbach in Washington, and lodged a protest under the '64 Civil Rights Act. Negroes were swimming in rivers, lakes, and ditches. On July 20, three Negro kids had drowned in the Pearl River. Five Negroes in Mississippi died from these closures. I asked the Feds to investigate.

After President Johnson signed that civil rights bill into law on July 2, 1964, we started integrating all public accommodations in Mississippi. We went into areas where white racists still kept Negroes scared and silent. We found local leaders, planted the spirit, and moved on. We started in McComb and Walthall County. Cops and white citizen deputies met us with guns. They called us "black bastards," but we walked to a McComb motel, sat down and ate, and registered to spend the night. When they saw we were willing to kill or be killed, over two hundred gawking highway patrolmen gave in.

One of our best campaigns was in Natchez. We chose it because it had mean cops and tight segregation. Whites there used to fire their guns into our civil rights churches. There were just a handful of decent Negro jobs in the whole town, but many good Negroes lived there, if we could organize them. I loved Wharlest Jackson, a tough, dark, heavyset Korean War veteran about thirty-five, who'd worked at Armstrong Tire and Rubber since '55. He'd survived the racist abuse at Armstrong, and around '65 he got promoted to mixer, a "white man's" job. Just to bring more hell on himself, Wharlest was active in the Natchez NAACP.

In May of '65, we integrated the Natchez hotels. I stationed boys at the Holiday Inn, with rifles. One night at the Eola Hotel, there were twenty civil rights folk doing some integrating and three hundred rednecks gathered outside, doing some segregating. Rednecks with knives and guns and homemade weapons were pecking on the windows like animals: "We'll get you when you come out!" Looking out over all those rednecks killed our appetite, but we ordered food just to make them serve us. We integrated that Eola Hotel.

White reporters covered all this. Peter Jennings who's so big on ABC News now—he was a greenhorn in the summer of '65. Peter's from up in Canada, and he couldn't believe how hot Mississippi was. Dan Rather likes hot weather, and me and Dan used to dog Peter Jennings about how hot he was. NBC News had Chuck Quinn there. UPI sent Reggie Smith there. These reporters were right in the midst of things. When we left the Eola Hotel, the Klansmen met us at the door. I had some great folks with me: Thomas Washington and Percy Chapman. Jeanie Bell was there, one of our staunch supporters. Doris Allison, former president of the Jackson NAACP branch. Wonderful people, and the Klukkers hated them.

One Klukker brandished a shotgun. Another held a twelve-inch knife and growled, "I'll kill this sonofabitch." I was ready to fly at him, but Reggie Smith put his big shoulders between us, and Chuck Quinn stepped in with his camera. Those newsmen had guts. Like Dan Rather in Jackson in '63, they didn't plan to be part of the civil rights movement. To them, it was a story to report. But they were part of the movement, because many times their presence, their notepads and cameras, saved us from being cut, clubbed, or shot. Klukkers hated the media as much as they hated uppity niggers. Reporters would grab a pay phone to call in a hot civil rights story—and find Klukkers had cut the phone wires.

The media took pride in being "objective." That always struck me funny. How can you be objective about white supremacy backed by violence? You either believe in it or you don't. There's no in-between. You could tell who these "objective" reporters favored in two seconds, by the questions they asked. Those who asked, "Aren't there Communists in the civil rights movement?" were against us. Those who asked, "What are the white folks doing to you?" were with us. Most reporters were with us. That night in Natchez Reggie Smith and Chuck Quinn kept me from getting cut. And if my blood had flowed, Negroes would have turned Natchez inside out. Instead, the bigots chased the newsmen, and I got in my car and drove to the Albert Pick Hotel. We integrated the Albert Pick that same night.

George Metcalfe was a fifty-five-year-old Negro. Like Wharlest Jackson, he worked for Armstrong Tire and Rubber in Natchez and risked his life serving in the local NAACP. George Metcalfe was president of our local branch and head of voter registration. He carried a petition to integrate the schools down to the Natchez Board of Education. The night of August 27, 1965, George Metcalfe started his car to drive home from the plant. His car blew up and broke one of his arms and one of his legs. Natchez Negroes swore vengeance. I told the Justice Department if white terrorism kept up, Negroes were going to punish the perpetrators.

The car bombing of George Metcalfe united every Negro in Natchez. We visited George in the hospital. We set up an armed protective squad, but I warned Negroes, "No bombs." I urged something better: a boycott of white Natchez business. Natchez deserved a boycott as much as any town that ever was. I nursed along the will to boycott. I said, "Don't grumble where the white folk can't hear you. Complain as a group. Boycott."

A few Negroes asked, "Why do we have to boycott?" I told them like Mama told me: God will deliver us—but we must help him. If we want God's help, we must register to vote and form cooperative stores, and sometimes we must boycott. I had to smile when whites howled about our boycotts. White folks *invented* boycotts. Soon as Abe Lincoln freed us from slavery, whites boycotted skilled Negro labor and held that boycott a hundred years! We never could freelance, always had to be *their* maid, *their* cook, *their* sharecropper. Isn't that a boycott? When white folks stopped buying Philco and Falstaff and Philip Morris in '55 because of rumors those companies gave to the NAACP, wasn't that a boycott?

Mississippi never had enough jobs, so they sure weren't going to let a Negro train to be a bank supervisor or a public accountant. They weren't going to let us train to be a state barber examiner or dental examiner. Mississippi had a Bond Commission, Building Commission, Fish and Game Commission, Milk Commission, Park Commission. Not a Negro on one of them. There were a few Negro extension agents in the Agriculture Department. There were Negro teachers in the

Negro schools. That was about all the state jobs we got. The federal government was almost as bad. Mississippi Negroes couldn't work for the Census Bureau, Weather Bureau, Food and Drug Administration, National Guard, or National Park Service—nothing but the Post Office. And with cotton now picked by machine, we couldn't even pick cotton. We had to work in a downtown store just to keep our families alive.

Negro women worked for whites six and seven days a week, for five and ten dollars a week. Getting robbed. We came into Natchez and pointed it out. All Charlie Evers said was, "If they won't hire you, they're boycotting your labor. Boycott them back. Don't give your money to people who hate you. Don't shop in stores that won't hire Negroes at thirty dollars a week." As Negroes got on southern juries, I said, "If whites hang a jury to save a white man, Negroes can hang a jury to save a Negro." If the White Citizens Council can phone the NAACP all day, tie up our line, warn us we're being watched, the NAACP can tie up the White Citizens Council's line, let them know *they're* being watched. I said, "Whatever whites do to you, do it right back. Return love with love and abuse with abuse."

And what set me apart from most civil rights leaders is that I was a businessman myself. I'd been amongst businessmen all my life. I knew how they thought. I knew the day segregation and racism became bad business, businesses would come around. Because a businessman loves green much more than black *or* white. You catch his attention by interrupting the green. He'll do most anything to start that green flowing again.

Sure, our boycotts in Fayette and Port Gibson hurt the white stores there, but most of them were years behind, with high prices, no selection and service. Close them up! That's free enterprise. I loved dialing a nasty white businessman: "This is Charles Evers talking. . . ." He'd hold his voice down and talk nice until I got through talking. Boycotts got white folks' attention.

Our '65 Natchez boycott had two goals: Show Natchez Negroes they were being robbed, and show the whites of Natchez that Negroes could protest in the street. I organized and ran that boycott. We began it September 1, 1965. We began marching six days later, fifteen hundred of us, up on the sidewalks, telling white folk how mean they'd been. Telling them, "No more."

We held that boycott the spiritual way: preachers and church choirs, sermons and speeches. But if a Negro bought from the wrong grocery store, we might take his groceries. If he bought gas at the wrong filling station, we might drop sugar in his gas tank. We threw brickbats through some windows at midnight, wrapped in paper with a warning. I can learn from Roy Wilkins and Martin Luther King, and I can also learn from the Klan. Klan brickbats said THE KLAN IS WATCHING YOU. Our brickbats said, THE NAACP IS WATCHING YOU. We never caused permanent injury, but some folk must be scared into doing right. If they break a boycott, you belt-whip them. I got many belt-whippings as a boy. No harm done.

The mayor of Natchez, John Nosser, was a wily old politician. He also owned a Natchez grocery store, Jitney-Jungle. He said in time he'd protect us, give us marching permits, but he never did. That was fine. I'd been studying whites a long time. I knew what the white power structure of Natchez would do. They played right into our hands by showing just how mean they were.

The Klan was dressed in white bedsheets, circling on horses, waving guns, shooting into our homes. I told my people, "We're going to march and sing in church, and if the Klan shoots at us, we shoot back." Whites gave us a curfew; we broke it. We had guns and hand grenades to defend ourselves with. But I said, "We ain't going to riot, either." We even told the Natchez cops where we were going and why, to head off any kind of riot.

I stayed with Mrs. Mamie Lee Mazique, sister-in-law of my Mazique friends in Chicago. Mamie was a doll. She joined our movement around 1964. Her husband had just passed, leaving her with five rent houses all paid up, so white folk couldn't reach her. She became our biggest backer in Natchez. She helped our marches, got us churches. Mamie hid me many times when my life was in danger. Sat up at night, guarding me while I slept.

From October 1 to 7, they arrested me and over five hundred Negroes in Natchez. Put half of us in the Adams County jail, sent the other half on buses to the state prison at Parchman. On October 7, we stopped marching to let Natchez breathe, but held the boycott. By October 12, local business was off 25 percent. The next day, we met with Natchez officials. At a rally, I announced Natchez was hiring a Negro cop and a Negro on the school board, making a biracial housing commission, integrating its hospital, and making city employees call us "mister" and "miss." But then Mayor Nosser denied making some of these concessions, so we held the boycott.

In December, Natchez cracked. Over twenty stores hired black clerks. The city not only hired Negro cops but let them police white neighborhoods. Natchez hired Negro salesman on its beer trucks, pop trucks, and bread trucks. It let Negroes stay in its hotels and motels. That's what unity and the dollar can do. We brought Negro women from five dollars a week to thirty dollars a week—six times what they'd been making. We gave Natchez Negroes new self-respect. We proved something to Negroes all over the nation. We registered many local Negroes, too. And after '65, the old segregated South burst wide open.

A good jackleg preacher sings well and prays well, and will preach at the drop of a dime. But he has no church. He stands out on a street corner, at the fairgrounds—anywhere he can draw a crowd. There may be good reason why he's got no church. He gets drunk or reckless, and folks snicker at him behind his back. But since jackleg preachers had less invested in the status quo than real preachers, they were stronger for civil rights. Jackleg preachers were important instruments of our movement.

We used a jackleg preacher named Russell in Natchez. Russell could rave all day about the evils of white folk and never get tired. One day we put him on the porch of Mamie Lee Mazique's house. When Chuck Quinn of NBC came by and turned on his camera, Russell went hog-wild, bragging he was going to shoot a white man. NBC put this on the Huntley-Brinkley news. Russell realized he'd been on national TV and almost had a hemorrhage waiting for the Klukkers to get him until we put guards around his house.

One night at a mass meeting in Natchez, a stiff, well-dressed FBI man told me: "Uh, Mr. Evers, I'd advise you not to go out that door tonight because they're going to kill you." I said, "*Who's* going to kill me?" Mr. FBI mumbled it was improper for him to reveal his sources. I said, "Well, hell, don't matter who it is! Can't you stop them?" He looked at me real cool: "No, our job is to make arrests after, not before." The bastard as much as told me, Go on, get killed, but don't worry—after they blow your head off, we'll look into your murder. Talk about closing the barn door after they stole the horse! I blew up:

"I don't need you around here, telling me someone's going to kill me! Get the hell out of my face!" Then I gave my assassin his chance. Walked right out the door. My guards and some state troopers were there, but a sniper from a second-floor window had a clear shot. No one tried to kill me.

In early '66, I heard my old school, Alcorn A&M, had been persecuting professors and students for doing civil rights. So in April of '66, I convened local Negroes and the NAACP and led three hundred marchers to campus. Alcorn's president, John D. Boyd, bowed to his white masters and got an injunction to keep us off campus. Governor Paul Johnson sent in two hundred and fifty national guardsmen to back the Highway Patrol. Many of the top professors and deans from my student days were still at Alcorn. Some resented me. Friends asked: "Don't you hate marching on your own school?" Not at all. I *preferred* marching on Alcorn than on Ole Miss. You clean your own house first, then reform the whites. Alcorn was my own house.

Two years later, in early '68, I was back at Alcorn. They had good teachers working for $70.00 a month. Chicken feed. But on the Alcorn farm, in the dining halls, in the laundry, they were paying Negroes 75 cents a day, $3.50 a week. Working them like slaves. Alcorn was acting worse than the white folks. I went back to J. D. Boyd: "You should be ashamed, working Negroes like this." I tried to reason with Boyd about it. He turned a deaf ear.

So on February 20, 1968, Reverend Allen Johnson and I led two thousand people to the Alcorn campus. Alcorn called out the Mississippi highway patrol. Five hundred redneck highway patrolmen, state troopers, and national guardsmen blocked us. I yelled, "You ain't nothing but murderers!" I stared down one little trooper: "You're sitting there with that gun in your hand, shaking. I've a good mind to walk right over you. Would you shoot me? Then shoot me, you sonofabitch!"

We moved in. Troopers beat us with billy clubs, sprayed tear gas in my face. It was just like the James Meredith march again. My eyes were burning. My clothes were stinking. I never ducked, stayed on my feet all the way. Reverend Johnson pushed me back: "Charles, let me go. They'll kill you. They'll just beat me." They beat Reverend Johnson down. My alma mater, Alcorn A&M, told the cops to throw us in jail and rough us up. The cops prodded us, jostled us with sticks, threw twenty of us in a little cell. But the only thing they had on us was power. We had righteousness. We rocked that jail with my favorite song, "Amazing Grace," and Martin's favorite, "Precious Lord, Take My Hand." We sang one of Fannie Lou Hamer's great songs, "Woke Up This Morning with My Mind Stayed on Freedom." But the loudest one we sang was "We Shall Overcome." That was the national anthem of the civil rights movement. And Alcorn slowly raised its pay scale.

In '67, Negroes did well in Mississippi elections, but the runoffs had twenty-two black candidates, and white election officials said none of our twenty-two won. Outright robbery. LBJ sent observers to push free elections in Vietnam, but not in Mississippi. Robert Clark, a Negro teacher in Holmes County, won his race. The man he beat challenged Clark's nominating petitions. Insurance firms harassed Clark. Fannie Lou Hamer threatened that if Clark wasn't seated, she and Aaron Henry would lead a march to the capitol from the north, and Charles Evers would lead one from the south. Clark was seated.

I led food marches, too. The federal Agriculture Department had tons of rice and cornmeal sitting in warehouses, eaten by worms and weevils, while taxpaying Negroes half-starved. In August of '67 we marched to the statehouse in Jackson. Troopers stopped us at the statehouse door. Paul Johnson refused us a crumb. Later that year he said all the Negroes he saw were "big, fat, black, and greasy."

Sunday, February 22, 1967, Wharlest Jackson asked me in Fayette, "Charlie, how can we change the white man's heart?" Five nights later, in Natchez, Wharlest Jackson got in his pickup truck after a long day at Armstrong Tire and Rubber and headed home to a wife and six kids. When he stepped on the starter, a bomb blew him to bits. I saw Wharlest's dead body and thought of all the work we'd done building the NAACP in Natchez. Wharlest's killers must have been the same ones who attacked George Metcalfe with the same kind of car bomb. But the cops never arrested anyone for Wharlest's killing—they never even investigated.

Local politicians put up a twenty-five-thousand-dollar reward for conviction of the killer. Armstrong Tire and Rubber put up ten thousand dollars, and paid a life insurance policy that Wharlest had with them. It wasn't near enough. Armstrong Tire and Rubber had been harboring Klukkers too long. On February 28, I helped stage a rally to protest the murder. I urged a national boycott of Armstrong auto tires.

Since Beckwith had killed Medgar in '63, white racists had killed forty-one more Negroes in Mississippi. The evening of March 1, 1967, me and some local preachers led sixteen hundred people on a silent protest march through Natchez. On March 4, we marched silently again. Wharlest's funeral was the next day. Gloster Current, Ruby Hurley, and Roy Wilkins came down, and mourners packed the Zion AME Church.

Our Woodville boycott worked. Port Gibson, Natchez, and Hazlehurst were all successes. I helped put cooperative stores in each of those towns. Indianola and Sunflower Counties built strong NAACP chapters. But it was hard, dangerous work. By 1970, about the only ones of the old folk left in the NAACP were me and Aaron Henry. About everyone else our age had been shot, bombed, or run out of the state. Many were burned out on the movement, no longer willing to pay the price. So we looked to our youngers. In civil rights work, you never stop recruiting.

CHAPTER 18

The Next Step up the Ladder

CHRISTIANITY IS BEAUTIFUL. The Christian Church helps hold the South together. Southerners, black and white, feel that. But to black folks, civil rights comes straight from Christianity. Both movements preach nonviolent liberation and teach us that love frees us from hatred, and violence enslaves us. For southern blacks, the church was a sanctuary from white violence.

But white southerners denied that civil rights came from the Christian church or from the South. They said civil rights was smuggled in by Communists and Yankees. When whites saw us using the church for civil rights, they hit our churches. I mentioned the gutless bombing of the Baptist church in Birmingham in September of '63. But killings like that were routine. Between '63 and '68, whites burned forty-two southern Negro churches. White politicians breathed hate at the podium. White ministers preached it from the pulpit. They'd sermonize a few times a year about the "brotherhood of man," but they told their white audience very clearly that white supremacy was Christian.

But we never gave up on the Christian religion. We had to win over whites, and politics can only do so much. Most women keep their heart open, but many men need religion to pry open their heart. The Hollywood Baptist Church off Highway 61 became Fayette civil rights headquarters. We reached out to white churchfolk all we could.

Do you know the difference between a preacher and a pastor? A preacher talks a good Sunday sermon but hides all week. A pastor knows how to preach—but he also knows when to stop talking and put his Christian ideals into practice. A pastor preaches on Sunday, feeds the poor Monday, visits the hospital Tuesday, the welfare office Wednesday, and the sheriff's office Thursday. Friday, a pastor finds some jobs, and Saturday night he's in the honky-tonk, giving them out. For too long we've had preachers instead of pastors. For too long we've been going to heaven Sunday and can't get work Monday.

Many a Negro preacher would tell his congregation, "We're not ready for civil rights, just don't covet thy neighbor's wife." Then he'd lay some married lady in his church choir while his flock fed the collection plate their very last dime. Or you had the cautious Uncle Tom preacher who obeyed the commandments, had a cozy house, maybe a little field. Whites greeted him on the street. He couldn't bear to risk losing all that. So he ignored civil rights and took the white man's crumbs. He wouldn't pay the price.

When I came back to Mississippi in '63, I told those Uncle Toms, "Preacher, civil rights won't hurt you. Civil rights will *help* you. Each time whites threaten you or burn a church, they unite your flock." And I told people, "No more Toms in the pulpit. If a preacher won't do right, tighten up on him. If he's getting one hundred dollars a week, cut him down to seventy-five dollars a week, until he does right."

Most black preachers accepted beatings, lynchings, and black poverty. They promised their flock heaven in the sweet by-and-by and asked them to live like dogs here on earth. That drove me crazy. Once I went down to a Pike County town in Alabama, trying to get Negroes to run for public office. There were seven hundred Negroes in town, just three hundred whites, but whites ran the town. A local Negro preacher denounced me from his pulpit, said I'd get all those who followed me either killed or fired.

I didn't rail at the preacher. He was seventy years old. He'd been scared of whites all his life. I understand that kind of honest fear. I can work around it. I said, "Preacher, you got a right to be afraid, but don't let your fears rule you." I returned the very next Sunday, gave the same message about bucking white folk, and the preacher led a song for us.

In all Mississippi, I only met two real civil rights pastors. Both were from Jackson: Reverend Allen Johnson and Reverend R. L. T. Smith. Reverend Johnson was a fine preacher, tough and strong. But Reverend Smith was even more: my stalwart advisor, almost a second father. He joined me on marches, in jail, got teargassed with me. Reverend Smith headed some Jackson boycotts. His store and home got blasted many times. He never gave up. He carried a gun and wouldn't have minded using it.

The NAACP chapter in Shreveport, Louisiana, was reviving and asked me to come speak at a Baptist church. Someone announced my coming over local radio and TV, and all hell broke loose. Whites acted like Satan himself meant to rabble-rouse their good niggers. Reverend Johnson said, "I'm going with you, Charles." We drove my Cadillac down Highway 80 toward Shreveport. We kept seeing Klan signs along the road. We were used to seeing them on state highways, but not every mile. We bought gas just short of Shreveport. A Negro attendant sneaked over, whispered the Klan was out in force, bragging I'd never leave Louisiana alive. Then the attendant laughed, "But they won't be expecting you in a Cadillac!"

When we reached the bridge into Shreveport, five hundred Klukkers were all over the road. I said, "Oh hell, they got us." Reverend Johnson said, "Don't worry. I'm going to pray. You just keep driving." Klukkers were peeking and peering at all the broken-down cars, but like the man said, they didn't expect a Cadillac. They saw us, but in that car they didn't recognize us. We went right through into Shreveport.

The Baptist church was packed. Cops circled the church, flashing red beacon lights, listening by loudspeaker. I told the cops, "You dirty bigots! One day the shoe will be on the other foot." Halfway through my speech, a redneck sheriff yelled, "Hey, boy, you ain't going to speak here." He began to run me off the platform. Outside, cops were beating Negroes, driving them into the church like cattle.

Reverend Johnson called up to the pulpit, "Come on, Charles." He pulled me out the back door, into the car. Someone shouted, "They're waiting for you at the bridge, Charles. They're going to kill you." I said, "They ain't going to kill nobody." Reverend Johnson said, "Charles, you're not going back across that bridge. I'm taking this car home. They'll think you're in it." Reverend Johnson drove my car. The Klukkers trailed him, waiting to catch it on a lonely stretch of road, but he escaped. Friends brought me to the house of the local NAACP secretary, hid me in the basement, and next day drove me out to the Shreveport airport. The cops never found me, but the NAACP had to call a private plane to get me out of there.

Port Gibson's a town twenty miles north of Fayette. It had three thousand people in '65, mostly Negroes. But only a few Negroes in Port Gibson were even registered to vote. I led a group to Port Gibson to show Negroes the power of the vote. Folks said, "Charlie, you can't change Port Gibson. They hate Negroes there." But I knew that 90 percent of Port Gibson's business came from Negroes, so a boycott could cripple the town. At the end of March 1966, we slapped a boycott down on all the stores that wouldn't hire us as clerks or treat us fair. The boycott was looser than I wanted, but we held it ten months, and it changed Port Gibson.

At the end of January 1967, I announced the boycott was over. We'd gotten Port Gibson to hire Negro cops and a Negro deputy sheriff. We'd integrated the hospitals, schools, and cafes. Police brutality had eased. Many whites in Port Gibson had stopped calling us "boy" and "girl." White businesses had hired fifteen Negro clerks. We told all the downtown stores, "Those who don't hire Negroes will stay on our list." We entered a selective buying campaign where we spent our money in stores that kept their word. We named a negotiating committee to watch these things in the future.

The boycott made us want more: better schools, streets, and sewers. We still controlled nothing. So we set up a Negro supermarket in town and sold twenty-five-dollar shares in it. Over one hundred Negroes bought in. We knew nothing about supermarkets, but I found a consultant to help us. In August 1967, we opened Our Mart. We paid investor dividends, and cut prices at the white stores.

The more we pushed Port Gibson, the more the whites resisted. Port Gibson hired a new police chief from McComb; a Negro-hating assistant chief, Jesse Wolf; and a big Negro cop named Rip to spy on us and intimidate us. One day in April of '69, Jesse Wolf and Rip arrested a young Negro who was drunk. Another young Negro, Roosevelt Jackson, asked them to just point the man home, like they did white drunks. Wolf and Rip claimed Jackson had interfered with an arrest. Jesse Wolf outweighed Roosevelt Jackson by one hundred pounds. He snatched him off his own porch and shot him through the stomach in his own front yard, in front of his sister, wife, and kids. Wolf and Rip let Roosevelt Jackson lie in his own blood forty-five minutes before they took him to the hospital. He was dead on arrival.

I was in Jackson at 10:00 P.M. when a friend called from Port Gibson: "Mr. Evers, hurry down here. They've just killed one of our friends and the people are mad. They're up at the courthouse." I said, "Get our people in church. I'll be right there." I jumped in my truck, took off ninety miles an hour down the Natchez Trace. I reached the church near midnight. Claiming a Negro had thrown a rock, whites had called out the highway patrol, even deputized white vigilantes, who were beating Negroes on the street. The church was in an uproar. Before I got inside someone shot a cop, and as they carried him out, I told the cops to leave.

The cops beat half to death a distinguished Port Gibson Negro named Horace Lightfoot. Horace was the first Negro elected to the Port Gibson school board since Reconstruction. We finally got him over to the hospital. No one knew which patrolman had beat him, but we swore we'd sue. When the cops heard "lawsuit," they charged Horace Lightfoot with attempted assault and battery on a police officer. Horace's real crime was getting elected to that school board. Horace was tried while he was in the hospital. I avoided the courtroom so as not to prejudice the jury, but a Negro boy ran up, "Mr. Evers, hurry. They're putting Mr. Lightfoot in jail."

When I got there, the judge was dismissing the jury, and the city prosecutor was saying he wanted Horace Lightfoot arrested right away. I said, "Your Honor, may I ask what this is about?" The judge said Lightfoot had missed his hearing. I said, "Look, the man's in the hospital. You broke his arm and his ribs. You beat in his head." The prosecutor said, "He's supposed to be here in court. I want him picked up and arrested now." I said, "No point arresting a man who can hardly move. We'll get him here when he's able. You all know Mr. Lightfoot. He's done all kinds of work for you. You know he won't run off somewhere. Give him a chance to get able." The prosecutor said, "Arrest him."

I said, "Someday the shoe will be on the other foot. I hope you'll be able to wear it." He said, "Are you threatening me?" "No," I said, "Just telling you." I asked the judge, "Can we leave him out till he gets better, Your Honor?" The prosecutor jumped up: "Shut up! You're interfering with me." I said, "Don't tell me to shut up! You're nothing but a two-bit attorney, doing what the mayor and aldermen say." The prosecutor shouted to the judge, "Arrest him! For disturbing the peace!" I said, "I been in jail many times for worse than that. Handcuff me. I'll go to jail." Then I told that attorney, "Just remember, you might be coming to Fayette one day." The attorney said, "You're threatening me again! Get your black ass out of here, right now!"

So I said, "Arrest this attorney, chief. I want to swear out a warrant for his arrest: insubordination, disrespect toward an American citizen, profanity in a public courtroom, and disturbing the peace. I want him arrested right now." The police chief's eyes were popping. I said, "I'm swearing out a warrant for his arrest." I signed the warrant. The chief turned around, filled out my warrant, and arrested the Port Gibson prosecuting attorney. Who knows why he obeyed the request of a Negro.

I refused to pay my $75 bail. The city attorney posted a $125 bond and left. They carried me to jail. A crowd gathered nearby. The police chief told me, "We're going to release you. We want to get you out of here." I said, "If it'll save the town, I'll go. We've got other ways to get this town." They let me out of jail. But that was the southern justice system in the '60s. A mockery.

Officer Wolf was arrested for killing Roosevelt Jackson, but unlike a Negro booked for murder, he was released on bail. When we protested that, the state highway patrol beat us. Wolf was held for a grand jury on a manslaughter charge, but the grand jury refused to indict him. Another whitewash.

Let me tell you about a civil rights leader named Floyd McKissick, because Floyd and I came off the same stalk: We were the same age, we both had strong parents, we both dreamed of being big lawyers, and we both wanted to run a Negro town. Floyd went about it wrong, but his trying spurred me to move into Fayette.

Floyd's daddy was head bellboy at the Vanderbilt Hotel in Asheville, North Carolina. When Floyd was a boy, his daddy said, "I'm the only Tom in this family. Work hard, get an education, do better than I've done." At thirteen, Floyd witnessed a road accident in Asheville and stepped out in the street to direct traffic. A white cop got so mad seeing a young Negro wielding power, he knocked Floyd down. Floyd hit the ground a civil rights man.

Floyd earned a Purple Heart and five battle stars in World War II. He helped rebuild old French towns, some so far gone it was like building a town from scratch. Floyd was the first Negro to attend the University of North Carolina law school. He had to sue to get in. Thurgood Marshall was his lawyer. Floyd loved legal work, but he never forgot building those French towns. He wanted to build Negro towns in the South, and lawyers weren't doing that.

Floyd practiced law in Durham, North Carolina. In '66, he moved to New York and took over CORE from James Farmer. Floyd made speeches showing how civil rights came from the Declaration of Independence and the Thirteenth and Fourteenth Amendments to the U.S. Constitution. If I'd have been a lawyer, that's just what I'd have done. Floyd talked about "being militant without hating." That's just what I wanted.

Floyd McKissick felt that the poor folk pouring out of the rural south weren't ready for city life, specially in the north. Liberals huffed, "Rehabilitate the slums! Clean up the ghetto!" Okay, spruce up Harlem. Bring ten winos off the street in Flint, Michigan. Floyd and I wanted more. We wanted Negroes to stay in southern towns, but as full citizens, with all our constitutional rights—without hassles from cops, banks, landlords, or the Klan.

And Floyd knew what very few civil rights leaders understand: Towns must be racially integrated *and economically* integrated. Jobs for the unschooled are what give blacks hope—not charity, not being called "people of color" instead of "colored people." Good pay for honest work is the foundation for better housing, a college, more stores, nicer parks, nicer names for being black.

Around '64, Floyd vowed to start a Negro town in North Carolina called Soul City. Floyd meant to build Soul City *from scratch,* with a water system, a sewer system—all the modern amenities. Floyd swore he knew what he was doing. All through the late '60s, Floyd said Soul City would be a clean, self-supporting Negro town, with industry, honest cops, and no racial violence.

I loved this idea of a Negro town, but I knew Soul City would fail. Floyd's wilder young aides boasted, "We'll have no honkies in Soul City." In '69, Floyd got the secretary of agriculture to pledge federal support to Soul City. Floyd said by the year 2000 Soul City would have fifty thousand Negroes. But I knew Floyd would miss that target, and that whites would end up owning 51 percent of Soul City.

Sure enough, to launch Soul City, Floyd needed big private money. That meant honkies. I said, "Floyd, don't be crazy. Don't try to build a big Negro town from scratch. Find an old redneck town, now mostly

Negro. Register the Negroes and get them to elect you mayor. Then your town's got a sewer system already built, it's got water, it's got electric power. It's got the infrastructure." Floyd turned a deaf ear.

Local rednecks who'd bucked Floyd when he wanted racial integration bucked him now when he wanted racial separation. They said, "Anything that bigheaded nigger is for, I'm against." But Floyd pushed on with his Soul City plan. In '72, Floyd backed President Nixon, and the Department of Housing and Urban Development, HUD, pledged to guarantee Soul City $14 million in land development bonds. It looked like Floyd's dream might come true in Warren County, North Carolina. The Feds had never before guaranteed a plan sponsored by a black business, or a plan outside a metropolitan region.

But the *Raleigh News and Observer* paper ran some harsh articles saying the federal grants and loan guarantees were a payoff for Floyd's work on Nixon's '72 campaign. The paper said Soul City had Floyd's cronies on the payroll, wasting lots of federal money. North Carolina Senator Jesse Helms asked the Justice Department to look at an audit of Soul City.

Floyd pointed out he'd first filed for federal help when Lyndon Johnson was president. He said HUD hadn't let him sell $5 million in guaranteed bonds. Floyd never apologized for switching parties and stumping for Nixon. He knew you can't get far without playing politics. But in '75, the federal government began backing away from Soul City, and from then on, Soul City slid downhill.

But in '65, I took for myself the advice I'd given Floyd. I moved from Jackson down to Fayette, Mississippi, and started planning to take Fayette over. I couldn't get a Negro elected mayor in a town as big as Jackson or Vicksburg, but in Fayette I could. Fayette was the Jefferson County seat in a county of ten thousand. Jefferson County had once been full of big slave plantations. By '65, it was mostly poor timber and cattle country, three-fourths Negro, but still run by whites. Fayette was an old Mississippi town, with three blocks of storefronts on Main Street, two traffic lights, and a Confederate soldier statue in the town square.

Fayette was near Alcorn A&M, and I'd been there in college. What a mean town it was! Whites there whipped Negroes just for wearing a white shirt on Main Street. Fayette had an old Negro cripple who couldn't afford a wheelchair. He wheeled around on a little wagon. One day, the cripple was on the steps of the town icehouse. A white constable ran up, "Nigger, get out of my way!" The old Negro tried to pull his wagon aside, but got tangled with the constable. The constable pulled his service revolver and shot him. The old Negro bounced down the steps, bleeding and crying. A constable tired of the heat shot the nigger in his way, went inside and placed his order for ice. No one arrested or even questioned him. That was Fayette for you.

By 1960, when I was living in Chicago, my daughter Carolyn was living in Fayette with one of her great-aunts. When I came south to visit Medgar, I'd slip into Fayette to see Carolyn. Whites in town warned me to stay out, but I kept my eye on Fayette. Medgar used to come by Fayette to see Carolyn for me. Lope liked Fayette, too. In the back of my mind, I thought of moving down there.

In '65, I finally made the move. As late as '64, there had been fifteen hundred voters in Jefferson County, and not one of them was a Negro. Not a one! But I kept thinking, "Three-quarters of the people here are Negro. We should have most of the power." I reached Fayette, and all over Jefferson County I began registering voters. The state registration law eased up, and I got almost eight hundred Negroes on the rolls. But that was all I could do until, bless the Lord and Lyndon Johnson, a federal examiner came. By December of '65, we'd registered almost two thousand more Negroes in Jefferson County. We had over twenty-seven hundred Negroes on the county voting rolls. We had the whites outnumbered. But we had to do two big things: convince all our people to vote, and get all our votes counted.

Fayette had two Allens staring each other in the face. R. J. Allen was the old white mayor of Fayette; Ferd Allen was the Negro head of our county NAACP chapter. They'd known each other forty years. R. J. Allen was a crew-cut old buzzard who'd been Fayette's mayor since 1951. We called him Turnip Green Allen because just before Election Day he'd try to buy the tiny Negro vote by handing out vegetables. Turnip Green's big farm just outside town was often short on labor. When a Negro got drunk in town, Turnip Green would fine him one hundred dollars. The Negro wouldn't have a hundred dollars, so he'd work it off on the Allen farm. Turnip Green was a good man, as white racists go, but he never imagined any Negro could be his equal.

Now, Ferd Allen had come up the hard way, one of twelve kids in a dirt-poor Negro family. He'd had to leave school after third grade.

Ferd was sixty years old, a hardworking grocer and vegetable dealer, and a good county head of the NAACP. Ferd Allen, some other Negroes, and I sent a letter to the white officials of Jefferson County saying let's forget this master-servant bullshit and elect some officials on merit alone, not race.

Once we had a voting majority in Fayette, we sprung a boycott. I'd just got concessions in Natchez, so Ferd Allen and I asked for nineteen concessions in Fayette. Hire more Negroes in stores and on the town payroll. Integrate stores and restaurants. Call us "sir" and "ma'am." The whites balked, so Ferd and I called a Christmas boycott in Fayette. Whites were dreaming of a white Christmas; merchants were dreaming of a green Christmas; the Negroes dreamed up a black Christmas. On December 24, town officials sicced the state highway patrol on our mass march.

Someone asked Turnip Green Allen what Ferd Allen was doing. Turnip Green gave Ferd a good reference: "He's a very good nigger. In fact, he used to work for my father-in-law. But he turned out to be the president of this thing." Turnip Green Allen never understood why good old Ferd Allen would boycott Fayette.

By the mid-60s, the Klan was having a hard time of it. The Klukkers hated the Jews and the hippies and the war protesters, and they loved and worshipped Jesus Christ, a long-haired Jewish man who preached against war. No wonder they were demoralized. The Klan drove into town with Confederate flags on their cars and staged a big "buy-in" in Fayette to help the white racist merchants. But whether by meanness or plain stupidity, they passed the merchants a big load of bad checks. So we got the last laugh. Our boycott cost the town lots of money, and many whites in Fayette never forgave us.

We fought for the right to be served in the new Holiday Inn instead of at the Negro inn. But by '66, there was no point claiming all Negroes were barred from getting a cup of coffee or a night's sleep at the Holiday Inn. A few Negroes were being served at those places. Now we had to take the next step up the ladder, to help deserving Negroes get decent-paying jobs—because if you can't *afford* the Holiday Inn, then you still can't stay there.

I told Negroes to shop in black-owned grocery stores and laundries and to open their own stores. Whites snorted, "Niggers can't run anything but a juke joint." So in '66, at the south end of Fayette, I opened the Medgar Evers Shopping Center. I graded the land, laid the foundation, and built that shopping center one piece at a time: grocery store, shoe store, liquor store, ballroom, restaurant and dance hall, radio repair shop, Laundromat, and dry cleaning plant. There was a community meeting room and my living quarters behind. It all revolved around the nice little grocery store. Nan and four of my daughters worked there as cashiers.

When Mississippi finally ended prohibition in '66, I slowed my bootlegging down to a crawl. My energy went to the Medgar Evers Shopping Center. I used the motto Conrad Hilton gave me in Chicago: "Own everything you can, and run nothing." I owned every shop in my complex, but I hired twenty good Negroes to run them. They'd been making about $7.00 a week. I paid them $1.25 an hour. Negro butchers made $25.00 a week; I tripled that.

Negroes liked my shopping center and bought less at the white stores. Whites raged that I'd stolen their customers with my boycotts. I never started a boycott to help my own stores, but I'd been in business all my life, and I stayed in business during our boycotts. Whites groused about idle Negroes begging for money—but when I played smart, worked hard, and made money, just like in Philadelphia, Mississippi, I found that whites liked seeing Negroes prosperous and proud even less than they liked seeing us begging and broke. They'd say, "Charlie Evers is high on the hog." I'd say, "You go to hell. I risk my life and work eighteen hours a day."

Governor Paul Johnson claimed, "No Negroes are hungry," so I led a rally to the state capitol. I addressed Paul Johnson and all his fellow racists: "Your mind and heart are sick, but the whole world is turning against you. Your time is near." I also warned my own people: "You can't win shooting off guns because Paul Johnson has garbage trucks and tanks, he has flunky boys coming out of the forest with guns." But I told Paul Johnson, "We won't let anyone turn us around." We were too smart to riot or to build from scratch like Floyd McKissick. It was all going to be peaceful. But I couldn't wait for the day when I'd be running Fayette.

CHAPTER 19

Lyndon Johnson Said, "We Shall Overcome"

EACH TIME I MET PRESIDENT JOHNSON, he impressed me a little bit more. He had a real handhold on power, and he knew every trick in the book. But he was also a man you could talk to. Far more than most politicians, he listened, and he called a spade a spade. The liberals loved making speeches of moment. LBJ could make a good speech, but what he loved was action. He talked in order to make things happen.

The Negro leaders who knew LBJ best were Roy Wilkins; Whitney Young, head of the Urban League; and A. Philip Randolph, head of the Brotherhood of Sleeping Car Porters. But if I was in Washington raising money and wanted to see Johnson, I never called on him that I couldn't get in. I could drop by the White House and talk about Negro rights with the president of the United States. Boy, I wish my daddy could have lived to see that.

Johnson was a busy man, and sometimes Lee White tried to block me. Lee was a little fella about forty who'd worked for President Kennedy, too. Kind of an advisor on race matters. He kept Johnson in touch with the Capitol Hill boys. Part of Lee White's job was making sure Lyndon didn't spend too much time on civil rights. But I could sneak a note into Johnson's office saying I was waiting outside. Mrs. Johnson helped me get in to see her husband. Lady Bird was such a wonderful First Lady. I only met her a few times, but we'd talk on the phone. I sent her notes. She was a natural hostess and made everyone feel they knew her and loved her. She got me in that Oval Office at least once.

More often I'd call the president's appointment secretary: "This is Charles Evers. I'm in Washington. Can I come give the president a progress report?" His secretary was a white gal, real polite: "I'm sorry Mr. Evers, the president is busy today." Well, you can't let them do that to you. I'd say, real quick: "How do you know he's busy? You ain't even been in there today." Pretty soon I'd have her okay to come by the White House. I'd say, "Just clear me at the gate, honey," because security at the White House gate never got used to seeing a big black man headed for the Oval Office. I'd have to wait until Lyndon had a minute between appointments, but when he learned I was out there, he'd send for me. He liked me.

I'd walk into that Oval Office, headquarters of the most powerful man on earth, with portraits of great presidents, Teletype machines, TVs, phones to Moscow. President Johnson always wore a coat and tie when I saw him, but just underneath he was a southern country boy. Talk to him three minutes and you knew he'd been raised in farm country. He knew all about hard work, and he knew when a man comes to see you, man-to-man, you tell the truth. He was a white Texan, but I came to feel we'd come off the same stalk.

Now, let me say a word for the white southerner. No one knows more than the Evers family that he can be a gutless assassin. But you can trust most southerners even when they're wrong. If a southerner agrees to something, you can put your foot on it. If a northerner agrees—well, you just hope he gets no outside advice to the contrary. So when LBJ told me he wanted all Americans to learn and to vote, that was *real* to me. I heard a real southerner talking. Johnson had been a teacher in a poor school system in Texas. He knew very well that small southern towns had no money to fund two good separate school systems. He wanted integrated schools not just for the Negro's sake, but for the whites too. And good schools and the vote were what the civil rights movement was all about. Many northern liberals said we'd never get civil rights from Lyndon Johnson, but Lyndon took us a long way.

I learned as a boy in the Holiness Church: A man converted is your best servant. He'll be just as much for you as he was against you. Hugo Black of Alabama was once a card-carrying Klansman, proud to belong to a group of head-beating murderers. But when FDR appointed him to the Supreme Court, no judge fairer to Negroes ever sat on the bench than Hugo Black. LBJ had been a stone racist and bigot at one time. But he'd converted.

And President Johnson grew so much in office on civil rights. He saw how mean America had treated Negroes and the poor, and he put through laws giving the common Negro some power in this country. He also looked for talented individual Negroes. In '66, he made a Negro, Robert Weaver, his secretary of Housing and Urban Development. Robert Weaver was the first Negro ever in the cabinet. Johnson named a Negro, Lyle Carter, assistant secretary of Health, Education, and Welfare. Johnson made a Negro, Carl Rowan, ambassador to Finland, and a Negro, Patricia Roberts Harris, ambassador to Luxembourg.

When LBJ made Ramsey Clark of Texas his attorney general, I couldn't help but be skeptical, because Texas hasn't exactly been a paradise for civil rights. But Ramsey Clark was a wonderful man, ten years ahead of his time. His father, Tom Clark, was a good, tough man on the race issue, and Ramsey was even tougher and better.

Lyndon Johnson cared about Negroes, and so did Lady Bird. That was something we could *feel*. All our lives, we'd seen white folks damn us, kick us, and find fault. To have the president of the United States and the First Lady care about us just swept us off our feet. Lady Bird went on a Dixie tour through Mississippi in '64, and the Negroes filled up the schools and churches trying to meet her—because they knew she wanted to meet *them*. The First Lady of the land wanted to meet poor Negroes! Having grown up under segregation, that meant the world to us.

President Johnson put at least one federal program in all eighty-two counties of Mississippi: the Office of Economic Opportunity, federal preschool programs and day care centers, Head Start programs. My high-toned friends told me we weren't black anymore, we were Afro-American. I told them great, now let's use these federal programs to get Afro-Americans some good jobs.

On March 15, 1965, Lyndon Johnson made a great speech to Congress. He'd been shocked by the violence at Selma, and he went to Congress to push through some bills to help the Negro vote. LBJ spoke to a joint session of Congress, and to the whole country over TV. Johnson talked about his school-teaching days in Cotulla, Texas. He said you never forget the scars that poverty and hatred leave on children, and that's why he believed in civil rights and voting rights. He said, "It's not just Negroes, but really it's all of us, who must overcome the crippling legacy of bigotry and injustice. *And we shall overcome.*"

Lyndon Johnson said, "We shall overcome." Not: "They shall overcome." Not "The damn niggers are trying to overcome!" He said, "*We* shall overcome." The President of the United States was quoting our song, calling racism his problem and civil rights his movement. In '65, we'd never seen a mayor or a Governor do that. To have the president of the United States do it showed that Lyndon Johnson was a very great man. I vowed that for the rest of my life, I'd defend his name against all defamers. I'm still doing it.

Lyndon Johnson sometimes lost his temper and bullied men into doing his will. But he and I saw eye-to-eye, so he never tried that "persuasion" bullshit on me. Of course, we crossed swords a few times. When he put the Voting Rights Act through in '65, I asked him to enforce it by sending federal registrars to every county in Mississippi. President Johnson was a master of what every politician must do: say no. Johnson said, "Charles, that's not the way to do it. I'm going to send federal registrars into Mississippi, but not eighty-two. I'll send enough to show the federal government means business, and that whites must give you a chance to vote." "Well," I said, "if you mean business, why not send registrars into every single county?" And we argued about that, but always in good faith.

Another time I asked LBJ to put a federal record-keeping center in Decatur, Mississippi: "Just one record building could employ all the jobless in my hometown. Decatur won't have a man unemployed." President Johnson laughed: "I'm sure that's so, but how do we get the congressmen to agree to put one in Charles Evers's hometown and not in their hometown?" I didn't quit: "How about a VA hospital in Decatur or Natchez?" Hospitals have lots of good-paying jobs. LBJ said, "We've got a VA Hospital in Jackson. If you want to pursue another one, work through your congressmen." I said, "Shoot, you know who my congressmen are," and we both laughed, because taking advice from Charlie Evers was low on their list of priorities. But Lyndon Johnson knew how to say no nicely.

I also kicked sand with LBJ because I wanted the Job Corps in Mississippi. Lyndon said, "Talk to Sargent Shriver." Sargent said, "Charles, your governor won't accept it." I said, "Can't we get Lyndon to order it?" Sargent said, "The president can't just order a state. It's a volunteer program. We can't go where we're not wanted." I said, "Who're you talking to? Have any *Negroes* said you ain't wanted?" No, he'd just heard from the Great White Fathers. I said, "Sargent Shriver, the Job Corps should go where it's needed. Mississippi needs you." But I lost that round. Mississippi didn't get the Job Corps until 1977.

How do you treat radicals? That was another place I saw eye-to-eye with LBJ. We both believed you bring radicals into the system, make them play politics through the system. Lyndon built his Great Society, poured money into departments like HUD, and expected the urban Negroes to thank him. But H. Rap Brown, chairman of the SNCC, raged about "lynching Johnson" and honky genocide conspiracies. Rap Brown told his people they were at war with the white man. I'd had those thoughts myself after Beckwith killed Medgar, with far better excuse than Rap Brown, and I'd snapped out of it. I warned my people to never give up on capitalism or on democracy, either.

In '67, Lyndon Johnson appointed Thurgood Marshall to the U.S. Supreme Court. Thurgood was already U.S. solicitor general, and Lyndon wanted to appoint the first Negro ever on the Supreme Court. Most civil rights folk loved the idea of Thurgood on the Supreme Court. But I'd never wanted Thurgood to be a judge at all. I wanted him to go back to marching and bringing civil rights lawsuits. I called him: "Thurgood, they're buying you off. If they get you on the Supreme Court, you'll never bring lawsuits again. You'll never again be the loudest mouth in this country for the legal rights of Negroes." Thurgood said on the court he could make damn sure every Supreme Court justice knew one Negro well, so when they heard a racial case, it wasn't "those stupid niggers," it was "Thurgood's people." Thurgood said he could tip the Court to the liberal side, push racial justice and First Amendment cases. He said, "Charlie, there's a lot of loudmouths. Get someone else to march and bring the lawsuits."

I said, "Thurgood, get someone else to sit up on the Supreme Court! Some smart, young, well-schooled Negro who's polite, believes like we do, and can sit on the Court longer than you can. But save that big mouth of yours. If you take that job, they'll shut you up." But Thurgood was tired. He said, "At my age, I need something like this. Charlie, when you're a lawyer, you don't turn down the Supreme Court." He'd dreamed of being on that court, and after all he'd done for civil rights, Thurgood had earned the right to settle down. He was a great Supreme Court justice, but I still wish he hadn't gone on the Court.

Wars have always been fought in this country. Ever since we fought the Indians, bayonets on tomahawks, we've been killers. Lyndon Johnson had war in Vietnam brewing when he took office. And like a fool, he fanned the flames and drew the country in.

The Vietnam War was wrong as it could be. White Americans raved about "Communist infiltration," but to blacks it was so clear: America hated the Vietnamese because they were dark and were bucking Washington. The Vietnam War was no more about Communism than the civil rights movement was about Communism. The Vietnamese were fighting for their freedom, but most whites can't stand a poor, dark-skinned country that bucks the United States. Fidel Castro, Ho Chi Minh, Manuel Noriega, or Saddam Hussein—if you're not white and won't kiss our ass—look out. I liked seeing the Vietnamese beat us down almost as much as I liked Fidel Castro throttling those roughnecks Kennedy sent in to invade the Bay of Pigs.

Some Negroes I'd fought with in World War II backed the Vietnam War. They'd laid down in the jungles in World War II, praying not to die. Now they were glorifying the U.S. Army, calling the Vietnam War a noble cause, and sending young Americans back into the jungle. It made me sick. I never forgot I only joined the U.S. Army to get the hell out of Mississippi.

Some Negroes felt civil rights leaders should ignore the Vietnam War. In '65, when Martin Luther King first urged peace in Vietnam, some Negroes objected. But Martin was right to take on the war. Killing "gooks" in Vietnam and killing "niggers" in Mississippi was part of the same thing. All that time and money we wasted in Vietnam we could have used fighting poverty and racism.

Senator William Fulbright of Arkansas never did shit for the Negro, but he was one of the first big men to oppose LBJ's Vietnam policy. It cost him his friendship with Lyndon Johnson, but he did right. Muhammad Ali refused to serve in Vietnam. It hurt his name, cost him millions, but it helped his heart and soul.

The way Negroes got drafted for Vietnam was a disgrace. No white family in Mississippi would have let their boy be drafted by an all-

Negro draft board and sent off to Southeast Asia. But there were ninety draft boards in Mississippi, not a Negro on one of them, and Negroes were told to march quietly off to Vietnam. I told these young Negroes, "Refuse army induction until we integrate state draft boards." I sent some fiery telegrams to President Johnson and the Justice Department. But it took years to get a half-dozen Negro draft boards.

Great big Lyndon Johnson got whipped by the Vietnam War. One day in early '68, he up and said, "I shall not seek and I will not accept nomination of my party as your president." Just like that, he took himself out of the race. Lyndon Johnson did more for the poor than any president in history, was one of our greatest presidents, and couldn't get reelected. All because of Vietnam.

Around '67, I began seeing more in George Wallace. Sure, Wallace backed segregation. He also loved law and order, school prayer, and seeing the U.S. Army kick somebody's ass. Wallace opposed many things: taxes and bureaucrats, hippies, busing, and do-gooder social programs. But I loved the way Wallace mocked liberal hypocrisy. I loved it when he mocked "the pointy-head intellectuals who can't park a bicycle straight." I loved his toughness and the way he stood flat-footed and never wavered. Most of all I loved hearing Wallace speak up for "the poor, the lame, and the halt," because so many of those people were Negroes. George Wallace knew in his bones what it meant to be poor in this country.

I started calling him. He probably growled "That damn Evers nigger—what the hell could he want with me?" But one day he was curious enough to take my call. You often hook someone the first time because they're curious. I talked straight to George Wallace, I made sense, and he liked me. After that, he took all my calls. We got to know each other. And I saw George Wallace was no bigot.

Black folk said, "Damn, Charlie, you soft in the head? That's not your place, with George Wallace! He loosed police dogs on us when we marched. He sicced dogs on children. Stay with the Kennedys." But the Kennedys were already with us. *Leadership isn't about sitting around with your friends—it's about sitting down with your enemies.* Finding common ground. Convincing them to see right and then do right. Bringing them into the fold. So what if George Wallace called us "niggers" and liberals promised us the moon? A century ago, liberals promised us forty acres and a mule, so we don't trust words and promises. A man converted is your best servant. We'd already seen LBJ change.

So I thought, "Let's go further. What big segregationist can work with us? What big white racist can join us?" I was always hunting for powerful bigots and ex-bigots, and I decided George Wallace was my man. Peckerwood to the core. Raised by a dirt farmer. Had driven a dump truck to make ends meet and married a sixteen-year-old who worked the counter at a five-and-dime. Been a GI, then a state legislator. He'd run for president in '64 and did well in some primaries before bowing out. Wallace scared and dismayed the liberals, but I liked seeing the liberals scared and dismayed. If George Wallace was a scary man, I wanted to work with him, keep him where I could watch him. Idealists hated George Wallace, but idealists have a way of running things straight into the ground. I stuck with Wallace.

When George Wallace took his message national, he didn't change it one bit. He preached the same in California as he did in Alabama. How many politicians can say that? And what he said was real. You could put your foot on it. The liberals were shocked how many folk in this country liked George Wallace. In '68, as an outsider running for president, the man got over 13 percent of the vote. I wasn't shocked. George Wallace was onto something. He was made of the same stuff as LBJ. Not too proud to change for good reason.

I told him, "Governor, you and I are fighting for the same people, the poor and the left-out. Pool our forces, and we could unite the South, maybe even the whole country." "Well," he said, "You know, Charles, we've got to do what's politically possible, now." I asked him, "Does being governor of Alabama really mean more to you than uniting the south, rich and poor, black and white? Come on, George Wallace! Let's join hands and shock the world!" George Wallace heard me out and said, "Charles, I'm a politician." I couldn't get him to go any farther than that—then.

Black Power

CHAPTER 20

In June of '66, James Meredith returned to Mississippi. He'd graduated from Ole Miss alive but still scared of the jeers, scared of being gunned down. James Meredith decided to face down his fear. He took a walking stick and started down Highway 51 for Jackson, walking toward towns he'd known: Hernando, Senatobia, Tillatoba. Near the start of his march, he made some friends, but near Hernando, a white bastard shot Meredith in the back. Meredith went down, and the white man shot him twice more. James Meredith lived, but a hospital took sixty pellets of #4 birdshot from his back.

Martin Luther King and Roy Wilkins, Floyd McKissick and I wanted to finish James Meredith's march for him. So did Stokely Carmichael. Stokely was a young SNCC field organizer in Lowndes County with big plans and a big mouth. In May of '66, a month before the march, Stokely had been elected to replace John Lewis as head of the SNCC. Stokely wanted to make the SNCC more radical. Martin, Roy, Floyd, Stokely, and I all talked to Meredith in the hospital and agreed to start a new, bigger march down Highway 50, in his name.

Martin and other marchers often stayed in my home in Jackson before a big march. The womenfolk slept in beds, and their men on the floor. Just before the second James Meredith march, Martin spent a week with me at my 2554 Queens Road home in Jackson. Martin was nonviolent all the way, like Gandhi in India. Whites jostled and beat Martin. He always turned the other cheek, saying "Unearned suffering is redemptive." In his "Letter from Birmingham Jail," he wrote about unearned suffering being redemptive.

I didn't believe that shit for a minute! I didn't turn the other cheek. Not a preacher in the world could convince me that an undeserved ass whipping redeemed anything. Not even Martin, in ten thousand speeches. I'd say "Martin, you must meet trouble with trouble. I accept whipping from no white man!" He'd laugh, but a week later, in another speech, he'd say nonviolent suffering can be dignified. I'd take off after him again: "Martin, how can suffering be dignified? It ain't dignified!"

See, I'd analyzed how the white man had always done us. Old Negroes used to say, "The white man mistreats us, but he don't know any better, he don't know what he's doing." But I felt the white man knew *just* what he was doing. He made all Negroes suffer real bad as kids, and the suffering stripped our dignity, made us think we couldn't open businesses, vote, or get rich! I knew I was right on this, but Martin knew he was right.

Martin knew I couldn't live without guns. He loved me just the same and rarely tried to change my mind. When he arrived that week at my place on Queens Road, he found my apartment full of pistols, rifles, and automatic weapons. With Dr. King as my special guest, I even posted security officers outside. If Martin had been self-righteous, he'd have preached down to me: "Give up your guns, my friend." But Martin just looked around at all that protection and chuckled: "Charles, I'm nonviolent, but I never feel safer anywhere, with anybody, than in your home."

But at one evening rally on the Meredith march, I told the crowd we'd need guns to fight off the white man. Martin saw the crowd was with me, so he interrupted and said Byron Beckwith lived nearby. Martin said, "Charles, if you're that violent, why don't you go up the highway to Greenwood and kill the man who killed your brother?" It was very rare for Martin to get so angry in public. But that night he did what a man must do: He stood up for his beliefs.

The James Meredith Freedom March should have been a big, strong, peaceful march to honor the courage of James Meredith and all the Negro James Merediths who'd tried to walk Mississippi roads to freedom. Why do white folk shoot us down? *And what will this state and this nation do about it?* That should have been our message. And walking down a hot highway should have been just part of it. I said, "Let's walk house to house and fence to fence and register Negro voters." I helped get most of the leaders of that march to focus the march on registering voters.

But not Stokely Carmichael. On June 10, 1966, Stokely looked out at the Negro sharecroppers hugging the highway, and he started shouting, "Black Power! Black Power!" Of all the dumb things to shout, when you don't have power. But the media jumped on it. Stokely made the phrase Black Power famous. Whites asked, "What does Black Power mean? Will you try to kill us?" And Negro kids asked, "Does Black Power mean we going to whip the white folk?" And what burned me up was Black Power meant nothing!

In Canton, Mississippi, twenty miles north of Jackson, I saw us moving to a head-on blow with the National Guard and the highway patrol. I warned our marchers, "These people don't play around. If you can't back up what you say, don't provoke them." Stokely Carmichael kept raving and cussing. Well, that day in Canton in '66, the Meredith marchers set up a huge tent on a Canton campground. The National Guard tried to force us off by sending out the biggest wave of tear gas I'd ever seen. It burned and stung our eyes and stayed in our clothes for a week.

The tear gas and highway patrol sent Stokely screaming like a drowning rat, "They'll kill us all!" He skedaddled, and I saw that he'd never make a civil rights leader. No backbone, no balls. I went easy on him: "Go on back home, Stokely. Cool down, baby." But later I snapped, "Don't hand me that Black Power crap! Screaming till the police come, then squealing like a pig in a crack! And don't talk that Black Power crap to my people. If you're mad, prove it. Register voters and vote a black man into office." The crackers arrested us and locked us in jail. Stokely was quiet until we got out, then he started hollering, "Burn the damned jail!" I said, "Stokely, they just released us from that jail. Why didn't you burn it down when you were in there?"

And Stokely Carmichael, preaching black separatism, had a white girlfriend. He'd tell Negroes to "close ranks," and him closing ranks at night with a white girl! In '67, H. Rap Brown followed Stokely as head of the SNCC. Rap Brown had been fooling with a white girl, too. Like I said about whites: Those who scream the loudest about the need to segregate the races are the same ones practicing nighttime integration. The Black Power folk who screamed "Kill Whitey" the loudest never fired a gun.

Or look at Louis Farrakhan today. Farrakhan flies to a new city, checks into the Holiday Inn, snores all night, eats the white man's breakfast, then makes a speech cursing all whites. When Farrakhan came to Jackson, I challenged him: "I'm an integrationist, so I can stay at the Ritz. But how can you blast all whites and stay in a white resort?" Whenever you see bigotry, hypocrisy is real close by.

Stokely exploited the old Negro dream of a proud, separate Negro nation. He blamed not only whites for keeping it from us, but also the teachers and preachers and NAACP men who warned us that freedom is a long pull toward a team goal. Forget teamwork; Stokely was for Stokely. He shook his black fist and yelled about Black Power, but there was no black power in that fist, no money, and no plan to get either one. But Stokely sure knew how to work the media. He ran from place to place making trouble, reporters put out his every word, and many aggressive young blacks bought into Black Power.

Too bad Stokely was marching in Mississippi when he made Black Power famous, because Stokely was a New Yorker, and Black Power was the kind of chant they liked in Harlem, where blacks were free to vote, and less than 30 percent of them registered! I saw a lot of Harlem in the '60s. Folk there yelled, "Say it loud, we're black and proud!" But they weren't black and proud enough to elect someone and make him deliver, weren't proud enough to start a bakery, control a few political jobs, or even to vote.

A real case of Black Power was in Hattiesburg, Mississippi, where the NAACP started a voter registration drive, and a local Negro named Vernon Dahmer collected poll taxes for Negroes scared to pay their poll tax. I'd helped bring Vernon deeper into the movement in the '50s. He was a husky, light-skinned man, always willing to help someone. But tough. In '66, Vernon pledged to pay the poll tax of anyone who couldn't pay. He got himself on local radio and almost *ordered* blacks to vote. The very next morning, before dawn, someone firebombed Vernon's home and grocery store. Vernon got out, fired his shotgun at the fleeing white terrorists, but then died of his burns. That hit me so hard. On his deathbed, Vernon Dahmer said, "People who don't vote are deadbeats on the state." That's paying the price.

But in Harlem, folk told me they never saw their "leaders" until election day. The Harlem congressman Adam Clayton Powell could have done so much more in Congress if he'd cared about the poor Negro. He'd say, "I've paid my dues, baby." That's leadership northern-style. A real leader keeps paying his dues.

As mayor of Fayette, I once spoke up north. I said that not all our problems come from whites. Afterward, some wild-eyed, bearded black kids running the program approached me, full of Black Power. They praised me for helping blacks, but told me to "stop defending Whitey." I said, "I defend anyone, black or white, who's right. I knock anyone who's wrong." I asked these kids, "Who owns this building?"

"Probably some honky."

"No," I said. "It belongs to a white American who thinks enough of you to let you use it."

"We're paying rent," they said.

"Yeah," I said. "Where'd you get the money?"

"Well, we got a grant from—"

I said, "Name me one black foundation!"

"Well, if whites give us the money, they owe us."

"No," I said. "No one owes you nothing but a chance."

I asked them, "What do you own? What do you control?" Nothing. I said, "Without green power, you can forget Black Power." Then I told them about Fayette, where Negroes called the shots.

These young blacks kept raving about "the honkies." I said "Whites never hurt you like they've hurt me. If I don't hate them, you've got no right to." These kids told me they were coming down to Mississippi. I said, "I'll have law and order in Fayette. Come down and break the law, you're going to jail, and without bail, because I'm judge and jury." I left their white-owned building, got in my car, and drove off. I kept Black Power folks out of Fayette and told Negroes all over Mississippi to throw them out when they came. It was hard enough killing white racism in Mississippi. I wasn't going to let black racism grow.

I couldn't blame Stokely for scrapping with Roy Wilkins. Hell, I was mad at Roy myself most of the time. And I didn't mind Stokely knocking the meek, measly preachers, either. But I hated to see Stokely attack the best old Negro pastors and businessmen. Some of those old folk had tricked white folks for us, cursing them under their breath and grinning at them to get the food to feed us. It's not fair to dismiss them all as Uncle Toms.

The oldest man in my county, J. P. Lewis, was a hero of mine. When no one else would sell me land for the Medgar Evers Shopping Center, J. P. Lewis did. Black kids called J. P. Lewis an Uncle Tom. But J. P. Lewis was one of our last living links to the old civil rights movement, which came forward through folks like my parents and Mark Thomas. The movement goes on to Medgar and me and everyone who paid the price in our time, and it goes on through all the people we've inspired. Stokely Carmichael was part of that movement, but he came near the end. He had no right to urge people to forget the beginning and the middle.

Stokely Carmichael left the SNCC in '67 to become "prime minister" of the Black Panthers, then left the Panthers because they worked with whites. The SNCC's next head, H. Rap Brown, was even worse. By May 1970, folk said he was living in Algeria. Algeria! Man, we needed help in Chicago and Jackson. Stokely moved to Guinea. He should have moved to Alabama, Mississippi, or Georgia and started hammering away, county by county, to elect black mayors, sheriffs, and police. That's real black power.

I admired some Black Panther community work. I liked their breakfast program. But extremists like the Panthers never get far in politics. They lose the white moderates by talking fear and hate. The Panthers wanted me to live like them, shooting off guns, calling cops "pigs" and whites "honkies." When I refused, they branded me a capitalist. Sure, I was! But those rascals were, too. Sleeping with rich blondes, riding around in Cadillacs—it amazed me how many white liberals fell for their radical political line. The Panthers bragged about all the guns they had. Listen: The Panthers didn't have guns enough to kill ten rabbits. What they had were big, bad words they used for "psychological warfare." When I was a boy, we just called it "bluff."

But there was one thing I liked about the Black Power boys and the Black Panthers: They changed Charles Evers from a "radical" to a "moderate." White moderates who feared the Panthers decided Charlie Evers wasn't so bad. I'd tell whites, "You better deal with me, because some wild-eyed Black Power haters are coming right behind me."

One day in Jackson, about '67, I was coming from a meeting. Across from the state office building, thirty military kids were drilling together. Twenty-eight whites and two Negroes, drilling their hearts out. White folk stared—from the street, from the windows of the state office building, from cars passing the drill ground. So many white eyes stared at the two races, working so crisply together. I got mad at those watching. I thought, "If you can just leave kids alone, they'll forget race." But I was staring, too. We all magnify our differences, watch too closely, wondering if racial integration will work, instead of *making* it work.

Losing Martin, Losing Bobby

CHAPTER 21

IN THE EARLY '60S, Bobby Kennedy thought a lot about how it felt to be poor and black in America, but until '67 he'd never seen how the poorest southern Negroes lived. Then Bobby got on Senator Joseph Clark's subcommittee on poverty and found out the Agriculture Department was overseen by Negro-hating southern politicians. Bobby learned that our federal food programs were designed to give farmers a good crop price—not to feed the poor.

One day in '67, Bobby said, "Charles, is poverty really that bad in Mississippi?" I said, "Bobby, words can't express it." He said, "I'm coming down." Joe Clark brought his subcommittee down. They hit Mississippi in the spring of '67.

A bunch of us talked one night in the Heidelberg Hotel in Jackson: Aaron Henry, Fannie Lou Hamer, Marian Wright Edelman, too. Marian was Marian Wright then, and had worked three years in Mississippi. A year later, she married Bobby's aide, Peter Edelman. Oscar Carr was there, a rich white planter who headed First National Bank of Clarksdale but had joined the civil rights movement after the James Meredith riot at Ole Miss in '62. Oscar Carr helped the Negro all he could.

We talked about the Mississippi Delta area, in northwest Mississippi. Bobby mostly listened. Aggressive as he was, he was also shy. The next day Bobby said, "I've heard enough about the Mississippi Delta. Now I want to go see it." At a job training center in Greenville, Bobby fidgeted while some bureaucrats talked about local employment. Bobby wanted to meet real families. So we carried him all through the Delta, driving muddy back roads in the heat. We went through the poorest part of the Delta, through some of those same Negro hamlets that had changed Medgar fifteen years before, when he was a young man selling insurance for Dr. Howard.

One afternoon, near Cleveland, Mississippi, we walked into the worst Negro shack I'd ever seen. Big holes in the floor, hardly a ceiling. A little stove in the corner. A bed black as my arm, propped up by bricks. Rats and roaches all over the floor. Piss and mildew so bad I could hardly keep the nausea down. In the tiny back room, Bobby met a boy four years old, wearing just an undershirt. Bobby followed that little boy around, looked at the kitchen with him. Miss Annie White came out wearing pitiful rags. Bobby introduced himself. We told her we wanted to help. She held out her arms: "Thank God." She had six kids. We saw a little girl with a swollen stomach rubbing grains of rice on the floor. Bobby spent five minutes talking with that girl, stroking, tickling, and poking her. She wouldn't respond.

Bobby said, "My God, I didn't know this kind of thing existed. How can a country like this allow it? Maybe they just don't know." The little boy came toddling out of the back room, stomach sticking out like he was pregnant. Bobby picked him up, sat down on the dirty, broken-down bed, and rubbed that little swollen stomach. Bobby stared at the child and some other local kids who'd appeared, and big tears streamed from his eyes, ran down his cheeks. Boy, that got me. We sat talking fifteen minutes, then Bobby said, "I'm going back to Washington to do something about this." His hand quivered. His eyes were lit with passion.

And the man kept his promise. He went back to Washington and worked his butt off to raise up the poor. I've never been fazed by famous men. I saw, as a boy, most "great men" aren't worth a damn. White culture told me that Jim and Jessie Evers were shit and James O. Eastland was a great man. But my family told me that wasn't true, the Bible told me it wasn't true. I just *knew* it wasn't true. I loved Bobby Kennedy not because he was famous, but because he lived like a man should. Reaching out, working hard, loyal to his family. Always learning and trying to help folks in need.

Byron Beckwith, the vicious killer of Medgar, was the complete opposite of Bobby Kennedy. In '67, Beckwith ran for lieutenant governor of Mississippi. He had no background in politics. His one "qualification" was killing my brother. His platform was "absolute white supremacy." He said whites were God's chosen people, and Negroes were "beasts in the field." I wanted to run against Beckwith, to show that Mississippi could rise above him. But when I told Bobby Kennedy my plan, he said, "Don't do it, Charles." Bobby sensed if I'd had to watch Byron Beckwith campaign every day, I might have tried to kill Beckwith. He said, "Charles, don't run out of spite. You'll get in trouble. You can do too much good in other places."

I said, "Bobby, I want to get back at Beckwith some kind of way." But after a long talk, I took Bobby's advice, stayed out of the race. Beckwith only got thirty-five thousand votes, fifth out of six candidates. That cold-blooded killer shouldn't have gotten one damn vote. But I didn't run against him because Bobby convinced me, "Charles, if you run, it's just hate against hate."

Then one day in '68, Bobby called me from California, told me he was running for president and needed my help. Now it was my turn to say, "Don't run." Most of Bobby's friends thought he'd run for president one day. But he was still young, and people thought Lyndon would run again. Bobby's people talked about '72 or '76.

Bobby liked the limelight, but he also had to carry out his brother's legacy. I felt the same doing Medgar's work. Neither of us could stand to let the haters win by killing our brother. To carry out John Kennedy's legacy, Bobby felt he had to be elected president. So I knew why Bobby was running. But I didn't like it.

Bobby and I wrangled. Young voters liked Eugene McCarthy because he'd pressed LBJ early to leave Vietnam. If Bobby jumped in, he'd be playing catch-up, not just against Lyndon but against another Irish-Catholic in Gene McCarthy. And, God, Bobby hated to lose. Also, I couldn't oppose Lyndon Johnson—even for Bobby. LBJ had done more for the poor and black than any American president ever. When Bobby said he planned to run for president, I said, "Against LBJ? No, Bobby." My friends Bobby and Lyndon, our two biggest voices for the poor, hated each other. I said, "Bobby, if you run against Lyndon Johnson, you'll split civil rights folk down the middle. Neither one of you'll be elected."

Before Bobby came in, I even urged Lyndon to stay in the race. I sent him a telegram and told him face-to-face, "Please don't step down. You run." Tough old LBJ shocked me with his weak answer: "I don't know, Charles. It's getting pretty rough." And he complained about his health. He said, "I don't feel too good. Some of the younger men can probably do a better job." I said, "Who? All those who might replace you, I have less faith in."

Many of Bobby's friends felt he should stay out of the race. Even Ted Kennedy advised Bobby to stay out. But when I urged Bobby to stay out, he bristled. He said Johnson was bleeding Vietnam. Bobby said, "He won't end the war. He's a hawk." I said, "Bobby, isn't America a hawk? Black and white, rich and poor—we're known to fight. Look how we stomped the Indians."

Bobby looked me in the eye: "If I run, will you support me?" I looked him right back: "Bobby, I can't oppose Lyndon Johnson. The man's done too much for my people. The two of you butting heads makes no kind of sense." We argued. Bobby said Gene McCarthy had already split the party wide open. Bobby saw Richard Nixon would be the Republican nominee, and Bobby hated the thought of *President* Richard Nixon. Bobby didn't like my opposing him, but he accepted it. Talking sense to Bobby was a kind of loyalty he respected. He liked men who thought for themselves.

I feared Bobby would get shot on the campaign trail. His staff worried about this, too. Bobby knew the danger of walking the streets when so many people loved and hated his family. But we never discussed it directly. Once I was heading back to Mississippi after meeting with Bobby. He said, "Be careful, Charles, because we don't need another Evers brother to go down." He knew that applied to him, too; we didn't need another Kennedy brother going down. But Bobby never talked about being killed. He made himself believe it wouldn't happen.

I kept telling Bobby, "Don't run," and Bobby kept saying, "If I do run, will you support me?" Finally, I said, "Alright, Bobby, if I have to tell you: No, I won't support you." Bobby pressed on, mailed me a letter saying he was running for president and needed my support. So I called him. I said, "You don't need me, Bobby. You got all those other play people." It was true he didn't need Charles Evers to run a strong race. But that "play people" stuff was to tease him. There was always a pack of smooth-mouth liberals and cocktail party activists hanging around the Kennedys. I'd tease Bobby pretty harsh, pretend he was still a rich kid who ignored the poor. I did that too much, and I never meant any of it.

This time Bobby took me dead serious: "Charles, what do you mean 'play people'?" Bobby couldn't stand to hear this from a friend.

I started to back down. I said, "You know, your people—" Bobby said, "Charles, you're my people." What could I say? I loved the man. I agreed to work for him. I said, "I don't want money for this. But if you win, remember my people." I knew he would. The poor and the outcast were becoming his people, too. Bobby made me and Oscar Carr cochairmen of his campaign in Mississippi, when it was unheard of down south to have white and Negro state cochairs.

On the evening of April 4, 1968, I was driving Highway 28 to Natchez. I had the radio on, but my mind was on that night's rally in Natchez. The next day I was supposed to fly to Memphis to help Martin with a Negro garbage strike there. Suddenly a white voice came on the radio: Martin had been shot in Memphis. He'd been staying at the Lorraine Motel. He'd walked out on the motel balcony for a breath of fresh air and got drilled by a dirty sniper. I started praying he'd be alright.

In Natchez, I went straight to Mamie Lee Mazique's house. Everybody there was hugging the radio, trying to catch news of Martin's condition. After the rally that night, we learned Martin had been shot flush in the face with a high-powered rifle. He was dead. Lord, that hurt to hear.

Martin knew many violent people wanted him dead. He accepted that. We'd talked about death many times. He used to say, "Charles, we're living in evil times." I should have known the haters would take him, but since they'd taken Medgar, the Lord knew I couldn't afford to let them have Martin. I'd come back a long way in the five years since they'd killed Medgar, and Martin was a big reason why. We'd counseled each other a lot, cheered each other up many times. But Martin's murder almost wiped me out.

In God's eyes, a poor Negro garbageman in Memphis is as good as the richest white man on earth. That's why Martin went up to Memphis to help that garbage strike. Senator James O. Eastland wasn't a bit more important to God than a garbageman. How long can Memphis stay beautiful if no one hauls garbage? Trust me, this could have been a beautiful world without James Eastland.

Martin's death seemed like Medgar's death all over again. The same cops who'd never tried to protect Martin launched a "manhunt" for his killer. Roy Wilkins, always so jealous of Martin, was broken up at Martin's passing. Very few Negroes had supported Martin properly.

I should have done more myself. And whites had been far, far worse. Then, as soon as he was killed, all these damn know-it-alls started bragging how close they'd been to Martin.

The FBI had never guarded Martin's life—they'd always been too busy bugging Martin's house, tapping his phone, tarring him as a Communist and sex pervert. That old tyrant J. Edgar Hoover kept huge files on Martin, snooped around, made private tape recordings of Martin. Hoover's boys had invaded Martin's privacy, even tried to blackmail him. Now they claimed they were pained by Martin's murder. They arrested a two-bit hood named James Earl Ray and said he'd shot Martin from the bathroom of a rooming house across the way. Ray had pulled little jobs across the country. He pled guilty to killing Martin and got ninety-nine years in jail.

The cops and FBI said James Earl Ray had killed Martin because Ray was a racist hungry for fame. They said James Earl Ray acted alone. Don't you believe it. Martin's killing was a well-greased conspiracy, white run, and whitewashed. James Earl Ray was paid to murder Martin by folk much bigger, richer, and smarter than he was. Come on, FBI! On Monday a dumb drifter can't stick up a gas station without his mama, and Tuesday he's moving across America and Canada, through Europe, like James Bond. Huge sums of money at his beck and call, forged passports and travel documents. The FBI asked us to believe James Earl Ray did all this on his own. There was big white racist money behind Martin's killing. I can't prove it, but you smell this kind of thing, and this stunk to high hell.

Martin was a famous man who never acted famous, a wonderful man, moral and true. There are talkers, and there are doers. Your soul craves great speeches, but you need a man to get things done. Martin was a great talker and a great doer who led us to freedom. Martin just wanted everyone to be free to enjoy all that God put on this earth. He never tried to hurt white folk. He prayed for them. Showed them the way. And one of them shot him dead.

I talked to Martin in '64 right after he won the Nobel Peace Prize. I'm a peace lover, but I love money, too. I said, "Martin, what you going to do with all the money from your Nobel Prize?" He had over fifty thousand dollars coming. He said, "Charlie, it doesn't belong to me." I said, "You're kidding." He said, "No, I'm not kidding. It doesn't belong to me." He drove an old car, lived in a rented home, gave everything to the movement. A beautiful man. Next to Martin, I always felt like a sonofabitch.

Bobby Kennedy had never been close to Martin. Maybe he regretted having the FBI wiretap Martin. But Bobby was hit hard by the assassination. Riots broke out all around the country at the news. When big parts of Washington, D.C., burned, Bobby and Ethel walked with Peter Edelman and Marian Wright Edelman right through the riot corridor. Later, Bobby took up many of Martin's issues.

They held Martin's funeral in his old church in Atlanta, Ebenezer Baptist. I went all to pieces, almost as bad as I had at Medgar's funeral. Just like after Medgar's death, Bobby Kennedy helped me with my grief. Before Martin's funeral, Bobby and Ethel consoled me. We all sat inside Ebenezer Baptist Church. Hubert Humphrey, Eugene McCarthy, Nelson Rockefeller. I was sitting with Earl Graves, Bobby, Ethel, Ted, and some friends of the Kennedys. I broke down in that church, and Bobby took me in his arms.

Then President Johnson walked in the church. Everyone sitting with Bobby jumped up, out of respect for the Oval Office—even Ethel and Ted. Bobby ordered them to sit down. With LBJ watching all this, Bobby just snatched them back down! That was so rude to Johnson and the presidency—and at a church funeral! I said, "You can't do that, Bobby!" But he did. Always a fighter.

Bobby and I left the church together, walking through a crowd of thousands toward the cemetery, for another service. A man shouted, "Hey, there's Senator Kennedy!" A crowd surged toward us. I told Bobby, "Stay in line. We'll walk straight on through." This was a funeral procession, not a damn campaign event. I walked on one side of Bobby, Earl Graves on the other. People pulled on Bobby, and Earl pushed them off, trying to protect Bobby. But Bobby Kennedy was a hardhead. He said, "Get out of the way, Earl. If they want to shake my hand, I want to shake their hand." The crowd pawed at him, climbed over each other to touch him. I said, "Earl, if he doesn't want protection, let them snatch at him."

Bobby was carrying his coat on his shoulder. I said, "Bobby, put that coat on!" At a southern Negro funeral, it was poor taste for a mourner to reach the cemetery with no suit jacket. Specially a rich white man. I knew someone in that crowd would snatch Bobby's suit jacket if they could. I said, "Bobby, put your coat on," but he walked on, jacket over his shoulder. A young white girl darted in, snatched Bobby's jacket, and took off running. Bobby jumped to go after her. I held him back. Today, that girl's a middle-aged lady. I bet she's still got that jacket.

Now Bobby was in his shirtsleeves and knew he'd done wrong leaving the funeral procession. I glared at him. Bobby looked sheepish: "Charles, you don't have to rub it in." I said "Can't tell you nothing. Next time, these people will snatch your cuff links and the shirt off your back." Bobby got back in line, and we passed on to the cemetery. Old hardhead Bobby sat up on the platform in his shirtsleeves, sticking out like a sore thumb.

Heading to the cemetery, Bobby and I walked with the reporter Jimmy Breslin. Breslin was surprised how few white faces were along that funeral route. He asked Bobby if the death of Martin would change anything in this country. Bobby said no, it wouldn't. Then Bobby turned to me: "You think this'll change anything?" All my old bitterness spilled out. Medgar, John Kennedy, and now Martin had all died in a country that encouraged its bigots to kill the leaders they hated. I said to Bobby, "This won't change nothing. It meant nothing when my brother was killed." I don't believe that now, but I believed it on the day of Martin's funeral.

When LBJ left the race, Bobby and I were as shocked as anyone. Politics was everything to Lyndon Johnson. Even with all his troubles, we never thought he'd head for the sidelines. But he did. And finally Lyndon and Bobby stopped butting heads.

In May of '68, Bobby won some Democratic primaries. He won the Indiana primary, won primaries in Washington, D.C., and Nebraska. If Bobby became president, I planned to be one of his advisors. I'd go on special assignment to Africa or Asia, do economic development there, help them get out of bamboo huts. But then Bobby lost the Oregon primary. At the end of May, he said if he lost California, he'd bow out. Bobby asked me to join him on the campaign trail.

So everything was on California, and when I got out there to campaign for Bobby, I worked like a dog. I hate taking orders, but I took orders from Bobby because the candidate must be boss of his own campaign. Bobby and his aides could make even real hard work fun. John Doar and John Seigenthaler were good men. Old Pierre Salinger always smoked big cigars. Ted Sorensen was one of the nicest guys I've ever known. We all knew we were doing something important. Excited people were everywhere: blacks, Mexicans, young girls, college kids, reporters. You saw the passion in Bobby's eyes and in those quivering hands. He kept saying, "This is a time to begin again." And, "We can do better." But sometimes you saw him riding by car from one campaign event to another, slumped in his seat, just staring out the window.

I'll always regret squabbling with Bobby the last day of his life. I rode with Bobby in a blue gray convertible through a black neighborhood on June 5, 1968, the day of the California primary. I was riding in front of the convertible, with Rafer Johnson and a few other Negroes, trying to keep the crowd from lunging into the car or hurting Bobby some other way. It was my job to keep him safe. I wasn't going to let anyone shoot him like they did Medgar.

But Bobby loved crowds. He told a roaring crowd in Watts that he'd end the Vietnam War. His tie was loose and his hair was ruffled. He leaned way out of the car. I could keep the crowd from lunging in, but I couldn't keep Bobby from leaning out. I yelled back over my shoulder, "Bobby! Stay in the car, damn it!" Bobby expected to be treated rough. I yelled, "What would happen if you fell out of this car?" Bobby grinned and said, "You'd pick me up." I lost my cool, said, "To hell with you!" and turned Bobby over to Rafer Johnson. Rafer had won the Olympic decathlon in '64. I figured he might be able to keep Bobby in the car.

That night, Bobby won the California primary. I sat around with Rafer and the football star Rosey Grier in Bobby's suite at the Ambassador Hotel, watching the returns come in on TV. Steve Smith, husband of Bobby's sister Jean, was there. Steve was a cool cat who'd been working for Bobby in California for months and had gathered lots of campaign staff. Frank Mankiewicz was there. Many others. Real nice, hardworking people.

Then Bobby sat down right in the middle of this big, tired, happy group, and together we watched those returns roll in. Very good news. We were about to win California. Not only could Bobby stay in the race, but the road was clear to the nomination. Maybe even the White House. But I was still ticked at Bobby for leaning so far out of that damn convertible. I was pouting.

Chuck Quinn of NBC, who'd covered so much civil rights action, was in Bobby's suite. CBS had already projected Bobby the winner of the California primary, but not NBC. I kidded Chuck Quinn: "Chuck, what the hell! Why not project Bobby the winner?" He said, "Well, no. We're going to make sure." I kidded Chuck Quinn that he was against Bobby, and Bobby played along.

As it sunk in we'd just won a big primary, I looked around that room at a bunch of Kennedy loyalists, relaxed, unguarded, bubbling over with joy. I stopped pouting. Bobby went around the room, shaking every hand. When he reached me, I said, "Don't thank me. I'm doing all this because I believe in you." I'll never forget those last few moments with Bobby. He knew he'd achieved something big, and he was able to enjoy it.

But Bobby always had to keep moving. Already we could hear the crowd downstairs in the ballroom chanting: "We want Kennedy! We want Kennedy!" All of us in Bobby's suite watched live network TV coverage of the ballroom. The crowd was dancing around down there. Balloons and streamers were out. Bobby had to go down, accept victory, thank his troops, and give a news conference. Our private moment in the suite was over.

Bobby said, "Okay, let's go." Everyone got up. Rosie and Rafer got up. I just sat there. I thought I'd watch Bobby's speech on TV. I was still pouting a little, and I've never liked thick crowds. I can't stand being packed in a tight space. Bobby saw me sitting there: "Charles, aren't you going?" I said, "No, you don't need all your black boys down there with you. I'm going to stay behind and watch you from here." Bobby said, "Aw, come on." I said, "No, I'll stay here." Bobby shrugged and left, but I knew he wanted me downstairs, and as soon as the door closed behind him I had a funny urge to get downstairs. I gave him just enough time to push through the crowd, then jumped up and went down after him.

The ballroom was even rowdier than it looked on TV. Noisy, happy, crowded. Balloons underfoot. I pushed my way through the crowd toward the speaker's platform. Bobby was just standing up to speak. He and I had a signal when he was speaking. He liked to see me in the crowd crooking a finger. I crooked a finger. Bobby saw me, smiled, and nodded. After his microphone was fixed, Bobby thanked all his helpers. The athletes: Rafer and Rosie, Don Drysdale. Cesar Chavez, who Bobby loved dearly. All the Kennedy staff. All the volunteers.

Bobby finished his speech and turned to leave the stage. Time for his news conference in the pressroom upstairs. I moved toward him. I thought he'd leave by the front door to go up the elevator to the pressroom, but he turned and left by a kitchen I didn't know was there. I was five feet from Bobby when he stopped, shook hands with two Mexican kitchen workers. The crowd was too thick for me. I moved to leave, caught Bobby's eye, and waved my hand, signaling that I'd catch up to him later.

That same second, I heard a loud ffat-ffat. I thought it was balloons breaking. But a little Palestinian punk, Sirhan Sirhan, had shot Bobby. He shot into the crowd about five times with a snubnose .22. The whole crowd near Bobby swirled together, writhing like one living thing. Rosey Grier pinned Sirhan Sirhan and took away his gun. Bobby had taken three bullets, one in the head. He crumpled and fell down on the concrete kitchen floor. Someone shrieked, "Oh, my God! They shot the senator!" People wedged together, trying to reach Bobby. Bobby had no Secret Service, and maybe he should have, but he had bodyguards, and they came swarming.

I plowed through that crowd like I was back playing football for Alcorn. I knocked down anyone in my path. When I reached Bobby, Ethel was crouched over him, screaming. Bobby was on the kitchen floor, surrounded by food scraps and cigarette butts, lying in puddles of his own blood. I could see right off that Bobby had a severe head wound.

Ever since Medgar had been killed, Bobby had been my best friend in the world. Now he was dying too, shot by another of the haters. This was almost worse than Medgar, because I'd never seen Medgar lying in his own blood—by the time I'd reached Jackson, he'd been all cleaned up. But I had to watch Bobby dying right in front of me, in all that blood. So insane. Such a waste.

On the last day of Bobby's life, I'd been scrapping with him. I always did too many little things to upset him. Leaning out of that campaign car was the most natural thing in the world to Bobby. Reaching out to strangers was what Bobby Kennedy was all about, and I'd snapped at him for it. I felt so bad about that when I knew he was gone.

I'd always thought I knew why the haters got Medgar: because he was a Negro, without bodyguards, without Charles Evers there to stop it. Bobby Kennedy was white, had plenty of bodyguards and me right there with him. And the haters still got him. As the cops took Sirhan Sirhan into custody, I tried to take it all in.

We got Bobby to Good Samaritan Hospital. His entourage arrived. Most of them still hoped some fancy surgeon could save him. But having run a funeral home, I'd seen too many head wounds. I knew if he lived, he'd be a vegetable. And Bobby could never have stood sitting in a chair somewhere, too dumb to understand. He'd have killed himself first. All night I stayed with Bobby at the hospital, praying he *wouldn't* make it, just praying he'd pass away clean, without pain.

As the sun rose, I sat on the front steps of the Ambassador Hotel thinking of Medgar, John Kennedy, Martin. Now Bobby. In five years, almost all my heroes had been shot to death. Everyone I was really close to. Everyone who offered the nation some hope of bringing the races together. Bobby lingered on for some hours, but the next day, June 6, 1968, Frank Mankiewicz came out and made it official: Bobby was dead. Part of me died that day.

Bobby truly believed "we can do better," and then that little punk killed him. The United States couldn't do any better than that. I stumped a little for Hubert Humphrey in '68, but not with my heart. I've rarely spoken about that day in Los Angeles. Aside from the day Medgar was killed, it was the worst day of my life. It was harder to take than the passing of my own parents, because the shock was so much bigger. It was harder to take than Martin's death, because no Bobby Kennedy could console and inspire me.

I flew back with Bobby's casket to New York on a presidential jet that LBJ had sent for Bobby and his family. Ethel was on that plane, pregnant again; Teddy Kennedy was on the plane, with his sisters, Patricia and Jean. Jackie Kennedy was there, and Coretta Scott King. In New York, I was too shook up to be one of Bobby's pallbearers. I came down to Washington by train. Since Bobby's death, nothing else has ever really hurt me.

Bobby was one of those very few men who always tried to make the world better, never broke his word, never hit you from behind. After Medgar, John Kennedy, and Martin were gunned down, Bobby seemed like our last hope. If Bobby had been president, he'd have bit the bullet on race and healed some of the terrible divisions we still have in this country. But in the end, the haters got Bobby before he had a chance.

Mourning Bobby, I saw I could give up—or work twice as hard to carry on Medgar, Martin, and Bobby's work. I took the second road, because I knew God had to be keeping me alive for some good reason. If Bobby had lived, I'd have never run for office. I'd have been a businessman, a hustler, an NAACP man—maybe even a political appointee—but I'd have never run for political office.

CHAPTER 22

Running for Congress: Evers for Everybody

IN JANUARY OF 1968, after twenty-one years in Congress, old John Bell Williams left to be the new governor of Mississippi. We had a special election to fill his seat in the third congressional district. The district covered twelve counties and had the second-largest Negro vote in the state. But no Negro wanted to run. A few friends asked me to run, real nice. I said no. Then in late January, Negroes started grumbling: "Mississippi Negroes will never be in Congress. Not even Charlie Evers can change that." That kind of sorry thinking made me *furious*. I brooded a few days, then announced for Congress.

I took leave as state head of the NAACP and got Lawrence Guyot to run my campaign. Lawrence was head of the Mississippi Freedom Democratic Party. The MFDP was full of racists and camera seekers, but Lawrence Guyot had a good political mind and happily paid the price. Once when Fannie Lou Hamer and some others got arrested in Winona, Mississippi, Lawrence Guyot walked in the police station alone, to check on bail. Cops beat and tortured him for hours, threatened to burn his dick off, then gave him to a local doctor who said he understood Lawrence had been in a car accident. Lawrence Guyot healed, looked those white bastards dead in the eye, and never stopped chasing civil rights.

Our campaign office was across the street from Jackson State, and Jackson State volunteers drove poll watchers and voters to the polls. The federal election observers were local whites, so we found our own lawyers to watch the polls. I loved campaigning. Waving to people, calling their names, hugging them, challenging them to vote and to make their friends and family vote—all this came natural. But I was running not just for Charles Evers, but for all Negroes. For Medgar. For Vernon Dahmer, whose killer was tried in Hattiesburg during the campaign. For Wharlest Jackson. For all who'd died for freedom. Win or lose, I meant to prove that a Negro could run for Congress in Mississippi and get many Negroes registered and voting on Election Day.

It sounds funny, but I was running for the white folks, too. Many Mississippi whites had never seen a Negro run for political office, never stopped to think what Mississippi Negroes needed. I made them stop and think. I needed white votes to win the race. My campaign poster said EVERS FOR EVERYBODY. I aimed to represent every man, woman, and child in that district. And I shared more with the whites than most of them knew. I believed in free enterprise and hard work. I was as proud of Mississippi as they were. I was so loyal to Mississippi, I'd risk my life for it.

Whites said too many Negroes took welfare. I surprised them by agreeing. You hear the word "workfare" a lot in politics today. I invented that word. I told folks you'll *work* for your government check. If you're handicapped, maybe it's piecework, but you will work. I promised to bring federal money into our schools and to expand Medicare, but on welfare I was a conservative. I promised to dredge the Pearl River and start shipbuilding on it. I told the voters I'd bring in textile mills and industry. Mississippi has always had lots of cheap labor. I said if the races could live in peace, new industry would put cash in all our pockets.

The first primary had about six white racist candidates, and me. The white vote split pretty good. I got all the Negro vote and won the primary by a plurality of seventy-five hundred votes. But I needed a majority, so the top white finisher, Charlie Griffin, and I had a runoff. Griffin had been a Washington aide to John Bell Williams for eighteen years and was pushing John Bell's same tired old policies.

The Board of Trustees of the Mississippi Institutions of Higher Learning banned me from addressing state-supported colleges. But white students at Ole Miss and Mississippi State sued just to hear me speak. Young whites had begun seeing that their parents were wrong about race. The next generation aimed to do better.

The kids at Mississippi College asked me to speak on campus. Mississippi College was a Baptist school west of Jackson. Lily-white. The most racist school you could imagine. Governor Ross Barnett had gone there. In '68, the school's board of trustees gave up its federal funding rather than admit Negroes. They wouldn't let a Negro in the door, even as a janitor. But students at Mississippi College invited the runoff candidates to speak on campus, including Charles Evers. School officials banned me, but the students won the right to hear me speak.

I reached the campus in early March of '68, so nervous I could hardly walk out on stage. I'd never felt so much like a dumb nigger. Cops and highway patrol were everywhere. I'd never heard of a lynching on a college campus, but this could have been one. Then I came out, and the crowd's roar struck me mute. When I spoke, they bowed their heads, and that released me. My voice carried, I cursed the scourge of racism, and those whites cheered my every point. Like I said, when white folk finally come around, they tend to overdo it. They opened doors for me, ushered me around campus like a hero. I told them to just listen to my words on behalf of the Negroes of this state. They listened. That meant the world to me.

The election was big news in Mississippi. Whites who disliked a Charlie Griffin used to say, "I'm going fishing." I said, "Go fishing! You might wake up with a Negro congressman." I scared some people. One white man offered me fifty thousand dollars to withdraw—in small bills, or any way I wanted it. I won't say who made the offer. No point making a scandal. But I'll tell you two things: I knew the man enough to know the offer was real. And I turned it down flat. I also got subpoenaed to answer a trumped-up charge of speeding. That's how the high-toned whites dealt with me.

Another group of scared whites came after me. One night, driving home with a week left in the race, I saw a car circling my house. I had no security in my campaign office, but I did what Roy Wilkins should have done for Medgar: I kept guards around my home. That night, volunteer Milton Cooper was on duty, behind a bush by my driveway. Five times the car circled my house. Then a white voice said, "Shoot the nigger!" and a shotgun shot up the house. Cooper shot three bullets back. The assassins took off with a lot of squealing tires and never came back. I stayed in the race.

I recruited sixty tough young Negroes to defend me and my crowds from anyone dumb enough to attack us. Whites called it my "goon squad." They could go to hell. That goon squad did nothing except to folks who picked a fight with us. We did lean on Negroes a little to vote for me, because our homes, jobs, and schools would never improve until Negroes held power. I expected those on my payroll to vote for me. What kind of man pays people not to vote for him? And I told my cab drivers, "Don't haul Negroes who get in your cab saying they won't vote for a nigger. Stop the cab and put them out on the street." But compared to what the Klukkers did at election time, I was a real softie.

Special elections get low turnout. They forecast bad weather this time, which also keeps voters home. But on March 12, 1968, 85 percent of those registered voted in the runoff. That district had never seen so many white voters. I'll take some credit for that. I got 99 percent of the Negro vote, but very few white votes. Moderate whites liked my message, but they still went for Charlie Griffin. Charlie got every cracker vote in the district and beat me eighty-seven thousand votes to forty-three thousand. That hurt. But getting a Negro candidate in a major state race was itself a victory. I raised issues never before heard in a Mississippi congressional race. My campaign inspired many Negroes and even brought some whites along on the race issue.

Election night, my campaign celebrated at the Masonic Temple in Jackson. I made sure those Jackson State kids were dancing because the Klan had put a fifteen-thousand-dollar contract on my head, vowed to kill me by Election Day, and here I was, alive and well. But more than Charles Evers was alive. The Negro cause was alive and well. I told the crowd we'd just become a political force in Mississippi. From now on, white candidates would have to discuss our issues in public. Congressman Charlie Griffin would feel heat from white *and* Negro. I thanked all Mississippi's Negro factions for joining hands and proving we could shift the balance between two white candidates. And until we'd built a state political machine, that's what I vowed we'd do. Help the white moderates. Campaign against the haters. Educate and train our people.

I went to Charlie Griffin's headquarters to shake his hand. He hadn't invited me, but I'd learned a long time before not to sit around waiting for invitations from white folk. Charlie Griffin was surprised to see me, but he couldn't have been more gracious. He shook my hand, told me I'd run a strong race. Three years before, I'd never have gotten that. Now Charlie Griffin wanted to shake my hand because that hand had forty thousand votes in it. That night I knew I could pick up a phone and dicker with the biggest men in Mississippi: Jamie Whitten, John Stennis, James O. Eastland. They didn't care a damn about civil rights, but they cared about votes, and I had forty thousand of them. The Great White Fathers stopped talking all that hatred as soon as we got all these votes. And you know what that means? They never really hated us. They used us.

By '68, lots of folk wanted black studies courses. It was so clear we'd never been taught one-tenth of the history of Negroes in America. Fannie Lou Hamer ripped black schoolteachers: "Why didn't you tell us a black man invented blood transfusions? Why didn't you tell us the first man to die in the Revolution was black? You going to have to teach what is necessary to teach!" I said, "Let's not have militant black studies programs teaching black kids only. Segregation in curriculum makes no more sense than any other kind. Let's teach black studies to all races." Whites must learn how blacks have served this country and have been abused here. Whites must grow up respecting what's best in black culture.

But I also said, "Not all black is beautiful." Some of it's a damn disgrace. Run-down homes, piss-poor schools, rape and robbery, picking cotton, getting beaten and lynched by drunken white thugs. Why preserve that? Give us jobs and clean, quiet neighborhoods—not some "authentically black" street where kids rip up my car.

The Bible says: "The son shall rise against the father and the daughter against the mother." In the '60s, we saw it. Negroes, white hippies rose up, too. White kids were ashamed that their ancestors had killed the Indians, stolen their land, bought African slaves. Crew-cut white folks couldn't understand why their sons would become freaks with ponytails. But as a Negro, I could, because hippies had been treated like Negroes. Politicians took cheap shots at them. Cops roughed them up.

The best answer to student unrest was adult unrest. But folks were scared to change. A white New Orleans boy asked me how he could tell his parents that everything they'd ever taught him about Negroes was wrong. I said, "Introduce your church and your family to your black friends. There's only so much your folks will do to their own flesh and blood. Work on them." At the same time, I had to keep angry blacks from drifting into violence.

In 1968 I helped Mississippi blacks move into the national political system. And I did it in my old stomping ground, Chicago. As '68 came up, a group of us, black and white, called ourselves the Loyal Democrats of Mississippi, or Loyalists. Aaron Henry was a Loyalist, and Patt Derian, an activist in Jackson. We had two lawyers from Greenville, Wes Watkins and Doug Wynn. The state Democratic Party shut us out, so we held our own precinct convention, our own county and state nominating conventions. We kept legal records of how the state party scorned us.

In June of '68, the Democratic party convention in Jackson chose sixty folk for the Mississippi delegation to the Democratic National Convention. I was one of just three Negroes chosen. But damned if I'd be a tool of the white Democrats of Mississippi. So we asked the convention to swear loyalty to the national Democratic Party ticket. They wouldn't. When no Negroes were elected among the twenty-four extra delegates, I resigned my post. Negroes came to Chicago with another delegation.

We Loyalists wanted to bring whites in, integrate the coalition. The MFDP had tough organizers like Lawrence Guyot and Harry Bowie, but they weren't exactly hoping to work alongside whites. Owen Brooks was a tough MFDP man who'd come south from Massachusetts and hated seeing whites among us. I said, "Owen, you don't understand us down here. We aren't going to be as mean to whites as they've been to us."

I wanted to unite the Loyalist Democrats and the regular Democrats so we'd have one strong Democratic Party and one strong Republican Party. But before the two rival Democratic parties could unite, you had to guarantee Negroes the right to vote. And in '68, Mississippi white folks weren't ready for that.

The national Democratic Party held its convention in Chicago in late August. It was jammed. Kids were protesting the Vietnam War, yelling at LBJ. Mayor Daley was screaming. Eugene McCarthy was there, pursuing the nomination in his sloppy way. Patt Derian and I forged the Mississippi Challenge, a biracial delegation of Loyalists pledged to unseat the Mississippi regulars. Patt and I led them into Chicago. Things were hectic, crazy. We went before the steering committee. We went before the nominating committee.

With young Hodding Carter and Aaron Henry, I fought the credentials fight. John Bell Williams and the regular Mississippi delegation were there, backing George Wallace. We said John Bell's group was racist, for one, and disloyal to the Democratic Party, for another. We said they can't have it both ways. If they milk congressional seniority, they must stay loyal to the national Democratic Party. We signed a loyalty pledge to the national party, and we unseated the lily-white Mississippi regulars. We had twice as many Negroes at the '68 convention as we'd had in '64 at the Atlantic City convention, but now we had a biracial group. We'd avenged how the white powers did us in '64. Chicago being my old stomping ground only made it sweeter.

Near convention time, they offered me Louis Martin's old job, deputy chair of the Democratic National Committee. A chance to shape national party policy. I took pause, because whites like to honor Negroes right out of power. I'd seen Negroes sell out cheap, become judges and forget civil rights. Did this lily-white group want to tie my hands? I warned Congressman Diggs, "I won't be window dressing. I'm going to be heard." They met my conditions, so I took a job—not as deputy chair, but on the Democratic National Executive Committee, highest policy-making group in the Democratic Party. I was the first-ever black Democratic national committeeman. I did damn good. I told the eleven whites on the committee about life as a Negro, in plain talk. And they listened.

At the '68 convention, some hoped to draft Teddy Kennedy. Teddy didn't want it, but Frank Mankiewicz was lining up delegates for him. One morning, I ate breakfast with Frank in a Chicago hotel. Oscar Carr was there, too. Frank was talking about drafting Teddy. I said, "You've done enough to the Kennedy family. Leave them alone." Al Lowenstein was saying, "We'll nominate Teddy and save the convention." I said, "No. You're not going to do it to that family a third time."

CHAPTER 23

Call Me "The Mayor"

IN THE SPRING OF '69, I decided to run for mayor of Fayette, Mississippi. Say it "Fay-YETTE." Fayette was the Jefferson County seat, with 1,626 residents, about 1,100 of them Negroes. We had the white folk outnumbered two-to-one, but we'd never had a Negro mayor. No biracial town in Mississippi had ever had a black mayor since Reconstruction. I'd moved to Fayette four years before, with the goal of getting a Negro mayor elected. But it wasn't supposed to be me. I'd planned to work behind the scenes.

Some of my friends had asked me to run. I always said no. Then a little old Negro lady I hardly knew came up to me in the Hollywood Baptist Church in Fayette and just ripped into me: "Charles Evers, we did whatever you asked us. We marched with you, boycotted with you, even got jailed with you. We stuck with you through all your tribulations. Now we ask you to run for mayor of Fayette and you won't do it." After she finished wearing me out, I had to run for mayor. I announced as an Independent.

Fayette was one hell of a place to try to get a black man elected mayor. It was one of the meanest white towns in all Mississippi—and that means one of the worst spots to be black anywhere on earth. No outside industry to shake things up, and no one looking to bring it in. A segregated school system bad even for Mississippi. White racist cops beating up Negroes as they pleased. One restaurant on Main Street in Fayette kept a sign in the window: "Every cent spent by a nigger to be donated to the Ku Klux Klan."

And I wasn't just any nigger. I'd been a tough civil rights fighter all my life. Medgar's work and his murder had brought great shame and controversy to Mississippi. The Evers boys had a high profile amongst the white racists of our state. But in '67, thanks to a lot of hard voter registration work, Negroes had elected four Negro election commissioners in Jefferson County. By '69, I thought maybe we had enough strength to elect a Negro mayor.

Turnip Green Allen was still mayor of Fayette in '69. Turnip Green was a seventy-seven-year-old white Democrat who thought Fayette was just fine: a sleepy little white-run town that "kept its niggers in line." Turnip Green never spent twenty dollars to attract outside industry, so we had no good jobs for the youth, and most of them with any ambition struck off north on Highway 61, headed for Memphis. We called it "going up 61." Turnip Green thought the niggers should love him. He'd given us three acres outside the city for a recreation area, so why shouldn't we vote for him? Once a nigger's had a little exercise, what else could he want?

I knew it'd be a big job to beat Turnip Green Allen in an election. Even with a voting majority, Negroes in the South weren't supposed to run for office. Negroes who voted "wrong" lost jobs and had mortgages foreclosed. Most Negroes in Fayette had family on some form of welfare. Whites told them, "Vote for Charles Evers and his slate, and you lose your welfare check." Many Negroes were scared to vote for me. Then there were Negroes who liked Charles Evers and weren't exactly scared, but didn't think mayor was a Negro job. They didn't think *any* Negro could run any town. White folk had messed with our minds for three hundred years. The shame in some of us went so deep. You'd get them registered, bring them to the polls—and they were so brainwashed they'd still vote for the white man they hated.

I had my work cut out. But I got helpers. We went house to house in Fayette, signing up Negro voters. I told every voter, "I don't care what you were last year. What are you doing tomorrow? Let's bring in the left-outs. The white man gives you nothing. Everything you need, you must take. We'll have police brutality until we get Negro cops. We'll have segregation until we have a Negro mayor. Don't vote just for Charles Evers. Come out and vote for the Negro race! Vote for yourself. Make history!"

Why beat around the bush? I told folk, "The white man's clever and informed. His mayor and aldermen take care of him. But who's looking out for black folk? Come on, black folk, wake up! Where black folk live, the dust begins. Where black folk live, the streetlights and the sewers end! Let's blacktop some Negro roads and put in some rain gutters! Those who put the sewers and sidewalks down and the streetlights up are the aldermen and the mayor." I said, "But Jefferson County is going to wake up with five black aldermen and a 230-pound black mayor. Not Evers and four white aldermen—no, sir! We're going to win it all and then shout from the rooftops, 'White folk: Let my people go!'"

That kind of talk fired up Fayette's Negroes. White folk saw I was making progress and started grumbling:

Evers says he cares about Fayette, but he wasn't born and raised here.

Evers is talking about brotherhood, but he's the one come from out of town to stir up our niggers.

This town ain't been the same since Evers brought in that damn nigger Christmas boycott in '65.

I ignored all the grumbling. Kept hammering away: "Mayors got the right to get all kinds of federal funds. In Mississippi, they ain't doing it. These mayors turn down federal projects because they'd have to be integrated. When I'm elected, we'll get those choice federal projects. I won't let Jefferson County be ignored any longer."

To the old folk, I said, "We need an old folks home round here, a decent place for the old to go." To the churchgoers, I said, "Holy folk! Pray all you want. It won't mean a thing until you get out and work for it. Elect some Negroes. Confuse the white man. Change his mind. It can be done, it's got to be done, and it will be done. Right will prevail!"

To those saying a Negro couldn't win, I said, "Win or lose, we're coming back. We're going to make a better Fayette for black *and* white." We reached out to white folk. They needed new jobs in town just as much as we did. We put up campaign posters: DON'T VOTE FOR A BLACK MAN. OR A WHITE MAN. JUST A GOOD MAN. EVERS.

By Election Day, June 3, we had 448 new registered Negroes. Our Negro election commissioners made sure the ballot boxes started out empty. And just before Election Day came outside help. Students from places like Brown University, Columbia University, Michigan State, and

Wayne State came down to shuttle Negroes to the polls. The Lawyers Constitutional Defense Committee sent us lawyers to advise us and watch the polls. John Lewis had just got married, but he came down. Three of Bobby Kennedy's old aides came down to Fayette to instruct my campaign. Paul O'Dwyer came all the way from New York. Thirty-six hours before the election, O'Dwyer and the others checked the voter registration lists, making sure everything was legal. Dead white folk weren't going to vote in this election. Neither were all the white folk who'd left town.

We had quite an election. At 7:00 A.M. when the polls opened, there was already a long line of Negroes at the brick firehouse we used as the polling station. Most of these Negroes were newly registered. By 10:00 A.M., almost 300 Negroes had voted. Of the 1,626 people in Fayette, 723 were registered voters, and 697 voted—a town record for turnout. We got 98 percent of registered Negro voters to the polls—and I'm still looking for that other 2 percent. When all the votes were counted, I'd whipped Turnip Green Allen, 433 votes to 264. I may even have got a few white votes.

White folks charged that we'd leaned on Negroes to vote Evers. Of course we had! That's how southern elections went. Negroes had a right to discipline our own. We sure as hell didn't threaten to kill anyone like white folk always did. Compared to how the whites played it, we were squeaky clean. So let them squawk; I knew I'd won the election fair and square.

I brought with me my all-Negro slate of five aldermen. Only one of those five had passed grade school, but they were good men, ready to serve. Two of the aldermen, Isiah Anderson and Howard Chambliss, had lost jobs for backing that Christmas '65 boycott the whites were always grumbling about. Isiah Anderson was an ordained minister who organized a United Mine Workers local, the first real labor organization in Jefferson County. Then there was James Gales, a good man. Another alderman, Will Turner, ran his own construction business. And the oldest, most deserving alderman was Ferd Allen, who liked to say, "I've come up the rough side of the mountain." He was sixty-five years old and had raised 21 children. He'd fought all his life for something like this.

I knew this day in Mississippi would touch folk all over the nation. I kept thinking of those who'd died for civil rights: Medgar, John

Kennedy, Martin Luther King, and Bobby Kennedy, too. They helped win the vote for all citizens of Mississippi. I thought of Nelson Rockefeller, and how much his family had helped Negroes through the years. I thought of Lyndon Johnson, who'd forced the Voting Rights Act through Congress. So many folk flashed through my mind.

Turnip Green Allen took defeat like a southern gentleman. He went so far as to place an amazing ad in the *Fayette Chronicle:*

> I bear no ill will toward anyone. I would like to see all of us work together for a better Fayette, and I will do my part in cooperating with the new administration.

Many whites in town hated Turnip Green Allen for placing that ad. I went to Turnip Green and thanked him for it. Then I asked him a favor: Would he personally swear me in as his successor? He thought about it. But for a man Turnip Green Allen's age, swearing in a Negro as town mayor was just too much. Turnip Green turned me down. Pet Thompson swore me in, a black man who'd just been elected himself as justice of the peace.

On Monday, July 7, 1969, a scorching hot Mississippi day, I took the oath and became mayor of Fayette—the first Negro mayor of a biracial Mississippi town in a century. Hundreds of people came to the swearing in. Black and white. Our inauguration program featured a drawing of two hands, one black, one white, shaking hands. We addressed the program to "the grandsons of former slaves and the grandsons of former slave owners." The program said, "Let us go forward together." I meant that.

Nearly every political bigwig in this country sent me letters or telegrams of congratulation—and lots of smaller ones did, too. I got sacks and sacks of mail from all over the country. Charles Evers, a sassy Negro from Decatur, Mississippi, got best wishes from President Nixon, Ted Kennedy, Hubert Humphrey, Ed Muskie, and Gene McCarthy. Nelson Rockefeller couldn't come because he was just returning from a long political trip through Latin America, but he flew some of my New York admirers down by jet: Ann Rockefeller; Ted Sorensen, John Kennedy's best speechwriter; Bill Booth, from the NAACP; the actress Shirley MacLaine. Lyndon Johnson's old attorney general, Ramsey Clark, came down to the ceremony. Paul O'Dwyer stayed on from the campaign. I got a personal, handwritten letter of congratulation from Jackie Kennedy. I got a nice letter from Ethel Kennedy, too.

These big white folk came down, hit Fayette, and their first question was, "Are the local whites cooperating with you?" That question always struck me funny. Here I'd just taken their town away from them, and the white folk hadn't blown my head off. That meant they were cooperating. But I tried to joke it off. I told my distinguished white guests, "Welcome to the Magnolia State, land of the brave niggers and the nervous white folk."

Lyndon Johnson missed my inaugural, with one of those light heart attacks he had. But he sent me a real nice telegram, and I called him in Texas. I said, "Mr. President, I'm the mayor because you pushed that voter rights bill through." Johnson chuckled, and he said, "No, you always did your own thing." I had to chuckle at that, too. We were both right.

Then all kinds of civil rights folk came, because we all knew if a Negro could get elected mayor in Mississippi, we could do it in any state in the country. Roy Wilkins, Gloster Current, Ruby Hurley, and all the other big NAACP folk in New York stayed away. Roy Wilkins didn't even send a telegram. But Whitney Young came, Julian Bond came. Myrlie came. The governor of the Virgin Islands came. Bless their hearts. Carl Stokes, the Negro mayor of Cleveland, Ohio, came to the ceremony. Two years before, Carl'd been the first Negro ever elected mayor of a major American city. He told me he wasn't too surprised I'd been elected in Mississippi, but to formally take power from the white power structure—*that* was something he had to come see for himself. Leontyne Price, the opera star from Laurel, Mississippi, not only flew down from New York, she opened the ceremony by singing "The Star-Spangled Banner" in her giant voice. Can you top that?

I had the world's greatest Inaugural Committee. I had Aaron Henry; Jack Young, the lawyer who chewed cigars, never smoked them; Dancing Sam Bailey; Father Morrissey, a local white priest; Professor Heidelberg, from Fayette's vo-tech school; my sister-in-law, Sadie McGee. Dancing Sam Bailey was an insurance man who used to dance up a storm at the Elk's Club in Jackson. Julius Heidelberg always supported me, whatever I did. Father William Morrissey was a big, burly, handsome priest with a diocese in Natchez. Father Morrissey always feared something would happen to me. I'd tease him, "Not with you as my protector. Pray for me, Father." And he always did. Oh, I loved my Inaugural Committee.

The natural place for the swearing in was the gym at Jefferson High School. But even with all these people of national note seeing Fayette for the first time, the white-run school board wouldn't let my Inaugural Committee stage the ceremony in any of the schools. We had to stage it in a damn parking lot, with my back to city hall. I was too happy to kick sand. Besides, we had the Mississippi state troopers directing traffic at my inauguration, and man, I loved that. Most of those troopers hated my guts, but they shut their mouths and did their job like pros.

Now, everyone in the crowd knew some Klukker might try to shoot me at the swearing in, or even bomb the whole inauguration. For once, I was glad to see those white goons from the highway patrol. But we were all nervous. Everyone supposed to be on the stage got up on the stage, *crack!*—the whole stage collapsed. The crowd screamed and gasped. Almost everyone on that stage ran or ducked for cover. It turned out the stage was just so badly built it had collapsed under our weight. We laughed and howled about all this later and mocked those who tore off that stage the quickest. But it wasn't funny then.

As I took the oath of office, I knew Mississippi could be the greatest state in the nation—just as good as it had been bad. I kept wishing Mama, Daddy, and Medgar were there. My next thought was for me. For forty-six years, whites had called me "nigger," "boy," and "Charlie." Never "Mr. Evers." Well, now they could call me "Mayor Evers," "Mr. Evers," or "The Mayor." I loved being "The Mayor" so much I even had Nan calling me "The Mayor." Papers all over the nation covered my inauguration. The *Chicago Defender*, my favorite Negro paper, gave me a glowing editorial and even called sassy Charles Evers "a first-rate diplomat."

We had an inaugural ball. A very classy one, too. In the city auditorium in Natchez—the very same holding pen they'd been using for years for arrested civil rights marchers. I'd been there many times before, but my inaugural was the very first time I wasn't there under arrest. That city auditorium held two thousand people, and we filled it. I told my guests, "Leave all your weapons at home. I won't let violence tear down what we've built."

I invited the white officials of Fayette and Natchez to the ball. None of them came. Too bad for them. They could have mixed and mingled with some classy folk. They could have seen some fine entertainment. We had the singer Eartha Kitt, we had Shirley MacLaine. Raymond Burr was there—you know that lawyer Perry Mason on TV that never loses a case? Here I'd always wanted to be a lawyer, and now we had old Perry Mason himself, sitting at the Charles Evers inaugural ball in Natchez, toasting Charles Evers and civil rights. Berry Gordy, head of Motown Records, threw me a party to celebrate. And the NAACP branches all over the country voted me NAACP Man of the Year for 1969. I'd come a long way.

But all this time, I knew praise shouldn't sit too close on Charles Evers. We're all God's children, He brought us here, and those He equipped to improve the world—we must do it. Not as braggadocios, now, but as helpers. All I did was my duty to God, my people, and myself. I got elected mayor out of it, I got the limelight and the inaugural ball at the city auditorium in Natchez. But all I deserved was a pat on the back. When I saw I was really going to be elected mayor of Fayette, deep in my heart I thanked everyone who'd ever worked for Negro rights in Mississippi. The black and white, the better known and the lesser known. All our slave ancestors, who did what little they could in the old days. Mothers and fathers, doctors and lawyers, pool sharks and cabdrivers. All the people with guts enough to stick up for the Negro. I was just one of them. God bless them all.

CHAPTER 24

Fayette Was Our Israel

I WAS DETERMINED TO BE MAYOR of all the people of Fayette. I said, "We've all won a great victory—not just the poor blacks, but the scared whites, too." I refused to belittle those whites who feared the rising Negro. They needed help as much as we did. Some Negroes were calling me "the Moses of Mississippi," ready to lead Mississippi to the Promised Land. Others called me a money-hungry, power-crazy demagogue who'd start a race war just to elect Charles Evers dogcatcher. Both sides were wrong. The only man who ever understood me was Medgar.

I ran Fayette fair and well. I was always out front, taking heat, catching hell. I held my ground against all comers, fought every day, and loved every fight. All over the state, white folk were spitting mad that a nigger was running a Mississippi town. Even some Negroes thought mayor was a white man's job. Some took years to accept a Negro in charge. But I always had a knack for knowing what was cooking in town, what folk were saying and doing.

Goal number one as mayor of Fayette was doing just what I'd always vowed I'd never do: beg for money. I planned to expand city services in Fayette, and when I took office our town treasury didn't have a damn cent. We couldn't even pay our outstanding bills. Garbage was piling up, and we couldn't pay our garbagemen. Some of Turnip Green Allen's folk and some of the aldermen had gone on a spending spree on their way out of office and busted the treasury. Turnip Green didn't condone the spree, and when we told him about it, he asked some of his white friends to help us get out of debt. But Turnip Green's office did leave us begging.

I hate begging because leaning on strangers is weak. But this begging was different. This money was turning the whole white-only system upside down. No Negro should be too proud for that kind of begging. And in politics, you never call it "begging." It's called "fundraising." You get up on stage: "Fellow citizens, I appeal to you today for sorely needed funds. . . ." That's what I did.

Now, if a state NAACP head was voted national Man of the Year by the NAACP branches for becoming the first Negro mayor in that state in a century, but he found his town bankrupt when he took office, you'd think the national NAACP would put some money in that town. Well, you'd think wrong. Roy Wilkins ignored everything we did in Fayette. When we got too big to ignore, he turned his back and said publicly that Fayette was Charles Evers's problem. He told my local NAACP chapters not to send Fayette one dime.

Roy Wilkins, I raised the money without you. I begged in Mississippi and all over this country. I begged for federal money and for private money. I told everyone, "Send money to Fayette Emergency Fund, City Hall, Fayette, Mississippi, 39069." And money poured in. Sacks and sacks of envelopes from all over the United States hit our little post office. An anonymous Mississippi donor gave one thousand dollars. I went on the *Martha Deane Show* in New York and got about thirty thousand dollars. And by late '71, a national poll showed more blacks respected Charles Evers than respected Roy Wilkins.

Louis Martin wrote a flattering column in the *Chicago Defender* on my election. A white Detroit man, William Kienzle, with the *Michigan Catholic* newspaper, heard about Fayette's debts, called and asked me how much Fayette needed. I said about $150,000. Well, the *Michigan Catholic* had a circulation of 150,000, so Mr. Kienzle wrote an editorial, "Dr. King's Dream Worth a Dollar?"

> In a day of the militant black, the Panther and the Manifesto, Charles Evers may be the last of the Martin Luther Kings. His philosophy is simple, black and whites can live together in peace, brotherhood and equality. . . . If each of our readers were to send one dollar . . . Fayette would be saved. No, more than Fayette would be saved. The dream of Martin Luther King might be dusted off and salvaged. . . . We plead with you . . . to send what you can, along perhaps with an encouraging word, to "Fayette Emergency Fund," City Hall, Fayette, Mississippi."

We got almost thirty thousand dollars from that appeal, from total strangers in a far-off state. And like the man suggested, many people sent us encouraging words, too. That was beautiful. Walter Cronkite, the anchorman at CBS News, saw the *Michigan Catholic* and asked if he could interview me. Cronkite promoted a one-minute clip where I asked CBS viewers to send a dollar. Cronkite got in trouble with the top brass at CBS, but in the next ten days CBS viewers sent us over seventy-five thousand dollars—more than Fayette's annual budget.

We paid off our town bills. We built Fayette a public health care clinic. Up in New York, I met with a fine white man named Gil Jonas who'd raised money for the NAACP. He helped me start the Medgar Evers Foundation, which raised money for the health clinic, a recreation complex, and a day care center. The mayor of New York, John Lindsay, called when he saw I'd been elected mayor and invited me up to New York. He had a surplus of garbage trucks up there. For one dollar, he sold me Fayette's first real garbage truck.

President Nixon helped with a Department of Health, Education, and Welfare (HEW) grant in '71. Negroes living in shacks got to live in a housing project we called the Martin Luther King Apartments. Just a little home, built to order, but they had running water and electricity, and they meant the world to my people. Jefferson County Negroes had never gotten federal building loans before. We told Negroes about the Federal Housing Administration (FHA), and helped them get decent homes.

We improved our health care like night and day. We got a $131,000 federal health planning grant for the Medgar Evers Medical Center. By '71, we had a $6 million health program in Fayette, paid by HEW grants. We saw over seventy-five patients a day there. We got three full-time doctors in Jefferson County instead of one. Three nurses, too. We got our first good dentists. Volunteer medical specialists began coming down from Michigan on two-week rotations. Drug companies gave us medicines. We set up a $680,000 community health program. We bought a $38,000 mobile medical unit. A friend gave us our first ambulance, fully equipped and air-conditioned. By '73, we were building a $400,000 center with day care, a medical clinic, dental clinic, cafeteria, and library.

Some said, "Why do you always go out of state for help? Let's solve our own problems." But our problems cost money! In '69, Fayette was the fourth-poorest city in the country. I don't know what three cities were poorer, but they must have been in Mississippi. I was never too big to ask for help. People said, "Damn these Yankees!" I said, "Who cares where they're from, if they can teach us something! Let's learn from the best." We got the Ford Foundation for $500,000. We got a federal grant from HUD. Between 1968 and 1971, Fayette got about $10 million from the federal government and our private fund-raising. I was never too proud or too scared to ask. I took every penny I could raise.

Some asked, "How do we know you're going to spend that money right?" I said, "You don't know. But give us a chance. See if we don't build the greatest little town in this country." And we did. Whites said, "Every white official in Fayette will resign before they'll serve under a nigger mayor." And many whites did quit. Only one cop stayed on. But the fire chief, Carl Werner, stayed on, and we built on that. With all the fires the Klan set, it was always a feather in its cap to recruit the town fire chief. But Carl Werner had been raised in Minnesota, where Negroes had rights. He rejected the Klan and served under Charles Evers. We brought in some of the best black firemen in Los Angeles to train our volunteer firemen. Learn from the best.

Whites whispered, "Evers wants Fayette to be all-black." Why in hell would I want that? Klukkers had tried to segregate us for a hundred years. Why should an integrationist like me do it for them? I hired seven new folk in city hall: an economic development team, a city clerk, an accountant, a bookkeeper, and a secretary. We set up a payroll of twenty-six. Ten of those folk were white. My office had portraits of John and Bobby Kennedy next to mementos of Medgar and a portrait of Martin. I told the Negro: Don't drive whites away. Negroes will be constables and justices of the peace, supervisors and school board members. But we aren't going to do white folk like they did us. Whites who want to help solve our common problems—let them serve alongside us, in harmony.

Goal number two was improving the self-image of Fayette's Negroes. We came to this country in chains. Abe Lincoln took the chains off in 1863, but in the mind, bondage goes on. Many Negroes who'd lived in Fayette all their lives had a hangdog look. I told them to act proud, wear white shirts any damn time they pleased. Help us build a new community. Fayette's Negroes had never known the mayor to ask for their help. They began bringing me and my staff all kinds of problems and ideas. We tried to help. We got rid of those hangdog looks and brought out a perky look, a bounce in the stride.

To make sure Negroes kept that perky look, goal number three was to overhaul the local police. Fayette had always had about three cops. All white. Maybe one of them could read. These cops had just one job: Keep the niggers down. Mayor Evers changed that. During my campaign, Fayette's police chief was dead set against me. Refused to change or grow. The day after I took office, I fired him and made a Negro teacher, Robert Vanderson, the first Negro police chief in Jefferson County in a century. Some said, "How can a teacher be a tough cop?" So I got Frank Rizzo, police chief in Philadelphia, Pennsylvania, to send us his top cop to teach Robert Vanderson how to be tough. And no one knew rough and tough like Frank Rizzo's boys. Alfonso Deal, fifteen years on the Philadelphia force, came to Fayette for a year on a ten-thousand-dollar grant and became our public safety director. Frank Rizzo and some of his detectives bought us a new Oldsmobile cop car. From New York, John Lindsay sent us a cop car and lent us *his* top cop, Richard Woodard.

I wanted an integrated police force so much I recruited white cops from Natchez and Brookhaven. Whites said we'd have no respect for law with Evers as mayor. They were dead wrong. I was a law-and-order man. I took back the chief's little bitty .38 pistol and gave him a .357 Magnum. Folk chuckled at Charles Evers, arrested so often, now enforcing the law. It wasn't funny to me. I never hated those who broke the law. I understood their games. I just arrested them, and some I locked up. You must have law.

But as soon as I gave Fayette's cops more power, I warned them: no more beating up Negroes. I was the only mayor in Mississippi in '69 who'd fire a cop for beating a Negro. "Keep the peace," I told my cops. "Preserve and protect the public, but beat them up and I'll fire you quick." I told them to fine the public for busting the speed limit: a dollar a mile, whites and blacks the same. No more giving civil rights folk mysterious speeding tickets for outlandish amounts. Turnip Green Allen had padded his salary with traffic fines. I never did. Within three years, all my white cops had quit on me, and Fayette had an all-Negro police force.

One day a Louisiana Negro came roaring into Fayette, way over the speed limit. A Negro cop stopped him and fined him $113. That

Louisiana Negro was flabbergasted we had Negro cops in Fayette and shocked one would fine him $113. Speeding in the South usually cost about $20. But I insisted on high standards and no favorites. We fined a white lady some huge amount for speeding, and she spit fire: "I suppose this money goes to the Charles Evers campaign fund." A cop told her, "No, ma'am, but after you pay the fine, if you want to contribute to Evers, we'll be glad to take that, too."

Goal number four was to create lots of good jobs. Half of Fayette was unemployed. Most of our Negroes took welfare. I hated seeing them on Main Street, lounging in doorways, playing the dozens, drinking whiskey and wine. So I went out and recruited business hard. We got Thompson Industries, a part of International Telephone & Telegraph, which made electrical wiring for cars, to put a fabricated wiring components plant in Fayette. One hundred and fifty jobs. A forty-thousand-dollar-a-month payroll. Commercial Chemical built a five-hundred-thousand-dollar plant. Another hundred-some jobs. A third firm built a concrete-mixing plant. We developed a 250-acre industrial park. Lavender House came to town, to make wigs and Afro clothing. A former mean white sheriff from Adams County opened a furniture store on Main Street, even hired two of my Negro supporters to work there. I teased the sheriff about turning over a new leaf, but I welcomed him. Fayette needed the business.

For a century, heavy industry in the South had followed segregated rules. I challenged heavy industry: Hire by skill, not race; judge workers by output, not race; set salaries by job, not race. Employment in Fayette jumped about 20 percent, and I trimmed the welfare rolls. Black women who'd been on welfare or getting three dollars a week as domestics started getting a hundred dollars a week in those plants.

Goal number five was education. Too many in Fayette, black and white, had poor schooling. We stressed education for all. We bought new schoolbooks and school equipment. We enforced school attendance harder than any other town in Mississippi. Steady truants, we jailed for a night. Their parents, too. They hated that, my liberal friends hated it, but the schools filled up. People said, "You can't require school. That's too much government. That ain't the American way." Then what is the American way? Government paying welfare? Not while Charles Evers was mayor. Make every child believe in the promise of school, and you can end welfare because we'll all be self-supporting.

With a federal grant, we improved our vo-tech training school. We taught seventy-five boys there a trade: carpentry, brick masonry, concrete and electrical work, welding. We paid them forty dollars a week to learn. I tried so hard to show Fayette's kids the good side of life so they could avoid the mistakes I'd made as a boy. We set up a child day care center and taught young people how to behave.

I also knew that schooling goes way beyond reading, writing, and sums. So many whites have abused and hated us, but I knew in my heart that nobody wants to hate. They learn to hate by watching others hate, and feeling hatred come down on them. Well, if they could learn to hate, they could learn to love and respect. I told Fayette, "Education. Training. Respect for all. We all need an education." I knew many of the old white folk would never change. They didn't want an education. But I knew they'd soon pass on. We had to teach their children not to hate.

Goal number six was discipline. Whites said, "With a nigger mayor, we'll have a race riot in town." I made sure Fayette had no race riot. A small-town mayor has to rule on all kinds of little husband-and-wife spats. People drink whiskey and go on a binge. The mayor has to fine someone or send them to the lockup. You want to be fair, use common sense, and never whip any man just for fun, like whites always had. But you also need discipline.

We had to be careful. Fayette was a pioneer black-run town. The eyes of the nation were upon us. I told my friends, "Fayette has got to succeed. *Fayette is our Israel.* If we fail here, civil rights in America will suffer. And if we can lick racism here, we can lick it all over Mississippi, and all over this damn country." I said, "We can't afford gambling here. Whoring and violence here keep industry out." Negroes who scrapped at my dance hall, I threw out and said, "Don't come back." Some said, "Aw, don't be so mean. Negroes have so little, so we get in scrapes on Saturday night." I said, "If you need work, apply to the Medgar Evers Shopping Center. I pay good wages. But being out of work is no excuse for fighting. Not in *my* dance hall."

I closed all of Fayette down tight at 1:00 A.M. Rolled up the sidewalks. No exceptions, not even me—and I'm a night owl. I never asked Fayette to do what I wouldn't do myself. Remember those five Negro aldermen who came into office with me? I fined one of them, Isiah Anderson, $160 for public drunkenness. Folk said, "Charlie, don't fine one of your own aldermen." Why the hell not? I'd have fined Mama if she'd come down from heaven and walked into Fayette drunk. Only authorized personnel could pack weapons in public. First time we caught you armed, it cost a hundred dollars. Second time, it was three hundred dollars, and we kept the gun. Third time, I was more than happy to jail you six months. Whites had never cared when Negroes killed each other. I did care, and I made sure my cops cared. We must have had the lowest crime rate in the nation.

I couldn't see why Negroes wanted to mingle in the street all day, why we were so quick to fight and to mock Negroes who tried to get rich. I thought I could change that, though I didn't fine or arrest for it. But I brooked no form of public profanity. Whites who used "nigger," "coon," or "ziggyboo" to a black man's face owed me one hundred dollars. Blacks using "honky" or "peckerwood" to a white man's face owed me a hundred dollars. You'll notice I use the word *peckerwood* myself— but not to a white man's face. It starts fights. I said, "If a white man calls me a nigger, I'll arrest him for disturbing the nigger's peace. If I call him a honky, he can have me arrested for disturbing the honky's peace."

People said, "There'll be a mass white exodus from town." I won't lie, some whites shuttered their windows and left. In a small town, you notice. Remember the white man who said every Negro cent spent in his restaurant would go to the Klan? The very day I took office, he rushed out of town. That was okay. He had revenge in his heart. We didn't miss him. But there was no mass exodus. The good white folk remained, and we made a happy biracial town. It just happened to be run by Negroes.

Something else I felt I owed Medgar was to divorce Nan. I had girlfriends everywhere. And as the mayor and a married man, all my girlfriends might tarnish what folks thought of Medgar. I didn't worry about what my girlfriends thought. I didn't care what folk thought of *me*. But I couldn't let the memory of Medgar be tarnished. So I cleaned myself up and divorced Nan. We still saw each other plenty, but we got off the books as husband and wife.

I donated my whole seventy-five-dollar-a-month salary to the Fayette General Fund. I didn't need it. I had nearly every Negro in Fayette behind me. I wasn't drinking, smoking, chewing, or gambling. Women were my only hobby. Besides, I earned good money from the Medgar Evers Shopping Center. In 1970, I bought myself a nine-unit white motel in Fayette and renamed it the Evers Motel, Restaurant, and Lounge. This was no dusty, rat-and-roach place. It had an air-cooled restaurant and a carpeted lounge. Negroes had never been allowed there. The day I bought it, Negroes asked me, "You going to let white folk stay there?" Sure, I let white folk stay. Like I said, in business the only color that counts is green.

Around '69, a Klansman fell sick in Fayette. Just forty-eight years old, and dying of anemia. All his blood had gone and left him plumb white. This man had beaten Negroes, helped kill Negroes, had once shot at an old Negro lady walking up the road. He'd once walked into the business office of our NAACP leader, Ferd Allen, and asked Ferd to come for a drive. Ferd was a little too smart for that. When that mean old Klansman got sick, God, he suffered. When his doctors told him he was out of blood, he begged, "Get me blood, any kind. Get me nigger blood. I just want to live." Before he died, that mean old Klansman ended up begging for a black man's blood. At the very end, even he realized that black or white, we're all the same inside.

Some whites wanted to help us but if they did too much, their family and friends shunned them. White folk who hardly knew me would call me and cry on my shoulder. So some whites helped us, some avoided us, and some bucked us any and every chance they could. Especially the older ones. When the highway patrol saw a car with an Evers sticker on the bumper, they'd often arrest the driver on some trumped-up charge.

We improved the roads and water system where Negroes lived. We lit streets, paved roads, put in water pipes and hydrants. We put in the first sewer in Fayette. There wasn't a playground in Fayette, nor a swimming pool. We put in a sixty-five-thousand-dollar swimming pool and welcomed whites to come swim with us. If they didn't want to, they could stay out and sweat.

We didn't assault whites with Negro progress, didn't fuss or brag. We just moved. White folk began to see they had to live with us, and some opened up to us. Any white who'd reach out his hand in friendship, we took it. We even put up signs showing a black hand shaking a white hand. The state Highway Department took those signs down. We put them back up.

The hardest thing I had to do was to fire our city attorney, Martha Wood, for breaking the miscegenation law. Martha Wood was a white woman, a good lawyer who backed civil rights. Around 1969, she fell in love with a local Negro cop named Jenkins. They married and tried to live in Fayette. Anyone could see they were in love. If Fayette had truly been a Christian town, they could have walked Main Street arm in arm and gone to bed in peace. But in '69, Fayette couldn't stand an openly mixed-race couple. Even Negroes grumbled, "Why can't Jenkins find himself a Negro girl?"

Public safety is part of the mayor's job, and we didn't have near enough cops to protect Martha Wood and Jenkins from the assaults bound to come down on them. I told them, "I got no time to be walking guard for you all day. If you want to be openly married, y'all have to leave town." I had nothing against them dating. Felicia, the love of my life, was a white girl. But I knew enough to keep Felicia out of Mississippi. And I couldn't have these two hanging around Fayette tempting the haters. For public safety, I told them to leave. I said, "I don't care if you're slipping around together, but you can't live together in Fayette." They wouldn't back down, so in December of '69, I had to fire Martha Wood as city attorney of Fayette. Martha was a fine attorney and one of the few whites in town willing to serve a nigger mayor. I loved Martha, but public safety comes before personal rights. Common sense comes before theory. The liberals don't understand that. That's why liberals make bad mayors.

Martha Wood and Jenkins went off to Illinois or somewhere. I didn't care where they went, as long as they left Fayette. I thought all this was behind me, but some of the northern liberal, fat-mouth media came to town and wrote a pack of stories: "Big civil rights Negro Charles Evers chased a good woman out of town because he can't abide nighttime integration." That was the national angle. Pure bullshit. Then the press left and again I thought the issue was past, but some mother hens in Fayette started whispering that Martha Wood was one of *my* women, and I'd fired her because I was jealous of Jenkins! Man, sometimes the mayor just can't win.

My toughest critic in town was the white lady editor of our weekly paper, the *Fayette Chronicle*, Mrs. Marie Farr Walker. She also became a dear friend of mine. Marie Walker was a short, stocky lady from a fine white family. She had strong ideas of right and wrong. She'd say, "Don't ever do anything you wouldn't want Jesus to be right there watching you." Some Negroes disliked her, but she was just a natural watchdog, defending Fayette.

Marie Farr Walker sat up in a little office with Confederate banners on the walls and wrote a weekly column, "Just Whittling," for the *Chronicle*. She said local whites were just "biding their time" while I was mayor. I'd fly off to Washington, soliciting federal money for Fayette, or spend long days making pitches for private money in New York, Los Angeles, Atlanta. Half the week I was off and gone. Marie Farr Walker said we in Fayette, Mississippi, didn't want money from the Feds, the Kennedys and the Rockefellers. Mrs. Walker said I traveled too much and couldn't hope to run Fayette from off in far places. Every time Mrs. Walker ripped me in her newspaper, the *Chronicle* circulation jumped. Even white folks in other counties wanted to read the paper where the lady editor attacked the nigger mayor. If I just dreamed of doing wrong, Marie Walker found out and cut me up in her column.

In March of '69, when I first put out word I was running for mayor of Fayette, some national news shows carried the story. But I didn't officially announce my candidacy in the *Fayette Chronicle*. Oh, Mrs. Walker got on me for that! Chastised me in print all through March and April, till I announced in the *Chronicle* in May. I spent thirty-three thousand dollars improving the streets of Fayette, and by acting quick, saved the town a bundle. But Marie Walker hit me in her column for improving the streets before publishing public notice. I'd pick up that paper and say, "Mrs. Walker, don't make a mountain out of a damn molehill!" But I loved reading her columns.

Around October of '70, I sent bulldozers to grade some land, including part of Christian Church Cemetery, an old Negro graveyard. The place was grown up in weeds. The graves were hard to see. The man on the bulldozer got careless, knocked down some Negro headstones. Oh, Marie Walker tore into me for that! Her next column claimed Charles Evers had hit an all-time low. Desecrating the dead. He can't even let the dead rest.

None of this bothered me one bit. I said, "Marie, honey, you write all them bad things about me, but that's alright. Just keep my name in there. I need the press." I liked Marie Walker and her husband, Jimmie Walker, too. Jimmie was a local lawyer who'd call me all the time to tell me what the racists were scheming. Mayors need folks like the Walkers. You get cocky. You need someone to keep you in line, tell you what your enemies are saying. And Marie Walker and I had a secret: When I was getting ready to run for mayor, she'd saved my candidacy.

I'd expected to run for mayor of Fayette with a Jackson residence. But Mrs. Walker heard Fayette meant to use the residency issue to keep me from running. She saw I had the guts and the contacts to get Fayette moving. She called me: "Get down here quick, Charles Evers. You've got to register a residence in Fayette." So I registered P.O. Box 605, Fayette. In Philadelphia, Mississippi, the Cole family and Lewis family had looked out for me. Marie Farr Walker did the same in Fayette. She had prejudice she'd drunk in with her mother's milk. She barked a lot and got up on her back legs, but she'd guard a Negro, and that's more than I'll say for most whites. Marie Farr Walker saw that Charles Evers was a leader, and she cared for me. I loved that woman.

Jimmie Walker and Mr. Ball, the druggist, owned lots of land just east of Highway 61, north of Fayette. With so many whites leaving town, I knew Jimmie Walker would sell that land for what he could get. I wanted to buy. Jimmie said, "Charles, how about twenty-five thousand dollars?" I said, "Noooo, indeed." I knew he'd come down. In January of '69 he sold me clear title to sixty acres of land for nineteen thousand dollars cash. The Walkers even asked me to dinner to tie up the sale. As a boy, whites never let me swim in a Mississippi lake. Now, I had my own land and money enough to build my own lake. With bulldozers, it only took a week and cost a thousand dollars. When I got mad at white folk, I'd go to that lake for some peace. Drive up on some red mud tracks. Sit on my own land, look out over the lake, watch the moss drip from the magnolia, and make my decisions.

People asked, "Ain't you scared whites will shoot you, like they shot Medgar?" The answer was no. I knew any man who said Negroes were as good as whites had signed his own death warrant. I was always ready to die. I kept up my precautions. I took target practice twice a week. I brought two bodyguards when I met big crowds. But leaders can't hide, and they shouldn't. If I was going to be killed, let me die working, mixing with folks—not hiding behind an office or a bodyguard.

Ever since '63, when I'd rejoined the NAACP, Klukkers had said, "Nigger, we'll kill you like we killed your damn brother." When I got to be mayor, the threats rose. I'd get five threatening letters a week. Many vicious threats came from Florida and New Jersey. I sent most of this hate mail on to the FBI.

Medgar's example helped me swallow all this hate so much better than I'd ever done before. Before Medgar died, if a man told me to go to hell, I'd knock his ass off. Now I found myself waiting things out, trying to see the good side. People broke into my house several times, tore it up, and I just said, "The Lord giveth, and the Lord taketh away."

Local folk phoned and threatened to kill me. No insurance company would write policy on my property, so I worried about bombings and arson, too. Some of my callers were dumb enough to give their name. They thought they could scare me, with Medgar and John Kennedy and Bobby and Martin all dead. But the guy isn't too dangerous who'll curse you out as nigger-this and nigger-that. Ask him his name and keep him where you can watch him. The man you worry about is the one walking around so full of hate he can't open his mouth. He's the one who might gun you down in cold blood.

Lord, I had hard nights. I had to live alone to keep my wife and daughters safe, and the white folk wore me out for it, called me a carpetbagger for keeping my family in Jackson. My unlisted line would ring late at night. I'd lift the phone with a heavy heart and hear some Klukker: "Nigger, there'll be one less smart-ass nigger around here pretty soon." He'd start in on all the little things he'd do to me before he killed me. I'd slam down the phone and try to put it from my mind. But that's hard to do. On a hot, quiet night, you hear things. You think things. Some folks go to bed with a good book. I'd go to bed with the voice of some mean peckerwood coward, rattling around my head.

On September 9, 1969, three men did try to kill me. I'd ordered a marble monument to Medgar, engraved with a Jomo Kenyatta saying. I'd put it in the county park near the old Confederate soldier monument. Whites in town were spitting mad. They said Medgar Evers never lived in Fayette and had nothing to do with Fayette. What fools! Medgar had *everything* to do with Fayette. Fayette was a living model of Medgar's work, a town where all folk could live as equals.

Turnip Green Allen complained he'd been mayor eighteen years and didn't put his daddy's tomb in the park, and here I put a monument there to a nigger who never knew Fayette. He said, "Think how that makes a white man feel, seeing Medgar Evers honored in the county park." He'd never wondered how Negroes felt about a statue of a Confederate soldier in the park. The park was county land, run by the all-white Jefferson County Board of Supervisors. They said, "Get that slab out!" I said, "You got your idol, and we got ours. You got the slave master Confederate soldier, and we got the freedom runner." But they ordered Medgar's monument off county land. I waited two months to show them they didn't scare me, then announced we'd move Medgar across the street to the Fayette city hall front lawn. You better betcha *that* was city land.

One morning just before we moved the statue, the phone rang in my office. A white woman's voice said, "Charles"—not "Mayor Evers"; as a white she used my first name—"Charles, I don't believe in everything you do, but we can't afford to have you killed. The Klan's going to kill you when you move that monument." I thought this was just one of my politer death threats. I yelled, "Go to hell!" and hung up. I tried to laugh off that little warning. We moved the monument to Medgar. No one tried to kill me, and I relaxed.

But six o'clock that evening a white man called. Probably the woman's husband. He told me the same: The Klan was about to kill me. I said, "They wanted the damn monument moved, didn't they? Well, we moved it this morning. Why are they going to kill me now?" The man on the line started raving, so I hung up. But then I took pause and began to fret. I'd gotten to be kind of an expert on death threats. These calls were polite and specific. These white folk weren't jiving. I told my cops, "I've gotten calls someone's trying to kill me. Look out for anyone strange." I went down to my shopping center and told my daughter Carolyn about the calls. She'd been seeing strange cars. I told her to keep her eye out.

At 7:15 that evening I was heading out for a bite when the phone rang. This time a Negro woman was on the line, probably the white couple's maid. She said, "Mr. Evers, I'm a friend of yours. Now don't hang up on me." I said, "Honey, what is it?" She said, "There are three men going to kill you." I snorted, "Aw, come on now." But the woman pressed me: "They're driving a 1968 Mustang. They got five guns in the car. They been on the road and bought some clothes for a quick change. One of them's in a motel in Natchez, with a getaway car." Well, when the callers get that exact, you listen hard. And that woman's next words chilled my spine: "They got a rebel flag on the car." I'd seen that

Mustang car, rebel flag on its antenna. I thought of Martin killed in Memphis, and I told the woman, "Thank you very much."

I told police chief Vanderson to stand ready with one of his best men. I packed my gun and left my office. The 1968 Mustang was empty, parked across the street. With Vanderson close, I walked to the store where Carolyn worked. The driver of that Mustang had bought gum in her store. I grabbed my papers and left. Next to my restaurant I stopped to greet some folks. Carolyn yelled, "Daddy, here comes that car!" Chief Vanderson was tailing the Mustang. I gave him a sign, and he and his man pulled the Mustang over. There was just one man inside, not three, but he had five guns alright: a carbine, three shotguns, and a .38 pistol.

The man's name was Dale Walton. He was forty-four years old, lived in Tupelo, and owned a general store there. A little white man, going bald on top. He'd been a chieftain in the Klan, but he'd found the Klan too liberal, too soft on the nigger. So he became a grand dragon in a more violent splinter group, the Knights of the Green Forest. He couldn't stand seeing a Negro with any power. Walton was a friend of Byron Beckwith. Two peas in a pod.

But we didn't find all that out for a while. When we asked Dale Walton why he had so many guns, he snarled, "I'm a Mississippi white man. I won't answer that." That didn't fly in Fayette anymore. Our police brought Walton to city hall. I said, "Don't you know it's against the law to speed in this town?" His eyes were like little snakes. He spit out, "I wasn't speeding!" I said, "Remember now, before you tell me, I'm the judge and mayor of this town. Whatever you say may come against you. So call a lawyer if you want." He looked at me with that ignorant face, full of hate, then drew himself up: "You must remember that I'm a white man."

At that moment I learned I was nearly all cured of the hate I'd felt when Medgar was murdered. Because if Dale Walton had said those same words in '63, I'd have knocked his teeth right down his throat. As it was, I flinched, but I didn't let him provoke me. I just told my cops, "Lock him up." We slapped him in jail, under a ten-thousand-dollar bond, for carrying concealed weapons. We held him for a hearing. Before we let him out, Dale Walton all but admitted he'd come to kill me. He told me, "You're fair. But I hate you."

After his lawyer came, I told Dale Walton, "I don't know your story. Why don't we sit down and talk?" He screamed, "I don't want to talk!" I said, "Listen, you don't know me, and I don't know you. I could have killed you right in your car, but I didn't. Now, why would you want to kill *me?*" Walton dropped his head. He'd heard Evers was a big, power-hungry nigger, but no one had told him I was a man. A smart, Christian man who tried to love everyone. At least for a minute, I made Dale Walton respect me.

Walton's hearing came a few days later. I couldn't sit as judge—had to guarantee him a fair trial. I gave the case to Ferd Allen, my mayor *pro tem*. We waited for Walton to get his lawyer. We put all his guns on display and bound them over to a grand jury, which met a week later. Walton wouldn't pay his ten-thousand-dollar bond, so he sat in jail six days, until the grand jury turned him loose. But the FBI was catching hell in the media and from friends of mine in Washington, so the FBI grabbed Walton for violating the Firearms Act. He got jailed forty-five days and fined $329.

Federal agents found Walton's two accomplices: one holed up in a Natchez hotel room, with a Thompson submachine gun, the other one, named Massengale, in Hattiesburg, a bodyguard for a big segregationist politician, Jimmy Swan. Because of the Thompson gun, they grabbed all three on federal gun charges. For years, I thought Dale Walton might return and kill me. He warned the FBI, "I'm full of that Evers nigger up to my head. I won't stand any more of that smart-aleck nigger." I always wondered if someone I knew in Fayette had asked Dale Walton to kill me.

We tightened security, I kept Nan and my daughters in our nice home in Jackson with a swimming pool—kept them out of Jefferson County all I could. But I knew the haters could get me. Friends tipped me that the Klan said, "We couldn't get Evers in Fayette, but we'll get him on one of those trips he makes." But if they got me, someone else would carry on. It didn't matter to me how long I lived. What mattered was, What did I do while I was here? Life's too short to go around worrying about death. Too many folks keep waiting on tomorrow, tomorrow, tomorrow. I did all I could each day. I said, "I'll worry about dying when I'm gone."

CHAPTER

25

A Black-Skinned Man Running for Governor

EVERY THREE YEARS, cops seemed to hit the Jackson State campus, guns blazing. At the first sign of a Negro campus scuffle, the cops would call in the highway patrol; the highway patrol would start squawking about Negro snipers, and then begin shooting down Negroes in cold blood. There was never a sniper.

I already told you about the '64 Jackson State riot. In '67, during another campus scuffle, cops fired into the crowd and killed a young Negro bystander, Benjamin Brown. Fifty Jackson cops stood by, and not a one tried to get Benjamin Brown a doctor. In May 1970, my fourth daughter, Sheila, was at Jackson State. Kids there hated the draft, the U.S. Army invading Cambodia, whites killing Negroes through the South. When a scuffle broke out at the college, I feared we'd see '64 and '67 all over again. I went on campus and warned the kids: "Cool it, because these bigots'll kill you. They killed Benjamin Brown. They killed Medgar and Martin, John and Bobby Kennedy. The same force that killed those men can kill you." Most of the kids cooled down.

That same night I flew to the funeral of the labor leader Walter Reuther. Reuther had run the United Auto Workers for almost twenty-five years. He was one of the few big labor leaders who wasn't corrupt and loved civil rights. He'd just died in a plane crash. Reuther's brother had come to Medgar's funeral, so when friends of Reuther's asked me to the funeral, I hopped on a plane to Detroit. We hit bad weather and stopped at O'Hare Airport, Chicago. I slept in a hotel; early the next morning, I was back at O'Hare.

Newsmen jumped me in the airport, said they'd heard I was dead. I joked it off: "Feel me, I'm alive." But then Hugh Hill, a serious reporter with CBS in Chicago, shot me a funny look: "Charles, we heard some whites had shot you." I said, "What you talking about?" Hugh said, "They killed two blacks in Jackson last night." It had gone over the wires. I called home to say I was alright. Sheila screamed, "Daddy! Thank God you're safe! They said you'd been shot." Sheila pleaded with me to stay away until things died down. Nan took the phone in a rage and said a black man had driven through Jackson State, enraging the students by saying white cops had shot me dead.

Back in Jackson, I found the students angry, but unarmed. The cops promised to wind down. But while students were still out in the street, the highway patrol arrived. Lloyd "Goon" Jones was there, the same highway patrolman who'd stood by in Oxford, Mississippi, in '62, as white folk rioted to keep James Meredith out of Ole Miss, and who'd teargassed us in Canton, Mississippi, in '66.

The highway patrol were never provoked and gave no warning to disperse. They just loaded their shotguns with their biggest, deadliest Double-O shot and, on the night of May 14, 1970, shot a damn 150-round fusillade. They claimed a sniper was firing at them from a building, and they shot up that building. A young Negro in a tuxedo, Phillip Gibbs, had just walked his sister home from a prom, and never threatened anyone. They killed him. A young Negro, James Green, passed on the far side of the street, coming home from a forty-cent-an-hour job. The highway patrol killed him, too. If Jackson State was a white school, they wouldn't have fired a shot, but cops killed two Negroes that night without batting an eye. One cop got on the radio: "Better send an ambulance, we killed us a few niggers here." Just like that. They wounded twelve other black kids.

The highway patrol shot up the building. The State wanted to replace the scarred building panels quick. Hide the evidence. We kept those panels as monuments to police brutality. And we wanted a memorial to our murdered. Jerris Leonard, deputy U.S. attorney general, came down to Jackson to meet with me and the head of Jackson State's student government. We gave the FBI our building panels only when they agreed to return them for our memorial.

The highway patrol insisted Negroes did the shooting at Jackson State. But most people saw through this. Some big northern whites chartered a Boeing 707 and came down to Jackson for the funeral. Senator Muskie brought five other U.S. senators: Tom Eagleton, Chuck Percy, Ralph Yarborough, Daniel Inouye, and Claiborne Pell. Adam Clayton Powell came with two other Negro congressmen: Charles Diggs and John Conyers. There were two students from Kent State, and Averell Harriman, ambassador to the Soviet Union. President Nixon called and sent a telegram.

We held the funeral in the same Masonic Hall where Medgar's funeral had been seven years before. On the stage above James Green's casket, I gave my eulogy: "How long, Lord, will our white brothers continue to destroy us?" I told that crowd, "There's no excuse for cops killing us. If the mayor of Jackson and the governor of Mississippi can't control their own cops, let's try them for malfeasance." I said we should arrest Goon Jones for conspiring to murder. And I challenged all the white folk from Washington to start a public federal investigation so this wouldn't happen again.

James Green's father worked for a grocery wholesaler. His foreman told Mr. Green, "You must feel pretty big with all those senators and reporters coming to your house." Mr. Green said no, he just wanted to get over losing his boy and get back to work. Well, they laid him off. I called Mr. Green's company three times trying to get him his job back. No luck. And a grand jury declared the highway patrol killings justified.

In May of '71, for the one-year anniversary of the killings, we held a week of events at Jackson State. We held memorial services and workshops. I gave a speech. On May 14, the first anniversary of Phillip Gibbs and James Green dying, we held an all-night candlelight vigil. We kept the news media off campus that week. Wanted no media circus, no sensational charges, just solid workshops and healing time. It did us some good.

In February of '71, Yale University, one of the world's great universities, made me a Chubb Fellow. I went up there, stayed overnight, mixed and mingled with some real smart professors and students, and gave a big speech. Charles Evers, from little Alcorn A&M, way out in the country, was made a Chubb Fellow at Yale. I was riding high in those days.

I ran for governor of Mississippi in '71 as an Independent. I was a huge underdog, but I didn't care. As Bobby Kennedy used to say, life itself is a gamble. I knew I could make Jackson a second Fayette and do for all Mississippi what we'd done in Fayette. Guess who was my opponent in the race? Bill Waller, the same man who'd prosecuted Byron Beckwith for killing Medgar. Waller had the Democratic Party nomination.

Bill Waller was a handsome man, with deep-set eyes, dark, slicked-back hair, and little sideburns. He was a smart corporate lawyer from Jackson. That got him big-business support. But Waller was never in the hip pocket of big business. He reached out to other groups. As district attorney, Waller had tried to convict Beckwith. That pleased the liberals. But when Beckwith got off scot-free, the rednecks forgave Waller, specially since Waller opposed busing and had a hillbilly accent. So Bill Waller had all three white votes sewed up: business, liberal, and redneck.

Here I was, neither redneck nor liberal, not even a white man, and trying to beat Bill Waller with no business support. And my staff was so young and raw. I had twenty-seven-year-old Ed Cole for my campaign manager, and twenty-two-year-old Jason Berry for my press secretary. A candidate must be tough on his staff, but we became a kind of family as we learned how to run for governor.

To win the race, I needed a coalition. We had 275,000 Negroes registered. I needed 250,000 of their votes. Eighteen-year-olds were now voting. I needed the votes of 25,000 young white rebels and 25,000 of their parents, white moderates who admired Martin Luther King and wanted to open up the white power structure. I thought 300,000 votes would win any election in Mississippi.

I decided I had to get Bill Waller knocked off in the Democratic primary, so I urged my supporters to vote in that primary—and to vote for Jimmy Swan. Jimmy Swan was the last man folks expected me to endorse. He was a hard segregationist country singer from Hattiesburg. A cheap imitation of Theodore Bilbo. Not only that, one of Jimmy's bodyguards had been part of Dale Walton's plot to kill me. But I told my followers to vote Jimmy Swan in the primary because I knew I could beat Jimmy in the general election. Backing Swan cost me some liberals: young Hodding Carter, Patt Derian, Wes Watkins. Some of my own staff were furious, but I'd do it again. Politics is a rough game. Sunday school teachers win no elections.

When Bill Waller easily won the Democratic primary, I heard whispers, "We've lost now." I said, "Hell, no! We've already won. Bill Waller likes blacks. We already know that Mississippi's next governor will be the first one ever to like and respect us."

My staff and I campaigned hard: in a Piper Cherokee three-seater, in fancy air-conditioned cars, in battered pickups, and many times on our own two feet. We mingled with the haves and the have-nots and the ain't-never-gonna-gets. I loved campaigning. Touching Negroes, pulling them close, squeezing backs—it was like a Holiness Church revival. These greetings were part of Mama's faith. And I loved coming into a little Mississippi town and seeing some old Negro in the crowd I hadn't seen for years.

I shook a lot of white hands, too, and shook up a lot of white stomachs. I saw white businessmen during that campaign scared to turn tail and scared to shake my hand. I'd look at them and think, "That's right, white folk! A black-skinned man from Decatur, Mississippi, is running to be your governor!" I spoke to poor whites, too, because discrimination hurt them, too. Hate loves to pit the haves against the have-nots, make each one fear the other. I knew I could help poor whites as much as I could Negroes.

I demanded police motorcades in each town. I had to show this was a serious campaign. No one would waste their vote on Charles Evers. I also had to show that a big black man could now get police protection in every little cracker town in the state. When some redneck town denied us a police escort, I'd say, "Get some cops out here with me, or we'll call NBC news on you!" I got the mayor of New York, John Lindsay, to come south and walk down some dusty roads campaigning for me. Lindsay had quite a name in those days and was preparing to run for president. Having him come south showed my campaign was for real.

I used my slogan from the Fayette campaign: DON'T VOTE FOR A BLACK MAN. OR A WHITE MAN. JUST A GOOD MAN. EVERS. Another poster said HANDS THAT PICK COTTON NOW CAN PICK ELECTED OFFICIALS. I said "Anywhere that's half Negro, let's run for office." In '71, I helped get Fannie Lou Hamer to run for the state senate.

I also told my life story in a book, my first memoir, *Evers*. A wonderful lady, Grace Halsell, had the idea. I said, "I can't write no book," but Grace told me to just talk, she'd gather it into a book. I was running around the country, ran poor Grace Halsell ragged, but she kept asking tough questions, and I never dodged her. She went off and wrote up *Evers*. We sold it at campaign events. That book stung some folk. It told about my running girls, bootlegging, numbers running for the Mob. Folk said, "You did *what*? Ran girls up in Chicago? Charles Evers ran a numbers game?" I'd say, "Yeah, and you heard it from me." I challenged my opponents to tell on themselves, too. They ducked my challenge. Some liberal idealists in my camp were kicking mad over that book being published. They said, "Uh, Charles, some of those confessions make . . . kind of heavy reading. . . . This is *not* the way to get whites to vote for you." They didn't want to bite the bullet.

But biting the bullet was the whole point of that book. Why let a political rival expose my mistakes? Confess your own sins and explain them. I could admit being a scoundrel because the South doesn't believe in saints. The liberal idealists said, "Charles, how could you live that way?" But the common folk forgave. I'd stand in front of big crowds of black faces: "I pray no other boy will ever be subjected to that kind of life. I was forced to live that way." It cleansed my soul to confess my sins and move on. With "Amazing Grace" playing on the organ, I'd tell crowds, "Let's sanctify Mississippi, turn away from evil, bury the hate, heal the scars." And the crowds forgave me, because they loved the church and believed in forgiveness.

Down here when a pastor says to "Vote Evers," his flock votes Charles Evers. And if the pastor tells his flock to stay home, those holy folk stay home! So I'd line up a pastor every stop I could, and on stage I'd say, "Pray for me, Reverend. Because I wasn't always a mayor." But I told folk, "Praying for us ain't enough. Campaigns cost money." I'd ask all the men in the crowd for five dollars. Folks said, "Charles, don't ask a lady for money." Why not? I'd ask for a dollar. Wives, mamas, girlfriends, too. They were poor, but they wanted political power. Then I'd add, "*I* can't be bought. They know because they've tried."

I told crowds, "Vicious as race hate is in Mississippi, it's a boil ripe to bust. All the poison will drain off. The scars will heal. All the suffering, the deprivations, all the murders and misery ain't been in vain! The new day dawning will spread its light all over this country!" I rode in a motorcade. I had my own dance troupe, the Everettes. I had a spiritual choir. Some days my daughters joined me. I had priests and nuns, whites and blacks, young and old, paid staff and volunteers—all working together. I wished Medgar, Martin, and Bobby could have been at those rallies to see a Negro bucking to be governor of Mississippi, making crowds of poor and black believe in themselves. But, God rest their souls, Medgar, Martin, and Bobby were all part of it.

I forced Bill Waller to campaign my way. In no one's hip pocket. Vowing to involve all people in government, improve Mississippi's reputation, start working again with the national Democratic Party. I forced Bill Waller to campaign for black support. No one had ever seen that before in a governor's race. I talked about things whites had always swept under the rug, like fixing Parchman Prison, where so many Negroes had suffered, and putting blacks on the highway patrol and in state government.

When the election came, whites harassed blacks in at least thirty-six counties. White employers told us, "If you vote Evers, if I see an Evers sticker on your car, don't bother coming back to work." Whites blocked many of my outside poll watchers from seeing the vote count. Ramsey Clark, advising my campaign, called on the Justice Department to stop this harassment.

On Election Day, we had the largest voter turnout ever in Mississippi history. I didn't get my three hundred thousand votes, nor even two hundred thousand. I got just 22 percent of the vote, and Bill Waller whipped me good. I didn't challenge his victory. He won by so much that a clean vote count would have changed nothing. But over three hundred other blacks in Mississippi ran for public office with me—for coroner, constable, supervisor, tax assessor, circuit clerk. About fifty of these Negroes were elected. But white folk stole some elections. I wanted to challenge the results in court, bring federal troops in to run our state elections. Again, I asked, Why can we send troops to Vietnam to ensure free elections, but not to Mississippi?

Waller had whipped me, but my concession speech was defiant. I said, "We may be beaten, but we ain't defeated!" Negroes had taken another step toward freedom. When Beckwith killed Medgar, he thought he'd killed civil rights in Mississippi. But by '71, we were ten times what we'd been in '63. By signing up two hundred thousand Negro voters, by running for Congress in '68, and by getting elected mayor of Fayette in '69, I'd done more to kill Beckwith than if I'd shot him dead. I hadn't gotten elected governor of Mississippi, but I'd prepared the ground. Someday, a black man will say, "Evers ran for governor. I can, too." And he'll win.

Now, guess which state supreme court judge swore in William Waller as governor? Old Tom Brady—the same man who made Byron Beckwith an activist back in '54, by claiming the federal government was itching to start a race war in Mississippi. The old order shook hands with the new. And Governor Waller *did* reach out to blacks. He put three blacks on the highway patrol, and he brought blacks into state government.

In all Mississippi, the best town for Negro candidates was Port Gibson, just up the road from Fayette. I was so proud when eight Negroes were elected in Port Gibson. Some of that had to be carryover from our work in Fayette. In late December 1971, at the swearing-in ceremony, you felt real change in the air. Civil rights had put blacks in Mississippi politics to stay.

CHAPTER 26

Scolding Richard Nixon about Watergate

In '72, some big wheels in the Democratic Party chose me as a committeeman at the Democratic National Convention. I wanted John Lindsay for president. He'd helped me in Fayette and stumped for me for governor. I told him, "John, if you get just one vote for president, it'll be mine." But the Lindsay campaign never got moving, and when the Democratic National Convention rolled around in July of '72, I threw my support to my old friend, Hubert Humphrey.

When I endorsed George Wallace for vice president, my friends said, "You're endorsing 'Segregation Now, Segregation Forever' George Wallace? Charlie Evers, you always had a strange sense of humor." But it was no joke. I preferred George Wallace a heartbeat away from being president to an untried, smooth-mouth liberal too blind to understand racism and poverty. Ask liberals why they use lily-white private schools, and they brag about not calling you "nigger." It's deeds that count, not words.

George Wallace wasn't ready to be president, but maybe someday he'd serve under a president like Ted Kennedy, Hubert Humphrey, or Walter Mondale. George Wallace, redneck vice president, serving whites, blacks, Indians, and Chinamen. He'd *have* to straighten up. Wallace never bragged about my endorsement, but he never refused it. I also courted George Wallace to get the backing of some rednecks for Charles Evers and civil rights. In '71, I helped striking pulp-wood haulers against the Masonite Company. Many of the strikers had Klan ties, but I stood with them. *Convert your enemy.*

273

On May 15, 1972, George Wallace was running for president in Laurel, Maryland, and some bastard shot him five times at close range. It brought me right back to June of '63 and Beckwith shooting Medgar. I visited Wallace in the hospital. When your brother's been assassinated, you never want to see even your worst enemy get shot. And by now, I really liked George Wallace.

Wallace spent almost two months in the hospital, under the knife, mostly alone. For a man who lived and breathed politics, that was like death. So I visited George Wallace. I was one of the first. Just like with Medgar, all the big politicians who never gave George Wallace the time of day when he was strong changed *quick* when he went down. Richard Nixon, Hubert Humphrey, and Ted Kennedy came. A South Dakota senator named George McGovern came. A Georgia governor named Jimmy Carter came. None of them cared about George Wallace as a man. They pretended to care because they knew he could no longer be president. They came courting his supporters. Wallace left the hospital, called himself a "viable candidate," and hit the campaign trail. Tough.

George McGovern beat out Hubert Humphrey as the Democratic nominee for president. McGovern was a smooth mouth who talked about helping blacks but never did much. Want to check if a politician's dealing straight on race? Check his staff. How many nonwhites are in his inner circle? Walter Mondale had brought blacks into his inner circle for years. McGovern's inner circle was lily-white. Folks like Ted Kennedy and Jacob Javits lived in rich white neighborhoods, sent their kids to exclusive white schools, and had no more than two blacks on their staffs.

The 1972 Democratic National Convention was no fun. The young left-wing liberals there spit on some of my old friends. Hubert Humphrey got pushed around pretty good. Mayor Daley of Chicago, a giant of the Democratic Party, was denied a seat at the convention! Seeing those two hammered made me feel like an old man. The Democratic Party needed a new chairman and vice chairman. George McGovern nominated a lady named Jean Westwood as Chairman, and the Democratic National Committee elected her quick. For vice chairman, McGovern nominated John Kennedy's old press secretary, Pierre Salinger. Stocky, cigar-smoking Pierre Salinger. We'd been in California together on Bobby Kennedy's last campaign. Pierre was a nice man, and funny. He'd been a hardworking floor manager for McGovern at the convention. Pierre hoped to be chairman but was willing to settle for vice chair. He expected to sail through.

But blacks needed a full voice in the party. The party had adopted some other reforms, but the United States had never had a Negro in a national leadership post. Liberals always talked equality. I thought, "Let's see them do something." Blacks were whispering, "Put a Negro up there," but no one spoke out. I found Basil Paterson, a black state senator from New York. New York had a big delegation, and I needed a man who could win. "Basil," I said, "if I nominated you, would you serve?" He said yes.

I raised my hand and stood up: "Much as I'd like to see you in there, Pierre, it's just not fair." I said, "If we're going to have a female chairman, we ought to have a black vice chairman. I place in nomination Mr. Basil Paterson of New York." The whole room went dead. You could have heard a rat piss on cotton. But someone seconded Basil Paterson, and then came booming applause.

George McGovern was the nominee of my party, and if he'd insisted on Pierre Salinger, I'd have folded. But McGovern was a liberal, so he said, "Either one of these very able men would be perfectly acceptable to me, and a great credit to our party." A furious Pierre Salinger withdrew his name quick. Basil Paterson became vice chairman of the party, and Pierre never forgave me. He wanted to bring Negroes into politics, but when we brought one too far and hurt Pierre's career, he showed his true colors. I still like Pierre. I've seen him since then. I don't think he likes me.

There was just one great scene at that convention. On July 11, 1972, Secret Service men and Alabama state troopers lifted George Wallace up to the platform in his chrome wheelchair. Just four days out of the hospital, still in pain, Wallace rolled up to the microphone, eyeballed a crowd of ten thousand liberals, and gave exactly the speech he'd give two hundred peckerwoods at a rally in Alabama: trashing taxes, busing, Negroes, and pointy-head social planners, and praising law and order, the army, and school prayer. I disagreed with most of his speech, but him giving it in the teeth of all those liberal Democrats made my eyes moist. I admire anyone with guts. I don't hate Klansmen for being racist. I oppose their racism and resent their violence, but I hate them for being gutless cowards who strike by night, hiding behind white sheets.

Neither Nixon nor George McGovern was much on civil rights. Nixon's Justice Department slackened off the civil rights record of Bobby Kennedy and Ramsey Clark. Nixon's federal judge nominees were awful. Nixon kept up the Vietnam War and kept sending too many poor and black soldiers there. A shame and a disgrace. Nixon was wrong to oppose busing.

But give Nixon credit: He cracked down on some racist unions, helped black contractors get hired and blacks get housing. Nixon had a black man, Robert Brown, right in the White House. He had a black deputy assistant secretary of defense. My friend Sam Jackson was assistant secretary of HUD. Richard Nixon sped up the integration of Mississippi schools. His White House forced some of the worst cracker schools to take black kids. President Nixon invited me when he spoke at a military base near Meridian, Mississippi. And when he saw the state police bar me from the podium, he touched my heart by seating me way up front, as his special guest.

And then in '71, Nixon had helped get Fayette our health clinic and the Martin Luther King Apartments. But then, Fayette got that from Nixon because I was a great salesman, and northern foundations had already given us the white man's seal of approval. To get this money from Richard Nixon, I had to pull it out between his teeth. Other black towns got nothing from Nixon's White House.

I voted for George McGovern for president, and even after all that had happened, I'd have campaigned for George McGovern if he'd asked me. He never asked me.

By '73, Mississippi had come over the hump on race. Segregation was dying. We had many black elected officials. No one looked up when I walked in a hamburger joint with my white secretary. Blacks once on welfare were making ten thousand dollars a year, with their kids in white public schools. By '73, I'd lived through the worst. I could have been gunned down, but I wasn't *expecting* to be gunned down, and that's a big change. For all our racial violence, we had more racial progress than Massachusetts, California—any of the big liberal states. I felt safer walking the streets of Jackson than in New York, Chicago, or Boston.

Whites from liberal old Massachusetts had always scorned the mean racist whites of Mississippi. But in '74, Boston had its own busing crisis, and the same folk who preached to Mississippi about racism said, "Don't school *my* kids with blacks." Liberal old Boston was a giant hypocrite. A judge in Boston handed down a school integration plan, and whites fought it like Ole Miss did in '62. I was so mad I sent telegrams to Ted Kennedy, to the black Massachusetts senator, Ed Brooke, to the Massachusetts congressional delegation, to George McGovern. I told them to get police protection for all students and parents being deprived of their constitutional rights.

In '73, I was reelected mayor of Fayette, with no opposition. Bennie Thompson got elected mayor of Bolton, Mississippi, just west of Jackson, and now we had two Negro mayors in the state. In fact, by '73, there were enough black mayors around the South for me to host the first Southern Black Mayors Conference and bring twenty black mayors and civic officials into Fayette. Howard Lee of Chapel Hill, North Carolina, was my cohost. We talked about the problems we shared, and how to get President Nixon's ear.

Every year since '64, on the second Sunday in June, we'd held a small memorial service for Medgar. My dear friend B. B. King often came. We were both proud, hardworking Mississippi black men, loyal to home but with time and money to travel. The year 1973 was the tenth anniversary of Medgar's death. We held his memorial service at New Hope Baptist Church in Jackson. From the pulpit, I said, "Medgar, it ain't all been bad, and you didn't die in vain."

But after the service, I got to talking with B. B. King about how young folk ignore our past heroes. B. B. was playing three hundred dates a year, ballrooms to prisons, Las Vegas to the Soviet Union. He'd cut "The Thrill Is Gone" in '69, his biggest hit. But B. B. could see that kids no longer wanted to hear a rural music about chopping cotton. Most of these kids ignored Medgar, who'd died to help them. I got so mad thinking of my own people, ignorant of Medgar Evers! I kept raving, "Who challenged the system? Who faced down the mayor of Jackson, and James O. Eastland, and Ross Barnett? Who took James Meredith into his house? Medgar! And no one even knows it. Martin Luther King took half the risks Medgar took! Martin left the South a lot. Medgar stayed in Mississippi!"

Finally B. B. said, "Alright, Charlie. Let's have Medgar Evers Homecoming every year." B. B. said he'd headline an annual three-day celebration of Medgar's life, with blues, jazz, gospel and rodeo. I loved the idea. Medgar didn't want us crying, hanging our heads, walking behind a fake casket, and that bullshit! Medgar wanted us to celebrate his life in civil rights. That's what we did in '73, and we've had a three-day Medgar Evers Homecoming every year since.

In '74 came my biggest tussle with the IRS. The IRS said I owed a fortune in back taxes. The IRS hated civil rights. Hodding Carter, the liberal newspaperman in Greenville, Mississippi, got audited every year. The IRS never forgave him for his editorials on civil rights. About thirty other civil rights folks in Mississippi got audited between '54 and '74. So when the Justice Department and a federal attorney in Jackson indicted me for income tax evasion in August 1974, I knew from the start it was political.

I wasn't blameless, because I'd hustled $200,000 up in Chicago, and hustlers don't pay taxes on money they aren't supposed to have. Since '69, big money had been flowing into Fayette, care of Charles Evers, and I wasn't always careful how I accounted for it. But stealing money, lining my own pockets at the expense of my people? Never. The IRS claimed I hadn't reported about $160,000 in income, hadn't paid about $50,000 I owed. Those numbers sounded real high to me, but I said, "I'll take my lumps and pay my bill."

Now, it so happened in '74 that the IRS also hooked my friend Nelson Rockefeller. They audited him for '69–'73 and found he owed over $900,000 in tax! Did the IRS threaten to jail Nelson Rockefeller? No. Nelson was from a famous white family, soon to be our vice president. The IRS said, "Oh, there, Nelson, just bring in those back taxes anytime. You know, 6 percent interest." Nelson's lawyers handled the case. Nelson probably wrote a personal check to settle it. I owed the IRS one-*twentieth* what Nelson did, but I was an uppity black man and no vice president, so the IRS tried to make me crawl like a dog. I cooperated, but I wouldn't crawl.

When they first came after me, I told my accountant to show the IRS auditor all my records. By law, I didn't have to do that. Most audited businessmen don't. But I said, "I'll make a clean breast of it, pay for my sins at 6 percent, like Nelson Rockefeller, and let's all go home." But the hotshot IRS agent on my case asked me: "Mr. Evers, what's your net worth?" I said, "That's your job. You tell me." Boy, that ticked him off. He was a white man used to asking all the questions. He said, "Mr. Evers, to cooperate with this investigation, you must tell us your net worth." He didn't know I'd been watching powerful white men all my life. I knew his game. I said, real quick, "What the hell's *your* net worth? What are your socks worth? What are your shoes worth?" Special Agent So-and-So hit the ceiling. I knew then he'd try to humble me.

We squared off awhile, then I told the IRS agent, "Let's calm down. You show me where I owe it, and I'll pay it. Send my accountant a bill." They said, "No, we're going to jail you." I said, "Mr. IRS agent, what can you do to me? Can you take away the loyalty that blacks show the Evers boys? No! All you can do is put me in some dirty jail. I been in a dirty Mississippi calaboose already. You can't do me no worse than that."

The newspapers implied I was a crook who wanted a plea bargain. The IRS people never offered a plea bargain, and I'd have torn it up if they did. I'd been a hustler and a good one, but I was no crook. The damn IRS people knew it, but they treated me like one. I'd broken some laws, but I'd built businesses, hired folks off welfare, sent money to charity. I'd given my share, probably saved the taxpayers a few dollars. I had no regrets.

I got myself a good New Orleans lawyer, Michael Fawer. He'd followed my civil rights work in Mississippi and called, offered to represent me. He met with officials of the Justice Department, but he couldn't keep me from being indicted. The white newspapers had a field day tearing up Charles Evers. That same year Inland Steel made $82 million net profits and paid no tax. Not a dime! Big business buys a jet and writes it off. A small businessman gives away a hamburger and gets charged with tax evasion.

Federal prosecutors tried me in June of '75. Michael Fawer and I fought them in court. After four long days of wasted time and harsh IRS testifying, the judge said the IRS testimony was so unfair to me that he had to call a mistrial. The white newspapers had to admit we'd beaten those federal prosecutors. I hung one of their newspaper clippings on the far wall of my office in Fayette. The bastards didn't lay a glove on me.

When Richard Nixon ran for president in '68, he promised to "bring us together," but his vice president, Spiro Agnew, split us apart. Leaders must want unity, not just on the stump, but in their souls. Richard Nixon never had freedom in his soul. In '68, I preferred my friend Hubert Humphrey. But when Richard Nixon was elected president, I made it my business to approach him. I wrote letters to Richard Nixon and called him many times. First, he ignored me, but I kept leaving messages. One day he took my call. We found we had a lot in common.

I got Nixon to invite me to the White House. I'd grown used to Lyndon Johnson, with his big staff hovering around. Nixon might have two or three men with him, and many times he'd send even them out of the room before we talked. Nixon was a history buff. He'd point to some chair: "Charles, you know Khrushchev sat in that chair." He knew who sat in which chair during which conference. That stuff bored me, but still we became personal friends. He was just as proud as I was of being tough, able to make a decision.

Watergate was a great shock to Richard Nixon. Most people thought Watergate was a terrible scandal. I didn't. People said Nixon was paranoid of his enemies, but that never bothered me. Nixon thought just like a black man: he liked to meet people one-on-one. He always suspected the powerful, never forgot that his enemies were setting traps for him, never forgave the snubs he'd felt from the golden boys when he was a poor, ugly child. As high as he rose, Nixon never stopped watching his back. Maybe he spent too much time doing that.

When news hit of the Republican break-in at the Democratic National Committee office, I grabbed the phone: "Mr. President, go on national TV and admit the truth. Tell the American people, as their commander in chief, you had the Democratic Party offices broken into to make sure they didn't aim to hurt this country. Some of the people will back you, some won't, but we'll all respect you for stepping up and taking the heat."

But Nixon couldn't admit he was a sonofabitch. When it came out the White House had used dirty tricksters to break into the office of Daniel Ellsberg's psychiatrist, I called Nixon: "For God's sake, Mr. President. Go on TV and say, 'Yes, I had Ellsberg's office burgled. George McGovern is dumb enough to give America to the Communists if I'd let him. I'm a sonofabitch, but I'm no one's sonofabitch but yours. Now judge me and be done with it, because this country has much bigger fish to fry.' "

But Nixon had to lie and say he didn't burgle Ellsberg, didn't break into the DNC offices, didn't lie and cover up, wasn't a crook. The lies kept growing and kept the Democrats and the press after him. I learned a lot about Richard Nixon during Watergate. Some of those dirty tricks he hatched made me lose some respect for him. Paying hush money, playing the FBI off against the CIA, wasn't right. But Richard Nixon was a good man who wanted to do right.

When I heard Nixon had been taping, I got on the phone a third time: "Mr. President, destroy the tapes. No one's got a right to hear a man's private conversations. The American people will support you on that. Tell them as chief executive and commander in chief, you had to destroy the tapes." But Nixon couldn't bring himself to destroy the tapes. The scandal grew up around him. In July of '74, the House Judiciary Committee voted the articles of impeachment. Whites thought Richard Nixon in jail would be an awful disgrace, but I'd seen too many good men jailed to agree. Prison's no disgrace unless you make it one. Even for the guilty, prison isn't the end of the world. I've told many prisoners what my daddy told me: "Okay, you made a mistake. Don't wallow in it. Just because you stumble ain't no excuse to lay down."

A month later, Richard Nixon resigned as president, but that sonofabitch never laid down. He kept working to rebuild his reputation until the day he died. We kept in touch. In March of '75, Richard Nixon asked me out to San Clemente. All kinds of dignitaries came to Nixon's funeral in 1994. People wanted me to go, but I'd already been to Nixon's funeral, in '75, in San Clemente. Man, *no one* would see him then! The guy went from head of the free world, able to get anyone on the phone, anytime, to being a pariah. No one would be seen with him, no one wanted to take his call. So he appreciated me going out to California to see him. Mrs. Pat Nixon was there, too, a lovely lady, but mostly Nixon and I talked alone, men talk. Nixon had hosted a lot of white politicians and business folk, but damn few civil rights leaders. We walked down on the beach. Nixon was an awkward man, with a bad knee and arthritis. He gritted his teeth and climbed those dunes.

Down on the beach, I asked Richard Nixon, "Why the hell did you do all that taping? If you were doing something wrong, why keep tapes?" Nixon was ashamed. He thought he was a master of the game of politics. Finally, he said the taping became a habit. He'd forget that the tapes were rolling, but he'd thought when he got older, he'd sit back, play all his tapes, and remember how it was being president.

Nixon said he'd hoped to sit down with his grandkids someday and play some of his tapes and teach them how government really worked—not the way they told it in the history books or the civics books.

I was so pissed off that this smart man had got himself in such a dumb mess. I asked Nixon, "When it all blew up, why didn't you burn the damn tapes?" He looked at me but said nothing. Finally he said, "Maybe I should have." He sort of laughed: "I wish I'd have listened to you." That's as far as he would go. He knew he'd screwed up on Watergate, but even months later, in a private talk with a good friend, he could barely admit it.

One day around 1975, I walked into a barbershop in Jackson for a shoe shine, and who was getting a haircut there but Allen Thompson, the old racist mayor of Jackson who'd let Medgar die. The very same Allen Thompson I'd thought about killing execution-style, back in '63. In those days, I bet he wished I was dead, too. I'd seen him since at a few official functions. We'd exchanged dirty looks. But seeing him now sitting back in a barber chair, my heart opened a crack. I looked him in the eye: "Well, I'll be damned, Allen! I never thought the day would come when you and I'd be using the same barbershop, me getting a shoe shine and you getting a haircut." He smiled, enjoying this as much as I was.

I kept on: "Allen, you know why I don't get my hair cut here?" I paused. "Because they can't cut black folks' hair right." The whole barbershop broke up laughing—Allen Thompson the hardest. We had a nice exchange that day, and my heart loosened. The next few years, we got friendly. We weren't no buddies, now. We never saw eye-to-eye. But we'd talk and laugh when we saw each other in Jackson. Making friends with Allen Thompson was a real milestone in overcoming hate.

In October of '76, I protested against Medicaid. Prescriptions and refills had been free for Medicaid patients, but our state legislature had decided to control costs by making them fifty cents each. Dr. Aaron Shirley helped me protest that. As usual, no one was looking out for the little man at the lumberyard or the Laundromat, the custodian at Mississippi Power & Light. I led three hundred demonstrators to the state capitol in Jackson. We protested in the capitol rotunda, and I lobbied our governor, Cliff Finch, in person. Fannie Lou Hamer sang

"This Little Light of Mine." We stared at a bronze statue of Theodore Bilbo and sang "We Shall Overcome."

In the same month, the mayor of Ruleville, Mississippi, Virginia Tolbert, declared Fannie Lou Hamer Day in Ruleville. We gave Fannie many awards. Amzie Moore rebuked the crowd, saying that only 40 percent of the registered Negroes in Mississippi were voting. As the featured speaker, I *ordered* them to vote in the next election, so Fannie Lou's work would mean something. Then I called members of the audience by name, told them Fannie Lou needed twenty-five hundred dollars to pay her doctor bills. I started us off with a five-hundred-dollar bill. We took up almost twenty-one hundred dollars for Fannie Lou that day.

Near the end of her life, Fannie Lou said folk must realize that "whether he's white as a sheet or black as a skillet, out of one blood God made all nations." In early '77, Fannie Lou went in the hospital in Mound Bayou with cancer, heart disease, diabetes. She was right with God, but she hated to die without seeing more racial and social progress. No one's heart was ever stronger than Fannie Lou Hamer's, but on March 14, 1977, her heart failed, and she passed on. Fannie did so much for our movement. She saw the truth clearly, and she always had the guts to speak the truth. She saw how racism kept America from being truly Christian. And Fannie Lou showed all the holy hypocrites what it meant to live as a true Christian. We all still miss her.

I endorsed George Wallace for vice president again in '76. Civil rights had made George Wallace a better man. On the campus where he'd stood in the door, the mostly white students elected a black homecoming queen, and Wallace crowned her queen. That same day, he visited a black mayors conference. This was more than cold politics. Personal suffering had worked on Wallace. Walking so close to death had made him look deeper at what a man is. Medgar's death brought me along, John Kennedy's death brought Bobby along. For George Wallace, being shot brought him along. As long as there's breath in the body, enlightenment can come.

Late in his political life, George Wallace began helping blacks in Alabama. When he ran for office the second time, he came into the black churches. I won't say I made him do it, because he'd embraced on his own the idea of uniting black and white. But I had a lot to do with it. George Wallace came into the black churches of Alabama and told how wrong it was to mistreat any people. We all knew he meant the hurt he and other whites had put on black folk down the years. It touched my heart when he said, "I will never stand in the schoolhouse door again."

Tuskegee, Alabama, had a black mayor, Johnny Ford, who married a white girl. I was sitting right next to George Wallace when he introduced Johnny Ford as "the greatest mayor we ever had in Alabama." For George Wallace to say that about a black man with a white wife— that amazed many of us. In his last term in office, George Wallace appointed more blacks to state government and more black state troopers than any governor in Alabama history. His son went to school with blacks, even had a black roommate.

Give me ten low-down dirty white bigots over ten liberals, anytime. Liberals work from the head, but bigots work from the heart. And once you've changed the heart of a low-down dirty bigot, then you've really got something. Because bigots do things. Bigots change things. When we changed George Wallace's heart, he was just as strong to help black folks as he'd been strong to hurt us before. Peace in his heart. God bless him.

George Wallace was the natural leader of millions of peckerwoods all over this country. He'd been through the fire of being shot. He was tough enough to take the heat in the street, smart enough to cut a deal. And he'd cast racism from his heart. It made no sense not to use this man for some high purpose. Why not vice president? I even wrote a column in the *Los Angeles Times* endorsing Wallace. I said the South was rising again, and this time we could win if whites and blacks would join forces. I said racism was not caused and kept by the George Wallaces of this world but by the liberals who promised us the world, but couldn't deliver.

But George Wallace's day as a national candidate was done. Another deep southerner, Jimmy Carter, got elected president in '76, using George Wallace lines: I'm not from Washington, the U.S. government has lost touch with the people. Carter didn't want Wallace as VP. Jimmy's wife, Rosalynn, came to Fayette in the '76 campaign, and I showed her the town. Rosalynn would have made a better president than Jimmy. Democrats said Carter had bit the bullet on civil rights and hung Martin Luther King's picture in the state capitol. But he'd also turned Martin away when Martin marched to the capitol. Jimmy Carter was a phony. Anytime you see a southern liberal, you know you got a phony.

Jimmy Carter had no more business being president than I got flying a jet backward to New York. A new president who doesn't know Washington needs advisors who do. As mayor of Fayette, I sought help from police and fire chiefs all over the United States—and Fayette's a town of fifteen hundred people! Jimmy Carter tried to run the whole United States by carrying half of Georgia up there to Washington. But most of Jimmy Carter's top advisors were either wimps or fools.

I was Fayette's mayor every day Jimmy Carter was president. I never asked for one federal grant or favor, not even a cup of coffee. He invited me to some civil rights events. I never went. Carter hired a few blacks. He hired Andrew Young as ambassador to the UN. That was a setup from the start. I said, "Andy, you ain't going to hold that job two years. You're going to quit or get fired." He said, "It's a great honor, Charlie." I said, "I know you, Andy. You ain't going to take all the bullshit they bring down on you." Jimmy Carter's White House was never straight with Andy Young, and when Andy met with some Arabs, Jimmy Carter, the great human rights hero, fired him. Beware of humanitarians.

Jimmy Carter was a prickly, Sunday-school-teaching wimp. Grinned all the damn time. Let all those Carter women jingle him. Wouldn't tie his shoes without asking Rosalynn, his mama, and his little daughter Amy. In November of '79, five hundred Iranian students took over the U.S. embassy in Iran and took fifty-some Americans hostage. Jimmy Carter wouldn't bomb the radicals, and the rescue mission he finally tried was pitiful. Carter looked weaker and weaker.

In 1978, two men who'd been out front for so many years stepped down. Hubert Humphrey, who'd always been so full of life, died in '78. Soon as I heard, I called Mrs. Humphrey and asked what I could do. Like Bobby Kennedy, Hubert saw injustice, called it by name, and tried to change it. Humphrey was jollier than Bobby Kennedy, but they both looked straight in your eye and *listened*. Hubert wanted me to be a congressman. Once as vice president, he came down to Fayette, saw me in back of the counter at my grocery store, and said, "Charlie Evers, you've got as much business running this grocery store as I do going back to Minneapolis to run my father's drugstore." I still miss Hubert.

The other one to step down was Senator James O. Eastland. After thirty years in power, he finally retired. I wanted his seat. So did Maurice Dantin, a Democrat and former district attorney, and Thad Cochran, a Republican. Folk said, "Charlie, don't run for the Senate. You'll split the Democrat vote, and we'll get Thad Cochran." Well, I liked Thad Cochran. All the Cochrans treated blacks right. Thad used to give me the soul handshake. He was the first Mississippi congressman with a Negro on his staff. One of his top aides was a black man, Nehemiah Flowers. I said, "Thad, you're my good friend, and one of us is going to be senator."

Aaron Henry, state cochair of the Democratic Party, wanted me out of the race. The doubters said, "A black man doesn't belong in this race." But tell me I can't do something, and I'm going to do it. I sat out the primaries, then jumped in the race as an Independent. I knew I could win. Some of my doubters became my biggest supporters. They were beaten-down people, raised up by my campaign. Muhammad Ali and Kris Kristofferson joined my motorcade. Ali paraded with me in Jackson, even made commercials for me.

I campaigned on my old platform: end racism, help the poor, bring industry to Mississippi. Make it a felony for daddies to abandon their kids. But I changed on busing. I'd led the fight for busing schoolkids back when busing meant a central school where you bused every local child, white and black. But in Mississippi, by '78, busing meant busing black kids only, and busing them thirty miles from home, stealing their identity. To hell with that.

I got 23 percent of the vote, Maurice Dantin 32 percent. Thad Cochran won easily with 45 percent. Maybe my running did keep Maurice Dantin out of the Senate, but I don't regret it for a minute. Maurice Dantin was no devil. Mississippi called him a moderate Democrat. But he was the darling and handpicked successor of Jim Eastland and his kind. Those people didn't know what Mississippi needed. So I'm proud I ran for that U.S. Senate seat. I just wish I'd won.

CHAPTER 27

Why I Became a Republican

AT HEART, I'M NOT A DEMOCRAT OR A REPUBLICAN. I'm an integrationist. I've had Democratic leadership posts, so people think I'm a Democrat. I was a Democrat because it was national Democrats who fought for civil rights. I was a Democrat because Bobby Kennedy was one. But I've always thought like a Republican, and I always knew that someday I'd register as a Republican.

I couldn't shake the feeling that the Democrats wanted to control the poor by keeping them in need. If I take care of you, I control you. For poor blacks, being called "nigger" isn't as bad as taking so much welfare they don't know who they are and where they stand. Like Daddy said: Produce something, or you mean nothing. And too many big civil rights folk sat in fat, do-nothing jobs, paid off and toeing the line. Not me.

Much as I loved Lyndon Johnson, he wasn't above installing a federal program to keep someone in line. Lyndon built too many social programs, told blacks to trust in HUD and the welfare office. And the liberals following Lyndon Johnson created new giveaway programs to satisfy the poor. No one should be satisfied. We should all work to get more and do better. I was seeing folk on welfare who were the children and grandchildren of welfare cases. The Democrats accepted that. I couldn't.

Liberals loved the Comprehensive Employment and Training Act (CETA) jobs program that was an eighteen-month dead end. I'd see young blacks on CETA, supposed to be picking up paper or cleaning washrooms for the city of Jackson. But since CETA paid the kids, the city let some of these kids sit around, smoking pot, drinking wine. After eighteen months, they were headed back on mama and daddy, or back on welfare. I said, "Let's do CETA right: Take three kids off welfare and make them clerks for a small businessman like me. After CETA pays these kids a year, if they work hard, I must pay them for two more years. That's my incentive to train them and advance them. Now we're all getting somewhere." I said all this, but the liberals ignored me.

Mississippi had white bigot Governor Finch from '76 to '80, but he invited blacks into the governor's mansion. On many things, Cliff Finch was dead wrong, but he let poor black folk know their government by inviting us in the mansion. He let us marry in the mansion, and for a twenty-year-old black girl from Fayette to plan her wedding party in the governor's mansion makes her feel so much more a part of the state. William Winter, who followed Cliff Finch, was a liberal who never let the word *nigger* escape his lips. But he never let the common black folk even near the gate of the governor's mansion. I got in there a few times to meet with William Winter, but very few blacks did.

Democrats say, "Don't spank your kids, put them in private school." They've got that reversed. Democrats give low-down, dirty criminals endless legal appeals. Brutal criminals must be cut down quick. Think that isn't Christian? Then do something Christian for the man's victims. And Democrats don't know that welfare's a sickness, which ruins families. Deep down, most Democrats want the poor to stay poor, so they'll always need the Democrats' protection. And deep down, most civil rights leaders want racism to live on, so we'll always need civil rights groups.

To hell with that. I say let's all climb out of poverty and vote whatever political party serves our needs. Let's kill racism dead and put the NAACP out of business.

Even with all our civil rights gains, the poor were still being ignored by the powers that be. The Democratic congressmen supposed to represent us were taking coffee breaks with lobbyists. So I aimed to honor Medgar's memory with a coalition to move amongst the big men in Washington and speak for the left-out. I knew Medgar would have approved.

So on January 28, 1979, in Fayette, I convened the first meeting of the Independent Coalition for Mississippi, a nonpartisan group to lobby the Great White Fathers on behalf of the poor of our state.

Nearly seven hundred people showed for that first meeting. Most were rural blacks, but some were members of the Mississippi Conference of Mayors, and some were white businessfolk. We elected a white businesswoman our secretary. The crowd elected me chairman by unanimous vote.

The Independent Coalition could help blacks start fresh and carry on Medgar's work. But Aaron Henry hated my Independent Coalition. Aaron thought he was carrying on Medgar's memory, and I was hurting it. Aaron sent letters round Mississippi saying an independent coalition would isolate blacks outside "the real political world." Aaron knew the Democrats weren't doing much for us, but he said let's educate and organize. Register new voters. Bring the Democrats in line. Aaron thought the Republicans would never care about blacks or the poor, and never hold power in the South. That's just what folks once said about Negroes.

By '79, blacks in Mississippi were showing power in our state legislature. In '65, just 7 percent of eligible blacks in Mississippi were registered to vote. By '79, it was 70 percent, the second-highest rate in the nation. By '82, Mississippi had 424 elected black officials, far more than any other state. We'd taken down the statue of Senator Bilbo from the rotunda in our state capitol. And as I walked around in public, whites would say, "Hi, Charles! Hi, Mayor!" instead of, "There goes that damn nigger, Evers."

But blacks were still outside the tent, peeking in. So were the Republicans. Republicans and blacks found each other and joined forces. Some said, "Charles Evers joined the Republicans and sold out the civil rights movement." Listen: Charles Evers will never sell out civil rights for anyone! But I'm a businessman and an integrationist, and the civil rights movement was antibusiness and segregated in the Democratic Party. The Democrats took us for granted. I watched Daddy cheat on Mama, so I know: The day you think someone will never turn on you is the beginning of the end. The day a political party thinks some ally could never turn on the party, that alliance is doomed.

The way things were going, in twenty years, the Republicans would be all-white and the Democrats all-black. Medgar would have hated that. Medgar never tied himself to one party. So I worked with the Republicans as a renegade Democrat or Independent. Aaron Henry already called me a Republican. He'd warn me, "When you lay down with dogs, Charlie, you wake up with fleas. And when you lay down with Independents, you wake up with Republicans."

Aaron said Republicans in the White House would cut aid to the needy, but I said no president could get away with taking food from a hungry child, not even that smooth old actor Ronald Reagan. I said, "If Reagan takes food from the hungry, I'll be the first to march on Washington. I'll get him on the phone or grab him by the hand if I got to." I'd brought Fayette back lots of federal money, but no one in Washington had ever given Charles Evers a quarter. When I went up there, I paid my own airfare, my own hotel bill, my own feed. I answered only to the Lord and the people of Mississippi. So if Reagan turned on the poor, I was ready to fight every Republican in Washington, from President Reagan on down.

In August 1980, the Democrats held their national convention in Madison Square Garden, New York. I stayed at the Hilton, alone. I was a Teddy Kennedy delegate. Out of loyalty to the Kennedy family, I went all over the country for him. I was one of Ted Kennedy's top black advisors, proud of being loyal to Teddy when other blacks and smooth-mouth liberals had fallen away.

National political conventions should honor those who carried the party through the wilderness. That's obvious. But the Democrats have never treated their heroes right. At their '72 convention, they kicked dirt on Mayor Daley of Chicago, and they kicked dirt enough on Lyndon Johnson to bury him alive! I went to Austin, Texas, many times in the '70s, and each time I said Lyndon Johnson was a great president, people gave me dirty looks. In Austin! The Bible says, "The prophet is never honored in his own land." But boy, it hurt to see the home folk reject Lyndon Johnson, who'd given so much to the Democratic Party and to his country.

But the 1980 convention was the worst. Ted Kennedy was heir to all the good work of the greatest family in the history of the Democratic Party—and at the 1980 convention the party faithful booed him. I'll never forgive that. Worst of all was seeing *blacks* boo Teddy—after all the Kennedys had done for us. Rosey Grier and Rafer Johnson had been right alongside Bobby Kennedy when he was shot—and Rosey and Rafer booed Ted Kennedy. That was my last Democratic convention. When H. Rap Brown and Stokely Carmichael had given up on the

Democratic Party in the '60s, I'd looked down on them for it. Now I was doing the same.

I challenged Teddy: "Why do you take this? Don't support Jimmy Carter, with his people cutting you up like this!" Teddy hated Jimmy Carter, but Kennedys work within the system, take the punches, serve their party. When Teddy chose to make peace with Carter and back his reelection, I knew I was no longer a Democrat. I've never talked real close to Teddy Kennedy since.

Before Ted threw in the towel, he made sure the platform stood with working people. He couldn't endorse Jimmy Carter with his heart, but in the end, Teddy went to the podium on that stage at Madison Square Garden, shook Jimmy Carter's hand, tried to smile and give the image of unity Carter wanted going out over TV. The day after he conceded to Jimmy Carter, Ted Kennedy made the greatest speech of his life: "The work goes on, the cause endures, the hope still lives, and the dream shall never die."

I pissed off many people by endorsing Ronald Reagan for president in 1980. Friends ripped me: "Charles, you're out of step." But I saw a leader's toughness in Reagan. Send Jimmy Carter back to Sunday school in Plains, Georgia. Reagan looked like a Nixon, an LBJ, and that made leaving the Democrats easier.

In November of '80, Reagan won in a landslide, so my civil rights friends were more "out of step" than I was. On December 9, I visited Reagan with Hosea Williams and Ralph Abernathy. Many blacks feared that Reagan hated black people. Hosea, Ralph, and I went to make sure that wasn't true. And it wasn't—Reagan promised me he'd be president of all the people. Reagan had promised to streamline government. I asked him to replace welfare with workfare, fire some of the federal bureaucrats, and stop telling black folk their life's best hope was a grant from HUD.

My first visit to Reagan in the Oval Office, I said, "Mr. President, let's do three things. First, fix the tax code. Tax everyone 5 percent, across the board: millionaires and welfare cases and Bethlehem Steel. No one pays more than 5 percent, but no one pays less. No slick exemptions or deductions. Anyone pays less than 5 percent, jail them. No more General Motors writing four jet airplanes off their taxes while Joe Smith can't afford bus fare."

"Second," I said, "keep illegal aliens out of this country, and stop coddling those here! Spend no government money on aliens. Third, any man who won't support his kids, make him a felon, and work him six days a week on a county work farm. Give him a decent wage, but send part of it to his family." Ronald Reagan loved hearing this, specially from a black man. I said, "Let's go ahead, then." He smiled: "Charles, we really can't do that." I got mad: "Mr. President, you're scared to bite the bullet." The whole Reagan White House was scared to bite the bullet. In this conservative Republican White House, if you talked about ending welfare, they thought you were crazy.

Before I left the Oval Office, I invited President Reagan down to see the blind and deaf in our Charity Hospital in Meridian. I told him to stop paying rich men like James O. Eastland $150,000 a year not to farm. "And another thing," I said, "Stop paying the ex-presidents. They got paid in their time. Cut off Mrs. Truman. Her husband was president forty years ago! Why does multimillionaire Jackie Kennedy need a presidential pension? Gerald Ford can't keep track of all the money he's made on corporate boards. Cut him off! And cut off Jimmy Carter down to the penny for leaving the White House such a shambles. Take all his peanuts, too, much as he screwed this country!" Ronald Reagan laughed his nice laugh. I said, "Mr. President, you could be the first one to renounce your pension when you leave office." He said, "I'll think about that, Charles." He never said another word about it.

Reagan invited me back to the Oval Office with other civil rights folk and told us he'd be cutting government. But he looked me in the eye and swore not to hurt those in need. I can read a face. He meant it. I said, "Mr. President, I'll hold you to it." But a young man who did Reagan's budgets, David Stockman, had a bunch of university degrees and not enough common sense to know how to pour piss out of a boot. People got hurt. Maybe Reagan was dumb, but he was smart enough to know how much he didn't know. He delegated. In the case of David Stockman, he chose the wrong man.

Reagan could drive home some cold bargains, roughshod his way, but unlike Nixon or LBJ, he always wanted to be liked. Reagan had blacks working around him, but he planned to veto extension of the Voting Rights Act. I got mad: "Mr. President, you'll take away everything we fought and died for." Reagan ended up renewing the act for forty years—even more than we'd asked for. Reagan once made a stupid comment that Martin Luther King might have been a Communist, but he also made Martin's birthday a national holiday.

Being mayor and judge and knowing everyone in town, I knew in '81 that Fayette was fixing to elect a new mayor. Bobby Kennedy told me in '64: If you stay too long, the same folks who screamed you up will scream you down. Well, the same folks who screamed me up in Fayette in '69 and '73 and '77 meant to scream me down in '81. I'd always been tough on people, taken no excuses, and they tired of my heavy hand. My opponent, Kennie Middleton, was a nice young black lawyer who wanted the job real bad. I refused to ease up on Fayette just to win an election. I figured, "Let Kennie run Fayette awhile." I barely campaigned.

Just before Election Day, four men broke into an old lady's little restaurant. I jailed them for six months. Guys broke into a farmer's co-op, stole some wrenches and all his tires. I jailed them six months, made them repay every penny, and fined the head thief $250. Those jailbirds and all their mamas and cousins said, "Charlie Evers, you're a dictator. We're going to beat you in the election." I said, "If Fayette has got to where it's okay to rob and steal from working people, I don't want to be your mayor."

I ran that town just like I'd done since '69. Didn't let blacks raise hell, cuss honkies, or come speeding down Main Street. I let no one tear up property. I wouldn't let men beat their women. Some of these dudes I fined, and some I jailed. I wouldn't let blacks congregate in the street. I told them to control their emotions, don't sing and dance—start planning their future. I wouldn't let them make fun of Negroes trying to get rich. I just didn't allow. Kennie Middleton implied I was a dictator. He used the slogan WE'VE SEEN WHAT FAYETTE CAN DO FOR ONE MAN. NOW LET'S SEE WHAT ONE MAN CAN DO FOR FAYETTE. Folks got out of jail and went straight to the polls against me, the law abiding voted for change, and Kennie Middleton was elected.

Kennie Middleton made a piss poor mayor. He knew nothing about the job when he came in, and learned nothing in office. He lost Fayette business and found none to replace it. I still like Kennie, but politics has got nothing to do with being nice. Being mayor, being out front, means pushing and pulling people to get things done. A good mayor gets things started in hard times. I sure did in '69.

People hold power tightly. The whites weren't ready to hand Fayette over in '69. I had to take it from them. I'd fought so hard to get ahold of Fayette, and now I wasn't ready to hand it over to Kennie Middleton. So in '85, I ran for mayor again and got Kennie out of there. Around '87, I did for Fayette what Kennie Middleton could never have done. I saw Sam Pierce, the secretary of HUD, in his Washington office.

I'd seen Sam at meetings for years. We came off the same stalk: black men the same age, both war veterans, both raised by tough small-time businessmen daddies, both protégés of Nelson Rockefeller. Sam had done things I might have done if I'd left Mississippi—become a lawyer, a cabinet secretary. HUD was that old Housing and Urban Development agency that Lyndon Johnson had pumped so big in the '60s. Now Reagan was knocking some of it down. When Reagan came in, HUD had over fifteen thousand employees, a budget over $14 billion. Reagan and Sam Pierce felt cutting HUD could save taxpayer money and help the housing industry, too.

"Alright," I told Sam in his office, "But don't cut the heart out of HUD. Don't forget the poor and the left-out." I asked Sam for a federal discretionary grant of three hundred thousand dollars to rehab some old low-income housing in Fayette. Walking out of Sam Pierce's office, I knew Fayette had that three hundred thousand dollars. We announced it at Fayette city hall. My visit to Sam Pierce convinced me HUD was alright. They'd made deep cuts, but they still cared for America's poor. And Sam Pierce was as good as his word; Fayette got the three hundred thousand.

Pierce and HUD later fell in a federal scandal. Reporters sniffed around at how I'd got the three hundred thousand dollars. A tempest in a damn teapot. I got that money fair and square, and we spent every cent wisely. But some stiff-backed folk said I'd got it because Sam Pierce was my friend. If being friends with Sam Pierce is a crime, I'm guilty. If helping your friends is a crime, Sam Pierce can plead guilty—after they've cleared the dock of all the white politicians around here since 1776.

In May of '89, I formally joined the Republican Party. My Republican friends cheered. Richard Nixon was delighted. My civil rights friends were not. My old campaign manager Ed Cole said, "Charles Evers has clout, but not a man alive can bring a lot of blacks to the Republican Party." That kind of talk inspired me. I always have to do what they say I can't.

Sometimes I tell an old black man to vote Republican, and he says, "Well, I don't know. I've been a Democrat all my life." I say, "You weren't nothing in politics till '65! Because you weren't registered." But I'm bringing a lot of blacks to the Republican Party. Connecticut's got a smart young black Republican in Congress now, Gary Franks. In '94, Oklahoma elected a smart young black Republican, J. C. Watts. Black voters will come.

In '89, Kennie Middleton challenged me again as I ran for a fifth term as mayor. Most of my old Washington contacts had retired. Civil rights wasn't in vogue. Federal support for little towns in Mississippi was way down. I couldn't get Fayette new plants because labor was cheaper in Mexico. Suddenly, 20 percent of Fayette was out of work, over twice the rate in Mississippi as a whole. I was sixty-six years old, and tired. I decided to leave the limelight, let a fresh man come out front. On May 4, 1989, Fayette elected Kennie Middleton.

Kennie was still a good man, but a bad mayor. He had no national contacts and brought Fayette no new jobs. I'd brought the town way up, but I couldn't hold it up for twenty years. Fayette settled down under me, and when Kennie Middleton came in, Fayette started sinking. We've got a new mayor now. Fayette's still sinking.

As I let go of Fayette a little, I started wanting to travel the world again. I wanted to see Africa, the place of my ancestors. I wanted to help countries in Africa do business with the United States, like I would have done if Robert Kennedy had lived to be elected president in '68. I hadn't let go of the idea of working as a bridge between Africa and a U.S. president.

Africa has so many resources! Copper and oil, sandy beaches for tourists. Africa should be so much richer than it is. I went to Senegal; Kinshasa, Zaire; and Cape Town, South Africa, to study the problem. I got Ronald Reagan to send me off on a trade exchange to Dakar, Senegal, with his daughter Maureen. I had my own bedroom on *Air Force Two*, my own staff, a big briefing book. Senegal was having its centennial. The country dedicated a square in Dakar to the United States, called it Jackson Square. I accepted on behalf of President Reagan. But this was more than a ceremonial visit. It was my chance to make contacts that might start economic development in Senegal—and in Fayette. I've been working on this ever since the mid-1980s. In January 1994, I went down to Fatee, Senegal, to push a swap with Jefferson County, Mississippi.

The Senegalese hate being called poor, ignorant Africans. They don't beg, they do business. Buying U.S. fish-processing equipment for plants in Senegal. Buying our chickens because theirs are tough as dogs. Since that first visit, I've had the mayor of Fatee and Senegal's minister of oil over for lunch with Governor Fordyce of Mississippi. They've struck oil in Fatee, and they need U.S. oil-drilling gear. I like doing business with Africans. I don't go through a hundred different committees. I meet one man, and he makes the final decision. We need more of that in this country.

Around 1982, I invited myself to South Africa and got White House clearance. I admire Nelson Mandela, but for a while I feared his ANC government would fail, because without know-how, you're shackled. If you've never been inside a government building, how can you run a government? If you've never been inside an airplane, how can you regulate an airline industry? You need advisors. I'd had Mayor Lindsay and Police Chief Rizzo in Fayette. I worried Nelson Mandela would have an all-black government, too proud or stupid to get advice from whites. I thought Nelson Mandela should be vice president, telling F. W. de Klerk, "We got the votes, but we don't know how to run a government. Teach us. In ten years, I'll be president." But the ANC has included whites in its government. South Africa will be alright.

Around '84, Jonas Savimbi in Angola asked Americans who believed in his cause to come to Angola. I rounded up two Alabama preachers, and down we went. Savimbi impressed me so much. His Unita movement was showing Angola how to make something from nothing. He wore a .45 Magnum with an ivory handle. He was fifty years old, with the drive of a man half his age. He charmed reporters in English, French, and Portuguese. Even if it meant cooperating with the South African whites, he was determined to get the Russians and Cubans out of Angola.

And he was doing it! Savimbi showed us the land he'd captured. His base was in the bush, southeastern Angola, but he looked ready to take the whole country. He was making the bush productive. Angola was making knives, cooking utensils, things of sand and ivory. He was turning powerless, dirt-poor Africans into free men and women living for a cause, and they loved him for it.

There was always something mysterious and isolated about Savimbi. But I've got a weakness for strong black leaders, and Jonas Savimbi became my friend. In June 1988, I went up to the White House and met with Savimbi, Ralph Abernathy, and President Reagan. I gave Savimbi the Medgar Evers Award one year, and Myrlie threw a fit. She disliked Savimbi's politics and his methods, and she said he wasn't fit to get any award with Medgar's name on it. I told Myrlie she could stuff it because I'd known Medgar twenty-one years before she'd ever seen his face.

Savimbi took me to one of his rallies, in a liberated zone of "the free lands of Angola." He brought me to the biggest crowd I've seen in all my life. Good God, bigger than the March on Washington in '63. Acres and acres of black people. Savimbi told me to talk to them, he introduced me, and I went on. I had no microphone, and very few understood my English, but I tried, out of respect for Jonas Savimbi and the pride he'd brought Angola.

Doing a job that big brings many enemies. Savimbi could never relax, never reveal where he was staying. I was his guest in Angola four times, and where he spent the night was always a huge secret. On my last trip to Angola, around 1992, Savimbi was getting real jumpy. Today, Jonas Savimbi's off his rocker. Fight, fight, fight. The Russians and Cubans are all gone, and Savimbi's killing his own people. He lost a fair election but won't give up power. He's killed most of his own advisors. What goes around comes around. Someday, they'll kill him. I'd have told him that to his face in Angola, but it was his plane flying me home.

American foreign policy is still racist. We're so hard on dark-skinned Manuel Noriega for sending us drugs. But do we go over to Sicily and take on the Mafia? No, because they're white. We lecture China on human rights. Well, how many blacks have been murdered in our country since 1619? How many Indians did the white man kill taking the West?

You know the biggest thing I've noticed in Africa? How much Africans are like the Negroes of Fayette. In Kinshasa and Senegal, they sing, dance, congregate in the street. Just like us. They scuffle and kill each other with no plan for the future. And they make fun of Negroes trying to get rich. And it hit me: *They're not like us, we're like them. We're still Africans.* No wonder we can't get rich in America. When I got home and told this to some of my civil rights buddies, they glared at me real hard. All of black folks' problems are supposed to be the white man's fault.

CHAPTER 28

The Bridge That Carried Us Across

I PLAN TO LIVE AWHILE. In '93, I had a hernia and a prostate operation and left the hospital in one day. I've put on fifty pounds through the years from too much soul food, but I'm still busy as a cat on a hot tin roof. I get an annual physical, top of my head to the soles of my feet. I tell my doctor, "Anything wrong in there, take it out!" As long as I don't drink, smoke, or get married, I'll be alright. And as long as I'm here, I'll be running something, not praying and hoping. The Lord has stayed with me seventy-three years. He might as well stay the whole way. I think He will.

In 1984, I toured Europe with B. B. King, and before I die I'm going to leave politics and do it again. I'd like to hit Paris and find Medgar's girl from the war. I've been in Paris several times since '45, but I've never known how to find that girl. I know she hasn't been sitting around waiting for the Evers boys to call. She must be married somewhere, getting to be an old lady. I'd like to hear her talk about Medgar.

But I'm not done with politics yet. I plan to be a Mississippi state rep. I won't be on any committees. I'll just introduce bills and push them through. We'll hire judges to hear rape, murder, and drug cases only. We'll end parole, take the phones and air conditioners out of the jails, cut back legal appeals, and give convicted murderers the chair within ninety days.

Before I start traveling with B. B., I'd also like to get to know my children better. I've got eight daughters by four different mothers. My daughter Pat manages a housing complex in Atlanta. My daughter Carolyn is in the temporary business in Jackson. Charlene Wilson, the oldest of my daughters, has been my receptionist and assistant at the chancery court clerk's office in Fayette, and a cook at my soul food restaurant. She married a hardworking eighteen-wheeler trucker who killed himself in a crash. When Charlene asked if she could move to Fayette and work with her daddy, I said, "Baby, come on." Charlene's a great help to me. My daughter Rachel is a teacher in Florida. My other two daughters by Nan are fine: Sheila lives in Hollywood, and Yvonne's a dental technician in Atlanta. I've got two daughters by Lois Williams: Cheryl, a teacher in Jackson; and Keta, a senior at Jackson State.

I don't mind that none of my girls loves business like I do. They can do what they want with my property and my companies when I'm gone. I've adopted them all, even when I never married their mothers, because a man must support his children. All my daughters love me, and none of them has ever been on welfare for one hour. None of them has gone through the trials Medgar and I did as kids, forced to dance for some peckerwood store owner. I'm here whenever my girls need me, with money in the bank.

What does bother me is that none of my girls truly understands me. Few people in Mississippi have. Those who called Charles Evers "the Moses of Mississippi" didn't understand—and neither did those who called me a demagogue just out for Charles Evers. But a man expects his own family to understand him, and I'm not sure my girls do. When they were little, I was getting daily death threats. I kept them away from me because I couldn't put their lives at risk. But little girls are so cute, and you never get those years back. Whenever I see a little girl, I feel sad that I never took my little girls shopping, never took them to the park or out for ice cream. They know why I didn't, but they're still real sensitive about it. If we'd spent more time together, I'm sure we'd be closer today.

Every man wants a son. If I'd had one, I'd have groomed him to take over my businesses, do my civil rights work. My girls weren't cut out for that. Maybe it was best having girls, with all the mess young black men get in these days. None of my daughters has ever been in trouble. But folks say, "Charlie Evers, you make everyone your son." I do love to invite local businessmen on my radio shows to talk up their business and get some of my fatherly advice: Stay in Mississippi. Build homes and businesses down here, where we got wildlife, open space, deep woods, and clean air.

But I don't fit into a family very well. I'm a loner. I don't follow a schedule—schedules make a tomcat's job harder and an assassin's job easier. I don't let people get very close to me, because those close to you are the only ones who can really hurt you. Few people still alive do I really love and trust. I admire a smart, independent woman who knows her mind but won't whine or try to change me. That kind is hard to find.

In a way, the Medgar Evers Homecoming is like my once-a-year family. B. B. still comes every year. We've had the Mississippi Mass Choir, one of the great choirs. We've had Muhammad Ali, Redd Foxx, James Earl Jones, too. Oprah Winfrey's a Mississippi girl. One of these years, she'll come. These guests give the locals pride in our Mississippi black talent. And of course I try to get Myrlie and her kids down every year.

Myrlie's made a nice career for herself. After Medgar's death, she moved her family to southern California, and the NAACP bought her a home. She finished school and worked as a college administrator, a commissioner of the board of public works in Los Angeles, an executive at Atlantic Richfield. She got on the NAACP board and moved to Oregon. How she could remarry I'll never know, but at least she kept the name Evers.

In February 1995, Myrlie got herself elected chairwoman of the NAACP. Now she's running it. I have real mixed feelings about that. I wish her all the best, but the NAACP's almost a defunct organization. Whatever you say about Roy Wilkins, he never would have let the NAACP get $4 million in debt. Myrlie appointed a new chief financial officer, put in a code of ethics, and improved the fund-raising, but people's memories are so short. If Myrlie can't fix it, I can see the headlines: EVERS DESTROYS NAACP. I'd hate that coming down on the Evers name.

Medgar and Myrlie's kids are all out in California. Rena married a man named Everett and is working. Darrell's a painter. He shows a lot of Medgar in his face and honors his middle name Kenyatta by wearing African clothes. Medgar's younger boy, Van, is a photographer in Los Angeles. I love all those kids. When they all come to the homecoming, we need about eight highway patrolmen to make sure some nut doesn't try to finish off what Beckwith started. The Medgar Evers Homecoming costs me plenty of headaches and thirty thousand dollars a year. But it's worth every penny. It's the only thing I run all year where I forget about turning a profit. And you know Charles Evers is in love when he isn't trying to make money. I just want Medgar recognized.

We play the Medgar Evers Homecoming up big on my Jackson radio station WMPR. Folks come on floats, in dance troupes or marching bands, on old buggies and backhoes, motorcycles, horses, or snorting along in race cars. They come driving the kind of heavy equipment whites didn't used to let us drive. We have lots of black folk, lots of barbecue, and the longest parade you've ever seen, snaking through Fayette. By '84, about a third of the crowd was white.

Thirty years I've had to explain to my kids and other black kids what happened to Medgar, without making them hate whites. It's not easy. But the Medgar Evers Homecoming is the best way to do it. The scars from '63 will never fully heal. But the homecoming celebrates Medgar and civil rights, and it shows how Medgar paid the price. Jomo Kenyatta spent seven years in a British jail, slept on a concrete floor, paid the price. Nelson Mandela did hard labor in a South African rock quarry, paid the price. I tell our kids: Have fun, play your rap music, but if you really want to do something, serve your people like Medgar did. Pay the price.

Medgar Evers Day 1993 was the thirtieth anniversary of Medgar's killing. About seventy thousand people took part, including hundreds of my old friends and cronies. We had three parades. B. B. King played blues. We had gospel concerts. I felt blue remembering Medgar, but how many people have a brother who died thirty years ago, and seventy thousand people still honor him? White politicians came, courting us. Thirty years ago it would have been political suicide for a white candidate to seek our vote. Now, here were white candidates passing out their campaign literature to poor blacks, working the crowd, *soliciting* our vote. I'd worked all my life to see that.

The Ross Barnett Reservoir is a man-made lake just east of Jackson. A group of eighty, half white, half black, took a yacht cruise on the Ross Barnett Reservoir. State troopers once kept Negroes off that reservoir by force. Now, we yacht on it. Thirty years before, Ross Barnett had said, "Americans everywhere must realize that integration is the primary facet of the conspiracy to socialize and communize America." The old Ross Barnett turned over in his grave when our mixed-race group hit his reservoir. But the new Ross Barnett understood. Because not long before Ross Barnett died in 1987, I'd persuaded him to attend the Medgar Evers Homecoming. At first, he was shocked to even get a call from me. He croaked, "What do you want to talk to *me* for?" But I talked him into joining the homecoming. As an old man, Ross Barnett rode in Medgar's parade.

As the racist barriers fall, Medgar's with us every step of the way. The honeysuckle thicket where Byron Beckwith crouched in wait has been gone for years. So is the sweet gum tree he hid behind. Blacks go to the best private schools now, serve as cops, on juries—and Medgar's there every time. But we still have a long way to go. In my chancery court clerk's office, we hire a white clerk, treat her well, but her friends ask, "You working for that nigger?" Before long, she quits. Whites know by now that racial integration won't ruin the South. Sandlot baseball, the Baptist Church, good fishing, Friday night football, and country music have all withstood the blow. Most whites accept integration now, but they still can't enjoy working for a black man. They can't stand for a year what they used to make us stand for a lifetime.

These kind of racial barriers are mental, and we blacks have them, too. When my daughter Sheila dated a white boy, I found out what those redneck parents faced in the '60s. Sheila asked me to meet her new man without telling me he was white. I saw him from the next room and had to collect myself before I could greet him. And even for me, it's hard to buck the old lie of a white man's job. Boarding a Delta flight at O'Hare Airport, Chicago, around 1984, I saw a black pilot in the cockpit. "Shit! How'd he get in there?" I saw the navigator was black, too, and thought, "Get ready for a plane crash." That's how deep that racist mess goes.

I'm shocked I'm still alive. I courted trouble as a boy so many times. Jimmy Boware could have killed me in his commissary. Japanese soldiers could have killed me in New Guinea or the Philippines. Klukkers could have killed me in Philadelphia, Mississippi. The Mob could have killed me in Chicago. The day I blazed into the Meridian bus station, I really *should* have been killed. The Klukkers wanted to kill me when I took over from Medgar. Dale Walton could have killed me in Fayette. I was the one meant to die young, but God sheltered me, and Beckwith took my brother's life instead.

Since I stopped being mayor of Fayette, I get few death threats. I wish I got more, because those who tell you they're going to kill you—they aren't going to kill you. Maybe some silent bastard plans to kill me before God takes me. I still carry a pistol after dark. I still sleep with a pistol near my hand. I don't answer my door at home unless I know who's coming. Someone breaks in at night, they got five locked doors before they reach my bed: front door, living room door, kitchen door, dining room door, bedroom door. But I'm still here for people. I answer the phone if it rings ten times a day or thirty. I never hide behind a secretary.

My high-toned friends tell me we're not black now, we're African-American. Fine, but now, let's keep on. We've beautified Mississippi and America, but let's open the system wider. Blacks are so much stronger than we were in '63, and this has made the whole nation stronger. Senator Bilbo warned the rabble that if they weren't careful, they'd find niggers representing them. Well, we do represent white folk now, all over the country, and whites who give us a chance like us. I wish Medgar could have lived to see it.

But too many black folk have forgotten the bridge that carried us across. We fawn over Louis Farrakhan and every new loudmouth down the pike. Why don't we honor Gladys Noel Bates, who paid the price to get equal pay for black teachers in Mississippi? Let's honor not only Martin and Medgar but Gladys Noel Bates and Vernon Dahmer, T. R. M. Howard and Fannie Lou Hamer, and all those who have struggled for civil rights, famous or not. Medgar's old home is boarded up, but Tougaloo College is making it into a museum. That's what we need. White folk, Japanese, Chinese people respect their heroes. Black folk should, too. We must stop acting like the white man was right when he told us we had no history.

Why are black folk failing in this country? Sure, we face racism. God doesn't want this world to be run by white males. But listen up black folk: Most of our problem isn't the white man. Medgar and Martin said study hard, do honest work, and respect all people. Medgar and Martin would cry to see all the black crime, drugs, gangs. These are *our* problems to solve. Whites won't respect us until we respect ourselves. In '63, blacks feared whites; now we fear each other. Haters don't need the Klan today, because we kill ourselves with crack and guns, while the last few pitiful Klansmen laugh up their sleeve.

Black folk don't know how to get rich. Our heroes are wrong. Even the good kids, who do their homework and try to get ahead, idolize Jesse Jackson. Now, I like Jesse, he's hardworking, but he's a hustler. He's a silver-tongued hustler for freedom, but he's a hustler. We don't need hustlers. We can't spend words. We need jobs, training, housing. I tell Jesse that, he laughs and carries on. I say, "Jesse, show me something you've done." George Wallace and Jesse Jackson might have become great men if they'd taken the advice I gave them. But they didn't take it.

Jefferson County is still badly run, but now our elected officials are black. Now it's our fault. We must do our blacks like we did the racist whites twenty-five years ago: If they don't help the poor, vote them out. White folks must understand how many problems they've made for us, and how they've made us hate. But black folk must realize that we can't blame the white man forever. It's mostly up to us now. We can be as free as we want to be. We must vote, build our own businesses, and take care of our own people.

Instead, we try to lighten our skin, straighten our hair, buy fancy clothes. We don't need new clothes; we need new ways of thinking. Martin and Medgar wouldn't want this Afrocentric bullshit. Let's organize ourselves by political party or region, not race. You must guard against becoming the thing you hate. The old jailbird's the toughest cop. The former whore is the loudest voice in the church choir. And blacks can be the worst racists. If I must be a bigot to be authentically African-American, then let it all go to hell. I'd rather be forgotten.

Have No Fear

CHAPTER 29

Byron Beckwith swore in court he hadn't killed Medgar. When the law questioned him, he'd pose as a peaceful Christian segregationist. But he loved being chief suspect in the Medgar Evers killing. And he'd brag to folks he knew of having "got rid of" Medgar. In '73, Beckwith was arrested in New Orleans, with a ticking time bomb and a map marking the home of a Jewish leader. The arresting officer asked Beckwith if he had a criminal record. Beckwith said, plain as day, "I shot Medgar Evers."

I tried to ignore trash like Beckwith. People told me things he'd said or done. I didn't care. After being convicted for his ticking time bomb, Beckwith had to sit for five years in the securest cells they had, or a black prisoner would have killed him. Beckwith got out, and he and his second wife moved to Tennessee. She thought he was innocent.

The old Jackson *Clarion-Ledger* would have closed down the damn paper before lifting a finger to hurt Byron Beckwith or help Medgar Evers. But in '82 the Gannett newspaper company bought out the paper. And in '89 when some *Clarion-Ledger* reporter found out the Mississippi Sovereignty Commission had messed with Beckwith's second trial, he wrote it right in the *Clarion-Ledger.* He showed how the Mississippi Sovereignty Commission had worked to keep Negroes and Jews off the jury. Man, those who ran the *Clarion-Ledger* in '64 must have turned over in their graves.

What the Sovereignty Commission did should surprise no one. That's just what the Sovereignty Commission was in business for. But folk got in a flutter. Out-of-town reporters came. Myrlie flew in from Los Angeles and asked the district attorney, Ed Peters, to reopen the Beckwith case. The statute of limitations isn't supposed to run out on a murder charge, but it does run out. People try to forget the past. William Waller was on record saying the hung juries he got were as good as a conviction. I thought the case was closed for good.

Ed Peters said he'd reopen the case if he found strong signs of jury tampering, but when he found none, it looked like the end. But his assistant, Bobby DeLaughter, pressed on. DeLaughter was a young white Mississippi man. A former defense lawyer. DeLaughter felt ashamed of how this gutless, unpunished killing had soiled our state's image. He wanted justice done so whites and blacks could join hands and raise up Mississippi.

DeLaughter had fits trying to prosecute Byron Beckwith. The state of Mississippi had tried to forget the Beckwith case. Court records had been thrown away, even the trial transcripts. The murder weapon was lost. Witnesses had died or left town. Without the transcripts, DeLaughter had no chance. But years before, Bill Waller had given Myrlie his own set of trial transcripts. She gave them to DeLaughter, and he got Beckwith indicted and jailed. He got Myrlie's court transcript made official. He had Myrlie and Bill Waller testify. Turned out DeLaughter's own father-in-law had the murder weapon. He'd kept it in a closet, as a souvenir.

DeLaughter got new evidence, too. His investigator found witnesses who stated that Beckwith had boasted of the killing. Beckwith always claimed to have been in Greenwood the night of the murder. DeLaughter found witnesses that Beckwith had been at Medgar's last civil rights rally in Jackson. DeLaughter said he'd have to exhume Medgar's body to prove he'd died by gunfire. That gave us pause. You let the dead rest, and besides, Medgar might have decomposed too much to prove anything. But we exhumed him in 1990. A second autopsy proved he'd died from gunfire. We reburied Medgar.

In December of '90, a year after the *Clarion-Ledger* story, Bobby DeLaughter got a grand jury to indict Beckwith for murder. Sheriffs in Tennessee brought a warrant to Beckwith's door. At his hearing, Beckwith told the judge the murder charge was "nonsense, poppycock, and just something to . . . incite the lower forms of life to force and violence against the country-club set." Beckwith felt he was in the country-club set. He had heart trouble, high blood pressure, but he vowed to fight the charge "tooth, nail, and claw."

Beckwith's lawyers argued Beckwith was being denied his rights of speedy trial and due process. Since he'd been tried twice before, some said he couldn't be tried again. Another year passed before Beckwith pleaded innocent, in October of '91. Then another year passed before the Mississippi Supreme Court approved a retrial. Beckwith said, "I didn't kill Medgar Evers. But he's sure dead! He ain't coming back." Beckwith would laugh when discussing Medgar's death. *Another* year passed before the U.S. Supreme Court refused to hear Beckwith's appeal.

Finally, in January of '94, over four years after the *Clarion-Ledger* article, Beckwith's third trial finally began, in the same courthouse he'd been tried in thirty years before. Myrlie wanted that trial so bad. She sat through it all in the front row. Darrell was there, too, looking like his daddy, showing Beckwith the face of the man he'd shot in the back. I expected another hung jury. Bobby DeLaughter was a good man, doing a terrific job on something important. But I couldn't get too close. A man must know himself. When Myrlie saw Beckwith in court, she wanted to punch him, right there in court. If I'd seen Beckwith smirk, I might have tried to kill him. I knew that about myself, so I avoided the courtroom. But I sure heard about the trial.

Beckwith was seventy-three years old, and looked poorly. He was just a shell of a man, eaten away by hate. In '64, he'd loved taking the witness stand, with almost all of white Mississippi rooting him on. Now, white Mississippi just wished he'd go away, and Beckwith never took the stand, just told folks to read his biography. On February 3, testimony ended. On February 4, the jury met, deliberated five hours, and deadlocked. We thought the jury was hung. Myrlie said forcing a third trial was a victory in itself, but we all knew that would be a hollow victory. We needed a conviction.

The judge sequestered that jury overnight. Next day came the verdict. Just like the old days, the jury deliberated an hour, then came back unanimous. But this time the jury had eight blacks and four whites, and this time they convicted Byron Beckwith of killing my brother. At 10:35 A.M., Saturday, February 5, 1994, they gave that bastard life in prison. Shocked the daylights out of me. I always knew Beckwith would get punished in the next world, but I'd stopped believing he'd get it in this one.

Myrlie hugged her family, friends, and well-wishers. Many whites in Mississippi were happy for Myrlie, too. They weren't in the courtroom with her, but she was in their thoughts. Beckwith sat still in his gray suit till two deputy sheriffs led him off. He waved a little to his family, but this man who'd vowed to fight on "tooth, nail, and claw" said not a word after he was convicted. His wife sat in the front row, crying. Beckwith's conviction cleansed some souls in the Evers family, and in the state of Mississippi. Myrlie went before the cameras, threw up her fists, and whooped with joy. She looked up at the sky and said, "Medgar, I've gone the last mile."

Reporters wanted my reaction. First, I was just glad it was over, but pondering the verdict, I got higher and higher. They'd finally convicted that bastard! Being elected mayor of Fayette the first time lifted me up real high, but February 5, 1994, had to be the happiest day of my life.

The guilty verdict transformed the 1994 Medgar Evers Homecoming. Beckwith wasn't at the state prison farm at Parchman, where he belonged, but he was still in jail. And Beckwith wasn't "the alleged killer" anymore. We could call him "the killer," and no libel lawyer in the United States could run a lawsuit at us now! Having Beckwith behind bars put peace in the souls of all the homecoming staff, the performers, the crowd.

Medgar Evers has a bigger name than his older brother, Charlie. No one else in history has ever brought so much attention to Mississippi, from around the world, as Medgar Evers. Many people only know me because of Medgar. I hear them say, "That's Charlie Evers . . . Medgar's brother." Reporters still write, "Charles Evers, brother of slain civil rights leader Medgar Evers. . . ." That's okay. For over thirty years now, I've been doing Medgar's work, and I'll keep on doing it till I reach the very end.

That's my life, the bad right up there with the good. I've made a lot of money in my life, done a lot of good, and some real bad things, too. I've been mayor of a Mississippi town that folk said would never have a Negro mayor. From '69 to '80, I think I was the best mayor in this whole country. As a civil rights man, I've been one of the best, and I've got forty-two plaques in my living room to prove it. I've got the "keys to the city" of twenty-one different cities. They don't mean that much to me. I tell my people, "Don't remember me as a politician or a civil rights leader, but as a man." A man honest enough to tell the bad along with the good, a man tough and smart enough to change some of the bad into good. I don't need forty-two plaques, if folks will say when I'm gone, "He told the truth, and paid the price." That's all the epitaph I need.

All the people who did me so mean in Decatur—Andy May, Jimmy Boware, and all the rest—they're likely all gone by now. All the army officers who abused me must be gone now, or wrinkled old men, trying to forget they were ever mean old racists. Most of the people who've told me they were going to take my life are dead and gone to hell. They've lost their lives, and maybe their souls. I'm seventy-three years old, still here, and still feeling good.

I've known most of the greatest leaders of my time, and they're all gone, too—Democrats like John and Bobby Kennedy and Lyndon Johnson, Republicans like Nelson Rockefeller and Richard Nixon, black leaders like T. R. M. Howard, Fannie Lou Hamer, Martin Luther King, and Medgar.

Life is never a sure thing. You can live cautious and wind up with cancer. You can shuffle and Tom and wrap your car around a pole, or drop dead from a heart attack. Lots of those I've loved most have gone violently. Until I was about fifty, I expected to be gunned down by a hater. I spent so many years marching and picketing, risking my life, living in turmoil. Now it seems I'll go quietly. I hate to think I might end up laying in bed, too senile to care for myself. I want to go down fighting and kicking. If it takes a few days lying down at the end, there'll be some good black folk watching by my bed. When it's time to die, I hope it's quick. Die rich and die fast. Cremate me, and sprinkle the ashes in Arlington National Cemetery, right next to Medgar.

Let me say one more thing. To all of you who still hold race hatred in your heart, I ask you, *please, give it up*. All of you sitting on the fence, come down on the loving side. Changing is hard, I know. But no one has more right to hate than Charles Evers, because they stole Medgar from me in the prime of his life—and I've stopped hating. Think you're too hotheaded to love another race? No one was ever more hotheaded than young Charlie Evers. I've cooled down. Niceness comes back to you. Kindness wins out. After they gunned down Medgar, I doubted it. But in the last thirty years, I've seen it.

You conservatives—all of you, even the bigots and ex-bigots—you must look deep in your heart, and drive out all the racism locked up in there. Don't hate anyone. Don't cast off anyone. Work with us. If you look deep behind your racism, you'll find fear of the darker peoples. Cast it out of your heart and then meet us freshly, smile at us, work with us. You'll make the poor and black move easier, and you'll move easier, too.

You liberals, don't be superior, now. You think you know how to treat minorities, but you don't. Don't be condescending. Greet us and hug us when we're right, but show us where we're wrong. Keep your standards high. Black folk deserve that much. And liberals, stop thinking so much about the words you use. Words aren't one-tenth of what this world needs. Stop trying to make speeches of great moment. Start creating jobs and teaching blacks the skills we need to make money and stand on our own.

To whites I say, blacks are the most loyal people on earth. But you got to be kind to us. Give us a little of your time. Show us you care. It isn't a monetary thing—it's about caring.

To blacks I say, there's still too much racism in this country. Of course there is! Don't wallow in it. Don't tuck your head in fear or in shame. *Never quit.* We're a tough race. You've got plenty of tough, smart ancestors, or you wouldn't even be standing here. Somewhere they're all rooting for you. Here we are today, the haves and the have-nots, a few of us rich, but most of us still left out and pushed back. Keep on pushing. Trust each other. Keep the Lord on your side. Study hard, work hard, and keep your hands clean. Make us proud of you.

To all people I say, it's not enough to live. You must make your life mean something. You can't let fear hold you back from reaching out to strangers. You must ask yourself, "What have I done on earth? How have I made this world better?" And if you haven't made this world better yet, then start today. Right now. In some little way, start doing it. It's never too late.

If you can't do anything else, at least come to Fayette, Mississippi, for the Medgar Evers Homecoming. We hold it every year, the first weekend in June. Join B. B. King and me, and thousands of other good folk, celebrating Medgar Evers. If Allen Thompson can join us, so can you. If Ross Barnett can ride in Medgar's parade, so can you. Come to Fayette. Ride in Medgar's parade. Have no fear.

SELECTED BIBLIOGRAPHY

Adams, A. John, and Joan Martin Burke. *Civil Rights: A Current Guide to the People, Organizations and Events.* New York and London, R. R. Bowker Company, 1970.

Barbour, Floyd B., Ed. *The Black Power Revolt: A Collection of Essays.* Boston: Extending Horizons Books, 1968.

Bartley, Numan V., and Hugh D. Graham. *Southern Politics and the Second Reconstruction.* Baltimore and London: Johns Hopkins University Press, 1975.

Belfrage, Sally. *Freedom Summer.* New York: Viking Press, 1965.

Bennett, Lerone, Jr. *Before the Mayflower: A History of Black America.* New York: Penguin, 1985.

Berry, Jason. *Amazing Grace: With Charles Evers in Mississippi.* New York: Saturday Review Press, 1973.

Branch, Taylor. *Parting the Waters: America in the King Years, 1954–1963.* New York: Touchstone/Simon & Schuster, 1988.

Brisbane, Robert H. *Black Activism: Racial Revolution in the United States, 1954–1970.* Valley Forge, Pa: Judson Press, 1974.

Brooks, Maxwell R. *The Negro Press Re-Examined.* Boston: Christopher Publishing House, 1959.

Caute, David. *The Year of the Barricades: A Journey through 1968.* New York: Harper & Row, 1988.

Chafe, William H. *Never Stop Running: Allard Lowenstein and the Struggle to Save American Liberalism.* New York: Basic Books, 1993.

The Civil Rights Act of 1964: Text, Analysis, Legislative History. Washington, D.C.: BNA Incorporated, 1964.

Crouse, Timothy. *The Boys on the Bus.* New York: Random House, 1972.

Evers, Charles. *Evers*. Edited and with an introduction by Grace Halsell. New York and Cleveland: World Publishing Company, 1971.

Evers, Mrs. Medgar (Myrlie Evers), with William Peters. *For Us, The Living*. Garden City, N.Y.: Doubleday & Company, 1967.

Fager, Charles E. *Selma, 1965*. New York: Charles Scribner's Sons, 1974.

Fairclough, Adam. *To Redeem the Soul of America: The Southern Christian Leadership Conference and Martin Luther King, Jr.* Athens, Georgia: University of Georgia Press, 1987.

Farmer, James. *Lay Bare the Heart: An Autobiography of the Civil Rights Movement*. New York and Scarborough, Ontario: Plume, 1986.

Fax, Elton C. *Contemporary Black Leaders*. New York: Dodd, Mead and Company, 1970.

Fleming, G. James, and Christian Burckel, eds. *Who's Who in Colored America*. 1950 edition. Yonkers-on-Hudson, N.Y.: Christian E. Burckel & Associates, 1950.

Frost, David. *The Americans*. New York: Stein & Day, 1970.

Gardner, Gerald. *Robert Kennedy in New York*. New York: Random House, 1965.

Garrow, David J. *Bearing the Cross: Martin Luther King, Jr., and the SCLC*. New York: William Morrow & Company, 1986.

Gregory, Dick. *The Shadow That Scares Me*. Edited by James R. McGraw. Garden City, N.Y.: Doubleday & Company, 1968.

Grier, Rosey. *Rosey: An Autobiography*. Tulsa: Honor, 1986.

Griffin, Winthrop. *Humphrey: A Candid Biography*. New York: William Morrow & Company, 1965.

Hilton, Conrad. *Be My Guest*. New York: Prentice-Hall Press, 1957.

Horne, Lena, and Richard Schickel. *Lena*. New York: Signet Books, 1965.

Hughes, Langston. *Fight for Freedom: The Story of the NAACP*. New York: W. W. Norton, 1962.

Huie, William Bradford. *Three Lives for Mississippi*. New York: WCC Books, 1965.

Jack, Robert L. *History of the NAACP*. Boston: Meador Publishing Company, 1943.

Kotz, Nick. *Let Them Eat Promises: The Politics of Hunger in America*. Englewood Cliffs, N.J.: Prentice-Hall, 1969.

Lewis, David L. *King: A Critical Biography.* New York: Prager Publishers, 1970.

McAdam, Doug. *Freedom Summer.* New York and Oxford: Oxford University Press, 1988.

McKissick, Floyd. *Three Fifths of a Man.* London: MacMillan Company/Collier-MacMillan, 1969.

Meredith, James. *Three Years in Mississippi.* Bloomington and London: Indiana University Press, 1966.

Mills, Kay. *This Little Light of Mine: The Life of Fannie Lou Hamer.* New York: Plume, 1994.

Milner, Samuel. *U.S. Army in WWII, The War in the Pacific: Victory in Papua.* Washington, D.C.: Office of the Chief of Military History, Department of the Army, 1957.

Moody, Anne. *Coming of Age in Mississippi.* New York: Dell Paperback, 1976.

Morgan, Chester. *Redneck Liberal: Theodore G. Bilbo and the New Deal.* Baton Rouge and London: LSU Press, 1985.

Morris, Willie. *North toward Home.* New York: Dell Publishing Company, 1967.

Navasky, Victor S. *Kennedy Justice.* New York: Atheneum, 1971.

Newfield, Jack. *Robert Kennedy: A Memoir.* New York: E. P. Dutton & Company, 1969.

Norden, Eric. "The *Playboy* Interview: Charles Evers." *Playboy*, October 1971.

Obst, Lynda Rosen, ed. *The 60's: The Decade Remembered Now by the People Who Lived It Then.* New York: Random House/Rolling Stone Press, 1977.

Parker, Frank R. *Black Votes Count: Political Empowerment in Mississippi after 1965.* Chapel Hill: University of North Carolina Press, 1990.

Rather, Dan, with Mickey Herskowitz. *The Camera Never Blinks: Adventures of a TV Journalist.* New York: William Morrow & Company, 1977.

Russell, Bill, as told to William McSweeny. *Go Up for Glory.* New York: Coward-McCann, 1966.

Sawyer, Charles. *B. B. King.* 1982 edition. London: Quartet Books, 1982.

Schlesinger, Arthur M., Jr. *Robert Kennedy and His Times.* New York: Ballantine Books, 1978.

Sewell, George Alexander, and Margaret L. Dwight. *Mississippi Black History Makers.* Jackson: University Press of Mississippi, 1984.

Smith, Robert Ross. *U.S. Army in WWII, The War in the Pacific: Triumph in the Philippines*. Washington, D.C.: Office of the Chief of Military History, Department of the Army, 1963.

Spofford, Tim. *Lynch Street: The May 1970 Slayings at Jackson State College*. Kent, Ohio, and London: Kent State University Press, 1988.

Stanley, Harold W. *Voter Mobilization and the Politics of Race*. New York: Praeger, 1987.

Toledano, Ralph de. *RFK: The Man Who Would Be President*. New York: G. P. Putnam's Sons, 1967

Warren, Robert Penn. *Who Speaks for the Negro? A Mississippi Journal*. New York: Random House, 1965.

Watters, Pat and Reese Cleghorne. *Climbing Jacob's Ladder*. New York: Harcourt, Brace & World, 1967.

Whitfield, Stephen J. *A Death in the Delta: The Story of Emmett Till*. New York and London: Free Press/Collier-MacMillan, 1988.

Wilkins, Roger. *A Man's Life*. New York: Touchstone/Simon & Schuster, 1982.

Wilkins, Roy, with Tom Mathews. *Standing Fast: The Autobiography of Roy Wilkins*. New York: Viking Press, 1982.

Williams, Juan, with the *Eyes on the Prize* production team. *Eyes on the Prize*. New York: Viking Press, 1987.

INDEX

Abernathy, Ralph, 139, 291, 297
Adkins, Ada, 36–37, 38
Adkins, Florene, 36
Africa
   Charles Evers in, 295–98
   and Negroes of Fayette, 297–98
African-Americans. *See* blacks
Afrocentrism, 305
Agnew, Spiro, 279
Alcorn, James Lusk, 56
Alcorn A&M (Agricultural and Mechanical) College, 56
   demonstrations against, 189–90
   Evers brothers at, 56–60, 70
Aldridge, Jesse, 168
Ali, Muhammad, 136, 210, 286, 301
Allen, Ferd, 201–2, 244, 257, 264
Allen, R. J. (Turnip Green), 201–2, 242–45, 249, 253, 261–62
Allison, Doris, 184
Anderson, Isiah, 244, 255
Angola, and Savimbi, 296–97
Arlington National Cemetery, 138, 141, 311
Armstrong Tire and Rubber, 190

Bailey, Sam, 246
Ballard, Mamie, 168
Barnett, Ross, 138, 162, 235
   on Medgar Evers's death, 131, 167
   on federal intervention, 122
   on James Meredith, 116
   in old age, 302–3
Bates, Gladys Noel, 304
Bay of Pigs, 113
Beard, Fred, 104
Beasley, Myrlie. *See* Evers, Myrlie
Beckwith, Byron de la, 127–31, 137–38, 158, 271
   and Tom Brady, 272
   lieutenant governor campaign of, 220–21
   trial and retrial of, 165–67, 168, 307–10
   and Waller as gubernatorial candidate, 268
   and Dale Walton, 263
Bedford-Stuyvesant, Negro poverty in, 176
Bell, Jeanie, 184
Belzoni, Mississippi, 85
Benson, Al, 100
Berry, Jason, 268
Bevel, James, 118, 180
Bilbo, Theodore, 29–31, 61, 141, 153
   as contributor to Alcorn A&M, 31
   death of, 64
   and representation by Negroes, 31, 60, 304
   statue of, 283, 289
   and Jimmy Swan, 268
Birmingham, Alabama, 122, 154
Black, Hugo, 206–7
Black Panthers, 218
Black Power, 215, 216–17, 218

318   Index

blacks (Negroes)
  and Africans, 297–98
  as Afro-American or African-American, 207, 304
  demoralization of by racism, 214, 242, 252
  as "Negroes" vs. "colored people," 59
  problems of, 237, 304–5
  racial barriers of, 303
  religion and, 36
  as remaining in South vs. moving to North, 199
  See also race relations in Mississippi and South; women, black
black studies, 237
Bland, Bobby, 107
Bond, Julian, 246
Booth, William, 175, 245
bootlegging, 40–42, 58, 71, 89, 109, 203
Boston, and school busing, 276–77
Boware, Jimmy, 1–2, 63, 303, 311
Bowie, Harry, 238
boycotts, 185
  in Fayette, 186, 202
  as integration tactic, 156, 185–86
  of Montgomery bus system, 91–92
  NAACP opposition of, 92
  of Natchez business, 185–88
  in Port Gibson, 196
Boyd, John D., 189
Brady, Tom, 128, 272
Brand, Mr. (voting clerk), 60, 62, 63, 143
Brazil, Evers brothers' plan to settle in, 126
Breslin, Jimmy, 226
Brooke, Ed, 277
Brooks, Owen, 238
Brown, Benjamin, 265
Brown, H. Rap, 209, 215, 218, 290–91
Brown, James, 108
Brown, R. Jess, 57
Brown, Robert, 276
Brown vs. Board of Education, 79–81, 92
Bunche, Ralph, 139
Burr, Raymond, 248
business(es)
  and CETA program, 288
  of Charles Evers in Chicago, 100–4, 107–9, 124
  of Charles Evers in 1955, 89–91, 95–96
  Medgar Evers as insurance agent, 72
  Charles Evers's brothels in Philippines, 50–51, 52
  and Charles Evers's childhood, 14, 24–25
  Charles Evers's enterprises in Noxapater, 71
  of Daddy Evers, 13–14
  of Evers brothers in college, 58–59
  Conrad Hilton on, 101
  in Jackson, 84
  as NAACP concern, 83
  and whites' envy of Charles Evers, 93–94
  See also economics
busing, 276–77, 286

Carmichael, Stokely, 213, 215–18, 290–91
Carr, Oscar, 219, 223, 239
Carter, Amy, 285
Carter, Hodding Jr., 75, 89–90, 239, 268, 278
Carter, Jimmy, 274, 284–85
  and Ted Kennedy, 291
  vs. Ronald Reagan, 291
Carter, Lyle, 207
Carter, Robert, 83
Carter, Rosalynn, 284, 285
Castro, Fidel, 113, 210
CCC (Civilian Conservation Corps), 45
CETA jobs program, 287–88
Chamblee, John, 131
Chambliss, Howard, 244
Chaney, James, 170, 172, 180
Chapman, Percy, 184
Chavez, Cesar, 228
Chess, Leonard, 107–8
Chicago Defender, 25, 135, 136, 142, 160, 247, 250
Christianity, and civil rights, 193–94. *See also* religion
"Christine" (wife of Charles Evers), 67–69, 70

church bombings, 154, 193
churches, Negro
   and civil rights movement, 141
   and Charles Evers's gubernatorial campaign, 270
   George Wallace in, 283–84
   See also religion
Citizens Councils. *See* White Citizens Councils
Civilian Conservation Corps (CCC), 45
civil rights
   and Black Power, 215, 216–17, 218
   boycott as method for, 156, 185–88 (see also boycotts)
   converts to, 206–7, 212
   and economic integration, 202
   economic vs. political approach to, 104
   and FBI, 113–14
   financing for, 83
   Freedom Rides, 114–15, 176
   Freedom Summer, 169–70
   grassroots vs. legal approach to, 146
   historical continuity of, 217–18
   James Meredith Freedom March, 213, 214–15
   and Kennedy administration, 113, 126–27, 136
   Kennedy family as backers of, 88
   marches vs. voter registration, 180
   March on Washington, 153
   Meredith's registration at U. of Miss., 115–18, 121
   and Mississippi Freedom Democratic Party, 152–53, 171, 182, 233, 238
   and Montgomery bus boycott, 91–92
   and NAACP vs. other groups, 83, 143
   public facilities integration, 183–85
   and reactions to Medgar Evers's murder, 136
   and religion, 36, 193–94
   Rockefellers as backers of, 88–89
   and segregation as business threat, 179, 186
   Selma march(es), 180–81, 207
   southern whites' view of, 80, 90
   and University of Alabama integration, 118
   unsung heroes of, 304
   and voting, 64, 66
   See also integration; NAACP
Civil Rights Act (1957), 104, 111, 137, 159, 162
Civil Rights Act (1964), 162–63, 179, 183
Civil Rights Commission, U.S., 180
Clarion-Ledger, Jackson, 25, 75, 80, 84, 131, 307
Clark, Joseph, 219
Clark, Ramsey, 207, 245, 271, 276
Clark, Robert, 190
Clark, Tom, 207
Clarksdale, Mississippi, 72, 73, 108, 137, 181–82
"Claudia" (Charles Evers's girlfriend), 67–69, 70
Clay, Cassius. *See* Ali, Muhammad
Club House, 109
Club Mississippi, 107
Cochran, Thad, 286
Cole, Ed, 268, 294–95
Cole, Harvey, 56
Cole, Howard, 90, 91, 95
Cole family, 89, 90, 94, 260
Coleman, James "J. P.," 77–78, 105
Collins, Ben, 115
Commercial Chemical, 254
Communism, 210
company store, 1
Comprehensive Employment and Training Act (CETA) jobs program, 287–88
Congress of Racial Equality (CORE), 83, 114–15, 143, 199
conservatives, 312
Conyers, John, 267
Cooper (white businessman), 27–28, 58–59
Cooper, Milton, 235
CORE (Congress of Racial Equality), 83, 114–15, 143, 199
Courts, Gus, 85–86, 96, 161
Cox, Harold, 114
Cronkite, Walter, 251

Current, Gloster B., 82, 83, 146–47, 148, 181
  with Medgar Evers on night of murder, 128
  and Fayette inauguration of Charles Evers, 246
  at Wharlest Jackson's funeral, 191
  for legal action only, 92
  and political endorsements, 149

Dahmer, Vernon, 216, 234, 304
Daley, Richard J., 238, 274, 290
Dantin, Maurice, 286
Davis, Ossie, 136
Deal, Alfonso, 253
Decatur, Mississippi, 1, 3, 11, 16
  Evers brothers first Negroes to vote in, 64
  Charles Evers's desire to leave, 21
  Negro vs. white voters in, 59–60
Decatur Consolidated School, 37–38
Dee, Ruby, 136
de Klerk, F. W., 296
DeLaughter, Bobby, 308, 309
Democratic National Convention
  of 1964, 171
  of 1968, 238–39
  of 1972, 273, 274–75
  of 1980, 290–91
Democratic National Executive Committee, 239
Derian, Patt, 238, 268
Diggs, Charles, 83, 87, 122, 139, 239, 267
Doar, John, 113, 117–18, 140, 226
draft boards, in Vietnam War, 210–11
Drysdale, Don, 228

Eagleton, Tom, 267
Eastland, James O., 74, 151, 162, 223, 237, 286
  and *Brown* decision, 80
  farm subsidy to, 292
  and FBI, 114
  on Senate Judiciary Committee, 84
  and teachings of white culture, 220
economics
  employment in Fayette, 254, 295
  importance of, 199, 202, 305
  Medgar Evers Shopping Center, 203, 217, 256
  as motive to reject segregation, 179, 186, 257
  Negro supermarket formed, 196
  plans for Mississippi, 234
  vs. political approach, 104
  strike of pulp-wood haulers, 273
  UMW as first labor union in Fayette, 244
Edelman, Marian Wright, 219, 225
Edelman, Peter, 219, 225
education
  black studies, 237
  and *Brown vs. Board of Education*, 79–81
  as "separate but equal," 37–39, 80
Eisenhower, Dwight, 84, 86, 104, 111
Ellsberg, Daniel, 280
Evers (memoir), 269–70
Evers, Charles (James Charles), xiii–xviii, 15, 310–11
  in Africa, 295–98
  at Alcorn A&M, 56–60, 70
  and assault on Medgar in bus, 105–6
  boyhood of, 3–4, 8–10, 12, 13–21, 33, 39–40, 48
  in Chicago, 59, 99–104, 106–10, 124–25, 131–32, 278
  congressional campaign of, 233–37
  death threats against (after mayoralty), 304
  Democratic National Conventions, 238–39, 273, 274–75, 290–91
  on Democratic National Executive Committee, 239
  FBI suspects of killing Medgar, 137
  gubernatorial campaign of, 267–71
  guns kept by, 151, 154, 171, 214
  health of, 299
  and Bobby Kennedy, 143, 171–77, 222–23, 229–30
  in law school, 51
  and Mau Mau killings, 150–51, 154
  memoir by (*Evers*), 269–70
  moves north, 96–97
  and 1960 election, 111

plots against life of, 94–95, 188–89, 235, 262–64, 304
as radio deejay, 90–91, 95
as Republican Party member, 294–95
return to Mississippi, 133
schooling of, 37–39
senatorial campaign of, 286
tax-evasion indictment of, 278
as teacher, 71, 110
in U.S. Army, 45–51, 53, 55, 70, 210
as Yale Fellow, 267
Evers, Charles, civil rights activities of, 110, 121, 310
  Alcorn A&M protests, 189–90
  Civil Rights Commission testimony, 180
  Clarksdale demonstrations, 181–82
  early activities, 64, 65–66
  early NAACP work, 72–74
  Fayette voter registration and boycott, 201
  food marches, 190
  Jackson demonstration (1965), 182–83
  and Jackson State shootings, 267
  James Meredith Freedom March, 213, 214–15
  Medicaid protest, 282–83
  as NAACP state field secretary, xvii, 145–52, 155–56, 181, 233
  Natchez boycott, 185–88
  Port Gibson boycott and arrest, 195–96
  protest of Wharlest Jackson's murder, 190–91
  public facilities integration, 183–85
  and Allie Shelby's murder, 180
  Shreveport speech, 195
  and voting (1946, 1947), 60–64
  and George Wallace, 211–12
Evers, Charles, as Fayette mayor, 244–45, 249–57, 310
  accomplishments, 251, 254, 257
  and accounting for financial contributions, 278
  election campaign, 241–44
  and Fayette as test, 255
  and firing of city attorney for open miscegenation, 257–58
  fund-raising, 249–52
  and HUD funds, 294
  inauguration, 245–48
  law-and-order stance of, 217, 253, 299
  loses to Middleton, 293, 295
  public insults prohibited, 256
  reelection, 277, 294
  and residency qualification issue, 260
  and size of town, 200
  and threats of murder against, 260–64
  and Marie Farr Walker, 258–60
Evers, Charles, and Medgar. *See* Evers brothers, relationship of
Evers, Charles, opinions and viewpoints of
  on Black Power, 215, 217
  on black racism, 305
  on businesses for Negroes, 83
  on capitalism and democracy, 209
  on child support, 292
  on economic integration, 199, 202
  on FBI, 113–14
  on hate, 270, 311
  on immigration, 292
  on Lyndon Johnson, 205
  on Bobby Kennedy, 159, 173–74, 220, 230–31
  on lawbreaking, 183
  on leadership, 211, 216
  on liberals, 273, 284, 312 (*see also* liberals)
  on marriage, 68, 70, 301
  on money-making, 173
  on Richard Nixon, 281
  on nonviolence, 214
  on pensions of ex-presidents, 292
  on prison, 281
  on punishment, 288
  on religion, 35–36
  on riots, 168, 203
  on school integration and busing, 81, 286
  on taxation, 291
  on Vietnam War, 210–11
  on voting, 155, 180
  on George Wallace, 211–12, 273, 283–84
  on Watergate, 280, 281
  on welfare, 234, 287, 288

Evers, Charles, women in life of
  at Alcorn, 67–69
  divorce from Nan, 256
  Felicia (love in Philippines), 51–53, 55–56, 59, 67, 68, 258
  marriage to Christine, 68–69
  marriage to Nan, 67–70, 151, 256 (*see also* Evers, Nannie Laurie)
  and memory of Daddy's straying, 19, 67, 68
  in U.S. Army at Ford Leonard Wood, 47
Evers, Darrell Kenyatta (son of Medgar Evers), 124, 301
  birth of, 75
  and father's death, 129, 140, 142, 309
Evers, Jessie Wright (Mama), 11–13, 18–19, 33–35
  and Charles's and Medgar's voting attempt, 60, 61
  and Charles's return home, 52
  death of, 106
  and peddlers, 43
  and teachings of white culture, 220
Evers, Jim (Daddy), 11, 13–21, 24–28, 34, 35
  and bootlegging, 40, 58, 71
  and Charles's and Medgar's voting, 61
  and Charles's return home, 52
  and company-store incident, 1–2, 63
  death of, 78–79
  as hero, 75
  and Medgar's U. of Miss. application, 77
  and teachings of white culture, 220
Evers, Liz (sister), 8, 9, 11, 12, 97, 99
Evers, Mary (grandmother), 17
Evers, Mary Ruth (sister), 8, 11, 12, 70
Evers, Medgar
  at Alcorn A&M, 56, 57–58
  applies to University of Mississippi, 77–78, 81–82
  assault on bus, 105–6
  boyhood of, 8–10, 12–21, 26, 35, 36, 41
  and Civil Rights Act, 104
  early civil rights activities of, 64, 65–66, 72–74
  Fayette monument to, 261
  French girl loved by, 48, 53, 55, 299
  funeral of, 138–42
  as insurance agent, 70, 71–72, 219–20
  on Clyde Kennard conviction, 105
  and Martin Luther King Jr., 93, 277
  marriage of, 69–70, 77 (*see also* Evers, Myrlie)
  memorial service and homecoming for, 277–78, 301–2, 303, 310, 312
  and James Meredith, 116–17
  murder of, 129–37, 143–44, 171, 209, 226, 229–30, 271, 283, 303
  and nonviolence, 154–55
  and party politics, 289
  schooling of, 37–39
  thoughts on death, 124, 128–29
  threats against, 84, 124, 126
  in U.S. Army, 46, 47–48, 53, 55
  and voting (1946, 1947), 60–64
  and White Citizens Councils, 81
Evers, Medgar, and Charles. *See* Evers brothers, relationship of
Evers, Medgar, as NAACP state field secretary, 82–88, 117, 125–26, 147
  and Freedom Riders, 115
  and Jackson campaign, 122–24
  and Jackson State College, 115
  and Martin Luther King Jr., 93
  and murder of Reverend Lee, 85
  and murder of Emmett Till, 86
  and poll tax campaign, 112–13
  and SCLC, 92
  terrorism against, 113
Evers, Mike (grandfather), 17
Evers, Myrlie (wife of Medgar Evers), 69–72, 77, 121, 301
  on award to Savimbi, 297
  and Beckwith trials, 165, 167, 307, 308, 309
  and death of Medgar, 127, 128, 129, 130
  at Fayette inaugural, 246
  and Medgar's burial, 138–40, 141, 142
  and succession to Medgar's NAACP post, 145

threats against, 126
Evers, Nannie Laurie (wife of Charles Evers), 67–69, 70, 71
  and death of Medgar, 132, 133, 140
  divorce of, 256
  and Charles Evers in Chicago, 96, 99, 108, 151
  and Jackson State shooting reports, 266
Evers, Van (son of Medgar Evers), 121, 124, 128, 129, 140, 301
Evers brothers, relationship of, 249, 310
  and Brazil plans, 126
  during Charles's time in Chicago, 124–25
  and economic vs. political answers, 104
  and Kennedy brothers, 143, 157, 158
  and Medgar's marriage, 69–70
  and murder of Medgar, 133, 154
  oath between them, 9–10, 64, 96
Evers Hotel and Lounge, 89, 107
Evers Motel, Restaurant, and Lounge, 256–57

Farmer, James, 114–15, 199
Farrakhan, Louis, 215–16, 304
Fawer, Michael, 279
Fayette, Mississippi, xvi–xvii, 200–202, 217, 241
  and Africa, 297–98
  boycott in, 186, 202
  economic difficulties of, 295
  grant from Ford Foundation, 252
  See also Evers, Charles, as Fayette mayor
FBI (Federal Bureau of Investigation), 113–14, 130, 137
  and Martin Luther King Jr.'s death, 224
  and Martin Luther King Jr.'s wiretaps, 225
  and threat on Charles Evers's life, 188–89
Felicia (Charles Evers's love in Philippines), 51–53, 55–56, 59, 67, 68, 258

Finch, Cliff, 282, 288
flat tax, 291
Flowers, Nehemiah, 286
food marches, 190
Ford, Gerald, 292
Ford, Johnny, 284
Ford Foundation, Fayette grant from, 252
foreign policy, American, 297
Forman, James, 118
Fort Leonard Wood, Missouri, 47
Foxx, Redd, 301
Franks, Gary, 295
Freedom Rides, 114–15, 176
Freedom Summer, 169–70
Fulbright, William, 210
funeral home of Evers family, 14, 18, 73, 79, 89, 90, 91
funeral home of Mark Thomas, 21, 45, 71, 89

Gaines, Bobby, 7, 42
Gaines, Margaret, 7, 42
Gaines family, 12–13
Gales, James, 244
Gardner, Junior, 9
Garroway, Dave, 104–5
Gibbs, Phillip, 266, 267
Goldwater, Barry, 175
Goodman, Andrew, 170, 172, 180
Gordy, Berry, 248
Graham, Alton, 60, 61
Graves, Earl, 169, 225
"Great White Fathers," 74, 151, 180, 237, 288
Green, James, 266, 267
Gregory, Dick, 123, 139
Grier, Rosey, 227, 228, 229, 290
Griffin, Charlie, 234, 235, 236–37
Grimm (first husband of Mama Evers), 11
Grimm, Eddie, 11, 20, 21
Grimm, Eva Lee, 11, 12, 18, 20
Grimm, Gene, 11, 20
Guyot, Lawrence, 233, 238

Hall, Carsie, 112–13
Halsell, Grace, xv, 269–70

Hamer, Fannie Lou, 38, 73–74, 118–19, 171, 311
  arrest of, 233
  on black schoolteachers, 237
  and bootlegging, 89
  and Robert Clark election, 190
  and Fannie Lou Hamer Day in Ruleville, 283
  on hate, 154
  and Bobby Kennedy, 219
  and murder of Medgar Evers, 135
  and NAACP organizing, 87
  in protest at Capitol, 282–83
  state senatorial race of, 269
  as unsung hero, 304
Hamer, Perry, 73
Harlem, 176, 199, 216
Harriman, Averell, 267
Harris, Patricia Roberts, 207
Hattiesburg, Mississippi, 216
Hawkins, Curtis, 70
Hazlehurst, Mississippi, 156, 191
Heidelberg, Julius, 246
Helms, Jesse, 200
Henry, Aaron, 73, 74, 82, 115, 181, 191
  and Robert Clark election, 190
  Clarksdale jail time, 181–82
  and Charles Evers's politics, 289–90
  and Medgar Evers's NAACP job, 147
  and Fayette inaugural, 246
  firebombing of home, 113, 122, 152
  and Andy Goodman, 170
  and Bobby Kennedy, 219
  as Loyalist, 238, 239
  and MFDP, 152, 171
  and murder of Medgar Evers, 128, 135, 144
  and murder of Emmett Till, 86
  and NAACP buildup, 176
  at 1968 Democratic Convention, 239
  police protection for, 137
  and SNCC vs. NAACP, 155
Henson, Matthew, 38
Hill, Hugh, 266
Hilton, Conrad, 101, 203
Hilton Hotel, 100
Hooker, John Lee, 107
Hoover, J. Edgar, 113–14, 137, 224

Horne, Lena, 123, 135
Housing and Urban Development (HUD) agency, 294
Howard, Theodore Roosevelt Mason, 64–66, 74, 81, 110, 311
  bumper stickers distributed by, 73
  at Medgar Evers's funeral, 139
  insurance company of, 72
  as speaker, 153
  and Emmett Till case, 87
  as unsung hero, 304
Humphrey, Hubert, 111, 162–63, 285
  Charles Evers's support for, 230, 273
  and Fayette inauguration, 245
  at Martin Luther King Jr.'s funeral, 225
  at 1972 convention, 274
  vs. Richard Nixon, 279–80
  and George Wallace, 273, 274
Humphreys County, Mississippi, 85
Hurley, Ruby, 86–87, 139–140, 148–49, 191, 246

idealists, 212, 270
immigration, Charles Evers on, 292
Independent Coalition for Mississippi, 288–89
Inouye, Daniel, 267
Internal Revenue Service (IRS), 278–79
integration
  as bar to whites' search for federal funds, 243
  blacks' demands for, 156
  and MFDP, 171
  of Natchez hotels, 183–85
  nighttime, 5, 87, 215, 258
  progress in, 303
  of public accommodations, 183–85
  of schools, 79–81, 276–77, 286
  whites' aversion to, 80, 303
  See also civil rights
IRS (Internal Revenue Service), 278–79

jackleg preachers, 188
Jackson, E. Franklin, 140–41
Jackson, Jesse, 153, 305
Jackson, Mississippi, xvi, 183, 208, 276
  demonstrations in, 122–23, 182–83

Charles Evers's homes in, 151, 213
Allie Shelby murder in, 179–80
Jackson, Roosevelt, 196, 198
Jackson, Sam, 276
Jackson, Wharlest, 183, 190, 234
Jackson State, 115, 167–68, 233, 236, 265–67
James, Elmore, 107
James Meredith Freedom March, 213, 214–15
Javits, Jacob, 163, 274
Jefferson County, 200, 242, 244, 251, 305. *See also* Fayette, Mississippi
Jennings, Peter, 184
Jews, 109, 127
Job Corps, 208–9
Johnson, Reverend Allen, 189, 194, 195
Johnson, Lady Bird, 205, 207
Johnson, Lyndon, 111, 159–62, 205–9, 311
   and Civil Rights Act, 104, 111
   Charles Evers's meeting with, 181
   and Fayette inaugural, 246
   and HUD, 294
   and Bobby Kennedy candidacy, 175, 221–22
   at Martin Luther King Jr., funeral, 225
   on Negro condition, 182
   and racist state agencies, 179
   retirement of, 211, 221–22, 226
   and social programs, 287
   and Soul City plan, 200
   staff of, 280
   as unhonored prophet, 290
   and Vietnam War, 210–11, 222
   and voting rights bill, 182, 201, 208, 245
Johnson, Paul, 179, 189, 190, 203
Johnson, Rafer, 227, 228, 290
Jonas, Gil, 251
Jones, James Earl, 301
Jones, Lloyd "Goon," 266, 267
Jordan, Charlie, 7, 15
Jordan, Frank, 9
Jordan, Sonny Boy, 7

Katzenbach, Nicholas, 183
Keating, Kenneth, 174–76
Keith, Johnny, 7
Kennard, Clyde, 105, 116
Kennedy, Ethel, 174, 225, 229, 230, 246
Kennedy, Jackie, 130, 142–43, 246, 292
Kennedy, Jean, 230
Kennedy, Joe Sr., 173
Kennedy, John, 111, 113, 116, 122, 130, 311
   assassination of, 157, 158, 173, 283
   and Bay of Pigs, 210
   on civil rights, 126–27, 136
   Charles Evers's visits, 142
   and Louis Martin, 160
   as speaker, 153
Kennedy, Patricia, 230
Kennedy, Robert (Bobby), 111–13, 143, 157–59, 267–68, 311
   assassination of, 229–31
   civil rights record of, 117, 176, 276
   and Medgar Evers's funeral, 138, 141
   FBI investigations pushed by, 137
   influence on Charles Evers, 252, 287
   and John Kennedy's death, 283
   and Martin Luther King Jr., 225–26
   and Thurgood Marshall appointment, 114
   and poverty, 219–20
   presidential campaign of, 221, 222–23, 226–28
   senatorial campaign of, 171–77
   as speaker, 153, 173
   staff of, 169
Kennedy, Teddy
   and busing crisis, 277
   Charles Evers as delegate for, 290
   and Fayette inauguration, 245
   and Bobby Kennedy's death, 230
   and Bobby Kennedy's presidential race, 222
   at Martin Luther King Jr., funeral, 225
   and 1968 presidential nomination, 239
   at 1980 Convention, 290–91
   staff of, 169, 274
   and George Wallace, 273, 274
Kennedy family, 88, 157, 172, 173
Kenyatta, Jomo, 75, 121, 150, 155, 165, 261, 302
Kienzle, William, 250

King, B. B., xiv, 6, 74, 277, 299, 301, 302
King, Clennon, 105, 116
King, Coretta Scott, 136, 230
King, Martin Luther Jr., 92–93, 143–44, 159, 190
  assassination of, 223–26
  Birmingham protests led by, 122
  and Jimmy Carter, 284–85
  Medgar Evers compared with, 277
  and Medgar Evers's funeral, 139
  and Medgar Evers's murder, 136, 143
  and fundraising for Fayette, 250
  J. Edgar Hoover's surveillance of, 113–14
  jailed for breaking probation, 112
  and James Meredith Freedom March, 213–14
  and Kennedys, 112
  and March on Washington, 153
  and Montgomery bus boycott, 91–92
  on nonviolence, 36, 214
  and Ronald Reagan, 292–93
  as speaker, 143, 153–54
  and Vietnam War, 210
Kitt, Eartha, 136, 248
Knights of the Green Forest, 263
Kristofferson, Kris, 286
Ku Klux Klan, 5
  and boycott breakers, 187
  and Byron Beckwith, 167
  and *Brown* decision, 80–81
  and Decatur fireworks at Christmas, 16–17
  Charles Evers's hatred toward, 275
  and Fayette, 202, 241
  and Liuzzo murder, 181
  in Louisiana, 195
  in Mississippi highway patrol, 117
  and murder of Chaney, Goodman, and Schwerner, 170
  and murder plots against Charles Evers, 94, 236, 262, 263
  at Natchez integration campaign, 184, 187
  and Emmett Till case, 87

Lamarr, Hedy, 23
Lavender House, 254

Lawyers Constitutional Defense Committee, 244
leadership, 211, 216
Lee, Reverend George, 85, 130, 161, 180
Lee, Howard, 277
Lemons, Mr. (school board member in Chicago area), 110
Leonard, Jerris, 266
Lewis, Chester, 163
Lewis, Clayton, 90
Lewis, John, 180, 181, 183, 213, 244
Lewis, J. P., 217
Lewis family, 89, 260
liberals, 284
  advice to, 312
  and CETA as giveaway program, 287
  and common sense, 258
  on improvement in North, 199
  vs. Bobby Kennedy as doer, 159
  promises of, 211–12
  and racism, 284
  and school integration, 81
  southern, 285
  and George Wallace, 211, 212
  and Bill Waller, 268
  Roy Wilkins as, 147
  words over deeds for, 205, 273, 312
Lightfoot, Horace, 197
Lindsay, John, 251, 253, 269, 273, 296
literacy test, 5, 74, 179
"Little Rock Crisis," 104
Liuzzo, Viola, 181
Long, Russell, 162
"Lope" (nickname for Medgar Evers), 33
Loper, Will, 33
Louis, Joe, 75, 136
Louis, Myra, 136
Lowenstein, Allard, 152, 153, 239
Loyal Democrats of Mississippi, 238
Luke, O. M., 131
lunch counter sit-ins, 122
Lynch, John Roy, 88
lynching, 5, 15
  black preachers' acceptance of, 194
  fear of, 25
  Gov. Johnson's condemnation of, 179
  and NAACP strategy, 82
  Negroes considered responsible for, 72

of Mack Charles Parker, 105
and "respectable" whites, 81
of Willie Tingle, 23–24

McCarthy, Eugene, 221, 222, 225, 238, 245
McComb, Mississippi, 170, 183, 196
McGee, Sadie, 246
McGovern, George, 169, 274, 275, 276, 277, 280
McIntosh, Henry, 9
McIntosh, Lizzy, 9
McKissick, Floyd, 198–200, 203, 213
MacLaine, Shirley, 245, 248
Magnolia Mutual insurance company, 72, 73
Mandela, Nelson, 296, 302
Mankiewicz, Frank, 227, 230, 239
March on Washington (1963), 153
Marshall, Burke, 113, 116
Marshall, Thurgood, 72, 81, 116
 and *Brown vs. Board of Education*, 79–80
 investigative trip to South by, 149
 and Martin Luther King Jr., 93
 as Floyd McKissick lawyer, 198
 as Supreme Court justice, 209–10
Martha Deane Show, 250
Martin, Louis, 112, 160–61, 239, 250
Martin Luther King Apartments, 251, 276
Masonite Company, strike against, 273
Massey, Sam, 26–27, 28
Mau Mau movement, 75–76, 81, 150–51, 154, 155
May, Andy, 7, 62, 63, 311
Mazique, Gladys, 99
Mazique, Mamie Lee, 187, 188, 223
Medgar Evers Award, to Savimbi, 297
Medgar Evers Foundation, 251
Medgar Evers Homecoming, 277–78, 301–3, 310, 312
Medgar Evers Medical Center, 251
Medgar Evers Shopping Center, 203, 217, 256
media
 absence of Negroes in (1954), 90
 and Black Power, 215, 216

and Charles Evers's tax indictment, 279
on firing of Martha Wood, 258
and integration campaigns, 184
and marches, 180, 181
"objectivity" of, 184
Medicaid, protest on, 282–83
Memphis Slim, 107
Meredith, Cap, 115
Meredith, James, 115–18, 121, 124, 139, 266
 at Beckwith trial, 165
 at Jackson State disturbance, 168
 in Kennedy senatorial campaign, 172, 176
 march of, 213, 214
Meridian, Mississippi, 106, 292, 303
Metcalfe, George, 185, 190
Meyers, Ed, 39–40, 41
MFDP (Mississippi Freedom Democratic Party), 152–53, 171, 182, 233, 238
Michigan Catholic newspaper, 250, 251
Middleton, Kennie, 293, 294, 295
military service, and race relations, 45–46
Milton (U.S. Marshal), 169
ministers. *See* preachers
miscegenation law, in Fayette, 257–58
Mississippi, racial relations in. *See* Race relations in Mississippi and South
Mississippi Burning (movie), 114
Mississippi Challenge, 238–39
Mississippi College, 234–35
Mississippi Economic Council, 179
Mississippi Freedom Democratic Party. *See* MFDP
Mississippi Mass Choir, 301
Mississippi Sovereignty Commission, 307
Mitchell, Oscar, 112
Mondale, Walter, 273, 274
Montgomery bus boycott, 91–92
Moore, Amzie, 73, 74, 86, 283
Morrissey, Father William, 246–47
Morsell, John, 83
Moses, Robert, 152
Motley, Constance Baker, 116
movies, and racism, 23
Muskie, Ed, 169, 245, 267

NAACP (National Association for the Advancement of Colored People), 66, 82–83
and Alcorn protest, 189
as assassination target, 137
attrition among field staff of, 191
and *Brown vs. Board of Education,* 80
and courts vs. direct action, 92
and "Emancipation Centennial (1963)," 121
Evers brothers' first involvement in, 66, 72–73
and Charles Evers as Fayette mayor, 250
Charles Evers as Man of the Year for, xv, 248
and Charles Evers in Shreveport, 195
Charles Evers as state head of, xvii, 145–50, 155–56, 181, 233
Medgar Evers as state field secretary of, 82–88, 117, 125–26, 147
Medgar Evers tribute from, 143–44
and Myrlie Evers, 145, 301
Charles Evers's opposition to (1950s), 83
and Medgar Evers's death, 131, 143
and Medgar Evers's U. of Miss. application, 78
and Fayette election, 246
and Freedom Riders, 115
and grassroots campaigns, 146, 181
and Lena Horne's visit to Jackson, 123
and Keating-Kennedy senatorial race, 174–77
and Martin Luther King Jr., 91, 92, 93
Mississippi investigation of, 105
political endorsement avoided by, 149
poll tax campaign of (1961), 112–13
and scholarship fund for Evers children, 136
and Shelby killing, 180
whites' resistance to, 80, 81, 84, 85, 86
Roy Wilkins as head of, 83, 91, 146 (*see also* Wilkins, Roy)
See also civil rights
Natchez, Mississippi, xvi–xvii, 156, 170, 183–89, 191, 247

National Association for the Advancement of Colored People. *See* NAACP
Needham, A. J., 61, 62, 63, 64
Needham, C. B., 61, 62, 63, 64
Negroes. *See* blacks
newspapers, Negro, 25, 75
Newton, Mississippi, 28, 48
Newton County Hospital, 78–79
New York Post, and scholarship fund for Evers children, 136
nighttime integration, 5, 87, 215, 258
Nixon, E. D., 91
Nixon, Pat, 281
Nixon, Richard, 279–80, 311
and civil rights, 276
Charles Evers for, 111
on Charles Evers as Republican, 294
Fayette helped by, 251
and Fayette inauguration, 245
and Jackson State victims, 267
and Bobby Kennedy, 222
Floyd McKissick for, 200
and George Wallace, 274
and Watergate, 280–82
nonviolence, 154–55, 213, 214
Noriega, Manuel, 297
Nosser, John, 170, 187, 188
Noxapater, Mississippi, 71
numbers racket, Charles Evers in, 101–4

O'Dwyer, Paul, 244, 245–46
Otis, J. R., 59, 68

Pace, Mrs. Lizzlie, 26, 28, 42
Palmer House, 101
Palm Gardens, 108
Parchman Prison, 271
Parker, Mack Charles, 105
Parks, Rosa, 91
pastors. *See* preachers
Paterson, Basil, 275
patriotism, 75
Payne, Mrs., 28–29
Payne, Robin, 28
Pearson, Otto, 27
Pearson, T. H., 115
peddlers, white, 43

Pell, Claiborne, 267
Percy, Charles, 163, 267
Peters, Ed, 307–8
Pettus Bridge, 180–81
Philadelphia, Mississippi, 71, 89, 94, 170, 203, 260, 303
Pierce, M. B., 154
Pierce, Sam, 294
Pittsburgh Courier, 25, 75
police brutality, 253
politics
   and civil rights in Mississippi, 272
   Democratic National Convention, 171, 238–39, 273–75, 290–91
   Democrats vs. Republicans, 287–90
   Charles Evers on Democratic National Executive Committee, 239
   Charles Evers joins Republicans, 294–95
   Charles Evers's congressional campaign, 233–37
   Charles Evers's gubernatorial campaign, 267–71
   Charles Evers's senatorial campaign, 286
   fixation on past victories in, 172
   as goal for Evers brothers, 31
   Bobby Kennedy presidential campaign, 221, 222–23, 226–28
   Bobby Kennedy senatorial campaign, 171–77
   Mississippi Freedom Democratic Party (MFDP), 152–53, 171, 182, 233, 238
   white politicians and black constituents, 302
   See also Evers, Charles, as Fayette mayor; voting and voter registration
poll tax, 5, 60, 74, 91, 95
   elimination of, 179
   NAACP campaign to pay, 113
"pom-pom girls," 50–51
Port Gibson, Mississippi, 59, 156, 186, 191, 195–98, 272
poverty
   and Independent Coalition for Mississippi, 288–89
   and Bobby Kennedy, 173, 219, 220
   in New York ghettoes, 176
Powell, Adam Clayton, 216, 267
preachers
   as accepting racism, 194, 217
   and Stokely Carmichael's criticism, 217
   jackleg, 188
   vs. pastors, 193–94
Preston (Chicago racketeer), 101–2, 103
Price, Leontyne, 6, 7, 246
prison, and disgrace, 281
Public Accommodation Act (1964), 142

Quinn, Chuck, 184, 188, 227–28

race relations
   aggressive vs. passive, 23
   diplomacy in, 22
   and military service, 45–46
race relations in Mississippi and South, 3–7
   and "agitators," 72–73, 121, 123
   and childhood friendships, 42–43
   and Daddy Evers, 14, 15–17, 20
   Medgar Evers on progress in, 303
   and highway patrol, 117, 140, 257, 265, 266
   and humiliation, 4, 37, 38–39
   and killing of Negroes, 6, 15, 201
   and Klansman's plea for blood, 257
   and Mau Mau movement, 75–75, 150–51, 154
   and mixed marriages, 52
   and Negro elected officials, 123
   Negroes demoralized, 4, 6, 214, 242, 252
   and Negro GI experiences, 55
   and Negro labor, 185–86
   and Negro newspapers, 25
   and Newton County Hospital, 78–79
   nighttime integration, 5, 87, 215, 258
   1955 conditions, 85–87
   1973 progress, 276
   public swimming facilities closed (1965), 183
   and "separate but equal" education, 37–39, 80
   and Mark Thomas, 21–22

race relations in Mississippi and South, *continued*
  voting barriers, 74–75
  and white peddlers, 43
  and white support for Beckwith, 138
  and white women, 44, 80
  See also violence, racial
racism
  in Alcorn textbooks, 57
  of Theodore Bilbo, 29–31
  by blacks, 217, 305
  blacks' absorption of, 303
  of conservatives, 312
  and Medgar Evers's experience with French girl, 48, 53, 55
  T. R. M. Howard on, 66
  Bobby Kennedy's reaction against, 159
  and liberals, 284
  in movies, 23
  in schoolwork, 38
  subtle forms of, 179
  in U.S. Army, 46–47
  in U.S. foreign policy, 297
  and Vietnam War, 210
radicals, treatment of, 209
Randolph, A. Philip, 205
Rather, Dan, 134–35, 184
Ray, James Earl, 224
Reagan, Maureen, 295
Reagan, Ronald, 290, 291–93, 295, 297
Reconstruction, Mississippi history books on, 38, 57
Reed, Eugene, 175–76
religion
  and blacks, 36
  Christianity and civil rights, 193–94
  and Evers household, 12, 18, 33–34, 35
  and pastor vs. preacher, 193–94
  revivals, 34–35
Reuther, Walter, 265
riots, 168, 203
Rip (Negro cop spy), 196
Rizzo, Frank, 253, 296
Robinson, Jackie, 66–67, 75, 88
Rockfeller, Ann, 245
Rockefeller, Nelson, 245, 311
  at funeral of Martin Luther King Jr., 225
  and IRS, 278
  and Bobby Kennedy, 172, 177
  and murder of Medgar Evers, 136, 137
  as role model for Charles Evers, 88–89
  and Sam Pierce, 294
Rockefeller family, 88, 173
Roosevelt, Franklin, 45, 152
Roosevelt, Henry, 17
Roosevelt, W. J., 17
Ross Barnett Reservoir, 302
Rowan, Carl, 207
Ruffin, Saul, 79
Ruleville, Mississippi, 283
Rushing, Reverend D. D., 180
Russell (jackleg preacher), 188
Russell, Bill, 135
Russell, Richard, 162

Salinger, Pierre, 226, 274–75
Sanders, I. S., 170
Savimbi, Jonas, xvii, 296–97
school integration, 79–81, 276–77, 286
schools. *See* education
Schwerner, Michael, 170, 172, 180
SCLC. *See* Southern Christian Leadership Conference
segregation. *See* integration; race relations in Mississippi and South; racial separation; racism
Seigenthaler, John, 226
Selma marches, 180–81, 207
Shelby, Allie, 179–80
Shirley, Aaron, 282
Shreveport, Louisiana, 195
Shriver, Sargent, 112, 208–9
Sirhan, Sirhan, 229, 230
sit-ins, lunch counter, 122
Smith, Lamar, 86, 130, 180
Smith, Reggie, 184
Smith, Reverend R. L. T., 194
SNCC. *See* Student Nonviolent Coordinating Committee
Sorensen, Ted, 226–27
Soul City, 199–200
Soul Food Cafe, xiv
South Africa, 152, 296

Southern Black Mayors Conference, 277
Southern Christian Leadership Conference (SCLC), 92, 143, 148, 155
Spingarn Medal, to Medgar Evers, 144
Stennis, John, 74, 151, 162, 237
Stockman, David, 292
Stokes, Carl, 246
Stringer, E. J., 82
Student Nonviolent Coordinating Committee (SNCC), 215, 218
  and Fannie Lou Hamer, 118–19
  and NAACP, 143, 155
Subway Lounge, 108
supermarket, Negro-owned, 196
Swan, Jimmy, 264, 268

Talmadge, Herman, 162
Tarborian Hospital, 65
Tarzan movies, 23, 43
T-Boy (cousin), 27
Thomas, Mark, 21, 41, 45, 71
Thompson, Allen, 123, 130–31, 150–51, 167–68, 282, 312
Thompson, Bennie, 277
Thompson, Pet, 245
Thompson Industries, 254
Thurmond, Strom, 162
Till, Emmett, 86–87, 118, 176
Tims, Archie Lee, 9
Tims, Cloris, 9
Tims, Jim, 12, 77, 81
Tingle, Willie, 23
Tobe, Old Man, 43–44
Tolbert, Virginia, 283
Tougaloo College, 115, 122, 304
Truman, Bess, 292
Turner, Will, 244

U.S. Civil Rights Commission, 180
University of Alabama, 118, 126, 176
University of Mississippi
  and Alcorn A&M, 56
  Charles Evers as speaker at, 234
  Medgar Evers's application to, 77–78, 81–82
  Clennon King's application to, 105
  James Meredith's admission to, 115–18, 121, 176, 266

University of North Carolina law school, Floyd McKissick in, 198

Vanderson, Robert, 253, 263
Vietnam War, 210–11, 222, 227, 265, 276
violence, racial, 5–6
  assassination of John Kennedy, 157, 158, 173, 283
  assassination of Robert Kennedy, 229–30
  assassination of Martin Luther King Jr., 223–26
  beating of Horace Lightfoot, 197, 198
  Birmingham church bombing (1963), 154, 193
  bombings, 170, 185
  and Christian foundation of civil rights, 193
  by Citizens Council against Charles Evers's businesses, 95
  Charles Evers against use of, 203, 247
  against Medgar Evers, 105–6, 113, 122, 124, 125
  Medgar Evers's murder, 129–37, 143–44, 171, 209, 226, 229–30, 271, 283, 303
  after funeral of Medgar Evers, 140
  against Aaron Henry, 113, 122, 152
  against T. R. M. Howard, 110
  against Jackson sit-in participants, 122
  Jackson State shootings, 265, 266
  lynchings. See lynching
  and Mau Mau movement, 75–76, 150–51, 154, 155
  media as protection from, 184
  Mississippi police coverup of, 84
  murder of Vernon Dahmer, 216
  murder of Goodman, Schwerner, and Chaney, 170
  murder of Roosevelt Jackson, 196, 198
  murder of Wharlest Jackson, 190
  murder of Rev. Lee, 85
  murder of Allie Shelby, 179–80
  murder of Lamar Smith, 86
  murder of Emmett Till, 86–87
  Negro voters threatened with, 85
  police torture of Lawrence Guyot, 233

violence, racial, *continued*
   rioting against Meredith at Ole Miss, 117
   at Selma marches, 180–81, 207
   shooting at Charles Evers's house, 235
   shooting of James Meredith, 213
   shooting into Negro churches (Natchez), 183
   shooting of Negro cripple, 201
   shooting of George Wallace, 274
   and tip on Charles Evers's would-be assassin, 188–89
   total of Negroes murdered (1963–1967), 191
voting and voter registration
   vs. civil rights marches, 180
   and election of Jefferson County election commissioners, 242
   Evers brothers' attempts at, 60–64, 93, 123
   Charles Evers on importance of, 155
   Charles Evers's radio messages for, 91, 95
   in Fayette, 201
   gains in Mississippi registration, 289
   importance of, 59, 64, 66
   and James Meredith Freedom March, 214
   and Lyndon Johnson confrontation, 160–61
   Mississippi barriers to, 74–75
   and Mississippi elections, 190, 271
   and Mississippi Freedom Democratic Party, 152–53
   and NAACP poll tax compaigns (1961), 112–13
   white coercion against Negro voters, 85–86, 94
   See also literacy test; poll tax
Voting Rights Act (1965), 182, 208, 245, 292

Wagner, Robert, 137
Walker, Edwin, 166
Walker, Jimmie (Fayette lawyer), 259–60
Walker, Marie Farr, 258–60
Wallace, George, 121–22, 211–12, 239, 305
   Charles Evers's endorsement of, 273, 283–84
   and integration, 118, 126
   at 1972 Convention, 275
   shooting of, 274
Waller, William, 131, 138, 165–67, 268, 271–72, 308
Walton, Dale, 263–64, 268, 303
Wansley, Bernon, 61, 62, 63
Warren, Earl, 79–80
Washington, Thomas, 184
Washington, Willie, 170
Watergate scandal, 280–82
Waters, Muddy, 90, 108
Watkins, Wes, 238, 268
Watts, J. C., 295
Weaver, Robert, 207
welfare
   and Charles Evers as mayor, 254, 279
   faults of, 287, 288
   Fayette Negroes on, 242
   and Reagan White House, 292
   as workfare, 234, 291
Wells, Houston, 129–30
Werner, Carl, 252
"We Shall Overcome," 190
Westwood, Jean, 274
White, Annie, 220
White, Lee, 182, 205
White, Walter, 66, 91
White Citizens Councils, 81, 94–96, 124, 138, 186
whites
   and blacks' problems, 305
   and burial of Medgar Evers, 140
   and Christian basis of civil rights, 193
   claiming to be civil rights supporters, 90
   as envious of Charles Evers's prosperity, 93–94
   Mama Evers on, 13, 38
   and Charles Evers's congressional campaign, 234
   Daddy Evers's defiance of, 15
   and murder of Medgar Evers, 130, 144
   and moral persuasion ('50s), 84

peddlers, 43
and Dan Rather, 135
schools for, 37, 38
and trustworthiness (southern vs. northern), 206
See also race relations in Mississippi and South; violence, racial; women, white
Whitten, Jamie, 74, 162, 237
WHOC Radio, 89, 90, 94
Wilkins, Roy, 83, 91, 146
  and *Brown* victory, 80, 81
  and Stokely Carmichael, 217
  and Charles Evers as Fayette mayor, 250
  and Charles Evers as Medgar's successor, 145–50
  and Medgar Evers's funeral, 139, 141
  and Medgar Evers's hiring, 82
  and Medgar Evers's murder, 136, 148, 235
  Medgar Evers's reports to, 125
  and Fayette inaugural, 246
  and Freedom Rides, 115
  and grassroots campaigns, 155, 181
  and Jackson demonstration, 122, 123
  at Wharlest Jackson funeral, 191
  and James Meredith Freedom March, 213
  and Lyndon Johnson, 205
  and Keating-Kennedy senatorial race, 172, 174, 176
  and Martin Luther King Jr., 92, 93, 143, 223
  and March on Washington, 153
  and NAACP debt, 301
  and respect of blacks, 250
Williams, Hosea, 180, 291
Williams, John Bell, 233, 234, 239
Williams, Lois, 300
Williams, Virgene, 36
Williamson, Sonny Boy, 74
Willis, Ruby Nelle, 36
Wilson, O. W., 107, 109
Winfrey, Oprah, 301
Winter, William, 288
Wofford, Harris, 112
Wolf, Jesse, 196, 198
women, black
  as civil rights leaders, 87
  in Charles Evers's boyhood, 36
  symbolism of dancing with (Johnson at inaugural), 162
  wages of, 186, 188
women, white
  and black separatists, 215
  sexual overtures from, 44
  southerners' touchiness over relations with black men, 80
Wonley, Ezra, 41
Wood, Martha, 257–258
Woodard, Richard, 253
workfare, 234, 291
Works Progress Administration (WPA), 45
World War II, 47–50, 55
Wright, Herbert, 83
Wright, Medgar, 11
Wright, Mose, 87
Wynn, Doug, 238

Yale University, Charles Evers as Chubb Fellow at, 267
Yarborough, Ralph, 267
Young, Andrew, 180, 285
Young, Jack, 115, 246
Young, Thomas, 129–30
Young, Whitney, 205, 246

Charles Evers (1922–   ) was born in Decatur, Mississippi. He served overseas in the army during World War II, and graduated from Alcorn Agricultural and Mechanical College, now Alcorn State University, in 1950. After graduation, he settled in Philadelphia, Mississippi, where he ran several businesses. He then moved to Chicago until the assassination of his brother, Medgar, in June 1963, brought him back to Mississippi. He assumed his brother's post as field director of the NAACP in Mississippi. Elected mayor of Fayette, Mississippi, in 1969 and re-elected in 1973, he became the first black mayor in a racially mixed southern town since Reconstruction. He currently divides his time between Jackson and Fayette, Mississippi.

Andrew Szanton, a gifted specialist in collaborative memoirs, honed his skills as an oral historian at the Smithsonian Institution. His first book was *Recollections of Eugene P. Wigner*, a collaboration with the Nobel Laureate in Physics. He lives with his wife and son in Somerville, Massachusetts.